ROBOTECTONIC

TY&A | **TYMDL**
Takashi Yamaguchi & Associates | Takashi Yamaguchi Media Design Lab

Contents |

ピーター・アイゼンマンの思考との対話
近代以降における建築の主要概念
(subject. object. context) の変容の考察

TAKASHI YAMAGUCHI | ピーター・アイゼンマンの思考との対話

近代以降における建築の主要概念
(subject. object. context) の変容の考察

Introduction

本書は、私の研究室の活動記録をまとめたものである。

私は長年、建築の理論研究、特にピーター・アイゼンマンの diagram 研究を行ってきた。さらに、理論研究のために、過去 14 年間、ハーバード大学、スタンフォード大学、コロンビア大学、MIT、プリンストン大学、中国清華大学などと、先進的なテーマについてワークショップ、講演会、シンポジウムを開催してきた。フランチェスコ・ダル・コー、ケネス・フランプトン、ピーター・アイゼンマン、サンフォード・クウィンター、マーク・ウィグリー、プレストン・スコット・コーエン、ビアトリス・コロミーナ、アキム・メンジェス、ナーダー・テラーニ、フレデリック・レブラット、シュー・ウェイグゥオ、デイビッド・ベンジャミン、ポール・デマリニス、アマール・アンドラウス、加藤邦男、工藤国雄、そして今回のパトリック・シューマッハなど理論家をメインに選んできたと言える。積極的に参加していただいた彼らに紙面を借りて感謝申し上げたい。

日本では、欧米の理論家の講演会は皆無である。書籍もほとんど翻訳されていない。日本の大学においては、建築論が蔑ろにされ、一般的な概観把握に留まり、体系化された系譜を怠っているのが現状である。したがって、日本の大学における建築教育は、建築論なき教育、すなわち建築家を育てる教育ではなく、デザイナーや設計士を養成する教育が行われている。理論探求を置き去りにした結果、機能性の追求と形態の遊戯で終わる演習教育が横行している。したがって、著名な建築家であっても、建築をデザインとしてしか理解せず、形態の美学を追求するだけである。展開する理論も詩的レトリックに過ぎないものばかりである。ほとんどは海外の建築の流行を追いかけるのみ。機能主義、ポストモダニズム、デコンストラクティビズム、コンテクスチャリズム、ミニマリズム等と海外の建築思潮の理論を探求するのではなく、流行をいち早く取り入れる器用さだけが目につく。さらには既存の計画学を崩そうとして機能構成の複雑化に走るグループ、ミニマリズムの美学に耽溺するグループなど独自の様相を呈し、日本の建築界はガラパゴス化してしまったと言っても過言ではない。こうした状況が学生達にかなりの悪影響を与えているのである。

こうした現状に抵抗する意味で、海外とダイレクトに交流する活動を続けてきたとも言える。

招聘した理論家は、建築思想にとって、重要と思われた人達ばかりである。

最初に、保守的なフランチェスコ・ダル・コーとケネス・フランプトンを選んだ。建築の基本的なフレームを紹介したかったからである。フランチェスコ・ダル・コーは、よく知られた通り、世界一のメディア、モンダドーリ社のカザベラ誌の編集長である。世界で最も長期に渡る編集長である。そのため、彼の言説は、世界の建築界を動かしているとも言える。また、

コロンビア大学のケネス・フランプトンは、その昔、批判的地域主義において、日本のテクトニック文化の継承者として、安藤忠雄を世界に紹介した人物として有名である。

その次からは、私が最も重要と思った現代の建築文化に影響を与えた人物達である。コロンビア大学で先進的な研究を行なっているマーク・ウィグリーを招聘した。1988年のMoMAにおける「Deconstructivist Architecture」（脱構築主義建築）の展覧会を実質的にキュレートしたマーク・ウィグリーは、新たな建築を志向する上で重要な役割を果たした。そうした先進的な企画を試みた人物である。ウィグリーは幾何学形態による安定性と秩序を追求する従来の方向性に疑問を持っていた。彼は、脱構築的操作によって、従来の建築の在り方を解体することを主張し、デコンストラクティビズムを提唱した。幾何学形態による安定した構築性を批判し、ユークリッド幾何学の静的適応にもとづいた構成では多様性に適応できないと批判し、新たな構築の方向性を示した中心的人物であった。2009年コロンビア大学と私の研究室とでは「Knowledge City」をテーマとしたワークショップを行なっており、そのファイナルとして、レビュー・レクチャー・シンポジウムを行なったのであった。マーク・ウィグリーを含め、シニカルで特有の視点を持って批評を行なっている彼の妻であるプリンストン大学のビアトリス・コロミーナ、ARX創立からの友人であるコロンビア大学のフレデリック・レブラットやハーバード大学のプレストン・スコット・コーエンと、中国清華大学のシュー・ウェイグゥオ、槇文彦とで議論したのであった。前衛と保守、理論家と建築家、年配と若手とが入り混じった構成メンバーでなかなか刺激的なイベントであった。

招聘はしなかったが、プリンストン大学ジェシー・ライザーと彼の妻でありパートナーである梅本ナナコとは、プリンストン大学、大阪産業大学、東大、中国清華大学とで、「Linear City」をテーマにワークショップを行い、海外での活動を共に行なった。2004年北京国際建築ビエンナーレで、ライザー・ウメモトが隣のブースだったこともあり、ナナコとはハーバード大学で「スマートシティ」をテーマに一緒に教える機会を持った。

ハーバード大学のサンフォード・クウィンターは、私が最も招聘したい理論家の一人だった。ハーバード大学に研究員として在籍中、彼との交流を持つ機会を得たことも幸運であった。彼には、アイゼンマンと同時に来日してもらった。アイゼンマンの理論に対して、次の世代として彼への批判を聞きたかったからである。特にobjectが持つ時間概念に関して、双方の異なる見解に興味があり、アイゼンマンのobject概念に対して鋭い指摘を期待していたからである。案の定、シンポジウムにおける議論は白熱した、アイゼンマンの妻であって、ANYやLOGの編集長をしているシンシア・デヴィッドソンが、二人の間に入って仲裁していたのが印象的であった。

クウィンターは、「Landscape of Change」という著書において、objectにおける独自の多様性の概念を提示したことで有名な人物である。個々のobjectが見せる形態とは、物質の流動システムにおいて不安定性の臨界を迎えた後、均衡状態として出現するものであるとする考え方に興味を持っていた。個々のobjectの様相も、連続性の中における特異点として立ち現れたものとする考え方、すなわち連続性から多様性が生まれるとする考え方は、次代の多くの先進的な理論家や建築家に影響を与えていた。今回、招聘するパトリック・シューマッハもクウィンターの影響を受けた一人である。パトリックはParametricismを提唱し、あらゆるものがパラメトリックに変化し対応していく社会の構築を目指している。

ピーター・アイゼンマンを招聘した理由は、現在の建築の方向性を大きく変曲させた人物だからであり、私自身の建築の出自として、アイゼンマンが存在したからである。私は京都大学で加藤邦男から京都学派系譜の建築論を学んだ。森田慶一の「建築論」は当時の愛読書であった。そこには、architecture の本来の意味が述べられていた。日本人が architecture を「建築」と誤訳してしまった問題点から、私の建築論への興味は始まった。その後、安藤忠雄からは、建築に対する真摯な態度と情熱を持った意志の必要性を学んだが、巨匠的直観性というブラックボックスへと全てを回収する在り方に不満を抱いていた。やはり最も多くを学んだのは、アイゼンマンからであった。それは京都学派の建築論のベクトルと一致していたからだ。アイゼンマンの建築理論がポスト構造主義との関係が密接であるため、私自身もデリダやドゥルーズの言説に興味を持っており、彼らの著書を読みあさっていた時期であった。ちょうどその頃、私と石丸信明は、インターンシップで、安藤忠雄建築研究所に来ていたフレデリック・レブラットと知り合い、彼が、その後アイゼンマンオフィスに入所したこともあり、交流を深めていった。その後、アイゼンマンオフィスのヌノ・マテウスが参加し、1988 年に、彼らと理論探求のためのグループ ARX を結成した。ちょうど、ドゥルーズが Le Pli（襞）を発表した年であった。ARX は、そうした時代に、理論探求と実践のためのグループとして結成された。ARX は、建築における作家性の解体を目指して、ニューヨーク、ジュネーブ、ベルリン、リスボン、日本を結び、ネットワークによる活動を始めた。当時、次代を変革させるアイゼンマンの先進的なプロジェクト（カーサ・グァルディオラ、レブストック計画、アーノフ・センターなど、そしてアイゼンマン独自の chora の概念を見い出した時代）に、ARX のメンバーである フレデリック・

レブラットや ヌノ・マテウス は、アイゼンマンのオフィスでプロジェクトに参加していた。アイゼンマンが大きく変革する時期であった。彼らとの議論を経て、アイゼンマンの建築理論に関して多くの示唆を得たのであった。そして 1991 年、ARX は、ベルリン・シュピルボーゲンコンペに参加し入賞を果たす。アイゼンマンの推薦による ANY への投稿。こうした機会を得て、欧米に連綿と続く建築論、すなわち正統性と先進性を持ち合わせた建築論をアイゼンマンから受け継いだのである。

われわれ ARX は、当時最先端の思想だったドゥルーズの「襞」における理論展開から、objectile 概念をわれわれの diagram に注入したのである。アイゼンマンの chora の概念の再解釈を継承した。ちょうどレブストック計画やアーノフ・センターの検討時期とも重なり、アイゼンマンが大きく変貌を遂げる時期であった。異なる観点の複数性はわれわれのグループの基本的な概念であった。われわれは、ベルリンのプロジェクトでアイゼンマンとは異なったアプローチを選択した。設計プロセスに、単一の視点を持ちながら複数の観点の間における読み取りを試みたのであった。さらに object は時間性を孕むものだとする考え方は、当時日本にいて、誰もが理解できない内容だった。現在でも理解している人はほとんどいない。アイゼンマンの学問的知見は、深く、ポスト構造主義の哲学から最新の非線形理論やカタストロフィー理論にまでおよんでいた。かつ建築的構築への指針として、多くの次世代の先進的な建築家達に影響を与えていたのだった。しかし、アイゼンマンの言説は、日本においては、難解すぎるとして、未だに彼の書籍は翻訳されていない。少なからず、ANY、A+U、SD という雑誌で部分的に紹介されただけで、アイゼンマンの理論の全貌は紹介されていない。当然、アイゼンマンの流れ

を汲む ARX が入賞したベルリン・シュピルボーゲンプロジェクトは、難解で理解できないものとして片隅に置かれてしまった。欧米のメディアが積極的に取り上げたのとは対照的に、SD 誌以外、日本のメディアからは完全に黙殺されてしまったのである。

私はこうした日本の状況に対してアイゼンマンの建築論を批判的に継承しようとして、大学での教育活動とともに、いくつかのプロジェクトの発表と理論研究を続けてきた。

こうしたプロジェクトの出発点になったプロジェクトを紹介したい。

Void Centers 1992

空間に散らばる subject どうしの superposition（重ね合せ）

1988 年、メンバーが離れて存在するテレコミュニケーションによって建築デザインをおこなうインターナショナルな理論研究グループが結成された。

そのグループは ARX と呼ばれた。正式名称は、造語である ARchiteXture (ARX)。architecture、texture、text の言葉からなり、建築は言葉であり、グローバルネットワークに展開する織物であるという、ARX 自身の概念を表出するものであった。複数の subject からなり、作家性を解体するためのものであった。

1992 年に、複数の subject がテレコミュニケーショナルに相互干渉する手法により、ベルリン・シュピルボーゲン都市開発国際コンペティッションに入賞し、ARX の理論を具現化した。コンペ案のコンセプトは、多くのアイデアが詰まったものになっていた。作家性の解体、同一時間でありながら異なる場所に存在する subject 群の並置、モチベーションという共通項の設定による interiority と exteriority との連続性、時間性を

有する diagram、objectile 概念の適応、diagram にパラメーターを挿入する事などである。

このコンペ案は、ドゥルーズの理論とアイゼンマンの chora の概念をベースに生み出された。すなわち、ドゥルーズが objectile（対象体）概念に重要な意味を見つけたが、われわれも建築や都市に対して、パラメトリックな適用を行なったのである。建築的には、diagram に、chora との連続的な関係により、パラメーター化を行ない、建築・都市構造を生成したのである。時間性を孕んだ敷地が有するモチベーションをパラメトリックに diagram 化したのであった。

われわれは、ドゥルーズの「襞」における理論展開から、objectile 概念をわれわれの diagram に注入したのである。それはアイゼンマンのレブストック計画にインスパイアされたからでもあった。

外部性である place のモチベーションを抽象化するところから始まる。場所性に時間性を導入し、モチベーションをもつインデックス化された記号を読み取り、建築の interiority へと連続させる事を求めた。すなわち歴史に沈殿する軌跡を、何世紀にも渡る時間幅における変異としてトレースした上で、それらを重ね合わせ、散逸された形象フラグメントをスイープすることで建築化する。このことは場所をとりとめもない恣意的な景観から離脱させ、新たなモデルとしての object へと転換しようとした試みであり、直接的に object を生成するのではなく、過去から現在に至る時間の流動性における変容をパラメトリックに写像するマッピングを diagram 化したのであった。

具体的には、変化する曲線群をベースにした。シュプレー川と S バーンの曲線群に接する円弧と曲線群との接点との交互の時間的変容の影響によって、diagram は構成される。（図

0-1）それは周辺環境や都市のコンテクストを、恣意的ではなく、モチベーションとして浮上させ視覚化したものである。それを新しい都市構造へと連続させる試みであった。その事により、時間も含めた外在する外部性は都市内部へと連続可能となる。こうして外部コンテクストと過去の異なる時間性とは、モチベーションとして浮上し、diagram を通して、建築と都市、外部と内部、過去と現在とが連続可能となったのである。これら変容した曲線群から発するポテンシャルは、ドゥルーズの言う所の襞そのものであった。われわれは、こうした diagram にパラメトリックな変化を与えることによって、変容する object 群を生成したのであった。それは、アイゼンマンの chora の概念を基底に据えたものであった。明確な figure（図）/ground（地）の従来の二項対立を超えて、硬直したモダニズムの完結性をズラそうとして、コンテクストに漂う関係性を diagram 化し、パラメトリックな操作を加えた。さらに重要な事項として、subject の問題の検討に着手したのであった。

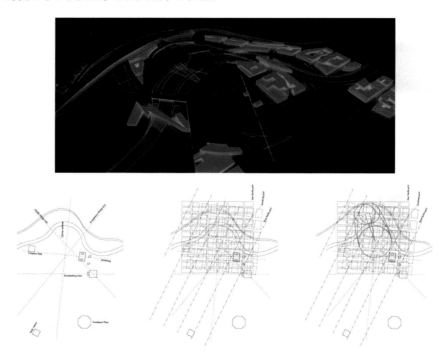

Fig.0-1　ベルリン・シュピルボーゲンコンペのコンセプトダイアグラム

次に、私自身は、さらにその方向を進めることになる。1997年に Cyberspace as Reference を発表した。（図 0-2）ここでは、自律的プログラムの問題を扱い、エージェントとしての他者性の視点を導入したのである。

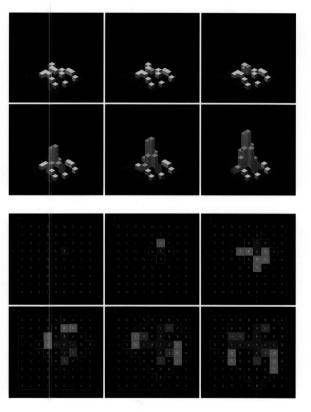

Fig.0-2　参照空間としてのサイバースペース
　　　　　空間の生成概念プログラム

アイゼンマンは建築の内部性を強く信じ、永遠なる原理を追求するという西欧の伝統的枠組みである統合性を維持する。しかし、アイゼンマンは、全てに原理が及ぶという統合性を求めながらも、全体の統合性を求めることの不可能性を証明した。そうした統合性を求めることの不可能性を回避する道を、diagram に求め、subject を object である作品に滑り込ませる、subject と object との融合という立場に立った。この立場は、object（作品）を宙吊り状態の成立不可能な状況に置こうとしたとも言え、diagram に、object に内在する interiority を読み取らせようとした意志自体が subject の優位性を温存させることになり、結局のところ西欧の伝統的思考の裏返しとなり、ここにアイゼンマンの限界があった。

そこで、一つの試みとして、アイゼンマンの diagram では、現在の著者、建築 object、過去から受け取る沈殿した subject の間の関係に焦点を合わせるエージェントとしての働きをしたものを、他者性の視点を持ったエージェントとしての働きを持つ自律的プログラムともいえる、subject と object との間に介在する参照空間を提示することを試みた。それは外在性における諸条件と建築 object との間の関係の沈殿を抑圧ではない、未来へ向かう可態性として格納するものであった。

ここでは、エージェントとしての AI による参照空間を策定している。この参照空間は、ビッグデータを超える全ての知の総体である anteriority（先在性）を格納し、subject と object とを介在するものである。それは、アイゼンマンの diagram を発展させたものとも言える。

この試みは、デジタルツインやミラーワールドの概念への先駆けとなるものであった。現実世界と仮想世界とが、鏡像関係に位置し、互いに呼応して、それぞれが連続していく。連続

性の流れは、現実と仮想との間にも生じてくるのである。そのことを、このプロジェクトは示していた。

コンピューターチップの演算処理能力のスピードは、ムーアの法則を超えて、シリコン以外の新しい素材が生まれてきているため、猛スピードで進化しつつある。ネットワークにおける度重なるジェネレーション革命を引き起こす処理能力と影響力を拡大しつつある。ポストヒューマン時代に登場する世界は、人間の身体の境界を超え、延長し拡張する。space とは、volume との関係を超えて、身体の意識が充満する世界となるであろうことが予想される。そうした意識の粒子が飛び交い変容し、volume を構成していく。建築の存在は、そうした流動性の中に解体していくものと思われる。

私の研究室では、アイゼンマンからの建築論の流れを研究し続け、アイゼンマンのリバースエンジニアリングを行なってきた。私の研究室の学生達には、新しいテクノロジーを元に建築論及び建築自身を解体し、新たな形式へと再構築させることを求めた。果たして、そうした方向の成果が得られたかどうかはわからないが、こうした活動は、日本では珍しく、ユニークなものであるため、今までの記録を書籍として発表することにしたのである。

日本では、アイゼンマンは、デコンストラクティビズムの建築思潮の一つとして捉えられ、さらに難解な理論のため、ほとんどの日本の建築家達には理解されないままブームが去ってしまった。

今回、アイゼンマンの建築論とともに、そこから導かれた私の建築論への展開の一部を本書に載せることにした。これらは、ARX 結成時から書き溜めておいたメモを核にして構成されたものである。

アイゼンマンの理論はル・コルビュジエから批判継承している

ので、ル・コルビュジエについても記述している。流れとしては、アイゼンマンの建築論を超えて、現代建築の問題点を探る形式になっている。さらに、アイゼンマン以降の、次代の建築についての私の試論を最後に載せている。すなわち、未来においては、ル・コルビュジエの volume 概念から出発したアイゼンマンの volume 概念を飛び越えて、パーティクルとして気化され、知能を持ったエージェントがそれらを構成するだろうことを予測しており、それはエージェントを超えて、知能を持ったパーティクルによる構成、すなわち Quantumetric が行われるだろう。その前段階においては、知能を持ったセグメントが object を構成するであろう。そうした Segmentmetric によって全体は構築されるようになるだろうと予測している。そうした一連の流れは、RoboTectonic によって行われるべきであるとしている。さらに、こうした動きが、ミラーワールドを構成し、リアルワールドとヴァーチャルワールドとの交流が行われるだろうと予測したプロジェクトを示している。しかし、こうした方向へ進むことは、利便性と同時に危険性も併せ持っていることも理解すべきである。

そのことを含みながら、われわれの研究室の活動は行われてきた。

Chapter 1

現代の建築の方向性

近代において、建築形態を覆うサーフェイスの単純化によって、建築のエレメントとしてのvolumeの概念の創出が試みられた。それはル・コルビュジエによってなされたものである。それまでの建築に見られるような、装飾という意味が付着した重いサーフェイスを軽やかでプレーンな面へと移行させたのであるが、それは骨組み構造という近代の新たなテクノロジーが、重厚な石積み壁を開放させた結果である。ル・コルビュジエは、そうした新しい建築の時代を切り開くべく、建築の概念を整理した建築家であった。いわゆる「近代建築の4原理」として、『volume、サーフェイス、プラン、規整線』を挙げた。[註1]
プランは建築の重力や機能およびサーキュレーションを受ける全体をコントロールする原理として存在し、規整線（図1-1）は面において、数比によって全体と部分を調和させるために使用された。特にプランは、volumeやサーフェイスの暴走を数比原理によってコントロールし、建築の全てを支配するものとして重視されたのである。そうした方向はギリシア時代以来の西欧における建築の正統な流れを汲むものであり、極大と極小の世界を数学的論理によって連続させようとする西欧的意思の現れでもあった。しかし、時代が進み、社会の欲望が肥大化し、複雑化しはじめると、旧来の数比原理（図1-2）のみによって内部と外部の世界を連続させること自体が不可能になると同時に、その意味が疑われはじめたのである。

モダニズムは人間を社会システム内の部品と化し、その存在を矮小化させるものとして、その問題性を露呈しはじめた。こうした問題に立ち向かうには、建築を司っていた旧来の数学的論理からの転換が求められた。すなわち、このことはモダニズム自体に孕む問題と同時に、建築に内在する生成原理自身の問題でもあったのである。しかし、当時、多くの建築家はモダニズムに攻撃を仕掛けた。その裏に潜む重要な問題を見つめることなく、その問題を温存してしまうのである。彼らが唱えたのは、合理主義と機能主義を攻撃対象とすることだけであった。
言い換えれば、近代以降、近代を再考する様々な運動が建築界に生じたが、そうした運動が生まれた根本的な理由はモダニズムがもつ不連続性にあったことに驚くほどに気がついていなかったと言える。すなわちモダニズムには、宇宙と呼応し、極大と極小の世界を連続させるという内部と外部との関係を担保する西欧の伝統的な意識がなかったことの重要性に、建築家は気がついていなかったのである。建築家達は、最適解への適応という外在的論理に関する命題のみを信じ、外部性を原理化することに邁進するだけであった。

註1）ル・コルビュジェ‐ソーニエ（樋口清訳）『建築へ』中央公論美術出版、2003年

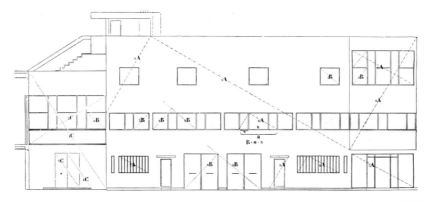

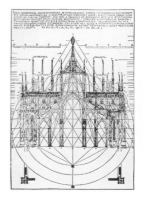

近代を再考する建築の運動において、二つの大きな方向性を観ることができる。そのひとつは、モダニズムを継承し、補強し、さらなる建築の外部性をより重視する考え方である。建築の外部にある社会システムの中に建築を開放させようとする考え、すなわち、社会の欲望すらもデータ化し、整理し、建築を生成しようとするレム・コールハースの建築に見られるような、過剰とも思われる外部からのアプローチである。この考えは、外在的原理を適応させようとする原理主義ともいえるものである。

しかし、もう一方で、建築の内部性を探る方向が存在する。ピーター・アイゼンマンに見られるように、建築自身の内部に建築が過去から連綿と続く真正なる力を見出そうと考える方向である。それは、建築内部に存在する内在的原理を凝視するものである。

着目するテーマは二つある。一つは内部性と外部性、それ自身に関わる問題である。すなわち、現代建築の流れと並行する二つの方向性、すなわち、建築生成における外在的アプローチと内在的アプローチに関する研究である。外在的アプローチとは、建築は如何に存在するか？（How is architecture?）という問いであり、都市のコンデンサーとしての建築、都市の中での建築のあり方、都市が建築を生み出していくプロセスを解明していくことである。いわば建築の外部に属する原理から建築を生成していくアプローチである。一方、内在的アプローチとは、建築とは何か？（What is architecture?）という問いに帰するものであり、建築が建築自身を生み出していく中に歴史性が沈殿していくプロセスを解明すること、あるいは建築の存在形式に関わる問題性を解明することである。それは、アイゼンマンの言説を読み解くことから始められる。

合わせて、内部性と外部性に関わる連続性の問題をも射程に入れている。すなわち、建築の内的論理と外的論理との関係性である。伝統的な西欧の建築概念において、数比を基とした内的論理によって生成された建築は、自律的に存在してきた。しかし、モダニズムの出現によって、今日、そうした自律性は

解体され、外部の論理が建築内部に侵入し、外部と内部は連続してくる。こうした自律性の解体を巡る探求が必要不可欠になってきていると思われる。本稿では、こうした二つの問題、内部性と外部性それ自身の問題と、内部性と外部性との連続性の問題を解明していきたい。

古典的には、プラトンのイデアに発する建築の内在的な問題性に対して、アリストテレスによってデュナミスとエネルゲイアという生成概念が与えられた。それ以降西欧の建築における論争は、イデアに代表される形式とそれらを生成する原理との対立バランスの中で展開されていく。中でも、カントによって「形」に重要性が置かれた一方で、ゲーテは発生論的な事物の特性に重きを置いた。建築においては、デュランのタイポロジーで、ビルディングタイプとして建築の「型」が設計の原理となり、古典建築は「オーダー」から「型」、「タイポロジー」に支配されることになる。

しかし、近代は産業革命と共に社会が大きな変貌を遂げ、建築を構成している材料、構造形式、そして社会に必要とされる建築の機能、規模というものが大きく変化し、従来のタイポロジーでは対応しきれなくなった。近代建築を象徴する「形態は機能に従う」という言葉に代表される機能主義は、一方で新たなビルディングタイプとしての建築を生み出しながら、もう一方で、建築の空間を生成する上で動線、空間を使用する用途、そこを使用する人数などの規模的な容量や人間の行動というものを抽象的に還元して、空間を設計するための新たな要素を生み出す、いわゆる現在の計画学の基礎となるものを築き上げた。その点において、近代建築における機能主義やサーキュレーションというアイデアは、建築を拡張するための新たな概念の萌芽であり、外在的アプローチの延長と位置づけることが可能であろう。

こうした状況において、内在的アプローチおよび外在的アプローチの二つのアプローチの位置づけこそが、今日最も重要な課題だと思われる。

さらに、近・現代の建築における、内部性と外部性との連続性への認識の変転にも焦点を当てたい。そのため、純粋な建築形態における内在的論理による生成論として、アイゼンマンの近代建築分析[註2]を採り上げる。また建築を外部から規定する社会システムとしてプログラムが扱われているコールハースの建築を扱う。それらは、特に従来の建築の要素間の関係と対比させながら検証されるであろう。

ル・コルビュジエの言説と作品に見られる連続性と不連続性の両義性

1-1：ル・コルビュジエの建築概念

ル・コルビュジエの功績は、テクノロジーの発展によって建築が進展するべき方向性において、新たな建築概念の創出をおこなったことである。特に volume の概念を創始したことである。この volume 概念は、後にアイゼンマンへと継承されていく。

ダグマル・リヒターは次のように指摘している。[註3]

"「フランス語の Vers une architecture（建築をめざして）」からの英語、ドイツ語への翻訳文を研究した結果、ル・コルビュジエの概念を巡る異なった言い回しが、この近代のパラダイムシフトの言外の意味を理解する上で、学問的困難さを引き起こしていることが明らかになったとする。ル・コルビュジエの最も重要な最初の概念は le volume であったが、mass

註2) Peter Eisenman, The Formal Basis of Modern Architecture, Lars Muller (2006)（以下 DT：DoctorThesis）
註3) ダグマル・リヒター「The Dom-in[f]o House」アンソニー・バーク、テレーズ・ティアニー編、(山口隆訳)『ネットワークプラクティス：建築とデザインにおける新たな戦略』鹿島出版会、2014 年、pp.134-147、原書:Anthony Burke ed, Therese Tierney ed, Network Practices; New Strategies in Architecture and Design, Princeton Architectural Press,2012
註4) ル・コルビュジエ（井田安弘・芝優子訳）『プレシジョン―新世界を拓く建築と都市計画（上）』(SD 選書 185) 鹿島出版会, 1984, ル・コルビュジエ（井田安弘・芝優子訳）『プレシジョン―新世界を拓く建

「マッス」として英語に翻訳され、一方、ドイツ語においては、Baukörper もしくは「建物のボディ」と翻訳された。このように、ル・コルビュジエの le volume の概念は誤解された。"

と記述しているが、日本においても、Vers une architecture「建築をめざして」の翻訳において、固形化した「立体」として、間違って翻訳してしまったため、同様の誤解と混乱を生じさせている状況は同じである。

「プレシジョン」[註4] の中で、" 内部が自ら広がり、その結果として外部が決定され、外部はいろいろな突出部をもつようになる（ラ・ロッシュ＝ジャンヌレ邸）" というル・コルビュジエの言説に着目するならば、ル・コルビュジエの volume 概念は固形化したものではなく、風船のように内部が膨張することを前提にしていたことと理解できるであろう。ル・コルビュジエの volume 概念はマッスで固定したものではなく、内部が膨張するという運動性を有していたものであった。

このことが、アイゼンマンが、自身の volume 概念に運動性を孕ませることの契機となるのである。

1-1-1：部品化 (『建築へ』[註5] より)　　(不連続性)

この書物の中で、建築と近代機械としての商船・飛行機・自動車が並置されている。

ル・コルビュジエは古典的建築概念の継承と近代機械の関係付けにおいて、文明という流れの中で建築を定義し直したと言える。それだけでなく建築自身を要素化しようとして、volume、サーフェイス、プラン、規整線を挙げる。ただし、具体的な建築 (ここでは新たな工場、倉庫といった建築) を例に挙げ、絶対的な幾何学的抽象性へと還元するのではなく、建築としての具象性を残した要素化を図るためのものとして volume、サーフェイス、プラン、規整線を提示したのである。

ル・コルビュジエの 4 つの原理を整理しておく必要がある。

1-1-2：ル・コルビュジエの 4 つの原理

建築の 4 つの原理として、volume、サーフェイス、プラン、そして規整線を挙げている。

前者 2 つはコントロールされる対象であり、後者 2 つは、それらをコントロールするためのものである。重要なのはプランであり、建築の重力や機能を受ける全体をコントロールするデヴァイスとして存在し、規整線は面において、数比によって全体と部分を調和させるために使用された。

築と都市計画（下）』(SD 選書 186) 鹿島出版会，1984 年
註 5) ル・コルビュジエ ‐ ソーニエ (樋口清訳)、前掲書

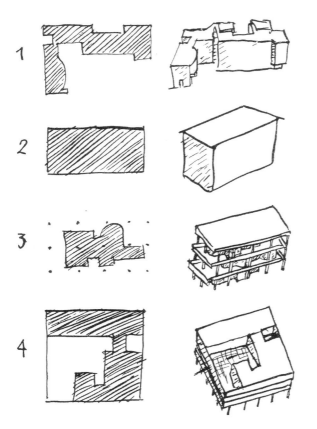

Fig.1-3 建築構成の四つの型（1929）
①ラ・ロッシュ＝ジャンヌレ邸、②ガルシュの邸宅
③カルタージュの家、④サヴォア邸

に従って、他の部分に隣接するというもの…つまり、「内部が自ら広がり、その結果として外部が決定され、外部はいろいろな突出部をもつようになる」というやり方…（オートゥイユのラ・ロッシュ＝ジャンヌレ邸）"、②"整然とした完全に純粋な外郭の内部に各部分を押し込めるというやり方…（ガルシュの邸宅）"、③"外側に見える骨組みにより、荒格子状の単純で明快、そして透明な外郭を形成し、内部は各層ごとに独自に構成し、フォルム、規模ともに、諸居室の必要volumeを設ける…（チェニスのカルタージュの家）"、④"外面に関しては第二の型式の純粋なフォルムを取り…、内部に関しては第一と第三の型式の利点と特色を備えたもの…（ポアシーのサヴォア邸）"。註6) ここでは、抽象的形態へと徹底的に還元するのではなく、具象性を残した要素的形態へと抽象化しているため、具象性に抽象性が孕むという両義的なものとなっている。つまり、それぞれはル・コルビュジエの作品を想起させるものでありながらも、単純化されたタイプ(型)として提示され、これまでの建築を単純な形態あるいは要素の組合せにし、それぞれに型を与えることでobject化(部品化)しているということができる。さらに自ら生み出したドミノも単純要素化された型の一つとして扱い、サヴォア邸の生成をそれらの型の複合として提示し、型の並置と統合が同時に示されている。

1-1-3：プランによるコントロール

ル・コルビュジエはプランによって、建築をコントロールしようとした。プランを基準平面と捉え、その基準平面においてvolumeをコントロールすることを求めた。volumeの配置、変形の操作をおこなうのである。コルネリアス・ファン・デ・フェンは以下のように述べている。

1929年に発表した「住宅構成に関する4つの型」（図1-3）について、ル・コルビュジエは「プレシジョン」の中で、次のようにタイプ分けする。①"各構成部分がその有機的構成理由

註6) ル・コルビュジエ（井田安弘・芝優子訳）、前掲書下、pp.25-26
註7) Cornelis van de Ven: Space in Architecture, Van Gorcum Assen / Amsterdam (1978) コルネリス・ファン・デ・フェン、佐々木宏 (訳)『建築の空間』丸善、1981年、p.189,l9〜l16

"ル・コルビュジエの第2の原理は「サーフェイス」である。それは彼にとって工場の形態の清潔さを意味している。それは新様式において装飾された拒絶すべきものではない。第3の原理として彼はそれを「プラン」に設定する。ル・コルビュジエにとってそれは形態の発生機を意味している。平面は、「volume」と空間の間を調整するものである。そしてかつてのフランスの理論家のブロンデルやヴィオレ・ル・デュクに従って、ル・コルビュジエは外部に対する内部よりもプランが先行すべきである。"と言明していること。さらに、続けて、"建物は石けんの泡のようなものである。外部は内部の結果である。"註7)

とル・コルビュジエは書いていることを示している。このことから、ル・コルビュジエの volume は運動性を孕むものであり、運動性のある内部の結果が外部を規定しているのである。すなわち、ル・コルビュジエの volume は、マッスで固定化された内部性から生み出されるのではなく、不安定で変動する volume が、プランによって明確に規定され、内部と外部との境界であるサーフェイスを決定していくという順序なのである。すなわち、無秩序に膨張する volume をプランによってコントロールすることによって、volume に秩序が与えられ、サーフェイスが決定されるのである。したがって、サーフェイスは二次的なものであり、コントロールされるものである。このようにコントロールして初めて、volume はソリッド化し object 化される。

伝統的に西欧はタンジブルなものに対する意識が強く、可視的で可触的な object 重視の意識に支配されている。ル・コルビュジエは、そうした西欧的意識の延長上にあったが、volume を最初からソリッド化させていない点で、新たな地平を用意したのである。

volume を、一旦は気化したものとして認識した上で固定化させ、次は、ソリッド化された object 間に存在する関係性へと向かうのである。これは、制作者の意識である。建築を設計するものにとって、volume は最初から固定化されているものではない。様々な要因によって、揺れ動き変動するものであることは周知の事実である。そして最終的に決定され固定化される、ル・コルビュジエは、そうした制作者としての建築家の立場から、このことを語ったのである。

サーキュレーションのコントロール

ル・コルビュジエは、建築家として、volume だけでなく、サーキュレーションの問題にも直面せざるを得なかったことは理解される。一般的にプランは volume の決定や配置だけでなく、サーキュレーションをも調整する。ル・コルビュジエによる volume のコントロールは、二次的にサーキュレーションをコントロールすることになるからだ。すなわち、ル・コルビュジエはプランというデヴァイスによって、volume だけでなく、サーキュレーションをもコントロールしていたと言えるのである。

すなわち、ル・コルビュジエは、節操のないサーフェイスの存在を忌み嫌い、無秩序になりがちな volume と同時にサーキュレーションをもプランでコントロールしようとしたと言える。ル・コルビュジエのプランは、そうしたコントロール装置であり、volume やサーキュレーションはプランによってコントロールされて初めて成立する概念であった。

1-2：ル・コルビュジエの両義性について

ここで言う両義性とは、ル・コルビュジエの作品における、要素形態である volume に孕む両義性のことである。その両義性そのものに二つの方向性が解釈され、それらはル・コルビュジエの作品とその成立背景を精緻に分析することから明らかになる、というよりはむしろ、前述した現代建築の二つの潮流、アイゼンマンとコールハースの設計思想を遡行的に眺めることから浮かび上がってくるものとして捉えている。

そこで、敢えて名前を付けるとすれば、一つは、volume 間の関係性としての内部性である。もう一つは、volume が持つ繋がりとしての外部性である。すなわち、関係性の内部性とは、例えば、要素 volume 間の図と地の関係などを示す。また外部性は、volume と機能的なつながりのことなどを言う。

こうした volume の関係性を内的原理として見るか、外的関係として見るかの差異である。

1-3：ル・コルビュジエ作品の両義性

ここでは、内在的論理、外在的論理というアイゼンマンやコールハースの異なるアプローチへとつながっていくル・コルビュジエ作品における内部性と外部性について、歴史的に概観していく。ここではその代表的なものを挙げる。その際に、ル・コルビュジエにおける内部性および外部性とアイゼンマンやコールハースにみられるそれらとは内容は必ずしも一致するものではない。それはあくまで、関係性の方向性（内部へ向かうか、外部へ向かうか）という問題であり、何を内部と捉えるかによって外部自身も変化していくものとして、本稿において内部性、外部性という言葉を使用している。

また、こうした西欧におけるル・コルビュジエの建築理論の批判的継承とは異なるもう一つの流れが日本にある事も記して置くべきであろう。すなわち、ル・コルビュジエ作品を、彼の弟子達を中心とする直截的な導入である。残念なことに、彼らはル・コルビュジエの建築理論の継承者にはなり得なかった。未来へと開く時間性からは退き、ル・コルビュジエの忠実な弟子として、彼の思考を維持しようとしたのである。新たな理論的な展開はなく、日本という地域へとル・コルビュジエの形態を定着させることを追求したのみで終わったのであった。

1-3-1：ドミノシステム

ル・コルビュジエは、近代建築を普遍化するにあたり「ドミノ住宅」（図 1-4）を提示した。ドミノは「柱」、「床」、「階段」といった object の配列による構成へと近代建築を古典的な建築から抽象化したものであり、ミース・ファン・デル・ローエがシュプレマティスムから影響を受け「点」、「線」、「面」へと抽象化したものとは大きく異なる。

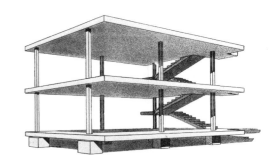

Fig.1-4 ドミノ住宅
階段とスラブと柱：ダイレクトな近代建築の一般化
object タイプ
エレメントを客観的・俯瞰的に捉えている

ル・コルビュジエの普遍化は、抽象化することではなく、建築の要素に対しては、Purism の立場から一つ一つの要素が機能的な完成品である object としてみなしていたため、それらの object を配置することが設計であった。あくまでも多様な具象的なものへと転換する以前の普遍的なシステムとして捉えており、ミースのように絶対的な抽象性へと結晶化させるものではなかった。ミースによって還元化された「点」、「線」、「面」としての柱や壁は、絶対的な空間を成立させるためにそれぞれの関係性が厳密に統合されたのに対し、ル・コルビュジエの object は、object 間の関係性に基づいた調整によって、あくまで並置されている。それらは、ガルシュの住宅やサヴォア邸において顕著である。また、近代建築の五原則としての「ピロティ」、「自由な平面」、「自由な立面」、「横長窓」、「屋上庭園」も同様なことが言える。

1-3-2：サヴォア邸　近代建築の五原則
ル・コルビュジエの object には機械の部品としてのメタファーがある。機械を構成している部品（object）はそれぞれの完結した機能を備えつつ、一つの統合体を形成している。

サヴォア邸（図 1-5）は、空間は視覚的には連続していながらも、アクティビティを引き受ける空間は部品化された独立性の強い空間である。すなわち異なるアクティビティが同時に多発し、視線は連続しているのに実際には連続しないというアンビバレンツな現象が出現しているのである。異なる平面構成をもつ各階も切断されている。透明で均質な空間を求めるのではなく、各部分が切断され、不均質で断片的な世界が表出されている。

ル・コルビュジエは、機械のような統合体としての建築を目指したものであったが、機械を詳細に模倣したものではなく、あくまでメタレベルにおけるものであった。そこには統合という言葉とは裏腹に、実際はそれぞれの object の並置であった。ル・コルビュジエは、この並置概念により、現前する経験を直接的に構成させ、不連続で機械的な部品化された空間を集積させているのである。そのことは、異なる方向性を孕んでおり、様々な解釈を生み出す。コールハースのアプローチのような新たな可能性を生み出し、一方でアイゼンマンのアプローチを生み出すのである。

Fig.1-5　サヴォア邸
ピロティ、屋上庭園、自由な平面、横長窓、自由な立面
：ダイレクトな（建築言語の中での）一般化、object タイプ

1-3-3：トラセ・レギュラトゥール（規整線）

古典的な比例やプロポーションの数比原理を対角線の平行と
垂直によって調和をとる手法へと視覚化した。（図1-6）すな
わち、目に見えない数値を見えるものとした。あるいは、数
学的な比率を具体的な建築設計の調和的手法として提示した
といえる。オーダーや木割りに見られる数比は寸法の数値の
比率を調和させるもので、視覚的な要素よりも実際の施工上の
合理的性質が強い。パッラーディオは数比を分割の比率として
視覚化した。パッラーディオとル・コルビュジエのガルシュの
家との相同性についてはロウの論証に疑うところはないが[註8]、
パッラーディオは分割の比率をXYZ方向にそれぞれ並置した
のみで、その比率どうしの関係性には至っていない。ル・コル
ビュジエはそれを二つの方向の関係性、すなわち矩形の比率
としてその比率どうしの関係性をトラセ・レギュラトゥール
（規整線）として古典的な比例やプロポーションの議論を整理
したということができる。

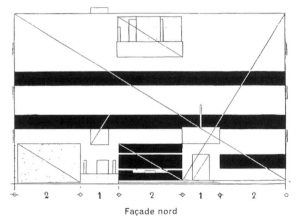

Façade nord

Fig.1-6　トラセ・レギュラトゥール（規整線）
古典的な建築を読み取る認識する手段であり、
同時に制作する手段として提示された

註8）Colin Rowe, The Mathematics of the Ideal Villa and Other Essays, The MIT Press (1982)

1-3-4：モデュロール　古典的身体×プロポーション

 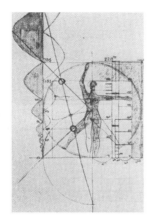

Fig.1-7　モデュロール
単純な平面幾何に結び付けられた古典的身体から幾何級数的な連続する幾何学へ
と身体を関連付け、
極小と極大を結びつけるものとして都市計画にも応用された

　そして、さらに前述の規整線を黄金比と人体寸法に関連付けることで絶対的な離散量として提示したのがモデュロール（図1-7）である。ここでは人体の各部の寸法は、機械の完成品の部材寸法であり、その寸法の値を黄金比と並置することで古典的な身体と幾何学の視覚的関係性に置き換わって、近代の科学と機械による精緻な身体が提示された。建築や都市を構成する上で寸法は細部を規定し、その積み上げによって全体が形成されている。そうした意味において寸法体系としてモデュロールの体系を用いることは、美しい調和へと建築を導くものと思われたが、実際に厳密にそれを適用することはル・コルビュジエでさえも難しかったと言われている。

Chapter 2

アイゼンマンの建築概念
diagram によって、建築の内部性の関係性を図式化する流れ[註1)]

2-1：力動的な diagram の基礎となる volume 概念の出自
2-1-1：volume 概念

本来ル・コルビュジエの volume の概念は固定化したものではなく、変動するものとして解釈しなければならないものであると思われる。ある意味で、アイゼンマンは、こうした後世の混乱したル・コルビュジエの volume の概念を検証し、再構築とさらなる発展を試みたと言えるのである。さらに、アイゼンマンは、volume なる概念をル・コルビュジエの概念を越えて再定義したのであった。ル・コルビュジエの作品にアイゼンマンは volumetric な原理であるムーヴメントを発見し、そのロジックを原理化していく。

アイゼンマンは、建築の volume がもつ力の関係性のロジックが建築をコントロールするべきであるという意識をもつ。そこには関係性という水平に横断していこうとする意識が存在するが、それを原理として抽出しようとしたところに、ル・コルビュジエが建築を内的論理が現れるプランというデヴァイスによってコントロールしようとする意識の延長があり、内的論理によってコントロールされるべきであるという正統で古典的な意識内にあると言える。リヒターが次のように述べているように、建築の真正性と真実性を求めるモダニスト特有の建築概念に未だ留まっていると言えよう。

" 正確に例示され、わかりやすい構築で、また可視的に示された異なる部分の集積であるべきという建築の真正性と真実性を求める叫びは、モダニスト特有の建築概念の基礎であった。"[註2)]

ただ、異なるところは、各 volume がもつ力の関係性への着目である。ル・コルビュジエの volume 概念が関係性への萌芽を孕むにもかかわらず、コントロール装置であるプランにしか意識が向かなかったのに対し、アイゼンマンは建築の volume がもつ力の関係性に着目するのである。また、後述のコールハースは、アイゼンマンとは真逆の方向で volume がもつ関係性に着目する。すなわち、最初に volume から意味を一旦切断する。その上で、現実の状況から得られた情報の関係性を整理し、その関係性を意味の剥がされた volume 群へと再び転化させるという正反対の方向をとるのである。これもアイゼンマンの方向とは異なるが、各 volume がもつ関係性への着目でもある。ここに、アイゼンマンが、ル・コルビュジエの volume 概念を発展させ、自身の volume 概念に運動性を孕ませることの契機が認識できる。このように関係性への探求は、ル・コルビュジエからアイゼンマンやコールハースへと受け継がれ、関係性をとりまとめるプログラムとして、次の新しい時代のデザインの方向性を展開していくのであった。このことに関しては、後述する。

註1) 本章は拙稿：山口隆「近代建築におけるプログラム的空間生成の萌芽」『建築設計 06』日本建築設計学会、2018 年、pp.85 ～ 92、を加筆修正したものである。
註2) ダグマル・リヒター、前掲論文、p.140,l36-p.144,l2
註3) 特にパリのラ・ヴィレット公園コンペ案において、建築や都市の設計における新しいコンセプトとして注目された。
註4) ルドルフ・ウィットカウワー『ヒューマニズム建築の源流』彰国社、1971 年

2-1-2：抽象化から diagram へ

アイゼンマンは、ル・コルビュジエの一般化を反復しながら、さらに抽象的なヴォキャブラリーとシンタックスに還元していく。object に結合する意味が反転することで、様々な捉え方が生まれる、静的な形式ではない矛盾を孕んだ両義的関係に着目し、図と地の反転から力学のベクトルを抽出し、関係性を diagram として全体性へと統合しようとした。

その一方で、object にデータや意味が結合することに着目し、object を操作することで、自己と他者との関係、外部と内部、ソリッドとヴォイドという立場のスイッチング、および object と機能や意味との関係を紡ぎ出そうとしているのがコールハースである。そして、アイゼンマン的な仮定では捉えられないル・コルビュジエの思考、すなわち、部品化された建築 object の並置の思考はコールハースへと引き継がれていく。社会のあらゆる事象を設計に組み込もうとする考え、すなわち、社会の欲望をデータ化し、整理し、機能を juxtapose（並置）[註3]させる思考である。この二つの方向性は後の建築思潮の流れを大きく二分することに繋がっていく。

ル・コルビュジエが建築を抽象化したものをさらにアイゼンマンは抽象化させていく道を選択する。それは、diagram の発想であり、建築の言語化であると言える。ルドルフ・ウィットカウアーのパラディアン・シェマの分析[註4]や、パッラーディオとル・コルビュジエの関係性の解明を行ったロウ[註5]の流れを汲むアイゼンマンにとって、この流れは当然と言って良い立場であろう。アイゼンマンはそうしたシェマを三次元の空間を生成する diagram として、ル・コルビュジエをはじめとした近代建築の分析から導き出すことになる。この点に関して本章において考察する。

2-2：アイゼンマンによる近代建築の分析
interiority[註6] を表現する diagram

前述したように、ル・コルビュジエはプランによって、建築をコントロールしようとした。プランを基準平面と捉え、その基準平面において volume をコントロールすることを求めた。平面だけでなく立面においてもコントロールの操作をおこなうのである。その基準は西欧の伝統的な美の価値観だった。すなわち面に投影された関係性が、静的な比例数理によって支配されるべきであると考えたのである。

アイゼンマンの博士論文において、本質的に、アイゼンマンは2つの方法において、形式性のアイデアを定義するために diagram を使用したという。

" 最初に、最も明白な形式性は美学から区別された。二番目に、さらに一層捉らえがたい関心事は、形式性が、建築の interiority における form の安定したセットとは異なっていると見られることだった。"[註7]

当時、形式性におけるこの違いは、特に近代運動に関連して、アイゼンマンの論文の記述では初期のままであった。この違いの本質は、アイゼンマンの論文において diagram を使用したように、diagram とは探求するものと見なされたものであった。

generic form とは、たとえば直線性 － 特定の直線に対立するものとしての － そして空間の中の form の関係性によって提案された form のプロセスのアイデア、たとえば回転とせん断、それはさらに form の実際のフィジカルな特徴と関係がなく、form 間の関係性の中に含まれた何かと関係があったものである。以前には、形式の diagram は、空間と時間の中の関係性

註5）コーリン・ロウ『マニエリスムと近代建築』彰国社、1981 年
註6）内部性もしくは内在性と訳されるが、アイゼンマンの重要な概念であるため、本稿では原語表記としている。Exteriority との対概念。
註7）DD p.51,l15-l21（筆者翻訳）

もしくは直線性については、めったに議論しなかった。形式のdiagramが機能と同様にformを扱った時、壁の厚さのような重要なものや、空間における記譜法としての形式のdiagramの可能な効果を無視しながら、そのようなdiagramは還元的で幾何学的な抽象概念となった。[註8]

アイゼンマンは、従来、建築が扱ってきたformは二次的なfigure（図）/ground（地）の関係を扱うゲシュタルトであり、三次元的な建築においては不十分であることを説く。[註9]
アイゼンマンは、そうした二次元の基準平面における操作を一歩進めて、movementとvolumetricという方法により、コントロールデヴァイスとして三次元化させていく。
そこには静的な比例数理という西欧の伝統的な美の価値観からは離脱していく可能性を秘めていた。
システムはformのヴォキャブラリーの一つの秩序である。それらはこのヴォキャブラリーの構文と文法が展開される範囲で枠組みを与える。システムとは本来的にあらゆる建物の意図や機能の秩序付けを明らかにするということから喚起されるように、それらの発展の中でコミュニケーションのすべての形式に必要な固有の構文と文法があるにちがいない。したがって、構文または文法の構成を制御する規則の基本的なセットは一般的な先例に由来しなければならないという。[註10]

こうして、アイゼンマンの態度は、過去の先例に倣って、原理を構築することを求めるのである。formのヴォキャブラリー、構文と文法を制御する規則は近代建築の事例から抽出されることによって、伝統的で静的な数比の論理を超えた新たな原理が継承されると信じていることが伺われる。アイゼンマンは、建築のformは言語というシステムと同等であるという認識から出発し、建築の言語も時間性の中で継続性をもちえる存在であることを前提にしている。過去の二次元的原理は不十分として、それに替わって、動きと方向をもった力という力学的なアナロジーに変換された三次元的原理を求めるのである。アイゼンマンはそうした操作を複雑に重層していくプロセスをとる。アイゼンマンの図式は、内的なエネルギーと外部の力とがせめぎ合うサーフェイスにおいて、調停されるべき状況において力学的なメタファーを使ったと言えるだろう。
どんなシステムの文法でも、特定の状況での形式的ヴォキャブラリーの実行に、基本的に関係している。したがって、一般形態からのひずみは、文法、つまりヴォキャブラリーの特定の用法とみなすことができる。そして、そのひずみを支配している規則は、システムとみなすことができる。アイゼンマンの思考においては、一般性から特殊性を導き出すという基本的な構えがある。そうした一般的なるものから特定の状況への移行においてのひずみに注目し、ひずみを支配している規則を抽出するのである。

diagramは、建築のinteriorityを明瞭に表現するための、ひとつの潜在的手段である。diagramはプランではなく、静的な実体でもない。むしろ、新しい形を生み出す潜在能力として、建築のinteriorityとanteriority（先在性）[註11]の上に流れる、一連のエネルギーとして考えられるともいう。[註12]アイゼンマンのdiagramについては次章において考察する。

2-2-2：アイゼンマンの形態操作における用語の定義
formは多くの誤解を生み出す言葉である。アイゼンマンのformの定義に入る前に、ここで、formについて定義を明確

註8）DD p.52（筆者要約）
註9）DT Chapter Two p.57（筆者要約）
註10）DT Chapter Three p.89（筆者要約）
註11）anterioriとは、先在する歴史上における全ての知の総体とも言えるもの。本書では先在性という訳にしている。

にしておくことは有意義である。form の訳語としては、主に形を表す形態と形式があてられている。英語では、視覚的に目に見える形に対しては figure、shape などの単語が相当し、form は視覚的に見えるものとしてだけではないどちらかというと形式に近く、それらと区別されて使われている。したがって、アイゼンマンの DT では、form について、generic form（一般的なフォーム）と specific form（具体的なフォーム）の二つのタイプに分け、generic form をプラトン的なものであるとし、そこからの変形、変容を specific form として捉え、generic form の特質を導き出すことの重要性を説いている。さらに generic form を線形的（linear）form と重心的（centroidal）form の二つのカテゴリーに分類し、それぞれの form の持つ固有の力学としての方向性や中心性といったものに、美的な嗜好性を超えた超越性を認め、普遍的性質をもつ generic form であることを説明している。

こうしたアイゼンマンの概念は、ル・コルビュジエの４つの原理（図 1-3）から出発したものと考えられる。アイゼンマンは、ル・コルビュジエの建築概念を巡って緻密な精査を加える。特にル・コルビュジエの volume の定義を再定義するのである。

form / volume / space

アイゼンマンは、form system について、以下のようにまずはヴォキャブラリーを定義づけていく。従来、建築が扱ってきた form は二次元的な図と地の関係を扱うゲシュタルトであり、三次元的な建築においては不十分であることを説く。そのため、三次元的な form を提唱し、volume として定義する。すなわち、volume は三次元的な form であり、さらに中立的でエネルギーを持たない space とは区別されるものとする。

volume はニュートラルな space の範疇の中にありながら、動的な性格を帯びるものと定義する。すなわち、内的なエネルギーを持たない中立で静的な space の動的な状況を volume と呼び、以下のように定義している。そこから volume による三次元的な図と地の関係を導き出していく。（図 2-1）

" この二つの語の重要な違いは、volume は動的な感覚で考えられるということであり、それは個別化され、限定された、内包される space であるということである。それは圧力を及ぼしているようにも、それにかけられる圧力に抵抗する能力があるようにも考えられる。このように連続で束縛のない状態として考えられる space という言葉は、たとえすべての form がその状態の中に存在することが認められなければならないとしても、重複的な言葉になる。space はそれ自身の正当性において、ふるまうこと、流れること、あるいは互いに貫入することもできない。建築の form は space の中に存在する volume として考えられる。 volume は space の動的な状態であり、境界を限定することと封じ込めることによってもたらされる、すなわちそれは限定された境界によって、活性化された space のことであるから、圧力のない状態の中では考えることはできない。" 註 13)

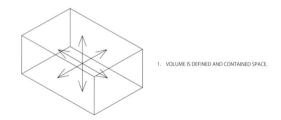

1. VOLUME IS DEFINED AND CONTAINED SPACE.

Fig.2-1　VOLUME IS DEFINED AND CONTAINED SPACE

註 12）DD pp.37-38（筆者要約）
註 13）DT p.59,l9-l19（筆者翻訳）

また、volume の動的性質について、以下のようにも述べている。

" まず、volume の動的状態は、それに作用している内包している力に抵抗する必要が生じる。これらの力はあらゆる物理的あるいは抽象的妨害から生じ、space の中立的条件に影響を与えるものである。その内部圧力は、境界を制限する状態への抵抗、すなわち、ムーヴメントあるいは動線と volume の中に配置された（マッスとして考えられる）ものを内包するサーフェイスとして考えられるかもしれない。さらに、再び内部と外部の特定の条件によって、あらゆる volume は与えるあるいは受け入れる両方の form としてみなすことができる。" 註14)

ここで重要なことは、volume の定義が space の特殊形であり、固体としての立体の意識を越えているということである。すなわち、volume はあくまでも space の一部であり、内包する力に呼応している動的状態というエネルギーを所有しているのである。そうしたエネルギーを封じ込める境界やサーフェイスによって圧力が生じ、中立的な space が動的な volume として定義されると認識している点である。この定義はル・コルビュジエの volume の定義を進化させたものと解される。このことに関しては後述する。

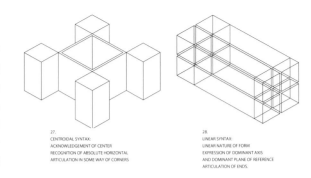

27.
CENTROIDAL SYNTAX:
ACKNOWLEDGEMENT OF CENTER
RECOGNITION OF ABSOLUTE HORIZONTAL
ARTICULATION IN SOME WAY OF CORNERS

28.
LINEAR SYNTAX:
LINEAR NATURE OF FORM
EXPRESSION OF DOMINANT AXIS
AND DOMINANT PLANE OF REFERENCE
ARTICULATION OF ENDS.

Fig.2-2　CENTROIDAL SYNTAX(左図), LINEAR SYNTAX(右図)

volumetric

この構文について、建築表現の基礎となる volume がどのように与えられるのか、すなわち volumetric に関して、マッス・サーフェイスシステムによるものとムーヴメントシステムによるものとして分析されていく。

まず、ロウの透明性の分析での、ル・コルビュジエのガルシュの住宅が、垂直スクリーンの連続として挙げられ、水平と垂直のスクリーンの統合としてショーダン邸を挙げる。さらにテラーニのカサ・デル・ファッショはそのような垂直スクリーンの連続とも、一つのマッスとしても捉えられる両義的な構成であることを説く。また、ル・コルビュジエによる「近代建築の 4 つの構成」について、ラ・ロッシュ - ジャンヌレ邸をマッスであるとし、ガルシュはマッスでもありサーフェイスでもある両義的な volume であるとし、カルタゴの住宅では、絶対的グリッドの中のマッスとして、サヴォア邸は、それら三つのパターンのどれとも捉えることのできる図と地の関係が曖昧なもの、弁証法的に昇華されたものとして解釈しなおされ（図1-3）、volume のゲシュタルトが定義される。

註 14）DT p.61,l16-l23（筆者翻訳）
註 15）DT Chapter Two pp.57-83

2-3：アイゼンマンの form system

2-3-1：ル・コルビュジエ

アイゼンマンが form の生成システムを導くにあたり、前提とされた建築 form の「属性」として、過去の建築が分析され、そこから form の「属性」が抽出されている[註15]。その分析対象のほとんどは、ル・コルビュジエの作品であった。この意味は重要である。

ル・コルビュジエの作品はそもそも、ル・コルビュジエ自身によって古典的な建築が解釈され、そこから近代建築へと一般化された作品であった。アイゼンマンも述べている通り、マス―サーフェイスシステムを初めに提示したのがル・コルビュジエであった。その意味でもル・コルビュジエは、アイゼンマンにとって重要な位置を占める。

volume の属性として、グリッドとの関係がル・コルビュジエの作品から抽出されている。中でもロンシャン教会堂については、マス（量塊）としての曲面と絶対的なグリッドとの関係性として捉えられ、規則的な二次元グリッドが引き延ばされたような構成として、次の時代のコンピューターによるメッシュ編集を予見させる。また、空間生成システムを発展させる最も中心となっている概念を導いたものが、ル・コルビュジエの著書「プレシジョン」で解説されている近代建築の4つの平面計画形式であり、それらをアイゼンマンは「古典的な図／地のシステム」として、volume をマス／サーフェイス／グリッドの関係として再解釈していることは既に述べた。（図 1-3）

さらにロウによる透明性の分析から着想を得て、volume を成立させているサーフェイスを、スキンによって全体を覆われたものと、プレーン（面）の連続した総体としての表面に区別している。（図 2-3）

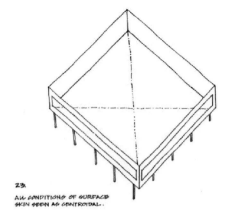

23.
ALL CONDITIONS OF SURFACE
SKIN SEEN AS CENTROIDAL.

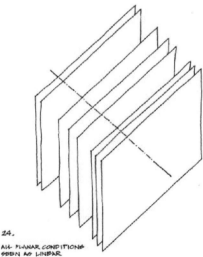

24.
ALL PLANAR CONDITIONS
SEEN AS LINEAR

Fig.2-3
ALL CONDITIONS OF SURFACE SKIN SEEN AS CENTROIDAL（左図）
ALL PLANAR CONDITIONS OF SEEN AS LINEAR SYNTAX（右図）

また、form の属性としてムーヴメントを導入し、その中の一つのカテゴリーである螺旋運動に対する形態として、「成長する美術館」とサヴォア邸のスロープが挙げられ、ライトのグッゲンハイム美術館を入れた 3 つのタイプのうち 2 つがル・コルビュジエの作品から導き出されている。さらに、ル・コルビュジエの 3 つの作品から 3 つの volumetric システムのタイプ；垂直面群による volume、水平面群による volume、格子面群による volume、を導いている。（図 2-4）

これらの分析の結果、アイゼンマンは DT 第三章の最後で volume のシステムを大きく二つのタイプ、中心性を持った volume と線形 (リニア) な volume に抽象化する。（図 2-2）さらに、volume の属性である面の構成の関係性を先のル・コルビュジエの作品をさらに抽象化させた図式として導き出している。ここでは、ル・コルビュジエの作品をトレースしたような壁の厚みは表現されず、シングルのラインで描かれた面どうしの関係性に還元されている。（図 2-5）

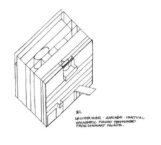 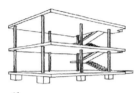 

Fig.2-4
VERTICAL VOLUMETRIC PLANES TENSIONED FROM DOMINANT FACADE (左図)
HORIZONTAL VOLUMETRIC PLANES (中図)、VOLUMETRIC PLAID (右図)

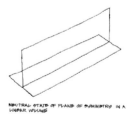 

Fig.2-5
NEUTRAL STATE OF PLANES OF SYMMETRY IN A LINEAR VOLUME (左図)
IN CORNER SITE WITH ONE SIDE DOMINANT SURFACE OF SYMETRY IS DISLOCATED TOWARDS THE DOMINANT SURFACE TO RESTORE BALANCE(中図)
ALL VERTICAL AND ORTHOGONAL PLANES ARE AFFECTED BY THIS DOMINANT SURFACE(右図)

註 16）モネオによれば、"アイゼンマンのテラーニに対する見方は、建築における統辞的なメカニズムの意味について理解させてくれる。「テラーニのフォルムの展開のプロセスは、対象を抑圧しようとする試み、あるいはコンセプチュアルな深い構造の視覚的な存在に同意したうえでの、表面構造の解読として理解できる」" ラファエル・モネオ『現代建築家 8 人の設計戦略と理論の探究』A+U、2008 年

2-3-2：ジュゼッペ・テラーニ

アイゼンマンのテラーニ作品の分析は、アイゼンマンのdiagram 研究において、最も重要な位置を占める。なぜなら、テラーニは、古典的なプロポーションやオーダーといった美のシステムを内部と外部の矛盾の調整によって建築の構成を試みており、そのシンタックスの中にアイゼンマンは生成的なdiagram を読み取っているからである。註16)

以下、そのことを詳述する。

カサ・デル・ファッショについてアイゼンマンは、まず、volume の属性としてマッス（量塊）からの、くり貫きの形態と面の連続としての形態の両義的な形態として抽出している。そしてそれらは内部状態（内部プログラム）を再現している

マッス（量塊）と、外部の力（外的なプログラム）を再認識させる表面（サーフェイス）との拮抗として分析している。つまり、この建物の内部と外部の矛盾の解決が、弁証法的に形態化されているという。それは純粋な建築形態の内部システム、とりわけ比例やプロポーションといった古典的命題のなかでの美しい関係性にとらわれながらも、現実的な機能的なプログラム、廊下の必要性や、開口部の必要性といったものとの葛藤が見られる。建築史や現実の世界において日常的にこのような葛藤があること、あるいは機能的問題のみに始終した場合、絶対的な美の問題に関わることもしないことのほうが現実には多いため、葛藤の末に行き着いた弁証法的、両義的な解決にアイゼンマンは形態生成の力学を読み取っている。（図 2-6）

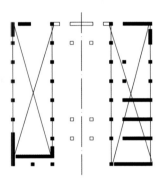

24 .
BALANCE ABOUT LONGITUDINAL AXIS
OF DOUBLE BAY OFFICES AND SINGLE
BAY OFFICES PLUS CORRIDORS

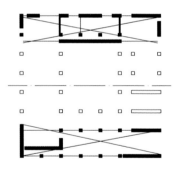

25.
BALANCE ABOUT TRANSVERSE AXIS
REAR OFFICES AND CORRIDOR WITH
ELONGATED ENTRY BAY

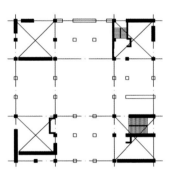

26 .
INTERNAL PLAIDING ACKNOWLEDGES
CENTROIDAL FORM

Fig.2-6　カサ・デル・ファッショ
内部プログラムと volume のバランス

サンテリア幼稚園も、カサ・デル・ファッショ同様に内部プログラムと外部プログラムの葛藤が見られる。カサ・デル・ファッショでは、その葛藤はマス(量塊)と表面張力(サーフェイス)との葛藤として認められたが、ここでは主に柱の方向性が内部と外部を調停し、統合する役目を果たしている。(図2-7)

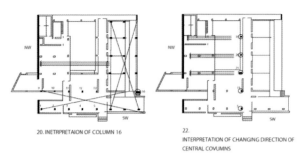

20. INETRPRETAION OF COLUMN 16

22. INTERPRETATION OF CHANGING DIRECTION OF CENTRAL COVUMNS

Fig.2-7　サンテリア幼稚園
柱の解釈(左図)、中心部柱の方向性の解釈(右図)

テラーニの作品は、ル・コルビュジエのようにobjectとして柱、床が存在するわけでもなく、ミースのように点・線・面といった抽象的な幾何学要素に還元されているわけでもない。ミースにおいては、表面と骨格はテクトニック的に分節され、ル・コルビュジエにおいては、白く塗りつぶされることで脱物質化され、抽象的な幾何学的volumeに還元された。テラーニにおいては、白く塗られ脱物質化されているが、柱と梁は面に穴が穿たれた面の一部として認識され、柱・梁といった分節がない三次元のフレームとして認識される。それはル・コルビュジエがvolumeの演算(ブーリアン)としてマス(量塊)を表現したこととも異なる。この発見はアイゼンマンにとって、その後のdiagram研究において重要な位置を占めたのである。
このテラーニの分析から導かれたdiagramが、基本となって

アイゼンマンのハウスプロジェクトに反映されている[註17]。

2-4：まとめ

2-4-1：volume概念の変遷と意味

アイゼンマンは、ウィットカウアーやロウの原理性を二次元的な形式性の中に固定化しようとする静的な分析から建築形態生成のプロセスを扱う動的分析への道を開いた。それらの分析の対象となったのがル・コルビュジエをはじめとした近代の建築家の作品であり、それらの作品の中に従来の古典的な幾何学や比例の図式だけでは説明しきれない力学を見出し、そこから形態のヴォキャブラリーと構文を導こうとした。それらがアイゼンマン独自のdiagramとして結実したのである。また、アイゼンマンは、volumeの概念をル・コルビュジエの概念を越えて再定義した。さらにル・コルビュジエの作品にアイゼンマンはvolumetricな原理であるmovementを発見し、そのロジックを原理化している。
当時翻訳として様々に解釈され、混乱したル・コルビュジエのle volumeの概念[註18]は、本来、内部のポテンシャルによって膨張収縮する気体のようなものとして解釈しなければならないものであると思われる。ある意味で、アイゼンマンは、こうした後世の混乱したル・コルビュジエのle volumeの概念を検証し、再構築とさらなる発展を試みたと言える。
アイゼンマンは、建築のvolumeがもつ力の関係性のロジックが建築をコントロールするべきであるという意識をもつ。そこには関係性という水平に横断していこうとする意識が存在するが、それを原理として抽出しようとしたところに、ル・コルビュジエが建築を内的論理が現れるプランというデヴァイスによってコントロールしようとする意識の延長があり、内

註17) アイゼンマンの自著『Diagram Diaries』(DD)のなかでテラーニのカサ・デル・ファッショとHouse Ⅰプロジェクトのdiagramの類似性について説明されている。
註18) ダグマル・リヒター、前掲論文
註19) Kostas Terzidis, Algorithmic Architecture, Elsevier Ltd. 2006,(邦訳)コスタス・テルジス『アルゴリズミック・アーキテクチュア』彰国社、2010年。本書では、哲学的な背景からアルゴリズムの一つであるスクリプト言語によって生成される形態の基礎的な事例が示されている。

的論理によってコントロールされるべきであるという正統で古典的な意識内にあると言える。

ただ、異なるところは、各 volume がもつ力の関係性への着目である。ル・コルビュジエの volume 概念が関係性への萌芽を孕むにもかかわらず、コントロール装置であるプランにしか意識が向かなかったのに対し、アイゼンマンは建築の volume がもつ力の関係性に着目するのである。また、コールハースは、アイゼンマンとは真逆の方向で volume がもつ関係性に着目する。

ここに、アイゼンマンが、ル・コルビュジエの volume 概念を発展させ、自身の volume 概念に運動性を孕ませることの契機が認識できる。このように関係性への探求は、ル・コルビュジエからアイゼンマンやコールハースへと受け継がれ、関係性をとりまとめるプログラムとして、次の新しい時代のデザインの方向性を展開していくのであった。このことに関しては、次章以降において詳述する。

2-4-2：ル・コルビュジエの建築概念の継承と発展

アイゼンマンの形態生成システムのほとんどはル・コルビュジエの作品より導かれた。それはル・コルビュジエの作品が近代建築の一般化から導かれた応用例として、原則を持っていたためである。すなわちル・コルビュジエの作品はそもそも、ル・コルビュジエ自身によって古典的な建築が解釈され、そこから近代建築へと一般化された作品であったからである。そのため、アイゼンマンは、ル・コルビュジエの作品に形態生成システムを導くための論理性が備わっていると理解したことが考察される。そして、アイゼンマンはそうしたル・コルビュジエの一般化を、さらに抽象的な図式 (diagram) へと

還元していくのであった。それに対して、ミースの作品がアイゼンマンの分析で扱われなかったのは、ミースの作品自体、ル・コルビュジエの作品のように矛盾を孕み、力学的な運動性を備えたものではなく、すでに絶対的な抽象性に到達したものであると見なしたため、それ以上の分析に及ばなかったと理解するべきである。それは逆説的にミースの作品の数学的な操作性に近似する意識を顕在化させていると言える。この操作性は、後述するコールハースらに見られる部品化と並置という方向性とはまた違った別の方向性として現代建築の一つの潮流であるアルゴリズミック・アーキテクチャー[註 19] 等に見られるコンピューター・プログラムの意識の中に見ることができる。それはさらにル・コルビュジエの後期の作品やモデュロールの試みにも通じている。そのことはル・コルビュジエのもう一面であるということもできる。

2-4-3：アイゼンマンの力動的な diagram

ギーディオンは、キュビズムにおける多視点による構成やル・コルビュジエの作品などに代表されるモダニズムの建築に、時間性や運動性が導入されているとして評価している。[註 20] すなわち各 object は静的で完結でありながら、その静的な object は観察者自身の認識や理解によって、時間性や運動性が読み取れるとしたのである。こうした subject による解釈可能な時間性や運動性は、アイゼンマンの目には、subject と object との関係において、何かしらの原理が存在していると映ったのである。アイゼンマンは、こうしたル・コルビュジエの作品における object と読み取る側の subject との間における時間性と運動性を解明しようとして、ル・コルビュジエの作品における力学的なメカニズムとして分析しようとした。その結果、

註 20) ジークフリード・ギーディオン『空間・時間・建築』丸善 1955 年

「図と地の反転による両義的な関係」、「静的な形式」を越えた「矛盾を抱えた関係」という特徴をル・コルビュジエの作品に見出していくのである。そして subject と object との関係性へと昇華させていくのである。

力動的な意識の萌芽をル・コルビュジエの両義的な建築概念の一方の連続性に見る。

ル・コルビュジエの建築的 object は次第に抽象化され、内部と外部の関係、部屋と部屋の関係、建物と周囲の関係、図と地の関係といったものが、壁で仕切られている空間をソリッドとする volume で考え、ソリッドとヴォイドが演算によって構成されることになる。こうした抽象化の側面に注目したのがアイゼンマンであり、アイゼンマンは統合という名のもとにル・コルビュジエの抽象化した形態の関係性を力学的なメカニズムとして解釈しようとした。

特に「四つの型」について、アイゼンマンは (平面ではない三次元の)volume のゲシュタルトとしてマッス／サーフェイス／グリッドとその複合と解釈している。

アイゼンマンは、ル・コルビュジエを中心とした一連の作品分析の中に、形態どうしの内在的な関係性、すなわち、図と地の反転による両義的な関係、「静的な形式」を越えた「矛盾を抱えた関係」という特徴を見出している。既に心理学、芸術の分野で見出されていたゲシュタルト理論の動的な関係性を、建築分野の内在的論理として「動的な原理」を抽出し、建築を生成する原理として適応させるべく diagram として、全体システムの統合を試みようとした。

一意に適応される関係性を内部化し、原理・法則を求めようとしたアイゼンマンのアプローチとは異なって、コールハースは、建築を構成しようとするあらゆる事象をそれぞれの object、すなわち、部品として捉え、建築や都市に見られるスケール間の断絶や空間的な断絶の直観的な把握から、各部品を並置することこそが、多様な意味を現出させるという設計思想に基づいている。(この点については後述する) その「部品化された object の並置」という概念こそル・コルビュジエの設計思想の流れを汲むものであり、このような問題意識は、object 相互の関係を外部化させるものである。

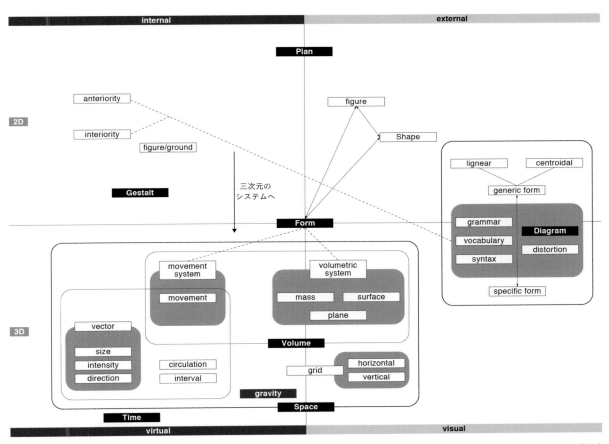

Fig.2-8 アイゼンマンの form システムまとめ

Chapter 3

平板的幾何学概念を越えようとするアイゼンマンの意識

建築論史的観点において、タイポロジーや、ル・コルビュジエ、ウィットカウアーやロウの立場が、二次元的で、ユークリッド幾何学的で、静的なものだとすれば、アイゼンマンのdiagramの立場は、三次元的で、位相幾何学的で、動的なものである。本章では、タイポロジーや、ル・コルビュジエ、ウィットカウアーやロウをアイゼンマンがどのように見ていたのかを通じて、アイゼンマンのinteriorityという概念の考察を行いたい。

これまで見てきたように、アイゼンマンは、ル・コルビュジエを中心とした一連の作品分析の中に、形態どうしの内在的な関係性、すなわち、figure（図）とground（地）の反転による両義的な関係、「静的な形式」を越えた「矛盾を抱えた関係」という特徴を見出している。既に心理学、芸術の分野で見出されていたゲシュタルト理論の動的な関係性を、建築分野の内在的論理として「動的な原理」を抽出し、建築を生成する原理として適応させるべくdiagramとして、全体システムの統合を試みようとした。

既に述べたように、ル・コルビュジエが建築を抽象化したものをさらにアイゼンマンはさらに展開させていく道を選択する。それは、diagramの発想であり、建築の言語化であると言える。ウィットカウアーのパラディアン・シェマの分析（図 3-1）や、パッラーディオとル・コルビュジエの関係性の解明（図 3-2）を行ったロウの流れを汲むアイゼンマンにとって、この流れは当然と言って良い立場であろう。アイゼンマンはそうしたシェマを三次元の空間を生成するdiagramとして、ル・コルビュジエをはじめとした近代建築の分析から導き出した。

3-1：過去の平板的建築概念に対する批判
3-1-1：タイポロジー、ボザール派 [註1] への批判

パッラーディオと初期モダニズムの間における建築論の変遷について、「Diagram Diaries」で、アイゼンマンは以下のように概観している。

" パッラーディオと初期モダニズムの間にはさまる年月において、建築理論が書かれ、断定的な論文として書き直された。それらは建築に対する規則と本質を展開した。建築の内部性は知ることができると思い込まれ、かように、標準としてありもしないのに想像された。
フランス革命が新しい制度をタイプ化し、刑務所・図書館・工場または病院を記号化する必要を起こした。それらは、新しい社会体制の記号になり、拡大していく建築の機能を組織化していく。建築論は、新しい用途のために典型的な構造を

註1) エコール・デ・ボザール（École nationale supérieure des Beaux-Arts パリ、フランス）、ボザールでの教育は伝統的、古典主義的な作品が理想とされ、これらの理想化された様式を踏襲させていく教育システムであり、ボザール様式と呼ばれるまでに至った。特に近代以前のアメリカは大きな影響を受けた。
註2) DD p42（筆者翻訳）
註3) ルイス・カーンの主要な建築概念であり、ライトはラーキン・ビルにおいて既に直感的にそうした考えを提示していた。

体系化していったのであった。 J.N.L. デュランの「Recueil et parallèle des édifices de tout genre」は、多くのタイポロジーのヴァリエーションにおいて定義されるように、建築の新しい機能を概説する。過去の前衛を当時の現在の interiority に関連付ける方法を提供するために、新しい機能を標準化と典型化する両方の必要性を示すのであった。"註2)

当時の建築論は、建築の interiority を捕捉できると思い込む。ありもしない標準型として想像され、断定的な論文として書き直され、建築に対する規則と本質を展開したと当時の建築論を、アイゼンマンは概観している。アイゼンマンは、タイポロジーでは、建築の interiority を捕捉することは不可能であると思っているのである。

タイポロジーは、参照のための、二次元的で固定化された型であり、そこには時間の概念は存在しない。タイポロジーは、二次元平面に投影され、視覚化されたものを分類しているだけであり、今までたくさんある中での解の一つに適合させようとするものと位置づけられる。むしろ、それらは幾何学を原型として持ち、それらの配置や構成が形の論理となる。いわゆる構成論の基礎となるものである。また、ディテールのタイプとも連動しているため、まったく新しい創造を望むことよりも、参照行為としての創造過程を援護するものである。

"さらに、アイゼンマンは、ボザール派についても論じている。新しい建物の機能は、互いに関係のある部屋という方式に変えた。パッラーディオの別荘は、いわゆるサーヴァントとサーヴド註3)の関係へと道を譲った。廊下は、パブリックとプライベートを区別する装置になった。個々の独立した主題は集合的な主題に変わった。タイプが、デュランの標準化された型の構造から、フランス・ボザール (French Beaux Arts Academy) へ移ったとき、タイプは、ボザール派として知られるものになった。ボザール派はタイプの特定の形である。ボザール派はタイプに建築の優美なドレープを加える。それは、建物の利用と経験に関する独立した理解に、建物のタイプを関連付ける方法であった。ボザール派は 19 世紀中ごろから 20 世紀中ごろにかけて、十分に前衛として君臨する状況であった。1968 年と同じくらい遅れて、多くのアメリカの建築学校で、タイプと diagram の対抗するものとしてのボザール派は、まだ流行っていた。タイプの規範の範囲内で受け入れられる特定のボザール派が存在した。たとえば、ボザール派は、建物の中心軸上の開口の中央に柱を置くことは不可能であると言っていた。ボザール派の構成のための特定の規定と規則が存在した。たとえば、入るところ、入り方、端と中央の関係、背面と正面の関係。これら全ては、より多くの規定構造で提案され、今世紀中頃まで英語とフランス語で建築に普及した。"註4)

ボザール派への移行においても、タイポロジーの単なる一形式に過ぎないと見て、批判しているのである。タイポロジーは、その後、デュランの標準化された型の構造から、フランス・ボザール (French Beaux Arts Academy) へと移り、ボザール派はタイポロジーの特定の一形式であるとする。

3-1-2：アイゼンマンの空間分析
アイゼンマンの言説において、diagram という言葉の最初の使用は、1963 年の博士論文に現れた。この diagram は、ウィットカウアーのパッラーディオのヴィラの解析と、ル・コルビュジエとパッラーディオの比較における分析的な論文を受けて、

註4) DD p42,43 （筆者翻訳）

こうした form のロウのさらなる発展に応じる形で進化したものである。ウィットカウアーは、パッラーディオのヴィラに普遍性があることを示した。すなわち、「9 square grid」である。さらにロウは「理想的ヴィラの数学」において、全く異なった時代背景において存在するパッラーディオのヴィラとル・コルビュジエの住宅において、同一性を読み取り、普遍的な「9 square grid」を抽出したのであった。アイゼンマンは、こうした建築内部に孕む普遍的な原理の存在を信じ、diagram として提起し、批判的に継承する。アイゼンマンは、「彼らの研究は、form の再検討における diagram の私の使用の出発点である。この文脈において、機能、伝統的美学、社会的関心および機械の隠喩は、私にとっては、常に、なんでも好きなことをする表現主義のための退屈な正当化であった。」[註5]と述べている通り、内的探求をおこなうウィットカウアーやロウの意識を継承し、機能、伝統的美学や社会的問題への関心および機械的な隠喩をおこなうだけのグループとのスタンスの違いを示している。

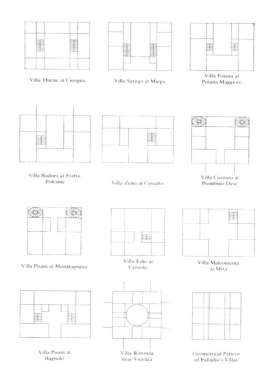

Fig.3-1　ウィットカウアーのパラディアン・シェマの分析

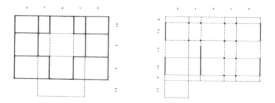

Fig.3-2　ロウによるパッラーディオとル・コルビュジエの比較図

註5) DD p49,l3-l11（筆者翻訳）以下原文：Clearly, Rowe and Wittkower were involved in what could be called the articulation of formal principles in architecture; their work is a starting point for my use of the diagram in a re-examination of the formal.

アイゼンマンの分析の立脚点となっている、ウィットカウアーのパラディアン・シェマの分析は、むしろ、建築の内部プログラムや柱や窓といった言語としての形態要素を削ぎ落とした結果、残るものとして建築の原型を導き出そうとするものであるが、規整線などと同様に、平板な図式にとどまった。さらに、アイゼンマンの学んだロウにおけるパッラーディオとル・コルビュジエの関係性の解明は、パラディアン・シェマの原理性に説得性を与えた。アイゼンマンはそうしたシェマを三次元の空間を生成する diagram として、近代建築の分析から導き出していることは、既に概観した。

中でも、次に見ていくアイゼンマンの初期のプロジェクトである住宅シリーズにおいては、テラーニの分析での diagram から展開を図っている。テラーニの場合、構造、機能、美学または象徴性では説明できない直観的に感じられたものを説明するための diagram であった。そうしたものから、建築の内部性への明瞭な表現の関係の本質をあばく方法としてアイゼンマンは diagram を用いているという。それらの関係を deep structure（深層構造）と呼んでいる。
テラーニの仕事と類似しながらも、異なっている点は、diagram が、建築の interiority と特定の建物との間にある関係性を同時に説明していることだとアイゼンマンは言う。敢えて機能または美学とは無関係なものを痕跡として挿入し、存在の不在についての考えを導入しようとしている。この建築のinteriority についてアイゼンマンがどのように考え、どのように建築として表現しているのか、住宅シリーズを通して概観していく。

3-2：力動的視点からの diagram 探求
アイゼンマンの form 生成システム「アイゼンマンの博士論文の解説を通じて」
3-2-1：動的な力学的視点と他分野との違いとしての建築の interiority

ウィットカウアーとロウの diagram は、安定性とアプリオリな状況としての form の解析に、本質的に依存していたが、アイゼンマンの diagram は、そうした静的な form に留まるものではなかった。すなわち、アイゼンマンの diagram は、先在する不安定性を内部へと diagram 化する際、可能性のある form の動的な開放を提案した。この事は重要である。
建築における形式主義のアーティキュレーションと呼びうるものに関係していたロウとウィットカウアーの研究は、form の再検討における diagram のアイゼンマンの使用の出発点であるが、アイゼンマンは、彼らとは、diagram の異なる使い方を提示し、異なる理論的根拠を提案した。すなわち、それは、単純に二次元平面に投影されている平板な form の表れよりも、その奥に内包された論理 deep structure である。伝統的な記名的建築家のデザインプロセスからも離れた建築自身のプロセスに関係する根拠である。
そのような論理は、form 自体の中で見つけられないものであった。むしろ、diagram のプロセスの中に見つけられることをアイゼンマンは信じていた。
その diagram のプロセスは、他の学問分野（とりわけ絵画と彫刻のような造形の学問分野）と建築における form／内容の関係性の間の違いを拡げる潜在性を持っていた。

アイゼンマンは以下のように、記述している。

" 絵画、彫刻と建築との diagram は、しばしば内容が似ている
と見られるとしても、それらの間に重大ないくつかの違いが
存在している。この絵画、彫刻と建築との diagram との違い
は、建築の instrumentality（媒介）と建築の iconicity（類像性）
との間の、機能と意味の間の、そして究極的に、記号と意味
の間に横たわる建築における独特な関係性の中に見出された
とする。
これは、建築がもつ interiority として定義されるべきものに
関する私の研究のための基礎であった。"註6)

このアイゼンマンの言説は、建築を絵画や彫刻と同等に見て
いたロウとウィットカウアーの平板的で静的な見方に対する
批判である。アイゼンマンは、建築の instrumentality（媒介性）
と iconicity（図像性）との間の関係性の中に、建築の独自性
が見られると主張し、建築の独自性を追求する。そのために、
意味と連動する記号の存在を見直し、建築の内部に宿る動的
な関係性を導き出し、建築の interiority の存在への信念を見
い出すのである。
アイゼンマンは、建築には、いかなる時期の政治、社会、美学、
そして文化状況を明らかにできる可能性があり、それは建築
の歴史において、diagram によって議論されてきたことを示す。
それは、建築に内在するものの明示である。それを interiority
（内部性）と呼び、建築は、単に表象することだけでなく、こ
れらの社会政治状況を転換させ、批評性をもつ可能性を孕ん
でいるのだということを宣言する。註7)
アイゼンマンの博士論文の diagram は、構築された作品の、
建築の interiority への関係性についてアイゼンマンが考えた
最初の重要なドキュメントとして残存している。

3-2-2：住宅シリーズと interiority の探求

アイゼンマンは博士論文での近代建築の分析から生成的な
form system を構想し、その実践として、初期のプロジェクト
である住宅シリーズで diagram の探究をしていくだけにとど
まらず、建築の interiority に関する論理をも制作という中で
展開していくことを試みている。主に以下に掲げる三つの項
目について建築の interiority の探究を行っている。

表層構造／深層構造

既に述べたように、アイゼンマンはアートの分野と建築とを
区別することで、建築の interiority を明晰にしていくが、アー
トからの影響によって、概念的な展開を図っているところも
随所に見られる。
中でも、コンセプチャルアートからの影響より、コンセプト
をより明確に表現するために、プロセスを視覚化することを
目的として、diagram を導入していることが挙げられる。こ
のプロセスの視覚化において、単なる生成の手順を説明する
ものではなく、建築の深層構造を暴くものとして、住宅シリー
ズの説明の中で以下のようにアイゼンマンは言う。

" 深層構造についての考えが一組の論理的関係によって定義さ
れる一方、建物における不在の mark についての考えが、建
てられた object から interiority までの認識を動かすように
意図された。次に、form の本質の１つから潜在的他者性の
diagram まで interiority についての考えを動かすように、最
初に、意図された。すべての完全なものが一つの form を持っ
ているとはいえ、diagram において見られるとき、form の美
学は重要でないと主張された。

註6) DD p49,l22-p50,l11 （筆者翻訳）
註7) DD p37 （筆者要約）
註8) DD p59,l15 -p62,l11 （筆者翻訳）
註9) DD p58,l11 -p59,l14 （筆者翻訳）

Chapter 3   42

むしろ、diagram の完全なものが実際のフィジカルなコンテクストに置かれたとき、それらの空間的関係性の、diagram のいわゆるシンタックスの、空間と固有の論理における異なる位置は、interiority への関係を明瞭に表現するだろう。これらの完全なものが存在に対立するものとしての不在であったとき、これらは interiority において原初の不在の潜在的条件を特徴づけるだろう。"註8)

いわゆる表層構造と呼ばれる、出来上がったものの美的関係や機能的な物質性は重要なものではなく、それらを可能な限り削ぎ落して、深層構造としての内在的論理が認識されるような diagram のあり方を探求していることがわかる。
このような意味で、住宅シリーズで行われている diagram の探求は、単なる思考のプロセスを表現するための diagram ではなく、既成の認識を揺り動かすコンセプチュアルアートに習って、コンセプチュアルアーキテクチュアを模索する試行であると言える。

subject と object の関係性の見直しへ
建築の内部性の探求と同時に interiority そのものも以下のように問い続けている。

" 建築の interiority は、以前には、本質的な機能が含まれていたと仮定されていたのであり、建築の interiority における深層構造についての考えが、形式上の本質についての考えと同義であると決して意味されなかったということ、・・・。
もっと正確に言えば、前提条件としての深層構造についての考えは、違いそのものの interiority としての建築についての

考えを明らかにすることが意図された。それは、自身の形式上の条件にのみ従順なものとしての form と、機能と意味を具体化するものとしての form との間の違いであった。
これら初期の diagram は、形式的本質にもはや頼るのではなく、むしろ diagram 自体の論理における可能性に依存する潜在的な状況に依存する論理の仮定を含んでいた。
diagram は、現代のプロジェクトにおいては以前に認知されていない何かを指す試みであった。そして、形のヴォキャブラリーが同じであると言われる一方、その論争的な価値は diagram によって確かに修正されたのである。"註9)

一つの本質を求めるべく内部性が探求されるのではなく、差異によって認識を動かすことに目的が見いだされている。住宅シリーズでの試みは、建築に関わるあらゆる認識を疑い、認識の主体である subject と認識の対象である object の関係性を見直すことの探求の連続として存在している。

建築の記号性の探究
既に述べたように、アイゼンマンは、絵画や彫刻との違いについて、建築の instrumentality（媒介性）と iconicity（図像性）との間、機能と意味の間、究極的に、記号と意味の間に横たわる関係性の中に、建築の独自性が見られると主張し、建築の記号性の探究を住宅シリーズの中で行っている端緒が以下のようにうかがえる。

" これまで、伝統的に、diagram は、イコン的記号として使われてきた。すなわち、diagram は、外部のいくつかの比喩的な存在を参照した。

しかし、今や、その代わりに、diagram は一連の指標の記号として見なされるのである。：差異のシステム、それは、ほとんど比喩的またはイコン的内容を持たない。しかし、むしろ他の形式的なシステムと異なるように理解される表記法のシステムとして見られるだろう。これらの指標的記号は、それらのイコン的な状態から、さらに interiority の潜在的状態として、ある種の中吊り状態で存在すると考えられたのである。"註10)

さらに、続けて

" 建築におけるいかなる diagram も、常に機能と意味によって正当化されるであろう。diagram は、他のいかなる意図をも最初は曖昧にする。明らかに、すべての建築は、事物を持ち上げることと、そして保護し、取り囲み、分割する意図と何か関係があるように見なされるだろう。要するに、重力と静力学の法則に、基本的に従っているのである。
したがって、例えば、柱と壁は、最初、記号として、ほとんど解釈されないが、しかし組み立てのインテジャ（整数）として解釈されるのは、ありそうである。柱と壁を、組み立てとして、または組み立ての記号として、人々が少しでも解釈するかどうかは、このコンテクストにおいては、明確ではない。この考えは、「建築は、本質的に散漫な傍観者によって眺められる」というヴァルター・ベンヤミンの論文によって確認されている。ここで開発された diagram の考えは、以下のことを提示した。建築は、組み立てのインテジャとして、そして、また、あるレベルで、指標として、すなわち、（機能、意味、美学に関係していない）記号の他の状態として振る舞う可能性の両方として存在するであろう。この他の状態は、機能、構造、意味の必要な状態に関する過剰の一つとして、特徴づけられた。

その時、過剰さゆえに、それは、潜在的でアプリオリな不在のある形式として、見られることができた。なぜなら、それは、もはや、現前に、すなわち、組み立て、機能などに結合されなかったからである。"註11)

これまで、イコン的記号の表現として建築が生成されてきたことに対して、指標的記号としての diagram による自己参照的な記号としての建築生成が住宅シリーズで展開されている。その表現の方法として過剰による認識の曖昧化と、不在の認識という手法がとられていく。

3-3：住宅シリーズの言説を通じて、interiority に収斂させようとする意識
アイゼンマンの diagram が進展していくプロセス
自己参照性、位相幾何学などの多様な試み
3-3-1：form の美学から diagram へ
form の美学は重要ではなくなった
アイゼンマンは、自身の住宅作品の設計を通して diagram 探求を行っている。当然のごとく、彼の設計行為は、単なる form の美学に耽溺するものではなく、実験的な試みであった。そうした実験によって、アイゼンマンは diagram を構築しようとする。しかし、その道程は、紆余曲折し diagram を巡る多くの問題を発見していくのである。diagram を探査するために、さらに、派生する問題を発見し、diagram 探査の方向は拡散していく方向にあった。記号論的な問題、すなわち構造と物質との意味の切断、不在の問題など、多くの拡散した問題がアイゼンマンの思考を巡るのである。
特に、初期の住宅のプロジェクトは重要である。なぜな

註10）DD p64,l5 –l16（筆者翻訳）
註11）DD p64,l19 –p65,l22（筆者翻訳）
註12）DD p62,l12 –l20（筆者翻訳）

ら、初期の住宅プロジェクトを設計するプロセスで、建築の interiority の本質を、form の二次元的美学から diagram へとシフトさせているからである。この事は、動的な form への一層の発展であった。

アイゼンマンの最初の2つの住宅プロジェクトは、diagram によって構築された form に関する建築の interiority の関係性の探査をおこなうものであった。そこでは、diagram が建築の interiority と類似したロジックを描写することができるだろうということをアイゼンマンは仮定していた。アイゼンマンの新しい diagram は、歴史的に正統と思われてきた建築に対抗し、言語学的なものであった。さらに、diagram は構築された建築物において読まれ得る事を目論んでいた。

重要な事は、diagram は、建築物の意味、美学、機能の記号との置換が可能となり、慣習的な建築の interiority が疑われた事である。

初期の diagram において理解されなければならない最も重要なことは、建築の interiority における深層構造と form の本質とが同じであると見なされなくなり、form の美学の重要性は消失し、form の美学に代わって、diagram が浮上するとアイゼンマンは主張するのである。

そうした意味で、初期の diagram は、形式的な本質を求めるものではなく、diagram の論理における可能性を探求するものであった。

3-3-2：差異としての diagram
本質の探究から動的なシステムの探求へ

前述の diagram の探求において、diagram とタイプ、interiority の関係について、アイゼンマンは以下のように述べている。

" 当時、私が使う diagram は、アナロジーというより、むしろ、こうした diagram が建築の中に潜在的に存在するという提案であった。diagram の存在は、建築の「生得的な」素材、機能的、及び美的条件によって抑制された。 この意味において、建築の interiority は diagram とタイプとの間にあると考えられた。しかし、差異としての diagram の考えであった。すなわち、機能、スタイルまたはイメージのような建築以外の差異としての diagram の考えであった。"註12)

本質へと向かう安定的、一元的な参照物が存在しなくなったという、建築や社会の状況において、動的な深層構造、あるいは、固定化しない動的システムを求める方法として、言語学や哲学分野の影響から差異のシステムが見いだされた。

また、このことから、わかるように、アイゼンマンは、diagram を建築の外に置くのではなく、内部化させようとするのである。生成する diagram が、object である建築内部に存在することを求めるのである。ここにおいて、伝統的に建築生成の担い手であった subject の立ち位置は崩れ、旧来の subject と object の概念は大きく変化させられるのである。

アイゼンマンは住宅シリーズという具体的なプロジェクトを通じて、タイポロジーの概念に対する diagram の概念について、概念的な差異にとどまることなく、あらゆる認識の根底に疑いをかけていく。すなわち、見る subject（主体）、作る subject（主体）、そして見られる object（もの）の認識の前提を疑う、デカルト的探究を建築の分野において試行しているのである。

3-3-3：解体の方法：二価性、自己参照性、過剰という方法

認識の根底に疑いをかけるために、アイゼンマンは差異によって認識を動かす方法をとる。それらは、テラーニの解体の概念から影響を受けていることは既に述べた。それらは、西欧社会の認識の基盤をなす二項対立的な関係性にブラーをかける（曖昧化する）方法、すなわち、二価性や、自己参照性、過剰という方法が、各住宅プロジェクトで様々な形で試行されている。

住宅シリーズの初期においては、形態の認識に向けられ、柱、梁といった形態の記号としての認識を二価性による過剰な構造や、カードボードのような曖昧なモノでブラーをかけることが試行され、次の段階として建築の interiority の関係性の純粋な diagram による自己参照的な形態の反復へと変化し、イコン的記号からインデックスへの探求へと向かい、建築の内部性の diagram の探求を深めていく。住宅 4 号あたりから建築の存在する時間性についての探求へとテーマがシフトし、本質と差異、言語的アナロジーから情動の状態としての建築へと向かっていく。また、建築の構想や表現の前提となるユークリッド幾何学の認識を動かすために、以降、位相幾何学と対峙させていくことになる。さらに、住宅 10 号では、diagram は、起源に回帰するのではなく、空間と時間に拡散する状態に導かれる。初期の住宅の diagram は、フィジカルな object を、モダニズムを通じてルネサンスからの interiority の軌跡に類似している安定した、知られた一つの領域に関連させてきた。しかし、住宅 10 号の diagram は、建築の interiority が、安定していて、既に知られているものではないという考えを示唆したからである。このことは重要である。アイゼンマンの diagram が古典的な枠組みから離脱し始めた契機でもある。そして、interiority の幾何学がユークリッド幾何学だったと

き、interiority の幾何学は、自身の表象として、紙の上に現れることができたが、幾何学が位相幾何学になったとき、それを、もはや 1 対 1 の関係で平らな紙の上に表現することは不可能になったことを知る。そして、既存の描画方法の限界のために、diagram は、このユークリッド幾何学の interiority のイコンから、位相幾何学のインデックスに移動し始めたのである。
内的論理を自己参照することで、生物的な自己増殖するプログラムへの方向性も探った。平板なる論理を超え、静止した時間性を超え、ユークリッド幾何学を超え、一元的な解釈を超え、生き生きとした presentness（プレゼントネス）を孕む diagram を探求しようとしているのである。

以下にアイゼンマンの住宅シリーズのプロジェクトを概観する。その過程で、アイゼンマンの建築の考え方の変遷をたどっていく。
ここでは、彼の作品論に向かうのではなく、あくまでも diagram を巡るテーマにおける探求であるため、作品の詳細に立ち入ることはしないことを最初にことわっておきたい。

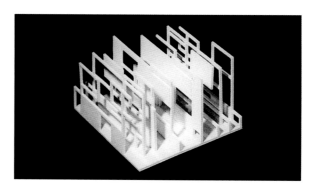

Fig.3-3　カードボードアーキテクチュア

註 13) DD pp.54-62, IO Chapter 3 pp.28-33：住宅 1 号に関する記述部分をここではまとめている。

3-4：住宅シリーズの操作プロトコルの図式

ここでは、アイゼンマンの初期プロジェクトである HOUSE Project について、「Diagram Diaries」を中心とした言説とそれぞれのプロジェクトについて出版されている図版等より、具体的な diagram の適用やその変遷を追いながら、アイゼンマンの diagram についての考察を行う。

まずは、HOUSE Project 全体について、具体的なクライアントや敷地があるものもあれば、純粋に diagram の試行のために存在するものもあり、思考の過程を表すものとして 1 号から 11 号といったように順序としての名前が付けられている。プロジェクト名の命名からも分かるように、具体的な敷地や形態を想起させるような名称とせずに、ニュートラルでジェネリックなものとなっていることからも明らかである。

さらに固定化しない動的なシステムの試行のために、批評性を常に意識し、それぞれのプロジェクトごとに前のプロジェクトで試行したことを前提として、新たな対応関係を次々に展開していく。特に subject / object の関係に対して、二項対立的な関係性に対して、様々な方法でブラーをかける試みを行っている。

以下、それぞれのプロジェクトごとに概観していく。

3-4-1：HOUSE Project　住宅 1 号[註 13]

存在の不在の考え方：不在の柱のマーキング
カードボードアーキテクチュア
壁、柱の二価性、ズラシ

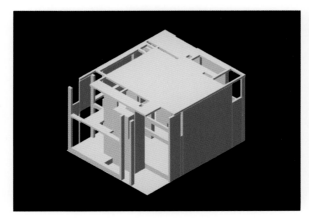

fig.3-4　住宅 1 号

HOUSE Project における form は、アイゼンマンの博士論文において generic form とされた、建築の interiority に由来する立方体、直方体が出発点とされている。

変形の diagram の存在を視覚化するために trace という概念が導入され、記されている。建築の内部性つまり、深層構造より導き出されたプロセスを diagram として導入している。

主要な表現としての物質的なマテリアル構造を使用することを疑い、構造的でないもの、すなわち、いかなる必要な機能を有しない、加算と減算の両方によって、壁でもあり、柱でもある記号の構造をもった"カードボードのような"壁柱で構成し、それをカードボードアーキテクチャー（図 3-3）と呼んでいる。

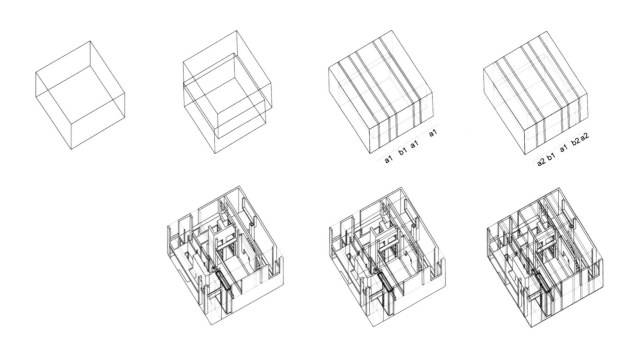

Fig.3-5　住宅 1 号生成の diagram

註 14）住宅としての機能（ダイニングやキッチンなど）を成立させていることが平面プランより読み取ることができる。
註 15）DD pp.63-68, IO Chapter 3 pp.34-39：住宅 2 号に関する記述部分をここではまとめている。

具体的には、求心的な正方形 volume から操作がはじめられる。ウィットカウアーやロウらの平板性からの脱却を図るために volume を前提としている。

さらに、「9 square grid」や比例関係といったアーティキュレーションを volume として定義していく。まずは、対角線方向にずらすことで一回り大きな直方体を得る。そのズラシの割合が最初の分割の基準となる。ここでは、ＡＢＡＢＡ型の古典的な分割形式を導き出す根拠となるだけでなく、三次元 volume の分割として平面性の脱却を図っている。

アイゼンマンのプロジェクトを通してみられる、二価性によって読み取る subject の認識をぼかそうとする（ブラーをかける）操作が随所に見られる。ここでも二つの比例分割が組み合わされ、それらを cross layering と呼んでいる。

基本的な三次元の分割面が定められるとその割合は対角線に対して線対称に転写され、三次元的なグリッド面が構成される。このグリッド面に対して厚みを持った壁としての volume が想定され、そこに開けられる開口と残された壁の部分の割合により、壁と柱の実質的構造的な二価性と記号としての二価性のもとにそれらの壁面が操作されていく。

さらに空間の関係性すなわち深層構造によりグリッド上に壁が出現したり、刳り貫かれたりしていく。（図 3-5）表層構造としての動的形態生成（サーキュレーション等）よりも動的な深層構造に重きを置き、固定化しないシステムを希求している。

大きな流れの中の分節は認識可能であるが、細かな分節は、必ずしも残された diagram と言説、図面だけでは解読できない部分が残っている。こうした細部の調整は、この住宅 1 号が具体的なプロジェクト[註 14]であることもあり、アイゼンマンは決して、表層的な機能性や物質性を消し去ったわけではなく、最終的に機能的な要素も調整が図られ最終形態に至っているものと思われる。

3-4-2：HOUSE Project　住宅 2 号[註 15)]

構造（柱グリッド、壁システム）の二価性、自己参照性、二つの起源の創出

過剰な方法による形式的な実態としての不在の表現

diagram ＝ object、ズラシ

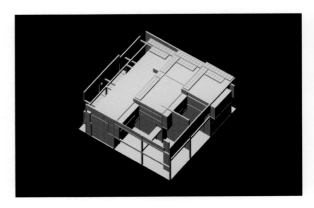

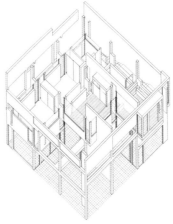

Fig.3-6　住宅 2 号

ここでは、住宅1号と同様に対角線方向に正方形 volume を
ズラすことから始まる。その volume が等価な「9 square
grid」に分割され、その分割をマークするものとして柱、壁、
volume という3つのモードがずらされた二重のグリッドの中
で取捨選択されている。volume は壁の残余空間として図と地
の関係の交錯を示し、さらに volume もズラシによって分節さ
れ、残余部分とメイン volume を交錯させることが試みられて
いる。全てが、最初の「9 square grid」に分割された volume
から自己参照的に操作が繰り返されている。対角線方向の分
節、高さ方向の分節が加えられ、三次元的な空間的な序列が
与えられている。（図3-7）
自己参照性という過剰のシステムによって、認識を動かす、す
なわちブラーをかけることを試みている。柱グリッドとずれ
た壁システムという二価性のシステムによる。二価性のシス
テムについて以下のように説明されている。

"住宅2号においては、柱グリッドとずれた壁システムのどち
らか一方だけでも、構造支持のためには十分なものであるに
もかかわらず、柱グリッドとずれた壁システムという構造シ
ステムの二価性として、自己参照性が過剰に示された。
そのような過剰によって、構造のシステムの一方もしくは他
の一方を記号として見ることが主張された。もはや、構造的
価値もしくは外的な参照物を参照するのではなく、むしろ内
部性を参照するのである。
柱もしくは壁のどちらでも、記号として見ることができたの
で、安定的もしくは一元的な参照物は存在しなくなったので
ある。"註16)

ここでは、まさに建築自体に内部化された diagram を確認す
ることができる。

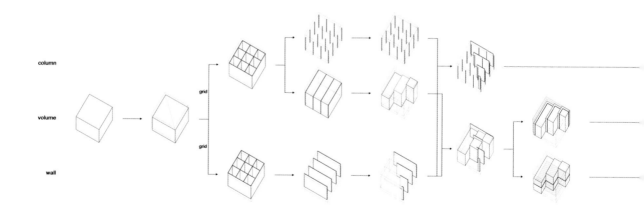

註16) DD p63,l13 –p64,l2（筆者翻訳）
註17) DD p67,l13 –p68,l2（筆者翻訳）
註18) DD pp68,69：住宅3号に関する記述部分をここではまとめている。

このように、住宅2号のdiagramにおいて、個々の柱、壁などは、組み立てのインテジャとしてのそれらの種類の単なる記号として見られるのではなく、それらは何か他のものを表現するものに見ることができる。 この構造システムの二重化において、柱と壁は、もはやただ単なる形式もしくは構造の実体だけではなくなり、むしろ、柱と壁は、形式的な実体として、不在を示しているという。すなわちdiagramによって介在されたinteriorityの実在を示しているという。 この住宅2号は、建てられたobjectがプロセスのdiagramになるという。このobjectとdiagramは一方であり、もう一方でもある。すなわち、diagramとして同時に働くリアルな住宅であるという。そして、diagramの役割は、プロセスの表明だけにとどまらず、次の課題が以下のように発見されていく。

"いやそれどころか、柱もしくは壁の配置は、形式もしくは構造的な意図のいずれかの結果であると見られたのではなく、む

しろ、diagramの存在（不在）を示した過剰の余剰を示す指標的な構造の結果であると見られたのである。単に言語としてではなく、差異のinteriorityの唯一の表明として建築を読むために、イコンを手段から引き離す必要が、次の一連のdiagramの重要な部分となったのである。"註17)

3-4-3：HOUSE Project　住宅3号 註18)
伝統的な読み取りのヒエラルキー（階層的な知覚）の曖昧化
ズラシ、回転（二次元）
住宅2号においては、物質的なobjectと建築の内部性の間の関係性を、二つの起源を創出することによって、diagramを通して曖昧にしている。住宅3号（1969年）では、リアルなobjectの認識の伝統的なヒエラルキーを曖昧にすることを試みたという。すなわち、認識の秩序にブラーをかける試みである。以下のようにアイゼンマンは説明する。

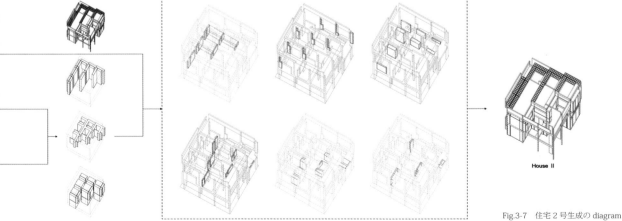

House II

Fig.3-7　住宅2号生成のdiagram

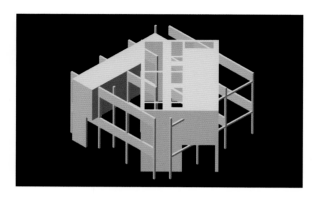

号は、最初の構造の考えをズラスことを試みた。 ここに、柱、部屋の分割－壁－そして部屋における開口には等しい価数が与えられた。 建築を読解することのわれわれの方法は、階層的に、すなわち、一番目、二番目、三番目のように事物を読むものなので、そのような階層的な価値に反して進むことは、結果的に、必ず視覚的に疑わしいものとなってしまった。住宅3号も例外でなかった。住宅3号における階層的な知覚を困惑させるこうした考えは、見られているものについて曖昧にすることで、新たな地平を開いた。さらに、そうした階層を曖昧にすることが建築の interiority の状態であったことも提案した。" 註 19)

住宅1号、2号、同様に正方形 volume からはじまり、45度傾けた volume が重ねられる。それぞれの volume が対角線方向にズラされ、「9 square grid」にフレーム、壁、volume が想定され、それぞれの操作で取捨選択がなされ、等価な操作で曖昧性を得ている。一つ一つの操作は必ず、ズラされた volume のどちらかでなされ、重ね合わされている。(図 3-9)機能主義的、計画学的なアプローチにおいては、必要な space の容量から出発するため、必要以外の space（余剰 space）を生み出すことが付属的になりがちであることに対し、form の内部性の操作において生み出される space は余剰 space が同時に生み出されていることがわかる。space の容量についてはアイゼンマンの diagram 等では語られていないが、グリットによる分割がある程度の容量の目安を作っていることは確かであろう。

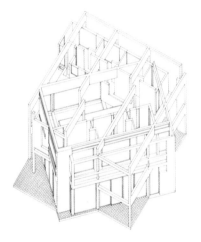

Fig.3-8　住宅3号

" 住宅3号においては、diagram は、伝統的な、一番目、二番目、三番目という視覚的な読み取りの区別を曖昧にすることを試みたものである。
構造システムが、空間的な組織化の最初のシステムだったため、住宅2号は、構造システムから始めたことに対し、住宅3

註 19) DD p68,l12 –p69,l8
註 20) DD pp69-76：住宅4号に関する記述部分をここではまとめている。

plan　　　　volume　　　line

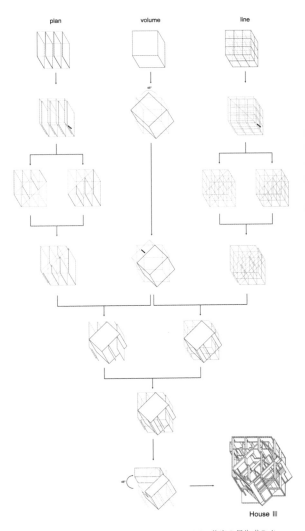

House III

Fig.3-9　住宅3号生成の diagram

3-4-4：HOUSE Project　住宅4号 [註20]

ウォールネス（壁性）の記号の導入
時間性（フリッカーフィルムの参照）
ズラシ、位相的対称性（正面、後ろ）、
コード化として白から黒へのカラーリング

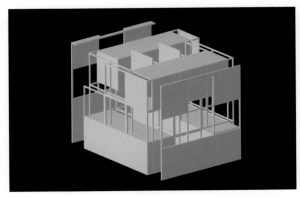

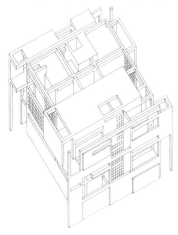

Fig.3-10　住宅4号

住宅 4 号（1971 年）は、最初の純粋な diagram によるプロジェクトであり、住宅 4 号の一連の diagram は単に組み立てのインテジャの階層だけでなく、マテリオリティ（物質性）に関係しているという。

line、plane、volume という形態に還元することで、物質性を消し去り、柱、壁という記号としての区別も消し去るために、壁性（wallness）という言葉を導入している。この壁性という概念は、絵画や彫刻との違いとして、平面性と対比して定義している。アートの概念に影響を受けながらも、常に建築を明確に他の分野と分節しようとしている。この wallness（壁性）の記号によって、object のマテリオリティ（物質性）だけでなく、その機能と意味を克服することを試みている。

"住宅 4 号の diagram も、また、機能の必要性を越えて、過剰の状態を暗に意味した。こうした過剰の概念は、住宅 2 号のものとは異なっていた。住宅 4 号の diagram が、最初に、単に後天的な説明装置だけでなく、発生装置でもあったのが主な理由だからである。この diagram は、一連の規則システムから始まった。いったん、その動きをセットすると、規則システム自身の真の性質を変化させはじめるだろう。生成力のある規則システムは、一連の動きをもたらすだろう。"註21)

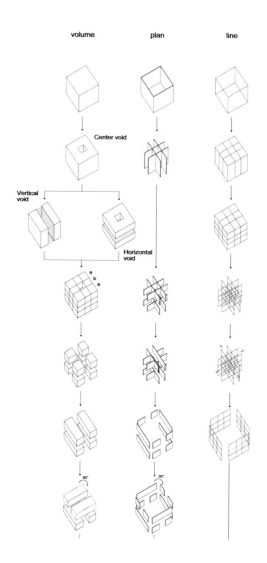

Fig.3-11　住宅 4 号生成の diagram

註21）DD p74,l8 -l18（筆者翻訳）

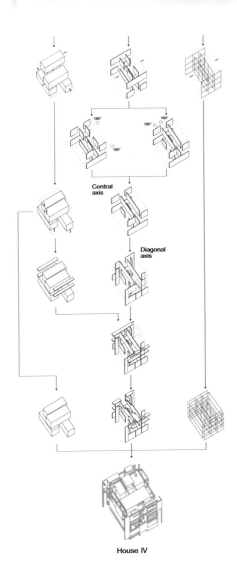

Central
axis

Diagonal
axis

House IV

住宅4号の diagram 建築におけるこうした最初の初期条件に
関係する記号システムを提案し、この記号システムを、機能
と意味が付加した幾何学による単純な方程式と区別したので
ある。

純粋な diagram からの出発ということで、純粋な立方体から
の出発となる。住宅1～3号までは、住宅という出発点があっ
たように思われ、二層程度の volume で generic form として
正方形 volume から出発していた。それに対して、住宅4号では、
これまでの方法と同様、「9 square grid」による分節、ズラシ
であるが、立方体からの出発であることで三次元的な分割が
なされ、対角線方向のズラシよりも、平行なシフトが主となっ
ている。diagram は、line、plane、volume の3つの状態がそ
れぞれの操作として並置して示されているのみで、最終形態
に至るプロセスは示されていない。これらの三つを重ね合わ
せた状態だけでは説明できないところで diagram はとどめら
れている。（図3-11）ここでは、時間性の導入として「フリッ
カー・フィルム」を参照にしたことが述べられている。ただし、
映画の線形性に対して、非線形なプロセスが提示されている。

"動きの論理的集合であるようだったものは、1973年のアル
ド・ロッシのミラノ・トリエンナーレのための diagram のフィ
ルムにおいて、断裂があることが示された。1000以上のフレー
ムが描かれ、「フリッカー・フィルム」と呼ばれるものに組み
立てられた。各々の空白、すなわち黒いフレームの後に、イメー
ジの白いフレームが続いた。イメージを脈動させながら。これ
らのドローイングは、プロセスの線形の物語であるようなもの
を生み出した。diagram が一つの見方で見られるようアレンジ
されたとき、それらはひとつの物語として理解されるだろう。

２つのドローイングを見た時、これはたとえ接続がないとして
も、目が、近接する異なるドローイング間のギャップを満たす
ために独自の接続をしようとするからである。たとえば、モー
フィング技術では、object A は、中間段階の作成を通して、異
なる object B に変換できる。映画において、そのような中間
段階が存在した。：明滅のため、目には接続をするための時間
がなかった。そして、目が見たものと心で記録されたものの
間の接続がなかったので、見られたものは意図がなく無秩序
のようであった。映像は、常に混沌から秩序を作ろうとする。；
diagram 化するプロセスにおいては、こうした自然の傾向の
効果を見られる秩序に還元することが必要である。住宅 4 号
の diagram は秩序を持っている。それは見えるだけではなく、
見る眼によって論理的にまとめられうる秩序である。これら
の diagram は、非線形、非階層的なプロセスの痕跡でもある。
そのプロセスはゼロに戻されることはない。このことは、フ
リッカー・フィルムの線形フォーマットにこれら diagram を
描く試みにおいて明白になった。"註22)

ここでは、住宅 3 号でも試みられた認識における順序を曖昧
化することと並行して、見る側としての subject（読み手）の
欲望、すなわち、線形的なプロセスに整序して見ようとする
欲望に対して、ブラーをかける試みであると解釈できる。そ
れはまた、読み手に対して解釈を委ねながらも、一般的な解
釈をズラシていくアイゼンマン特有の批評性の組み込まれた
ものと次第になっていくのである。

3-4-5：HOUSE Project　住宅 6 号 註23)

グリッドの生成と form の生成の diagram
三次元的対角線における位相的対称性
実際の空間認識としてのユークリッド幾何学から位相幾何学へ
暗号化としてのカラーリング
大地の概念の曖昧化

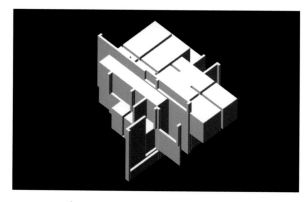

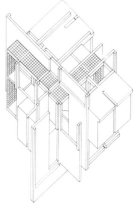

Fig.3-12　住宅 6 号

註 22) DD p75,l4 –p76,l16（筆者翻訳）
註 23) DD pp76-83：住宅 6 号に関する記述部分をここではまとめている。
註 24) DD p77,l3 –l22（筆者翻訳）

住宅6号（1972-75）は、さらに映画のプロセスのアイデア
をさらに発展させるために、diagram を使ったという。住宅4
号との違いを次のように説明している。

" 住宅4号は、単一の時間フレームへと圧縮されるようなこ
れらのステージを明らかにすることを試みた。構築された
object においては、そのような共一同時性が白と黒では表現
されないので、色を diagram に導入した。初期の住宅において、
diagram は、色をもたず、基本的にマテリアル性とは無関係で
あると理解された。このような非マテリアル性は、住宅のコー
ド化の要素として、diagram のプロセスに関する表象として、
表現された。住宅6号は、もはや diagram のプロセスの表象
でなく、実際、プロセスそのものであったので、もう一つのコー
ド化、つまり、カラーリングが必要とされた。diagram だけ
でなく住宅にも。これに加えて、コード化は、ソリッドとヴォ
イドのレベルを示すために重要であった。住宅4号において、
diagram は、ソリッド、ダブル・ソリッド、ニュートラル・ソリッ
ド、単一のヴォイドとダブル・ヴォイドという表記法によって、
サーフェイスである壁を示した。" 註24)

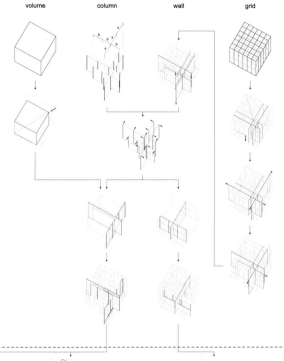

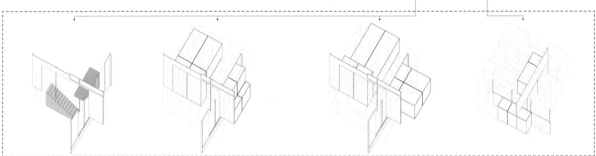

Fig.3-13　住宅6号生成の diagram

これまでの住宅では物質性を消去するためにニュートラルな白で全体を均質化していたが、ここでは、物質性としてではなくソリッドとヴォイドのレベルを示すためのコード化として色が導入された。

さらに、これまでの住宅では、レイヤリングという形で分割軸の取捨選択がなされていたが、ここでは明確に、グリッドの生成とformの生成としてdiagramが区別される。グリッドの生成では、これまでのように正方形volumeを等分割したものが、対角線上にズラされてできている。これは、ユークリッド幾何学の根拠となる座標を形成している。そのグリッド上にformが形成される。ここからの方法はこれまでの住宅で試行されてきた壁性、volumeの操作がなされていく。まずは、直交する二対の壁が生成される。平面におけるX，Y軸のように配され、かつ交差する長さは均等ではないため、対角線方向の暗黙の方向性を暗示させる。ここでは新たな試みとして空間の認識における位相的対称性が以下のように試行されている。これはすでに住宅4号で試されていたが、それは前後のサーフェイスの反転として、正面から後ろへ人が移動するときの認識上の対称性であったのに対して、ここでは三次元的な対角線を対象軸としての位相的対称性を試行している。（図3-13）

"住宅6号はユークリッド幾何学から位相幾何学へのシフトを、さらにコード化することが必要であった。このシフトは、diagramの中でだけでなく、住宅の実際の経験において、理解されなければならなかった。一番上の後部の1つのコーナーから一番下の正面の1つのコーナーまで、中心の対角線を走る位相的な軸に沿って、この住宅は暗号化された。この軸を明瞭に表現するために、2つの階段は、赤と緑に塗られた。；

赤と緑を混ぜることは、住宅のニュートラルな軸という灰色を生成する。白が最初の4つの住宅のためのベースカラーであったので、灰色は、今や、位相的な中心軸をマークするニュートラルな色になった。この文脈において、白は1本のポールに、センターの点になり、ニュートラルな軸としての灰色の線が存在した、そして、黒は他のポール、すなわち想像された外部の囲いであった。それから、赤と緑は、目に見えない、さらに、ニュートラルで位相的な概念上の軸の記号であった。赤い階段が、緑の階段に平行で、ダイレクトに越えるならば、赤い階段はユークリッド空間において対照的であろう。

赤い階段が90度回転されたとき、赤い階段はユークリッド空間で非対称になるが、住宅の一番下のコーナーから一番上のコーナーへの線に沿って、位相的に対称形となった。赤と緑の階段は、灰色の位相的な軸が存在したというアイデアを暗号化した。一旦それが読まれるならば、この住宅において、もはや、右側上方または逆は存在しない。；この住宅は、定位において、大地との概念上の関係性を持たず、リバーシブルになった。このことは、建築に関して定義している状況としての大地から立ち去るプロセスにおけるもう一歩であった。・・・・

住宅におけるすべての垂直と水平のサーフェイスは、いろいろな灰色の濃淡で色付けされた。この同じマーキング装置は、マテリアルをもったサーフェイスにおいても効力があった。白い点から外へ向けて、ガラスの平面はより不透明になり、透明から半透明に、グリッドの半透明から不透明に移りながら、このように、マテリアルを帯びた垂直と水平のサーフェイスとそれらのカットの全ては、インデックスでコード化された。"註25)

住宅6号では、建築空間の成立における前提としてのユーク

註25) DD p78,l3 –p80,l18（筆者翻訳）
註26) DD pp83-88：住宅10号に関する記述部分をここではまとめている。

リッド幾何学そのものに対して、認識を動かすことが試みら
れ、位相幾何学へのシフトが導入された。さらに、diagram に
とどまらず、実際の空間の経験としての位相性の認識をユー
クリッド幾何と並置することで二価的なあいまいな空間を提
示し、複数の視点の存在を暗示させている。それらの認識を
補完するものとして、暗号化やカラーリング、インデックス
によるコード化が行われている。diagram は並置され、その階
層性、時間的線形性の解体が試みられている。

3-4-6：HOUSE Project　住宅 10 号 [註26)]
el form（エルフォーム）の導入
複数の主体、過剰な視点
終わりのないプロセス、空間と時間に拡散、設計プロセスの解体
部分の散乱

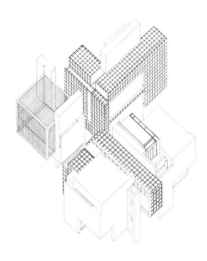

Fig.3-14　住宅 10 号

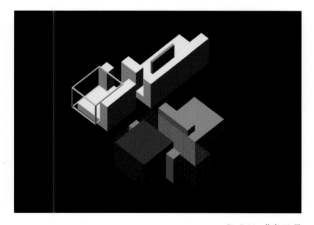

Fig.3-14　住宅 10 号

住宅 10 号（1975-78）の diagram は、先述のように、形態
そのものではなく、空間における状態を生み出すことを試み
たという。
自身でも以下のように語っているように、一つのプロセスや
階層では読み取れないほどの、diagram とそれを検証する模型
が存在する。具体的な敷地とプログラム（住宅としての）が
存在したということにも起因するが、多くのスタディがあり、
それぞれの関係性を読み解くことは困難である。

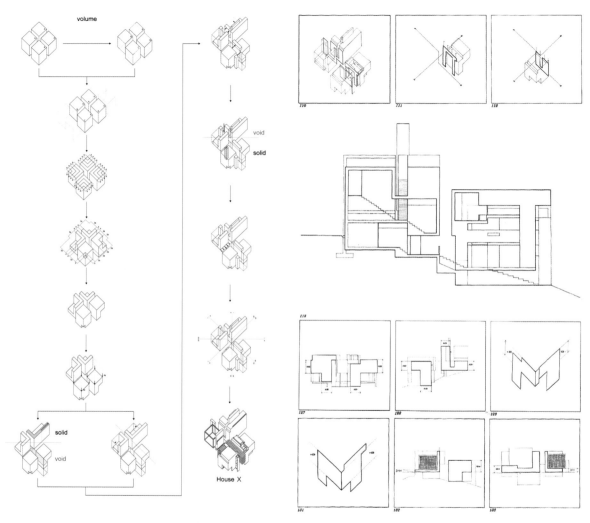

Fig.3-15　住宅 10 号生成の diagram

Fig.3-16　住宅 10 号　数ある部分の検討 diagram の中の一部

註 27）DD p83,l3 –l22（筆者翻訳）
註 28）DD p86,l1 –l8（筆者翻訳）
註 29）DD p86,l3 –l13（筆者翻訳）

" それは、もはや、若干の単純な幾何学的起源から、階層的に読まれないであろう。たとえ、そのような起源から読むように見られたとしても。統一の始まりからの読みが試みられるたびに、そうした解釈は逸脱していくであろう。diagram は、起源に回帰するのではなく、空間と時間に拡散する状態に導かれた。それは、もはや、全体的でも、階層的でも、安定的でもなく、絶えず変動する。これらの diagram は、最初に、住宅 6 号で開発された位相空間の考えに基づいていた。住宅 10 号において、2 つの不完全な起源が存在したという考えであった。すなわち、el（エル）キューブと el（エル）ポイント、失われた各四半部。この el（エル）form は黒いキューブと白い点の両方に向かって動いた。これらの二つの操作は、等しい有効性の最終ポイントであった。こうして、住宅 10 号は、住宅 6 号のような、グレーを通して、黒から白まで行ったコード化を明らかにした。" 註27)

住宅 6 号からの連続としてグリッドが想定されている。ここでは四つの象限が位相的に等価な変形を加えられながら、四つの異なる空間を生成している。これまでは、line、plane、volume の分節による生成であったが、ここでは el（エル）form（以下エルフォーム）という立方体の一点から相似な立方体の欠きとられた形、を四つの象限に与えることから出発している。これは以降のシリーズの共通の出発点となる。volume とヴォイドの状態のレベルにカラーが与えられながら、これまで培われてきたズラシや回転による差異化によって、二重化が行われている。ただし、その方向性は位相的関係性の認識が前提とされ、様々な角度から位相関係が調整されている。（図 3-15）その検討はあるときはコーナーから、ある時は正面や断面から、あるいは下から見上げる、上から見下げるといっ

たように、部分の関係性の調整によって、全体が整えられていく。（図 3-16）アイゼンマンは以下のように語っている。

" 一連の diagram としては、順々には動かなかった。空間や時間における一元的条件に向かって移動するたびに、それらは不安定化された。これは、テラーニの Giuliani-Frigerio の diagram に似ていた。それは、トポロジカルなコーナーから始まった。Giuliani-Frigerio は、カサ・デル・ファッショと同様に、ファサードからではなく、コーナーから説明された。" 註28)

部分と全体から部分の散乱へ

" 住宅 10 号の diagram の作業は、単一の視点と複数の観点の間における読み取りの似た考えから発展した。加えて、diagram は、また、単一の subject（主体）と複数の subject の間で、位相幾何学と位相幾何学の間で働いた。住宅 10 号において、コーナーと中心から、また内部からの複数の視点があった。住宅は象限に分割された。そのため、見ている subject が外部に立つだけではなく、トポロジカルな対称性の点という内部に立っていた。" 註29)

これは設計における設計者の視点であるが、あらゆる角度から全体を調整することなく、その都度部分を調整していくことを繰り返していくようなプロセスであり、最終的にどこが最初で終わりなのかも区別がつかないほど試行が繰り返されている。いろいろなスケールの図面を描くことや多くの模型を作って検討していくこれまでの設計プロセスと似ているようであるが、視点のめぐらせ方が異なっている。また、部分と全体の関係において全体性を調整することが目的ではなく、

部分の調整のプロセスの順序を曖昧化することで、決して終わらない部分の調整のプロセスが時間の中に解き放たれている。すなわち、建築生成における subject に内在する問題を扱っているのである。従来の一つの観点から建築 object を生成する考え方、すなわち単一性を排除し、多様性を object に導入しようとする意識の萌芽が読み取れるのである。

3-4-7：House El Even Odd 1980[註30)]
表現方法としてのアクソメから形態生成のデヴァイスへ
アクソメとステレオトミーの二重化
三段階のスケーリング、自己再帰性
住居の記号としての住宅から、記号としての住宅へ、批評性のためのプロジェクトへ

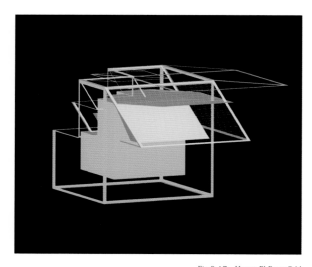

Fig.3-17　House El Even Odd

House El Even Odd では、これまでの住宅シリーズでの表現方法としてのアクソノメトリック（以下アクソメ）という方法そのものの認識を動かしている。それは住宅 10 号のためにできていたアクソノメトリック・モデルから始まったという。

" このプロジェクトは、object に関して subject（主体）の遠近法的な見方の優位性に関わる。このプロジェクトは、住宅 10 号のためにできていたアクソノメトリック・モデルから始まった。ある特定の視点から単眼方式で見られるとき、このモデルは「リアルに実在する」モデルと見ることができた。現実とアクソノメトリックな投影法が幾分互いに関係しているという考えを与えながら、現実のモデルのように、壁は、垂直と水平であるように見えた。House El Even Odd は、その diagram としてのこの考えを採用し、アクソメの３つの段階を経て、この考えを発展させた。最初のステージは、住宅 10 号からパビリオンの１つを使う直交の投影だった。第２のステージは、45 度角度で傾けられた同じパビリオンのアクソメ投影であった、第３のステージは第２のステージのアクソメの投射のさらなるアクソメ投影であった。そして、それは、まったく奇妙なことに、平面のような平らなプランを生み出した。結果は、3 段階の三次元的 volumetric な重ね合わせだった。逆さまにし、そして反転させ、それはある状態を生み出した。・・・・こうして、diagram の重ね合わせは、アクソメとステレオトミーの認識の混同を引き起こした。ステレオトミーとは、同一のものを立体的に読み取るための、各投影面の平面による通常の直角投影である。"[註31)]

註30）DD pp88-92：House El Even Odd に関する記述部分をここではまとめている。
註31）DD p89,l1 –p90,l8（筆者翻訳）
註32）DD p90,l9 –p91,l2（筆者翻訳）

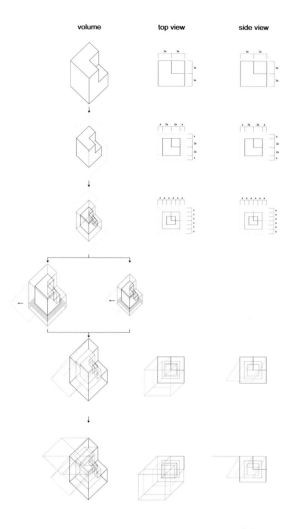

volume	top view	side view

Fig.3-18　House El Even Odd 生成の diagram

ここでは、一つの generic form としてエルフォームを出発点として、二次元のアクソメを変形することによって、生成される３種類の立体が重ね合わされている。重ね合わせる際には、差異化としてスケーリング（拡大縮小）が行われている。現代の３D技術では容易に３Dメッシュのポイントを平行移動することによって求めることができるが、容易にできることが返って、その視点の意味性に無頓着であることに気づかされる。（図3-18）

表現手段としてのアクソメを形態生成のデヴァイスへと変換したことと、それを表現するための House El Even Odd そのもの意味について、以下のようにアイゼンマンは説明する。

"House El Even Odd の diagram が、居住することの考えに関して建築的記号の考えの継続的な変容を提示するのを見た。House El Even Odd において、この diagram は記号となった。プログラムの記号に関する記号、そして非妥協的かつ柔軟的に居住することの考えに関する記号である。三段階の diagram の投影が、自己再帰になったとき、三段階の diagram の投影は、object としてだけでなく、自身の表現として、存在した。自然を模倣する建築から自身の object を表すものへのシフトが、住居を作ることの伝統的な必要性を脱臼させるために、要求されたことが主張された。"註32)

居住の記号としての住宅から、記号としてのみの住宅へとシフトしたことを説くものであり、もはや住宅としての機能性も、具体的な敷地にも関係のない、批評性のためだけの住宅が提示されている。

アクソノメトリックという図法と視点による介入を施すことによって、壁は、垂直と水平のいずれにも捉えられるものと

して存在し、リアルなモデルとアンリアルなモデルとの混交を生み出している。もはや、object が、リアルな世界における単一の存在物を超え、アンリアルな世界にも跨ぐものであることを示している。このことは、object 自身の存在形式の問題として、リアルな世界に拘束されていた object がアンリアルな世界へと結びつくものとしての理解は、次の時代へと連続していく可能性を開いた。

3-4-8：Fin d'Ou T Hou S（1983）[註33]
外在性の導入（テクスト）
diagram がプロセスの軌跡や記録であったものから、
言語という人間の思考そのものを取り込む事へとシフト、思
考の補完、拡張された diagram

Fin d'Ou T Hou S（1983）は、以前の住宅から別の変化を表しているというように、表現されている資料の少なさのせいでもあるが、住宅であることはもはや読み取ることはできない。

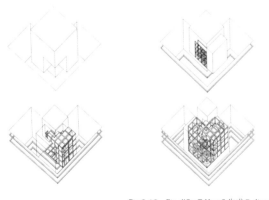

Fig.3-19　Fin d'Ou T Hou S 生成の diagram

スケールや内部、外部の判読は困難である。読み取ることができるのは、エルフォームがスケールを変えながら位相的な反転やズラシが行われている。その過程でヴォイドと volume のレベルがフレームや volume、割り貫きという痕跡を残している。大きな変化は大地の表れである。（図 3-19）大地に対する刻印がこれ以降現れてくることになり、外部へとつながっていくこととなっていく。この変化はその命名にあるとアイゼンマンは次のように言う。

" このことは、このプロジェクトへの diagram の特別な関係性の中に見られた。初期の住宅は、変換とそれら変換の記録であった。; それらは、建築の形式的な interiority を、住宅自身の形式的な状態に関連づけた。これらの住宅は、大部分、ユークリッド幾何学に基礎づけられた。Fin d'Ou T Hou S は、当時、テクストであると宣言された最初の住宅であった。最初のテクストはその名前においてであった。それは異なる読み取りを引き起こした。それは、「Find Out House」「Fine Doubt House」、または、8 月（工事の時であった）の終わりには「Fin d'Aout」と読まれた。住宅は、インデックスとしてのテクストの概念についてであった。このインデックスをマークするために、一連の変換の diagram が生み出された。位相的な係数装置としてエルフォームを使用しながら。 この住宅は、不確かな始まりをさらに示した。: それは、点と完全な立方体から始まった。 この考え（それは住宅 6 号と 10 号で始まった）は、この住宅の中で、自身を、余す所なく探求した。" [註34]

この Fin d'Ou T Hou S は、住宅 11a やカナレッジョのプロジェクトの後に試行されている。建築の interiority の探求から、外部への連続性に向かいつつあった状況の中で、さらに何か

註 33）DD pp92-93：Fin d'Ou T HouS に関する記述部分をここではまとめている。
註 34）DD p92,l7 –p93,l7（筆者翻訳）
註 35）DD pp211-215: The Diagram and the Becoming Unmotivated of the Sign より要約
註 36）DD p50,l18 –l22（筆者翻訳）以下原文：My initial idea in the use of the diagram was that the substrate of form, here referred to as an aspect of architecture's interiority, could be detached from such

を見つけ出す（Find out）ためのプロジェクトそのものであった。このことは、diagram が思考のプロセスを表現するというよりはむしろ、言語を導入しようとする事で、人間の思考を補完するもの、拡張するもの（アルゴリズム・プログラムやパラメトリックなもの）としての位置へとシフトしてきたことを意味していると思われる。このことの意義は重要である。テクストをプログラムとして扱うことの拡張性を示したのである。

3-5：まとめ
3-5-1：アイゼンマンの概念の整理
アイゼンマンの理論は、デリダの理論を下敷きにしている。パロール優先の西欧的思考を否定するのである。デリダは、パロールが話す主体の優位性を担保することに対して攻撃を仕掛け、エクリチュールの重要性を説く。ロゴス中心主義はパロールを充満とみなし、形而上学はパロールが起源に属する状態であると仮定する。アイゼンマンも同様に、そうした立場を取る。建築も言語と同様にパロールであり、現前の優位性を常に有していたとアイゼンマンは言う。記号をモチベーションの有無で区別し、モチベーションをもつものが建築であり、モチベーションをもたないものはビルディングであるとする。そして、diagram が存在の形而上学を封印するエクリチュールであるとする。[註35]

アイゼンマンが、デリダに倣って、意味と form とを切断しようとしたことは重要である。このアイゼンマンの意味と form との「切断」は、後に詳述するコールハースの意味と objectとの「切断」が向かう外的方向性とは異なっており、内的方向へと向かう。ウィットカウアーやロウの静的な方向とは異なり、アイゼンマンは動的なものへと向かう意識をもっていた。しかし、彼らと同様、あくまでも内的な方向性を堅持するのである。外部への連続性を試みるのであるが。
「建築の interiority の相として、ここで、言及される form の基板が、そのようなプログラムの関心から切り離されるだろう」[註36] ということがアイゼンマンの考えからわかるように、アイゼンマンは、あくまでも、機能、意味、美学への、仮定された必要な関係性から、form をズラスということを考えていたのである。「Diagram Diaries」で、アイゼンマンは以下のように記述している。

〝 私の博士論文と一番目の住宅プロジェクトとの間の５年間における diagram についての考え方の変化は重要である。新しい diagram に対するモデルは、建築的－歴史的と対照的に、明らかに言語学的であった。これらの diagram は、存在を乗り越える考えを提示したほどには、建てられた object におけるマテリアル性の明瞭な表現の還元における文体論的な表現をそれほど提示しなかった。このようにして、diagram は、表され、構築された人工物において読まれることができた。〟[註37]

このことからわかるように、アイゼンマンの diagram は、それ自身ではなく表現された object において読まれるものであった。object の存在を超越しようとするアイゼンマンの意識とは裏腹に、アイゼンマンの diagram は object に依存しているのである。還元された文体論的な明解な表現として diagram を抽出することはできなかった。アイゼンマンの diagram は、明確な表現として確立されたものではなく、アイゼンマン自身の解釈によって変動する曖昧なものであった。それは、object

programmatic concerns.
註37) DD p53,l19 –p54,l6（筆者翻訳）

を、subject と object という二項対立的な視点である分離したものではなく、object と subject との二項対立にブラーをかけ、object に subject を分有させようとする意識を孕んでいた。すなわち客観性という立場を乗り越えようとするものであったのだ。そのため客観的に外部化されない diagram となり、object の内に閉じ込められた、いまだ主観の内部に閉じ込められたものであるとも言える。そうしたアンビバレンツな位置に存在する特異なものであった。すなわち、アイゼンマン独自の主観に依存するものであった。アイゼンマンの diagram は、既存の意識を超越するものであり、限界でもあった。

しかし、それでも、住宅 10 号に見られるように、diagram が、起源に回帰するのではなく、空間と時間に拡散する状態に導かれたことは重要である。

初期の住宅の diagram は、フィジカルな object を、モダニズムを通じてルネサンスからの interiority の軌跡に類似している安定した、知られた一つの宇宙に関連させてきた。しかし、住宅 10 号の diagram は、建築の interiority が、安定していて、既に知られているものではないという考えを示唆したからである。このことは重要である。アイゼンマンの diagram が古典的な枠組みから離脱し始めた契機でもある。住宅 10 号において、この diagram 的なインデックスは、この不安定な内部性の本質を構築するものに関して、もはや 1 対 1 の表象を提示することはできなかったことをアイゼンマンは認識する。そして、interiority の幾何学がユークリッド幾何学だったとき、interiority の幾何学は、自身の表象として、紙の上に現れることができたが、幾何学が位相幾何学になったとき、それを、もはや 1 対 1 の関係で平らな紙の上に表現することは不可能になったことを知る。そうして、既存の描画方法の限界のために、diagram は、このユークリッド幾何学の内部的なイコンから、

非ユークリッド幾何学として描かれ、位相幾何学のインデックスに移動し始めるのである。

3-5-2：interiority に関する二つの問題
平板的で静的な概念に対する批判
関係性をより力動的に捉え、平板的な関係性を
捉える側面を持つユークリッド幾何学を超えて、位相幾何学
によって、さらに動的に捉えようとする野心的態度

住宅シリーズを通じて diagram が進化するにつれて、interiority に関する二つの問題が明らかになったとアイゼンマンは以下のように言う。

"（1）diagram は、価値に関して、interiority が先天的な条件であったと思い込んだこと。すなわち幾何学的なイコンの安定した集合と。

（2）建築へと diagram の幾何学を変換することにおいて、建築になるために、単に diagram から幾何学自身を変換するのではないことが理解された。

建築は幾何学以上の何ものかである。；壁は厚みを持っており、空間は密度を持っている。それゆえ価値は、いかなる幾何学の上にも君臨したのであった。ーユーグリット幾何学もしくは位相幾何学の上にー interiority に関わる先天的な条件は、常にある建築的内部性に左右されるであろう。それゆえ、ユークリッド幾何学から位相幾何学へシフトされた diagram と同様、ある幾何学の代用は、幾何学自身をシフトすることなく、ユーグリッド幾何学に与えられる価値を、単に移しただけであることが見られた。これは別の問いを生じさせた。；なぜ diagram は、潜在する幾何学から、必ず発展したのか？なぜ diagram は、

註 38) DD p169,l7 –p172,l22（筆者翻訳）
註 39) Generic Form に対する Specific Form であり、アイゼンマンは自身の Form システムにおいて、近代建築の分析から Generic Form を抽出し、それらを展開して Specific Form が生成されていくものと考えていることは第二章において述べた。

実体に関する安定条件としては見られない建築のinteriority
から始まったのか？

もしinteriorityが不安定であるならば、diagram化にふさわ
しい変形以外の他の何かが他を処理することが可能だろうか。
これらの問いの最初の答として、分解プロセスのアイデアは、
建築のinteriorityがひとつの複雑な現象として見られうる事
を提案した。その複雑な現象から、objectのより複雑でない
状態が蒸留されるだろう。この意味で、interiorityは、もはや
純粋で安定的なものとも、もしくは必ずしも幾何学的なもの
とも見られなかった。建築が、常に幾何学に立脚しているので、
建築が具体化されたものとしてのフォーマルな宇宙の価値は、
いまだ存在していた。これらの具体的な価値をズラスために、
一連の他のdiagramは、幾何学にもとづかないdiagramのプ
ロセスに導入された。それは、以前に定義されていたような
内部性に関係し、しかし同時に、そこから遠ざけられたいく
つかの方法において見られうる。それゆえ、建築のinteriority
において具現化され、内在的で、最終的に動機づけられたか
に見えるものを移そうとする試みの中に、一連の外部テクス
トは導入される可能性を孕む。

これらの外部テクストは、建築のinteriorityにおいて、具現
化された、もしくは内在的ないかなるものに与えられた普遍
的価値を問うた。もしdiagramが、建築の内部からであろう
と外部からであろうと、価値のそのような起源から、出発し
なければならないならば、それらは常に先天的な具体性を持
つだろう。―それらは動機づけられたdiagramなのであろう。
同時に、次の問いが尋ねられた。；言説を捨てることなく、そ
のような具現化は永遠に不在でありうるだろうか？　すなわ
ち、建築外部からの、表面上ランダムで恣意的に見えるテク

ストに関するアイデアが、建築の具現化のinteriorityもしく
は建築の記号の動機づけを克服するための試みに導入された
のである。そのような恣意的なものが存在する一方、常にあ
る偶発性が存在する。

diagramは、恣意性に偶発的構造を求め始めた。その構造は、
リアルな三次元空間に挿入される時、介在するもの、感情であ
るもの、ぼやけさせるもの、条件としての図形的であるものの
オルタナティヴな条件を生み出すだろう。建築的anteriority
において沈殿され存在しているレトリックと言葉の綾を開示
しうる条件である。"註38)

住宅1号と、その後に続く初期の一連の住宅プロジェクトに
おいて、アイゼンマンのシンタックスで構成されたdiagram
は、specific form註39)を提示するものではなかった。むしろ、
組織化へと向かうまだ形を成さないが、可能性として存在す
るものとして考えられたのであった。

アイゼンマンの作品における自己参照システムには、外部参照
形態を導入しようとするsubjectの直接性、すなわちsubject
の直接的意図を排除しようとしている事がうかがわれる。

しかし、操作は複雑になったが、建築家自身のsubjectから導
き出されたものであることには変わりが無かったと言える。

こうしたアイゼンマンの、形態操作は、次代のアルゴリズム・
プログラムへと継承されていくのである。

すなわち、subjectが直接行っていた複雑な操作をプログラム
として外部化させる方向へと向かわせる影響をアイゼンマン
は与えたのである。

Chapter 4

アイゼンマンの diagram の意義 ^{註1)}

この章では、アイゼンマンの言説を中心としてアイゼンマンの diagram の意義を検証するものである。あわせてアイゼンマンの建築の批評性について言及し、アイゼンマンが提示した建築の interiority の批評的意味から派生する subject の問題にも触れたい。

アイゼンマンの diagram に対する姿勢・考え方は、建築論の歴史において重要な通過点として見逃すことができないものと捉える。その意味で、アイゼンマンが diagram をどのように捉えているのかを、アイゼンマンの著書「Diagram Diaries」（以下 DD とする）をもとに概観してみたい。

「Diagram Diaries」の構成

1999 年に出版された本書はそれまでのアイゼンマンの作品の作品集の体裁を取りながら、diagram に関する論考のテクストが並置されている。作品はインデックスとして本書中央部に収録され、そのインデックスを境として前後に interiority および、exteriority に関する論考とイメージが掲載されている。

はじめに、ロバート・E・サモルによる寄稿；「The Diagrammatic Basis of Contemporary Architecture」から始まり、アイゼンマンによるテクスト「An Original Scene of Writing」によって diagram の出自およびドゥルーズやデリ

ダの思想を通して、エクリチュールとしての diagram を提起し、アイゼンマンの考える建築における diagram を定義していく。続く「Diagrams of Anteriority」では , anteriority と interiority および、diagram の関係について、歴史的な経緯が語られている。「Diagrams of Interiority」では、建築の interiority として grids、cubes、el-forms、bars がサブタイトルとしてつけられ、diagram の実際の使用について自身の博士論文から住宅シリーズへの展開が述べられている。

後半の「Diagrams of Exteriority」では、外部参照としての Site、Texts、Mathematics、Science がサブタイトルとしてつけられ、対応する作品においてどのようにそれらの外部参照が使用されたか記述されている。

最後に「The Diagram and the Becoming Unmotivated of the Sign」と題するテクストでは、サインとシニフィエの動機づけられた関係から、デリダによるサインと存在、パロールとエクリチュールの問題を踏まえ、建築における trace（痕跡）という概念を定義している。

4-1：diagram の誕生と問題性

4-1-1：タイポロジーと diagram の問題 ^{註2)}

タイポロジーと diagram は、異なる方向へと向かう二つの

註 1) 本章は、拙稿、山口隆「ピーター・アイゼンマンの diagram に関する考察」『論考　建築設計 03』日本建築設計学会、2018 年、pp.3-8、を加筆修正したものである。
註 2) DD pp.41-42（筆者要約）
註 3) デリダの presence と absence の概念の二項対立的深層を敷衍しながらアイゼンマンが措定した造語。著作 DD より後の論考となる著作 WV では、being-only-once や建築のエクリチュールとして、object としての現存在だけではない別の存在の状態として定義している。

抽象概念であるとアイゼンマンは認識する。すなわちタイポロジーは標準化へと向かう還元的な抽象概念であり、一方、diagram は、diagram 自身を越えて何かを生じさせる可能性をもつ抽象概念であると位置づける。

アイゼンマンによると、この二つの方向の差異は、現在の問題を暴くとともに、表現と diagram の関係という問題をも示していると言う。

ここで言う、presentness（現在性）[註3] は、標準化された建築の interiority に object が回収されない状況に留めおく生き生きとした状態であり、object が批評装置として作動する前に留めおく。presentness におけるこうした臨界レベルが、第二段階の表現としての diagram に宿るとアイゼンマンは言う。

これは、明らかにデリダの影響を受けての言説である。デリダはフッサールの時間概念を批評的に継承し、フッサールの現象学を現前の形而上学として批判したことはよく知られている。デリダは、［現前］が［存在］と特権的な共犯関係を結んでいることを炙り出し、現前中心主義をロゴス中心主義として批判し、覆すことを試みる。すなわち出発点としての起源の特権を解体し、現前による抑圧からの解放を目指すのであった。アイゼンマンは、こうしたデリダの構図をズラしながら、建築に導入するのである。すなわち、アイゼンマンも presence（現前）という時間の捉え方が重要であるとして、標準化されたタイポロジーが固定化されて、今という presence に発話されることを抑圧として捉え、批判する。新たに、presentness（現在性）を提起し、標準化され固定化されない状態、すなわち、建築の interiority に、未だ object が回収されない状況に留めおく状態として定義する。そして、この presentness における生き生きとした臨界レベルに何か宿るものとして、diagram を

提示するのである。すなわち、アイゼンマンは、タイポロジーが固定化し強大なロゴスとなって、object に現前することを批判し、そして、標準化以前にある固定化しない diagram という第二段階の表現こそが、現前からの抑圧を克服できるとするのである、

4-1-2：バブルダイアグラム [註4]
外在的客観データだけの閉じた関係性を求めるものとして批判

ボザール派のアカデミズムに打ち勝とうとして、ヴァルター・グロピウスとバウハウス出身の人々は、バブルダイアグラムをアメリカの建築の言説へと導入した。実際は機能の絵文字であったバブルダイアグラムは、現前の建物に含まれる anteriority の存在の根元を削り去ったとアイゼンマンは指摘する。

バブルダイアグラムは、近代建築が存在することの時代精神を表現しようとしたために、批判的に振る舞わず、むしろ、いかなる過去をも否定しようとして、現前を標準化し固定化することを試みたのだった。すなわちそれは、anteriority の否定だけでなく interiority の否定でもあったとアイゼンマンは指摘する。標準化しようとする意識は、diagram が絶えず置きかわろうとすることを抑圧しようと絶え間なく試みる。それは、標準化された interiority へと向かうことに対する［現前］の違反行為、すなわち、diagram のズラシを否定し、生き生きとした建築の出現を拒否しているとアイゼンマンは批判するのである。

註4) DD pp.27,43（筆者要約）

近代建築の落とし穴

近代建築の落とし穴の１つは、diagram に置き換えるよりはむしろ、その存在における時代精神を表現しようと試みたということであったとアイゼンマンは観る。結局、近代建築はグローバルな資本によって吸収されてしまう。正確に言うと、モダニズムのイデオロギーが、批評的であるというよりはむしろ、懐柔され、普通で一般的なものになったからであると指摘する。

そのようなグローバルな資本の可能性は、今日、自身の歩みを逸脱し置き換えることをモダニズムが怠ったことの現れである。時代精神を示すその試みにおいて、近代建築は、diagram の置き換えと presentness に対する可能性を失い、diagram の能力を失ったのであると、アイゼンマンは批評するのである。

4-1-3：パッラーディオにおける標準なるものの違反
生成原理として生き生きとしたものを捉えようとする意識

パッラーディオは巨大なオーダーと小さなオーダーを融合させ、互いに異なるスケールを衝突させた。そして、標準化されたものへの関係を置き換えることを生み出した。こうした標準なるものへの違反行為は、現前に関して重要な状況を引き起こしたのだとアイゼンマンは指摘する。アイゼンマンは、パッラーディオが標準化されたものへのズラシの関係を生み出したことを評価し、次のように記述している。

すなわち、パッラーディオの図面は、実際の建物の立面図や平面図というより、むしろ、建物の抽象概念であり、建てられなかった図面も含めて、それらを沈殿させ、事実そのものを刻印することを越えて、何か別の建築の表現を開始したの

だとアイゼンマンは捉えている。パッラーディオのこれらの図面は、第一段階の表現としての建物自体の平面と断面を越えて、第二段階の表現と呼ばれうる。すなわち、第二段階の表現のほとんどの事例は、モデルまたはコピーのような表現ではなく、むしろ、沈殿させたものの置換を試み、潜在的な臨界に対して anteriority を開くものであり、あるレベルをもつ意味で、diagram 的であるとアイゼンマンは指摘する。

4-2：建築の interiority と anteriority
4-2-1：アイゼンマンの diagram[註5]

アイゼンマンは、diagram への探求の理由として、建築の外部へ執着する伝統的な態度に対する批判からはじまった事を述べている。すなわち、建築は外部に注目しすぎていたことを指摘し、アイゼンマンは、それを修正しようとする。建築は、伝統的に外部に存在する事象、すなわち、政治、社会状況、文化的価値などに関係しているため、建築は、理論的に、自身の言説、建築の内部に存在する事象を、滅多に検討してこなかったことに問題意識をもったことを記述している。

アイゼンマンの diagram 研究は、そうした問題意識を受けた考察である。それは、建築が自らを明らかにすることができ、実現された建物において自身の内在性を明らかにすることができるという内部の事象の存在の可能性を信じる問題意識である。建築は、自身の職務を務めるために、その全く同じ精神を、批評的に超え、置き換えなければならない。建築には、いかなる時期の政治、社会、美学、そして文化状況をも明らかにする能力があり、それは建築の歴史において、diagram によって議論され続けてきたことを示す。すなわち、それは、建築に内在するものの明示である。それを interiority と呼び、

註 5）DD p.37（筆者要約）
註 6）DD p.27,160-173（筆者要約）
註 7）ドゥルーズのダイアグラムをスーパーインポーズと評し、自身の diagram は superposition であると差異化しているため英語表記としている。

建築は、単に表象することだけでなく、これらの社会政治状況を転換させ、批評性をもつ可能性を孕んでいるのだということを宣言する。

さらに、建築の interiority には、アプリオリな歴史も、また存在するとも言う。すなわち、建築の interiority に存在している蓄積された全ての先在する知識である。この建築の先在する総体を anteriority と呼び、その扱いが重要だとしている。アイゼンマンは、こうした建築の interiority を明示し、建築の anteriority を開こうとする構えを見せるのである。そこには、建築の object に刻み込まれた anteriority を見通せる観点としての subject の存在を策定していることが理解できる。

4-2-2：アイゼンマンによる diagram の定義

アイゼンマンは diagram を構造でもなく、抽象概念でもなく、関係性を説明するものとして、定義している。

そして、アイゼンマンは diagram の二面性を捉えている。分析的側面と生成的側面の二つである。生成的側面においては、実際の建築物と建築の interiority との間に介在する存在として捉えている。そして、diagram と幾何学的なスキームとの違いに注目する。

4-2-3：diagram は、interiority だけでなく anteriority でもあるとし、内部性の拡張を求め、歴史性を連続させようとする野心

diagram が建築の interiority と anteriority に関わる重要な問題を以下のように提示している。[註6]

パッラーディオとセルリオは、幾何学的な図式を念頭にもって、時に明白に、時に暗示的に、自らのプロジェクトを描いているのだが、パッラーディオがおこなったプラン上の寸法の表記は、実際のプロジェクトに一致しておらず、diagram に一致しているものであると主張する。作品に暗に示されるこの決して描かれることのない diagram は決して明白にされることなく存在すると言う。例えば、建築における最古のパランプセプトの図面の中で、しばしば diagram の図式はインクを付けられることなく、尖筆で表面に描かれるか刻まれている。このパランプセプト上に、実際のプロジェクトに関する、後の墨入れは、その時、diagram の痕跡の superposition[註7] である。これらドローイングの多くにおいて―後期ゴシック建築からルネッサンスにかけて―実際には、その重ね書きが diagram の刻印の全てを掬い取るというものではなく、部分的な跡のみであるが、diagram が建物のプランの実際の一部である箇所とは異なり、ページ上のインクの質が変化している箇所において、インクは diagram 上を走っていると読み取る。このような不可視の線と diagram の痕跡という一つの建築の歴史が存在するとアイゼンマンは主張する。

これらの線は、建築の anteriority と interiority と呼ばれうるものとの間に存在する中間の状態（すなわち、diagram）の痕跡であるという理解のもとに、実在しうるプロジェクト同様、その歴史の総計の中の実際の建物と痕跡とにおいて、インデックス化されている、と主張する。この指摘より、アイゼンマンの建築に対する意識を知ることができる。すなわち、diagram は、建築の interiority だけでなく、連綿と続く歴史そのものである anteriority でもあるという認識である。こうしたアイゼンマンの考えは、建築の内部に、歴史に沈殿する意識を有

するべきであるとする建築のあるべき姿を宣言するものと理
解できる。

4-2-4：anteriority の更新
アイゼンマンは、建築の interiority において明白に現れる
anteriority を更新するための差異の反復を重視する。ここに
もデリダの影響が見て取れる。

建築が、批評的であるためには、同じことの反復より、むし
ろ差異の反復であるべきであることを示している。建築が過
去において明示されたものとは異なるように presence（現前）
において存在させるためである。こうした過去の総計は、建
築の interiority において明白であるような anteriority である
が、建築の presentness として、唯一の価値を存在させるた
めに、デザイン・プロセスの中で差異の反復は活発でなけれ
ばならず、そうしたプロセスを経て、デザインは object を生
成しなければならないとする。こうした object は、interiority
と anteriority を、現前へと、同時に関連づけるというプロセ
スを提示するとともに、interiority と anteriority、そして現前
との関係を明らかにさせるのだと主張する。

4-2-5：建築の anteriority と subject の問題
アルベルティは、『ウィトルウィウスが、建物は構造的である
べきであると意味したのではなく、それらが構造的なように
見えるべきであると意味した』と示唆したのだとアイゼンマ
ンは指摘する。

すなわちアルベルティによって、初めて、建築はその存在自体
のみならず、建築の表現に関与することが示されたのである。
すなわち、構造パラメーターは、ギリシア、ローマ、そして
ゴシック建築へと徐々に発展していく。したがって、構造と
して知覚されたものは、15 世紀において、subject の目に映っ
た構造的に見えるべき先在していたものであり、これは、表現
における状態、予測を生み出す。そして、ノーマルという意
識が浮上してくる。ノーマルについての考えは、アルベルティ
に見出されなかったが、クロード・ペローとグァリーニによっ
て、後に見出されるのであるとアイゼンマンは述べている。
「構造とは、構造的であると、見る人の目において現れるもの
である。」
ここに、「のように見える」という状態は、建築の anteriority
との関係で重大な問題を持つとアイゼンマンが指摘する。同
時に subject の問題をも孕むのである。

4-3：diagram の形而上学上の問題
4-3-1：エクリチュールの diagram への侵入
アイゼンマンは建築の interiority と anteriority に言及しつつ、
さらに、エクリチュール（writing）の diagram への侵入へと
言及していく。

アイゼンマンは、文化に関わる歴史的記録としてのアーカイ
ブ、およびアーカイブ的マテリアルの科学的研究としてのア
ルケオロジーに関するミッシェル・フーコー（以下フーコー）
の理解は、建築の interiority と anteriority として解釈され
うるとする。建築の interiority と anteriority は、すでに、
presence（現前）、動機付けされた記号、そして、二つの図と

註 8）DD p.31,l52-p.32,l18（筆者要約）

地に関連する subject による図形描写へと向かう精神的欲望を含んでいるという理解をする。そして、抑圧の集約としての建築の interiority と anteriority に言及し、その問題点を暴こうとする。

デリダにとって、最初に、エクリチュールとは抑圧された記憶の状態である。またエクリチュールが持つ抑圧は、抑圧された記憶が持つ抑圧でもある。そしてそれは現前を脅かす。建築は、現前の形而上学にとって不可欠なものであるため、建築の interiority において、現前を脅かすいかなるものは、抑圧されることが推定されるだろう。この意味で、建築の anteriority と interiority は抑圧の総和として捉えることができる。デリダは、すべての言説は抑圧を含み、次には、抑圧は、オルタナティヴな内部の表現を含むと反論するであろうが、建築が、現前の形而上学の必須条件であるため、現前を脅かすいかなるものは、建築の interiority において抑圧されると仮定されるとする。この意味で、建築の interiority と anteriority は、抑圧の集約とみなされうると理解する。デリダの思考を受けて、表象の form が、建築の記号のモチベーションがなくなるものとして、建築の interiority において、すでに存在しているとアイゼンマンは推測する。表象に関するこの抑圧された形式は、建築に対して、内部へと向かう方向だけではなく、先在する過去へと向かう方向にも存在するという理解を示す。
建築におけるこの表現こそが、またエクリチュールと呼ばれ得たものである。こうしたエクリチュールが diagram にいかに侵入するかが、建築にとって重大な問題になるという理解を示すのである。註8)

この考え方は、デリダの現前の形而上学批判の完全なる裏返

しとも言える。デリダは、現前の形而上学を批判する。デリダが批判するパロールを重視する態度は出発点の優位性を担保するものである。それに対して、エクリチュールに重きを置く態度は、出発点の優位性を葬り去り、ロゴス中心主義を覆す。すなわち、起源なるもの、すなわち、正統性、作家性の意味を解体する企てがある。デリダは、そうした企てにより、抑圧からの解放を求めようとした。しかし、アイゼンマンは、そうしたデリダの試みを、建築へと読み換えることで、反転させ、逆に建築の特殊性を示すのである。すなわち建築は現前の形而上学そのものであることを提示してしまうのである。したがって、建築の interiority と anteriority は抑圧そのものの集積であることの認識を前提とするのである。

4-4：diagram における subject と批評性
4-4-1：object の中に注入された diagram
著者としての subject を超える
エージェント・他者性の視点
アイゼンマンは、diagram を、subject（著者）と object（作品）の間のオルタナティヴな関係性を提案するものとして、位置づけている。
ここに、subject の問題が浮上してくる。アイゼンマンは古典的意識から一歩進んだのであった。diagram は客観性を備えた手段となり得ると、それが、著者としての subject を超えることであるという意識である。脱構築主義以降、アイゼンマンはポスト構造主義の思想に影響を受けながら、他者性の視点を導入しようとした。著者という subject を離れた diagram の存在を求め、そこに先在する建築の総体が注入され、建築の interiority として浮上し、建築が構築されることを求める。過

去の建築の総体である anteriority によってつくられる立場である。 註9)

4-4-2：diagram と subject-object
subject/object の歴史 註10)
diagram 自体は、建築における長い歴史をもつ。そのような歴史をたどることが可能である一方、この文脈において、より関連することは、建築の interiority と anteriority を明確にさせるプロセスとして、その進化をたどることである。アイゼンマンの diagram の進化は、そのようなプロセスである。
アイゼンマンの思索において、subject/object という二項対立、（すなわち、世界に関する神中心の古典的な見方から人間中心的なものに、さらに人間を囲む object 世界で新しく進化する関係性）を説明するために開発されるものが必要であった。新しく進化した subject-object は、神からの啓示によって、もはや説明されえない、新しい意識への答えが必要であった。
アイゼンマンは、こうした問題に着手したのであった。こうした歴史は、subject において人間以外の存在を許す可能性を開くことになる。アルゴリズムや AI である。そういう意味でアイゼンマンの diagram は過渡的な存在であったと言える。創造の源泉を原理的なプログラムと気が付きながらも、diagram として object に格納した。

4-4-3：diagram は、異なる subject の状態に焦点をあてる
アイゼンマンは、透視図の導入が表現のパラメーターを変えたことを指摘する。これは、観るという subject の観点と object の間の活発な関係性を、建築の interiority へと回収させたという。ブルネレスキが透視図の形式において数学と物理学から外在性を導入する一方、アルベルティは、言説に関する歴史の必然としての anteriority の考えを導入したことを対比しながら、透視図などのような可視的なものの interiority への沈殿は、究極的に、diagram の考えに影響を及ぼすという。

例として、ブルネレスキの教会のサン・ローレンツォとサント・スピリトの二つの違いを採り上げ、diagram が、それらの異なっている subject の状態に焦点をあてることでサン・ローレンツォとサント・スピリトの違いをはっきりさせることができるとする。その二つの視点とは、ひとつは、一点から円錐のビジョンを介して空間を見ている静的な subject を要求するものであり、もう一つは、動く subject を要求するものである。（図 4-1）

註9）　ポスト構造主義は読み手の理想的な形式をずらし、その意味を転換させた。中でもロラン・バルトが「作者の死」を主張したことは周知のとおりである。ここに、作者と読者の二重の作り手の問題が潜んでいる。
　　　アイゼンマンは、こうしたポスト構造主義の影響を受け、diagram として、現在の subject 以外のものを持ち込もうとしたのである。
註10）DD p.38（筆者要約）

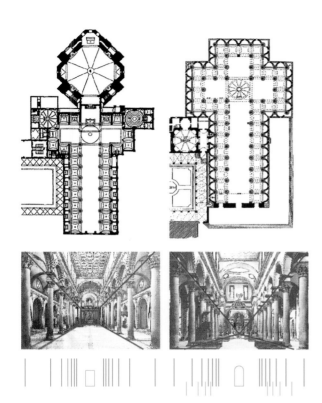

Fig.4-1　Brunelleschi: The Vision of the Subject
サン・ロレンツォ教会（左図）とサント・スピリト教会（右図）

を還元することをともなう曲線の系列が存在する。これこそが襞なのである。対象はもはや本質的な形態によって定義されるのではなく、パラメーターに枠づけされた曲線族を変化させるものとして純粋な機能性に帰着し、可能な変化の系列と不可分、あるいはこの対象自身が描きだす、可変的な湾曲をもつ表面と不可分である。この新しい対象を対象体（objectile）と呼ぶ。

ベルナール・カッシュが示しているように、これは技術的な対象のまったく現代的な概念である。それはスタンダードの観念がまだ本質という外見をもち、恒常性の法則を課していた工業中心時代の初期（塊りによって、塊りのために生産される対象）などとは無関係である。この状況では規範の揺らぎが法則の恒常性にとってかわり、対象は変化による連続体の中に位置し、コンピューター支援システムや数値の指令による機械が板金作業に置き換えられるのである。対象の新しい規定は、もはや対象を空間的な型に、つまり形相 - 質料の関係に結びつけるのではなく、時間的な変調に結びつけるのだが、これは質料を連続変化にみちびくだけでなく、形相の連続的発展をもたらす。

（中略）

系列の法則は、連続的な運動の中にある「同じ線の軌跡」として諸曲線をとらえ、この軌跡は連続的にそれらの交差する曲線に接触されるというとき、ライプニッツは変調を定義していた。これは対象についての、単に時間的ではなく質的な概念を示している。マニエリスム的な対象であって、もはや本質主義的な対象ではない。つまりこれは event となる。

対象〔客体〕が根本的に地位を変更するとすれば、主体にも同じことがおきる。

これは厳密には一点ではなく、一つの場所、位置、地勢、「線

こうした見解は、ドゥルーズの「襞」に記された objectile（対象体）からの影響と思われる。観るという観点によって、異なる subject を生み出すことである。

ドゥルーズは、「襞」で以下のように述べている。
"接触する、または接する曲線の「唯一つの可変性」に諸変数

的な焦点」、複数の線から出現する線である。変化あるいは屈折を表象するのだから、それは観点とも呼ばれる。遠近法主義（perspectivisme）の根拠とはこのようなものである。遠近法主義は前もって決定された主体に依存することを意味するのではない。逆に、観点のところにやってくるものが、あるいはむしろ観点にとどまるものこそが主体である。だからこそ対象の変形は、主体の相関的な変形にかかわるのである。つまり主体（subject）とは下におかれるもの（sub-jet）ではなく、ホワイトヘッドのいうように「自己超越体」（superjet）なのである。対象が対象体になると同時に、主体は「自己超越体」となる。変化と観点との間には必然的な関係がある。それは単に観点の変動が理由ではなく（後に見るように、目覚ましい変動があるわけであるが）、第一にあらゆる観点は、何らかの変化に対する観点であるからである。

（中略）

遠近法主義とはまさに一つの複数主義であり、それゆえに距離をともなうのであって、不連続性をともなうのではない（たしかに二つの観点の間に空虚は存在しない）。ライプニッツは、延長（エクステンシオ）を、地勢あるいは位置の、つまり観点の「連続的反復」として定義している。延長がそのとき観点の属性であるからではなく、観点の間の距離の秩序として延長は空間（スパティウム）の属性であり、それがこのような反復を可能にするからである。

一つの変化に対する観点が形態や形状の中心にとってかわる。最も知られた例は円錐曲線のそれであり、円錐の先端とは観点であって、われわれは円、楕円、放物線、双曲線を、また曲線と点を、切断面の勾配に対応する同数の変形部分としてこれに結びつけるのである（「遠近画」）。これらすべての形態は、一つの「平行投影図」が自分自身を折り畳む仕方そのもの

となる。そしてこの「平行投影図」は、遠近法の古い概念にこのような特権を負っている円などではなく、いまや円もその一部にすぎない第二段階の曲線からなる曲線族を変化させ、また描きだす対象体なのである。この対象体、この平行投影図は、あたかも拡げられた襞のようである。"[註11]

（ドゥルーズ、襞）

このことは、観点と subject との関係性がドゥルーズによって、導かれているが、アイゼンマンもその影響を受けているものと思われる。さらに、event（出来事）概念をアイゼンマンは重視する。時間性を孕んだ object 概念を提示するのである。この時間性を孕んだ object に関しては後ほど述べるとして、以下に subject の問題について述べたい。

4-4-4：subject としての建築家
subject とエージェント

アイゼンマンは、subject の問題を射程に入れる。そこでは生成力のあるエージェントに言及している。

diagram は、現在の著者、建築 object、過去から受け取る沈殿した subject の間の関係に焦点を合わせるエージェントとしての働きをする。

アイゼンマンは、subject の存在が時間軸上で変化していくことを理解し、先在するものとして沈澱していった過去の subject 群を、現在の subject である著者と区別している。そうして、subject すらも anteriority として過去から受け取り、現在の subject である著者とともに重ね合わせ、それらの関

註11）ドゥルーズ、宇野邦一訳『襞』第2章　pp.34-38
註12）堀口徹、小野田泰明、菅野實「建築批評家ジェフリー・キプニスにおけるシングル・サーフェイス概念の研究その1、その2」『日本建築学会計画系論文集』第560、第575号等
註13）WV　Chapter12 pp.96-99（筆者要約）
註14）プラトンのイデアの分有になぞらえて、アイゼンマンの diagram に対して、筆者の充てた造語。

係式として diagram を考えている。diagram のプロセスは、subject からのある精神的インプットなしでは決して作動しないものと位置づける。それは、生成力と形成力のあるキャパシティーを制限する抑圧を開放し、建築の anteriority と subject の両方の内部で構成された抑圧を開放するものであるとする。アイゼンマンは、作品という object が生成する立場をシフトすることで、subject を論じているのである。そのことは、object 自身の問題に収斂することになる。

4-5：まとめ
批評装置としての diagram
4-5-1：アイゼンマンの批評性
アイゼンマンの批評の立場は、ソモルやジェフリー・キプニスの批評[註12]とは異なる。建築の interiority そのものが批評であるという立場である。ソモルのように、喧噪慌ただしく、ノイズを散撒くことが批評でもなく、キプニスのように外部から批評を建築に押し込むことが批評ではないとするのである。アイゼンマンは、建築の記号と意味とが引き合うモチベーションがゼロになることが批評であるとする。すなわち、従来の意味が記号から切り離された時こそが批評が現れる時であるとするのである。[註13]

4-5-2：分有された subject [註14]
subject と object の連続性、その関係性を射程に入れる
アイゼンマンの diagram は、明確に外部化されたものではないことが、本章においてみられた。まずはアイゼンマンが外部化の否定に固執したことについて概観したい。標準化へと還元する類型ではなく、標準化を克服する diagram を目指したアイゼンマンの意識を捉えたい。そこには批評性を建築に内在化しようとする意識が見て取れる。そのため、アイゼンマンは、常に建築の既成概念をズラスのである。たとえば、デリダとの書簡の交換の中で、西欧の二項対立から離脱するデリダをも批判する。デリダが提示した現前と不在を二項対立として批判し、アイゼンマンは新たに presentness（プレゼントネス）を提示する。そこには西欧のロジックでは落ちこぼれるものを掬いとろうとする意識がある。批評性を侵入させたいがための presentness の問題を取り上げるのである。アイゼンマンの diagram は外部化されないものである。それは object に内包され、それを読み取ることを求める。いわば作品という object は subject 自身の分身ともいうべきものである。それは subject と object の区別すらも無くそうとするアイゼンマンの態度から生まれたものである。そうした subject が分有された object が、彼自身の問題意識を継起する時系列上に存在する。それこそが、建築の anteriority である。作品はそれを包含する interiority である。それは開かれたものではなく、それを理解することのできる subject を策定して扱おうとしたのであった。

アイゼンマンは、“パランプセストにあらわれた痕跡の線は、建築の anteriority と interiority と呼ばれうるものとの間に存在する中間の状態すなわち、diagram の痕跡である。”[註15]と述べている。

アイゼンマンはこうした痕跡を diagram として掬いとろうとするのだが、決して標準化という外部化は行わなかった。その理由は、硬直化した静止状態ではなく、動的な批評性を温存させたかったからである。そのことは、presentness をどう捉えるかという問題に関わってくるのである。それは、批評装置と

註 15）DD　p.28,17-l15（筆者翻訳）以下原文：Thus, there is a history of an architecture of traces, of invisible lines and diagrams that only become visible through various means. These lines are the trace of an intermediary condition (that is, the diagram) that exists between what can be called the anteriority and the interiority of architecture; the summation of its history as well as the projects that could exist are indexed in the traces and the actual building.

77

しての diagram を志向していたとも言える。アイゼンマンは、diagram に subject と批評性を持ち込もうとしたのである。

アイゼンマンは、パッラーディオが巨大なオーダーと小さなオーダーを融合させ、互いに異なるスケールを衝突させたことについて、標準化されたものへの関係をズラスことを生み出したと評価した。批評性の特質であるズラシは、いきいきとした動的な状態で維持されるべきであり、標準化された静止状態になった時、重要度が消失し、創造性を発揮することはできないと考えたのである。そうした生き生きとした批評性が diagram として、object に留まることを望んだのである。

Chapter 5

コールハースの建築概念 [註1)]

近代建築を再考する二つの大きな方向性として、建築のイデアを純粋に求める内部へと向かう方向と社会の事象を設計に組み込もうとする外部へと向かう方向の二つが認められ本論文で対象としている。前者の方向を推し進めた建築家であるアイゼンマンについては、これまでに建築の interiority に関する探求の推移と考察を行った。本章では、後者の建築家であるコールハースを対象とする。ここでは、コールハースの建築思想を取り上げ、中でも特に、現代の建築思潮に大きな影響を及ぼしていると思われる並置の概念について、その出自を考察するものである。

すなわち、コールハースの建築概念が、既に述べたル・コルビュジエの建築概念を継承していることを示したい。第二章ではル・コルビュジエによってもたらされた図と地の反転のダイナミズムを内的に深化する方向へと導いたアイゼンマンの分析から導かれた diagram について概観した。

本章では、そうしたダイナミズムの内的な探求ではなく、object を並置することで object どうしの多様な関係が生まれ、関係性のダイナミズムが生まれることに着想を得て、ル・コルビュジエのもう一つの両義性である部品化された object の並置を継承したコールハースについて論ずる。

ー不連続性から連続性への反転ー

ベルナール・チュミの言説

モダニズム以降のプログラムに関する建築思潮：ベルナール・チュミの言説より

ベルナール・チュミのラ・ヴィレット公園計画案を生み出す元となった考え方が記された彼の著作「architecture and disjunction」（「建築と断絶」）[註2)] のプログラムと題した第二章において、建築におけるプログラムの歴史的概観が年代および思想史ごとに描かれている。その中で、1950 年代生れのモダニズム建築の理論について

"…建築を形態的・スタイル的な操作として定義していることには変わりないとし、利用に関する考察の不在を巧妙に隠すものである」と指摘している。また、「建築を容易に把握できる静的な対象として捉えているだけで、空間と event との相互作用として捉えてなく、形態の論理に関するあらゆる言説から、身体とその体験が除外されている "とチュミは説いている。

これは、ウィットカウアーやロウの分析 [註3)] の立ち位置に対する批評としてとらえることができ、アイゼンマンのスタンスもこの中に一部属するものと思われる。アイゼンマンが、ウィットカウアーやロウなどの静的な分析から建築形態の動的分析への道を開いたことは、これまでの章において示した。

註 1) 本章は、拙稿、山口隆「レム・コールハースの並置概念の考察」『論考　建築設計 03』日本建築設計学会、2018 年、pp.9-14、を加筆修正したものである。
註 2) Bernard Tschumi, Architecture and Disjunction, MIT Press (1996). Ⅱ program pp.98-168、（邦訳）ベルナール・チュミ（山形浩生訳）『建築と断絶』鹿島出版会、1996 年
註 3) パッラーディオのナインスクエアグリッドの分析や、Transparency に関する論考
註 4) Rem Koolhaas, Delirious New York（以下 DN とする）: A Retroactive Manifesto for Manhattan,The Monacelli Press (1994)

本章では、コールハースの「動的」なものの解釈を捉えることを目的とする。ここでチュミの言う「静的な対象」に対する「動的」なものがあるとするならば、その「動的」なものの解釈がアイゼンマンとコールハースとでは異なり、本章ではその違いを重要なものと捉えている。

チュミの言説は以下のように続く。

1970 年代：モダニズム批判は自立的対象の固有の性質ばかりに注目し、建築を詩学のお手軽な対象とし、記号理論と手を結んだ。「利用形態やプログラムは、主体や内容ではなく形態の一部になれるのか？」という疑問を投げかけながら、ロシア・フォルマリズムは、内容に関する考察を排除するのではなく、それを作品の様々な構成物の全体性としてとらえるようになり始めていたとの考察から、内容も形態的になり得ると示唆している。

チュミによれば、「建築はデザインの条件に関することではなく条件のデザインに関すること」であり、形態は、すなわち利用形態（プログラム）のことを意味し、ここまで考えなければ建築は捉えきれないとしている。そうした上でプログラムを定義している。

チュミは、こうしたプログラムの考えによって object を選択し、配置する。しかしながら、そこではプログラムによって object が単純にコントロールされているのみである。こうしたチュミの態度は、外在的な条件に基づくアプローチのみであり、anteriority と interiority を重視するアイゼンマンにとって、まさに正反対な態度であった。

「切断」の概念

コールハースは、こうした外在的条件のプログラム使用において、さらに一歩踏み込み、意味を object から切断する。アイゼンマンも「切断」ということを述べているが、それはコールハースの「切断」とは異なっている。

アイゼンマンが、デリダが記号と意味を切断したことに習って、意味と form とを切断しようとしたことは既に見た。しかし、コールハースは、意味と object を切断する。両者の違いは、切断対象が form と object の違いである。この違いが両者の立場を明確にする。前者は内的な方向へ向かい、後者は外的な方向へと向かう。このコールハースの外的な方向に向かう「切断」の概念が、その後の新たな豊饒なる建築生成を生み出していく。こうした「切断」という概念は『デリリアス・ニューヨーク』[註4] でのリサーチにおいて得られたとしているが、実は、object の「切断」という考えの源流はル・コルビュジエにあり、コールハースはそれを発展させたに過ぎない。それらのことを本章では扱う。まず、ル・コルビュジエの作品と言説の両義性については既に述べた。ここではコールハースの作品ごとに「切断」と「並置」に着目し詳述する。さらに、コールハースの建築概念として、コールハースの手法について詳述し、コールハースの手法が、どこから生まれてきたのかという問題、およびそれによって開かれた可能性を論ずる。

本章では、コールハースの並置概念の背景として捉えられるロシア・アヴァンギャルドにおける類似概念を考察し、コールハースの作品に直接的にも間接的にも多くの影響を与え、並置概念の直接の源泉と考えられるル・コルビュジエの並置概念の萌芽とコールハースへの影響を考察する。その後、実際に、並置概念に対するコールハース独自の展開を導いたと思われるニューヨークのリサーチから見出された並置概念について詳述する。さらに、並置概念がはじめて示されたプロジェ

クトであるラ・ヴィレット公園設計競技について、その並置
概念がいかに表現されたのかを詳述する。最後に、この並置
概念というものは、前述した建築のイデアを求める方向性と
現代建築において対を成すものであり、建築における外在的
アプローチと内在的アプローチの関係について考察を行なう。

5-1：コールハースの思考　切断と並置
ここでは、コールハースの作品ごとに設計手法と並置概念、お
よび subject の問題に着目し詳述する。

5-1-1：「デリリアス・ニューヨーク」「Ｓ、Ｍ、Ｌ、XL」[註5]
一義的なモダニズムを乗り越えるために過剰な欲望と求心
性、批判性を解体していったニューヨークをコールハースは
リサーチした。 AA スクール卒業後、ニューヨークの IAUS で
の研究活動の主テーマが、ロシア・アヴァンギャルドとニュー
ヨークの研究であった。これらのテーマは互いに関連し、ロ
シア・アヴァンギャルドが改革の原動力とし、それらを視覚
化しようとした「社会的コンデンサー」[註6] が無意識に生成し
てきたのがニューヨークであり、真の「社会的コンデンサー」
とはニューヨークの摩天楼であるとの洞察のもとに行なわれ
た研究が「デリリアス・ニューヨーク」である。

この研究では、誰も語られなかったマンハッタンのゴーストラ
イターとしてコールハースは、マンハッタニズムという重要
な概念を提示した。高層の摩天楼において、各階で意味の切
断を引き起こしていることを見出す。その後、ブルース・マ
ウとの「Ｓ、Ｍ、Ｌ、XL」において、コールハースはビッグネ

スという概念に到達する。建築のスケールが巨大化したとき、
建築はビッグネスという属性を帯び、建築内部の論理をサー
フェイスに表出させるべきという意識が消失させられるなど、
拡大したスケールは内部と外部とは無関係になるという内外
の不連続性を引き起こす。そうした状況においては、古典的
な枠組みが無意味なものとなっていくのを発見する。コール
ハースは、スケールすらも部品化させ、量的な幅を規定させる。
そのことによって、量的な変化が質的な変化をもたらすこと
を発見していく。[註7]
建築の巨大化現象において、建築の内部では、こうした切断
現象が現れ、全てが部品化されていくことを予見する。すな
わち社会の欲望によって様々なプログラムが生まれ、繰り返
される予期せぬ衝突や交配を建築が孕むことを肯定し、コー
ルハースは、こうした建築的ロボトミーを提案する。[註8]
過密であるが故に、全く別々の機能が並置される現象が起きて
いる場、それがニューヨークの魅力を形成しているのであり、
並置のコンセプトはその裏返しで、過密を可能にしているも
のこそ、並置という現象にあることを見出している。
そして、その並置の概念を加速させたものとして、柱、床、階
段という建築の要素のみを重視するル・コルビュジエとは異
なり、コールハースはエレベーターというテクノロジーデヴァ
イスを挙げる。エレベーターはル・コルビュジエがドミノシ
ステムに内包しなかったエレメントである。既に、ポンピドー
センターで古典的な建築のエレメントではない設備的エレメ
ントをサーフェイスにおいて、外部化されてはいたが、それ
は狭義のデザインとしての領域に留まっていた。しかし、コー
ルハースは、文明の欲望の増大が新たなテクノロジーデヴァ
イスを生み出し、その産物によって建築自体が大きく変容してい
く方向にあるとして、その重要性を見出した。マンハッタン

註5) Rem Koolhaas, Bruce Mau, Hans Werlemann, S M L XL（以下 SL とする）, The Monacelli Press (1997)、（邦訳）
　　　レム・コールハース（太田佳代子、渡辺佐智江訳）『S, M, L, XL+：現代都市をめぐるエッセイ』筑摩書房、2015 年
註6) ロシア革命による社会主義体制のプログラムとしての共同施設；新しいタイプの共同住宅、クラブ、労働宮殿、工場等
註7) SL　pp.495-516

はまさにそのテクノロジーと人口爆発による欲望の肥大化が、垂直方向への機能空間の並置を加速した場であった。そこにコールハースは過密時代の可能性を見出した。註9)

さらに、こうしたリサーチから機能と建物の形態に関係性がなく、そこに切断があることを暴き出した。部品化された建築エレメントの並置はル・コルビュジエの特徴であるが、マンハッタンの分析において、「切断」という現象が見られるとして、コールハースはル・コルビュジエの思考を批評的に継承する。註10)

コールハースは、ル・コルビュジエを相当意識していたことが伺われる。「デリリアス・ニューヨーク」において、以下のようにル・コルビュジエを批判している。

" 彼は自分の理論的仮定世界の黒ビロードの容れ物にアメリカ製摩天楼を隠し、次にそこへジャングル（できうる限り純粋な形態の自然）を加える。そうした上でこの偏執症的批判法たるトップ・ハットに入った相容れないこれらふたつの物体をかき回してやる―すると摩訶不思議！―、中から水平の摩天楼が出てくるではないか。これこそル・コルビュジエにおけるデカルト的ウサギである。この手品によってマンハッタン摩天楼とジャングルは元の姿がわからなくなる。つまり摩天楼はデカルト的（＝フランス的＝合理的）な抽象となり、ジャングルは複数のデカルト的摩天楼をまるごと支える緑の絨緞に姿を変えているのだ。"

ル・コルビュジエは理想的な高層建築を求めていた。しかし、それはル・コルビュジエが発見する以前、既にマンハッタンに存在するものであった。ル・コルビュジエは、一旦それを否定してみせることで、自身の案にするマジックを使用したと

する。すなわち、マンハッタンの重苦しいファサードを近代的なガラスで包むことで、自然と太陽に満ちあふれた理想的なル・コルビュジエの作品としたのである。そしてコールハースは、こうした態度を取るル・コルビュジエを否定してみせることで、マンハッタンを強調する。しかし、これも一つのマジックである。このマジックは次のことを示している。実は、マンハッタンそのものが、ドミノシステムが垂直に連続したル・コルビュジエの高層建築の作品であること。そのことは、皮肉にも、コールハースの思考はル・コルビュジエの思考を意識していることを逆説的に示している。

周知の通り、ドミノシステムにはエレベーターは排除されている。つまり、コールハースがエレベーターを重視したことこそ、ル・コルビュジエを意識していたもう一つの理由である。またサヴォア邸において、各階には独立した自由な平面が見られる。こうした異なる平面構成の違いが、各階に異なる意味を並置させ、各階の意味の切断を具現化させているのである。さらに、こうしたことを概観すれば、ル・コルビュジエが既にマンハッタンの建築に見られる各階の切断に新たな建築の可能性を見出していたと言うことも可能であろう。註11)

以上のように、コールハースは、ル・コルビュジエを批判的に継承していく。そして、形態objectを抽象化し、ヒエラルキーをつくらず、全てはパラレルとして並置させ、浮遊させる。さらに意味と切断され部品化された形態objectに、リレーショナル・ダイアグラムによってデータ化された機能を適応させている。部品化された形態objectは、機能を表出するものではなく、むしろ機能等の関係性が適応されていく対象とされ、近代の機能主義を反証している。彼のリサーチは、並置の概念の形成を促しただけでなく、その後の彼の設計活動における立ち位置を決定づけ、さらに後に続く世代にデータスケー

註8) DN p.100 LOBOTOMY
註9) DN pp.29-108 Coney Island: technology of fantastic, Double Life of Utopia: The Skyscraper
註10) DN pp.235-282 Europeans: Biuer! Dali and Le Corbusier Conquer New York
註11) DN マンハッタンの最初のゴーストライターは、コールハースではなくコルビュジエだったとも言える。

プという設計姿勢を導くことになる。[註12]

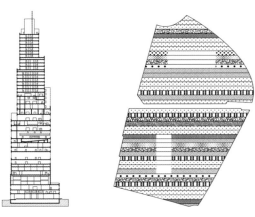

Fig.5-1　スカイスクレーパー断面（左図）
ラ・ヴィレット公園案機能の再分配（右図）

5-1-2：ラ・ヴィレット公園コンペ案

ニューヨークの調査をベースとし、スカイスクレーパーを構成
しているフロア間の関係性は空間の形態とは関係ないが、そ
こで展開されているアクティビティの組合せの面白さに、並
置の可能性を見出している。そのスカイスクレーパーを横に
寝かせたように公園のプランニングを提案する。（図5-1）こ
こでは、帯状に並置されたアクティビティが主題となる。

近代建築までの建築は、プログラムと空間に強い関係性はな
かった。つまり、どんなプログラムも受け入れられる、互換
性がある空間であった。デュランによって建築類型と建物用
途であるプログラムはまとめられたが、古典主義建築に用途
を与えたにすぎなかった。

機能主義はある部屋や空間をそこでなされる行為を形式化す
ることによって規定した。寝るところは寝室というように。

しかし都市空間や建築のアイデンティティを規定しているの
は、機能ではない。その場所のはたらきを規定しているのは、
使われ方、すなわち人の活動、出来事であることにコールハー
スは気づいたのである。近代建築の機能主義における機能と
は、プログラムとほぼ同義である。このプログラム（機能）と
形態の間に何のヒエラルキーもなく、空間という容器は機能
をいろいろ入れ替えることができるところに、コールハース
は event 性を見出した。そこで、むしろ分断された個々のプロ
グラムを空間として近接させ、並置させることで、それによっ
て起こる event（出来事）、プログラムでは予期されないストー
リーが発生する可能性があるところに、コールハースは空間
の可能性を見出した。

その空間的手法とは、一つはレイヤーであり、もう一つは切
断された異なるプログラムを並置することであった。すなわ
ち部品化されたプログラムがパラレルに（帯状に）配される
ことである。[註13]

5-1-3：ボルドーの住宅

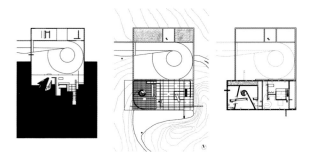

Fig.5-2　ボルドーの住宅平面図

註12) 例えば MVRDV など
註13) チュミもラ・ヴィレットのコンペにおいて同様のコンセプトでプログラムを考え、レイヤーという手法を選択した。
註14) 構造システムについて詳しくは文献：セシル・バルモンド（山形 浩生訳）『インフォーマル』TOTO 出版、2005 年、レム・コールハース「OMA@work.a+u：レム・コールハース」吉田信之編『a+u：建築と都市』
　　　2000 年 5 月臨時増刊

ル・コルビュジエのサヴォア邸を転換させたプロジェクトである。それぞれのフロアで全く異なる平面が並置されている点は、ル・コルビュジエのサヴォア邸から抽出したものと解釈される。(図 5-2)

サヴォア邸は建築の各システム；柱と床と階段からなるドミノシステム、スロープによる動線システム、volume とヴォイド、サーフェイスの図と地の関係からなる形態システム、機能空間としての空間システムなどが並置されたものである。コールハースは、このプロジェクトで、柱と梁で支えるという構造を異なった構造システムへと移行させることでル・コルビュジエのドミノの転換を試みている。[註14] 特に、このプロジェクトでは切断と横断、この相反する二つが並置されている点が重要である。このプロジェクトの中心として、上下に動的に移動するスラブの存在がある。横断という概念は切断という概念を前提とする。

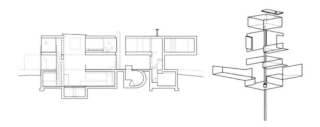

Fig.5-3 ボルドーの住宅断面図、エレベーターダイアグラム

さらに、ル・コルビュジエが近代建築の可能性として導入したスロープに対して、現代建築の可能性としてエレベーターの概念の転換を図っている。従来の階段の補助的な役割としてのエレベーターを、移動手段ではなく場そのものを移動させ、場を変える装置として、身障者であるクライアントの条件を

転換している。これは、分断された場が上下に動的に横断していくものであり(図 5-3)、建築空間が交通空間になるのである。このことの意味は大きい。ル・コルビュジエのドミノシステムの特徴である床によって切断され、固定されたものとしての静的 volume 概念から上下に流動しうる動的 volume 概念へと移行させ、自由な空間へと開放させた。しかし、こうした概念は床による上下階の分断というドミノシステムに基礎を置くものである。

5-1-4：エクゾダス

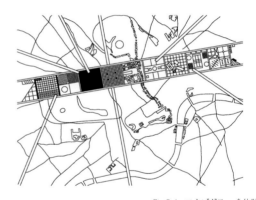

Fig.5-4 エクゾダス 全体計画図

AA スクールの卒業設計として提出されたこの作品は、現実のロンドンの都市にアイロニカルなユートピアを並置し、読み手に対してそのどちらをとるのか選択を迫る。レオニドフのマグニトゴルクス重工業都市計画を想起させる形式に volume が与えられ、現代社会に対するアイロニカルなユートピアのシナリオが二つの壁の間に並置されている。(図 5-4)

コールハウス自身は、二つの壁の間の世界こそが自分の提案するユートピアであることを主張しない。現実にとどまってもよし、未知なる世界へ踏み込んでもよしとする。ただし、一度入ったら戻ることはできない。そのような選択は著者自身がおこなうのではなく、他者に迫るのである。すなわち、subject としての自己を確定しない、決定を他者に委ねるものとして、並置を用いる。むしろ、そこに並置の可能性として subject をオープンにしうることを見出し、西欧の伝統的 subject を解体しようとする。[註15]

5-1-5：クンストハル、エデュカトリアム

クンストハル、エデュカトリアムでは、「切断」という「不連続性」から、一転して「連続性」という意識が強調される。「切断」という意識は「デリリアス・ニューヨーク」で見出されたとされているが、ル・コルビュジエのドミノシステムに既に胚胎されていたことは既に述べた。コールハウスはル・コルビュジエのドミノシステムに孕む問題性を発見し、未だ「不連続性」の範疇にあったル・コルビュジエを越えようとした。

ル・コルビュジエは、volume をプランでコントロールしようとすることを中心に置いていた。すなわち、「volume は、平面のコントロールのもとで分節されるべきである」という意識を持っていた。平面が規定する壁によって volume は限定される。そうした意味で、ル・コルビュジエは、未だ「不連続性」の範疇にあったと言える。

しかし、ル・コルビュジエはスロープという流動的デヴァイスを発見している。それは未だ部品化されていない建築エレメントの一部ではあるが、次の時代を開くものであった。[註16] コールハウスはそうしたル・コルビュジエの意識を継承し、

建築内部をスルーしていくサーキュレーションを建築化していく。そして折り曲げられたスラブが上下に連続していくトランジェクトリーを生み出す。断面を交差するスラブを挿入することにより、ドミノシステムという平行スラブによって切断されていた建築の可能性を拡張した。(図5-5) すなわち、それは流動する「連続性」の意識の創成でもあった。こうした連続性への可能性の拡張は、実はル・コルビュジエの「不連続性」を前提とし、そこから出発し、発展させたものであった。その試みは切断された volume を流動化させることであった。コールハウスは、平面から断面への操作範囲の敷衍によって、「プラン」に執着していたル・コルビュジエの「不連続性」を越えたのである。

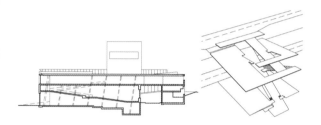

Fig.5-5　クンストハル断面（左図）, 連続する床面（右図）

5-1-6：フランス国立図書館コンペ案

この案は、意味の充満した volume をコントロールするものである。さらにその意味は数量化されデータ化されている。ル・コルビュジエが、プランのコントロールがなければ volume は風船のごとく無秩序に膨張するものであることを危惧していたが、コールハウスは、膨張する volume 相互の関係を diagram 化して、その関係性をコントロールする。そこではコントロールするものとしてのプランは、関係性の diagram へ

註15) SL pp.2-19
註16) 奥田 真也「＜斜床＞とは何か – 問いを発し続ける＜L.C＞（ル・コルビュジエ）」『建築文化』51(600)、彰国社、1996年10月、pp.138-144

と、その地位を譲っている。

詳しく見ていくと、ル・コルビュジエによる近代建築の一般化を含む、近代建築を否定ないし、昇華するプログラムを展開させているものとして、ル・コルビュジエの並置の概念から派生しているものと解釈され、以下の7つの項目に読解できる。

①ゾーニングから領域の関係性へ
　接続・包含・貫通
②平面的な動線計画から立体的な動線へ
　それぞれの諸室に通ずる独立したエレベーター
③二次元的な断面計画から多層・多重的断面計画へ
　入れ子状、内包空間
④近代建築の四つの型の再読
　volume ／サーフェイス／グリッドからソリッド／ヴォイド／三次元グリッドへ
⑤ドミノシステムの昇華
　柱・床・階段（建築オブジェクト）からエレベーターシャフト・volume・エレベーターへ
⑥コアの集中から分散へ
⑦要素主義の昇華
　要素に volume を与え配置配列から要素の内包／要素のくり貫き（ブーリアン）へ
　ヴォイドという形象へプログラムをかたどる。

これは、ル・コルビュジエのドミノシステムに対する特殊解と捉えられる。すなわち、ドミノではセクションは均質でプランは自由である。それに対して、このコールハースの案はセクションが自由で立体構造を断片化している。すなわちプランによってコントロールしようとしたル・コルビュジエの意識をセクションへと拡張させ、さらにル・コルビュジエの並置概念をブーリアン演算というデヴァイスにより三次元的に発展させている。近代建築は中心の喪失として、平面において拡散し、セクションは重力との対応で、自由にすることは困難であった。そういった意味において、コールハースは近代を継承しながらもさらに発展させている。

コールハースの散乱した幾つかのプロジェクトにおいて、この案はデータの処理のみで出来上がっているのではないことを強調しなければならない。ミースがプランへの還元を成功させた重要性と同様、セクションへと三次元的な拡張を示した意味で、建築概念の発展において重要性を孕むプロジェクトとして評価される。

ル・コルビュジエはドミノシステムを唱えながら、それはあくまで、建築の原則として、それが向かう均質性への抵抗として、自らの作品においては、崩している。建築家個人の均質化に抵抗がみられる。コールハースは「不安定な総体」として、統合でない不均質なものの集合、バラバラな状況はバラバラなまま共存させている。統一体をつくるのではなく、バラバラな部品が共存できる非階層的な場をつくっている。線形的な従来の設計行為から、アクティビティのプログラムという非線形的設計を試みている。そこに建築の可能性として、人間の行為、アクティビティを活性化させることを試みているのである。また、カーンのサーヴド／サーヴァント・スペースという空間概念をも昇華したもの、すなわち階層的な機能の配列を超えたものと捉えることができる。

5-1-7：シアトル図書館

並置概念の発展系とも言えるプロジェクトであり、並置したvolumeをズラスという形式が様々なシステムを統合している。それは、既存のプログラムの変換であり、周辺環境との内外

の視線のシステムでもあり、リサーチによって得られたデータから導き出されたものとして示されているものでもある。

リサーチの結果、現実は蔵書が増える一方でパブリックスペースが切り詰められている状況が大半であることが判明し、多様な変化に対応できる柔軟なパブリックスペースと、蔵書に対する具体的な解決案の提案が不可欠であると判断する。

そこで、プログラムを二種類の空間に分割；物理的な収蔵品を柔軟に収納できる空間、絶えず変化するパブリックスペースとして機能しうる空間。言い換えればモノゾーンとヒューマンゾーンを分けている。機能プログラムをボックスに変換し、似通ったプログラムを5つに分類、各プログラム群の必要サイズを計算、それをボックスに置き換え、プログラムどうしの関係を念頭に入れ、実際の敷地に落とし込み、ボックスを押し出す。周りの状況とリンクした、繊細でアイコン的で合理的な形態が誕生する。コミュニケーションの手段として、リサーチで得た情報をグラフなどで視覚化している。(図 5-6)
このシアトルのプロジェクトは、データそのものを建築化している。一つのパッケージの中にデータを閉じ込めているのであり、その後の世代のデータスケープを予見させるものである。

Fig.5-6　シアトル図書館ダイアグラム
データによる要求書室の再分配、再構成

5-2：コールハース的視点の歴史的背景

コールハースの制作の背景として、ニューヨークとロシア・アヴァンギャルドの研究があること、および、ニューヨークの研究について彼の制作のアイデアの多くをその研究から得ている事を既に見た。ここではそうしたコールハースの歴史的な背景として、ロシア・アヴァンギャルドとオランダの都市計画的伝統におけるデータの分析による近代都市計画について詳述し、並置概念と後の世代へと伝わっていくデータスケープの兆候に着目する。

5-2-1：コールハース以前の object の並置概念
ロシア・アヴァンギャルド[註 17]
社会のコンデンサー＝社会のプログラム
社会制度の変革が建築，都市計画のプログラムになった

コールハースはアイゼンマンの主宰したニューヨークの「建築・都市研究所」に在籍中に、ロシア・アヴァンギャルド、とりわけイワン・レオニドフの研究を行なった。彼の初期の作品、例えば AA スクール時代の卒業設計であるエクソダスなどにはそうした歴史からの影響を多くみてとることができる。

ロシア・アヴァンギャルドにおいては、同時代的な建築と芸術の運動であるオランダのデ・スティルの面による空間構成に対して、volume による空間構成が新規性として登場した。それは芸術におけるシュプレマティスム[註 18]という新しい傾向と社会改革の新しいプログラムがその形式と結びついた。建築の機能要素 (プログラム) と形態との結びつきは、ジュリアン・ガデの要素主義の流れによるル・コルビュジエのソビエトパレスのコンペ案などにもみられるものであるが、ル・コルビュジエのアプローチは内外の要請の調停の結果として成立する

註 17) ロシア・アヴァンギャルドは 1910 年代からソビエト連邦誕生時を経て、1930 年代初等までのロシア帝国・ソビエト連邦における各芸術運動の総称であり、レイヨニスム、シュプレマティスム、ロシア構成主義の主に三つの芸術理念がある
註 18) ロシア・アヴァンギャルドの中の芸術運動一つであるシュプレマティスムは、キュビスムと未来派の影響を受けたクボ・フトゥリズモ (立体未来主義、立体＝未来) の集大成という位置づけでマレーヴィチが主張した。その内容は「絶対象」という意味で、禁欲的な完全な抽象絵画であり、ミースなどに影響を与えた。

volume であることに比べると、ロシア・アヴァンギャルドのアプローチは、新しい社会が新しい形式を必要とした、より形式的な性格が強いといえる。この形式とプログラムの恣意的な関係をこれまでの建築の歴史との断絶と捉えるか、新たな建築の可能性として捉えるか、コールハースは後者と捉え自身の建築を展開している。とりわけ、イワン・レオニドフの 1930 年の「文化宮殿」のプロジェクトはコールハースに限らず，その後の建築家に大きな影響を与えている。(図 5-7)

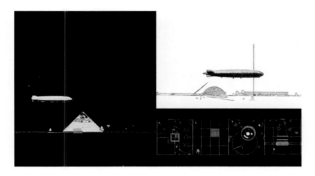

Fig.5-7　イワン・レオニドフの「文化宮殿」

幾何学的立体を一つの完結した object として捉え、一つの完結した機能を備えた object として扱った。社会の変革は、新しい機能をおさめたそれぞれの object が並置されたものを 1 セットとして社会のコンデンサーが提示された。シュプレマティスムはそれら object の並置の中に絶対的な構成、関係性を見出そうとした。そこに統合という幻影を見出し、社会の統合とオーバーラップさせた。

立体幾何学の複合的な表現は、プログラム的な要請に対応している。建築が機械に近づいていくことを意味する。力学的な機械では機能に応じた部分をもち、それらが連結され、そ

して作動する。この力の伝播関係は目に見えるように「構成」されている。しかも、機械は当然「正確」に構成されなければならないが、この与件は機能が複雑になればなるほどに不可欠なものとなる。

ロシア・アヴァンギャルドからコールハースはもう一つのものを吸収した。それはあらゆる事象を数値化し、科学的方法として客観化することである。これはコールハースによって展開され、現代においてあらゆる事象を量子化することへと繋がることとなる。

例えば、ギンスブルグの率いた「オサ」というグループは科学的方法を建築の実践に組み込むことを標榜し、発生期にある社会主義社会にとって必要な計画内容や形式的形態を公式化する課題を自らに課し、エネルギー配分や人口分散といった幅広い緊急問題にも、同様に関心を払った。「オサ」の主要関心事は、第一に共同集合住宅の問題と適正な社会単位の創出であり、第二に分配のプロセス、すなわち、あらゆる形式の輸送であった。(図 5-8)

ロシア・アヴァンギャルドがコールハースだけでなく、現代の建築思潮に影響を与えているもう一つの面がある。前述の事象の量子化と根元を同じくする、科学的客観性のもとに事象を数量化しようとする動きであるが、「オサ」との違いは単なる数量化ではなく、数式化あるいは、数学的・力学的な法則に従って研究しようとした動きであり、「ヴフテマス（国立高等美術工芸工房）」によってなされた。

「ヴフテマス」の基礎デザインは、純粋形態の表面のリズムを描写すること、あるいはそれと対照的に、力動的形態の成長と減退を、数学的級数の法則にしたがって研究することであっ

た。演習では、幾何級数的に変化する空間を扱い、その大きさや位置を加減、変化させたりした。例えば、「空中レストラン」という作品では、その透明性と奇抜なアクセス方式は、生産主義の豊かな実用主義を反映していた。主観的なコンポジションではなく、より客観的なコンストラクション（構造）へ傾倒し、テクノロジー、生産と結びついていた。とりわけ、タトリンの「第三インターナショナル記念塔」はその先駆的作品であり、螺旋の内部に四つの巨大で透明な立体が吊り構造で作られ、この四つの立体は、それぞれ映写機関、情報機関、行政機関、立法機関の目的に充てられた。こうした動きは、現代におけるコンピュータによる数学的形態生成、アルゴリズミックデザインの萌芽とみられる。

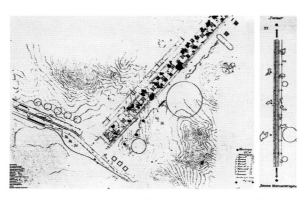

Fig.5-8　「オサ」のマグニトゴルクス重工業都市計画

5-2-2：近代都市計画　オランダの伝統　リサーチ

オランダという国自体が伝統的に干拓によってできた都市、すなわち人工の都市であり、緻密な分析やデータを基にした計画なしでは成り立たなかった。近代化にともなう都市計画（アーバニズム）は調査とデータ作成、分析が主となった。そ

れは"量"の問題と関わり、もはや都市の全体像がそうした調査の結果としてのデータでしか把握できなくなったことによる。人口の少ない村社会や単一の生産活動で集団が生活していた社会においては、一対一の対応、すなわちアナログ的な関係で全体を掌握できた。それに対して、人口が爆発し、人々が多様な活動を営むような社会へと劇的に変化した近代化は、その集団自体を掌握する手段の変革をも余儀なくされた。とりわけオランダは、前述のような理由から、そうしたリサーチやデータの表現、さらにそれらを計画へと落とし込んでいく合理性といった土壌が近代以前から築かれていた土地であるといえる。

中でも、ファン・エーステレン[19]とファン・ローヒュイゼンによる都市計画におけるスタンスは、コールハースの前身を行くものであった[20]。例えば、エーステレンによる「五分間タウンプランニング」と呼ばれる計画は、正しいデータさえ揃えられれば都市計画家は五分間で正しい答えに行き着くと言う考えの基に成立していた。これはまさにデータ至上主義、狭義の機能主義的な合理性を標榜するものであり、背景として都市的な規模の計画を扱うことの客観性を保証するものとして捉えられ、いかにして subject としての計画者の恣意性を排除するかといった問題性に対する一つの解答であった。ここに計画における subject の問題が都市的レベルでは、建築の計画以上に多くの人に関わることとして浮上したということができる。こうした subject の問題としてオランダの近代都市計画とコールハースの設計における subject の扱いに連続性を見て取ることができる。具体的にはエーステレンとヒューィゼンの二人が関わっていた機能主義者グループ Opbouw グループによる 30 年代の余暇 diagram とコールハースが横浜でのワークショップでつくったアクティヴィティ・ダイアグラムの類

註 19）アムステルダムの都市計画局長であり CIAM の議長でもあり、それ以前にはドゥースブルクの助手でもあった。
註 20）この点詳しくはバート・ローツマの前掲論文「現実のバイト：第二機械時代のリサーチの意味」参照のこと。
註 21）詳しくは SL、五十嵐太郎、南泰裕編『レム・コールハースは何を変えたのか』鹿島出版会、2014 年など。

似性の中にそれぞれのアプローチの連続性が認められている。
また、あらゆるものを計算し、新しい都市のための空間的帰結へと変換していった統計的方法をコールハースは、建築が量を扱う事へとシフトしているとの洞察の基に、建築へと適用した。むしろ建築が都市的なものへとシフトしていることでもあり、都市と建築を分けて考えることの矛盾にそれまでのリサーチによって気がついているともいえる。
さらに、コールハースはそうした統計的手法によって平均的な均質空間に陥る危険性が近代都市計画の見落としている部分であることを十分に把握し巧みにはぐらかしている。

5-3：コールハースの建築概念
関係性を一度断ち切って、不連続化させる構えが見られる。
データを object に添付する
その後、object をコントロールし、関係性を構築する
関係性を連続化させようとするアイゼンマンとは異なる態度
関係性を、いったん不連続化させているため、一般解ではなく特殊解となる
第一章で考察したように、ル・コルビュジエの二つの両義性、内部化と外部化の方向性の一方、すなわち、建築を外部化していく方向へとコールハースが進んでいることを措定した。ここではそのコールハースの手法について、詳述していく。とりわけ、こうしたコールハースの手法が、どこから生まれてきたのかという問題を扱う。

5-3-1：コールハースの視点
コールハースの手法は、ル・コルビュジエの二つの両義性、内部化と外部化の方向性の一方、すなわち、建築を外部化していく方向へと進んでいる。
コールハースの手法は、以下の3つに大別される。
①ヴォイドの戦略：あるスケールの建築を複数組み合わせることで、次のスケールの建築を生み出す。
②ピクセル化：スケールが大きなものを細分化することで低次のスケールに達する。
③ズームの方法：スケールが小さなものを組み合わせることで高次のスケールに達する方法と、スケールが大きなものを細分化することで低次のスケールに達する方法を合わせたもの。
一見してわかるように、これらは、いずれも、外在的なアプローチであり、内在的な意味を消去した操作的なものである。建築の内部性の問題はひとまず括弧にくくり、データをパッケージ化した object を操作するというプログラムに特徴がある。[註21]

5-3-2：制作の背景とプログラムの建築へ
コールハースの制作の背景には、ニューヨークとロシア・アヴァンギャルドの研究が直接的にはあることは既に述べた。さらにオランダの文化的歴史的背景としてオランダの都市計画的伝統におけるデータの分析による近代都市計画があることが読み取れた。そのデータ分析による都市計画とは、プログラムをすれば自動的に建築が生み出されるという考え、すなわち、都市計画家は軸線や規範性といったものさしを創ろうとし、そのための計量化であり、その容量を再配分するというものである。コールハースの扱うプログラムは、都市、アーバニズムに対して建築を開いていくもの、データにおいて建

築が関係付けられている。そのコンテクストの中に場所性があり、場所性も何もかもすべてが抽象化されている。

従来のタイポロジーは建築という狭い枠組みの中の論理であり、建築という特権的立場の中での一般性を抽出したものである。[註22] そうした枠組みでの場所性、ゲニウス・ロキは、ものとしての建築における概念であり、静的な分析と捉えられる。ポストモダン的状況におけるアーバニズム、都市はスタティックに止まっている状態ではなく、もはや静的なタイポロジカルなアプローチで建築を構成することは、目まぐるしく変わる時間に対応することは困難である。そうした巨大化と複雑化をともなう都市の欲望に対して、古いタイポロジーでは対応できない現状を、ニューヨークのリサーチによって、コールハースは認識したのである。

コールハースの動的な計画としてのプログラムは、切断による object の並置とデータによって大きさや形態が変化する外部化によって可能になっていると言えるのである。

5-3-3：特殊解としての建築

コールハースは収斂していく一般解としての建築を求めていない。全一性から離れていく。抽象化していく特殊解のようなものである。コールハースの制作の根幹とすることは、資料、データ、diagram、分析といったあらゆるものであり、従来の空間概念である「軸」、「グリッド」は身体を基準とした空間との概念であり、それだけで空間は構成されていないという認識がある。[註23]

データ、分析、統計学、合理性の規準によるイメージを建築化している。データをイメージ化、グラフィカルに美しくまとめ、建築化、構築化している。美しいイメージのもとに構成して

いる、すなわち、イメージを建築化している。建築のイメージを用い（カモフラージュとして使いながら）、全くフォームとは関係なく、データによって成立させている。収斂していく一つの一般解のモデルを突き詰めていったミースやル・コルビュジエに対して、コールハースはあくまで特殊解であり、再生産されるポストモダン的タイポロジーを逆説的に提示している。敢えて建築としてのタイポロジカルな個性を消去することで、他の建築家との差異化を図っている。

5-3-4：価値基準の解体

コールハースは、subject が解体されていくという必然性を歴史が持っていることを認識している。モダニズムは、最適解としての主流の欲望だけをみて、他は捨象した。すなわち多様なベクトルを最適解によって整理しているとも言える。その価値基準がモダニズム的なものであり、ある種のヒエラルキーが存在し、遂行されることで一義に決まるものである。[註24] そうしたモダニズムの価値基準を解体しているのがコールハースである。価値基準をシャッフルし、一義に決めるのではなく、ヒエラルキーをつけるのではなく、特殊解として提示するのである。どんな些細なことでも全部、分析のエレメントとして取り上げていく。コールハースは、固定的で静的な枠組みではなく、映画におけるデータを扱う編集者としての態度を取り、その手法を建築的な職業の実践に応用した。そうした考え方がコールハースの diagram へと集約していく。

註22）計画学に根付いている形態と用途の関係に限定された型であるということ
註23）セシル・バルモンド、前掲書、pp.17-56、ボルドーの住宅の構造的発想についての図式 (pp.28-29) に一般解と特殊解の違いが示されている
註24）例えば、バブルダイアグラムなど
註25）コンピュータープログラミングにおける object 指向。

5-3-5：コールハースの diagram

コールハースの diagram は、建築を構成しているあらゆる事象 (形態だけに限ることなく) を対象とするため、それぞれの事象を内部的論理の成果品、すなわち、部品として捉えることで多くの複雑な事象を扱うことを可能としている。さらに、建築や都市に見られるスケール間の断絶や空間的な断絶の特殊解的な把握から、部品どうしの関係性を情報として整理・分析することこそが、多様な意味を現出させるという思想に基づいている。あらゆるものが部品として扱われ、スケールそのものも部品化されていく。スタッキングやバインディングといった下位のスケールの集積化や、ピクセル化といったスケールの分割化などの操作がおこなわれる。そしてこうした部品化された情報の整理によってもたらされたリレーショナルダイアグラムをもとに、部品化された object を操作するというプログラムをおこなっている。既に詳述したル・コルビュジエの設計思想の流れを汲む「部品化された object の並置」という概念は、部品化された object を操作することで object に結合する意味が反転することに着目し、両義的関係から、自己と他者との関係、外部と内部、ソリッドとヴォイドという立場のスイッチング、および object と機能や意味との関係を紡ぎ出そうとするものであり、関係性の設計手法の一つである。このような問題意識は、object 相互の関係を外部化させるものである。原理を抽出するために、そうした関係性を内部化しようとしたアイゼンマンの思考とは方向が真逆である。内部化においては、object 自身は消失してしまうが、コールハースの外部化は、object 自身を顕在化させ、object 相互間の多様な関係へと展開する。データと object とを接合させるという現代の object 指向[註 25]にも繋がるプログラムの思考そのものである。

5-4：並置概念からもたらされたもの
5-4-1：新たな場所性

コールハースは、建築、アーバニズム、地域計画を連続したフィールドとして捉える方法を発見した。[註 26] すなわち、建築を外在的アプローチで設計する手法を切り開いた。そのフィールドの中で起こる様々なパースペクティブから様々なコンテクストの中で建築、アーバニズム、地域計画を操作することを可能にした。関係他者、たとえば政治家や私的組織とは丁寧なコミュニケーションをとって仕事をする。通常、建築家の世界がいわゆる他のものと鬪う[註 27]という関係ではなく、デザインプロセスに関連するあらゆる人の欲望というものを取り込みながら、それがどのような空間的な帰結をもたらすのかということを、プロセスを経て示すことによって、互いにコミュニケーションさせ対面させ社会との議論を開く、そうしたことによって、建築の目的として説得力のある方法を見つけたと考えられる。

その方法論の中心にあるのは、建築とアーバニズムが組織を試みる、そういう現実の大部分の考え方が全てのものは計量可能であるという真理に支えられている。データというものがその建築を成立させるランドスケープを構成するという考え方である。データにおけるランドスケープというものは、計量可能なあらゆる力の視覚的表象になり、作られる建築作品に少なからず影響を与え、建築というものを定義し、コントロールするということである。

たとえばこれは計画学の中で、建築法規、造園法というものの考え方の延長であり、投資、ディベロッパー、建設業者によって展開されてきた建築を都市化するときの経験則、技術的制約からの延長であり、また、自然条件、法律というものとも

註 26) 文献 SL に見られるようにサイズは建築、アーバニズム、地域計画を包含し、現代の建築の領域としてそれらを区別できないということ
註 27) 例えば、安藤忠雄など、多かれ少なかれ従来の建築家は社会に対して批判的な態度を示してきた。ケネス・フランプトンのいう批判的地域主義といったスタンスにもあたる。

絡んでくる。それから政治的な組織の内外の利益団体の政治的な圧力というようなものも関係してくる。建築の依頼という、要求・欲望というものは、しばしば矛盾する多くの力によって制限されているが、そういった力を全て視覚化することによって、これまでの伝統的なサイトプランがより新しく複雑なものとして生まれ変わる。すなわち古典的な建築の考え方においては、地形というランドスケープの上にデータというもう一つのランドスケープが重なっている。それは人間が作り出した社会構造が色濃く反映され、その二層構造の中で建築が生まれると考えられる。

殆どの建築家はそういった社会条件、社会的制約に対して戦いを挑むのが通例であるが、その二重のランドスケープ；自然条件におけるランドスケープの上にデータのランドスケープを重ねるというコールハースのような考え方は、交渉条件、交渉というプロセスを建築の創造的プログラムの中に導入することを可能にする。データスケープという考え方をデザインプロセスにおいてツールとして現実的かつ実用的に利用することを試みている。

そうしたデータスケープ的な考え方が明確にしていくものは、建築における過去の伝統的な建築設計の考え方は限られた役割しか果たしていないということである。

環境を形成するというのが社会の勤めであるが、その社会を生産する問題というものに対して、建築の設計が限られた役割しか果たしていないということが問題となってくる。それは、社会が建築を形成する、その社会を基盤とした社会からの要求条件というものが矮小化しているという現実に行き当たる。たとえば、硬直した官僚システム、利権構造のそれぞれの政治的なテリトリーでの戦い、そういったものが、社会

全体が硬直していて、建築・都市に対する要求というものが明確に現れるのではなく、非常に屈折して建築の余条件を規定している。たとえば、地方自治体における談合の問題、箱物行政の問題というものがまさにその例であり、そういう硬直した社会というものの中に建築家が自ら入っていきながら、そういう要求条件を整理し、そういうものを建築設計の中に取り入れていくという考え方が近年非常に重要になっている。牧歌的な古典的なアーキテクトとクライアントという関係を変えつつある。クライアントが単純な個人のオーナーではなく、社会構造、社会全体がクライアントというものになってきている状況においては、まさにそういう方法が重要になってきている。それはクライアント自身の問題に関わってくる。社会構造自体がクライアントの意識を望む方向にもっていっていないというような現実から引き起こされるものの問題に建築家がメスを入れて入り込んでいこうという、まさに、コールハースのような考え方は社会的な問題と建築家との接点に一致する職能の問題に関わると考えられる。

近代社会というものが、社会システムが抽象的なシステムとして、システムの多様性によって支配されている。法律規則等というような関係が明確に規定されながら、未だ抽象的であり、その近代社会の構造が揺らいできているということが重要な大きな問題である。マンフレッド・タフーリによって現代建築はニヒリズムとして捉えられたが[註28]、それに対してコールハースや MVRDV の建築がその社会システムの中に設計を組み込もうとする考えは、ニヒリズムから脱却しているように思われる。

コールハースの立場は、建築を成立させている社会状況の中に求めようとしていることである。その計量的アプローチの中

註28）タフーリがミッシェルフーコーの「言葉と物」に触発されて「私室の中の建築」という 1976 年に発表した論文で、建築が現実に関する程度についての問いを立てている。また、1973 年の「建築神話の崩壊」の中で、自由のためのどんなアヴァンギャルドの力も、最終的には資本主義システムの中に必ず吸収されてしまうことを示した。建築家が如何に社会と適合する建築をつくったとしても、資本主義社会のシステムの中に吸収されてしまうひとつの歯車であり、建築家が何かやろうとしてもパフォーマンス程度にしかならないという判断、ニヒリズムという考えが現れている
註29）ミースの提唱した、床および天井と最小限の柱と壁で構成される、ユニヴァーサル・スペースが、どのような用途にも対応できる空間であること

で用いられる数字とデータが建築を成立させる新たな場所性
（ランドスケープ）となり、建築言語に取って代わると言う認
識である。ある意味、建築がアプリオリにある三次元的文化
表象であるという思考を停止するという考え方、そういう問
いかけをしない、ということであると思われる。

データは前述したように、他の言語への媒介的、ある語を他の
言語へと翻訳するプラットホームであり、データというものが
あらゆる言語に取って代わるという、普遍的な国際言語、貨
幣がかつて果たしていた役割をデータが受け継いでいる。デー
タへの過信、魔術化されていくデータへの過信というものは批
評の対象になる。すなわち、データによって人間の感情さえ
計量可能であるという批判、あらゆるものが計量可能である
ということの批評性。データ化を突き詰めて考えていくとど
ういうことになるのかということを見据えて、安易に乗っかっ
ていいのかということを批評的に眺めていく必要がある。
コールハースらの試みは、データスケープ＋ランドスケープ
＝二重の場所性、二重の場を見出した。社会の欲望を整理し
たところの欲望のトポロジー（第二の場所性）を重ねあわせ、
社会システムを上手く取り込んでいる。アイゼンマン後期にお
いても、二重の場所性を示唆している。しかし、それは現実
の場所性以外に原理化可能な状況を抽出した地平であり、そ
こがコールハースとは異なっている点である。
MVRDV は、そのデータそのものを形象化し、全体を統合する
ことを意識的に行っていないが、コールハースの建築には、アイ
ゼンマン的な統合がある。最終的に、全体の形象にプログ
ラムを焼き移しているところがみられる。

5-4-2：subject の変容　データスケープによる subject の位置の差異

近代という問題解決のところ、コールハースは subject という
ところでモダニズムを考えている。ミースは、subject は匿名、
不特定多数であり、顔が見えない subject を入れ込む均質空間
をつくった。[註 29)]
コールハースはそれだけではない。一つの要素としてモダニ
ズムを取り込んでいる。モダニズムは主流の欲望だけをみて、
他は捨象している。計画学では決まり易いようにベクトルを整
理している。その提示の仕方の価値基準がモダニズム的なも
のであり、ある種のヒエラルキーがある。一義に決まる。そ
このモダニズムの価値基準を解体しているのがコールハース
である。価値基準をシャッフルし、一義に決まるのではなく、
ヒエラルキーをつけるのではなく、一つの特殊解を見つけて
いる。どんな些細なことでも全部、分析のエレメントとして
取り上げてしまう。
一方、コールハースのプログラムは、作品や言説にみられるよ
うにアロアンスとしてのプログラム、入力する subject をオー
プンにしている。subject をあいまいなオープンなもの、拡散
したものにしている。読み替え、あるいは、入力する subject
をオープンにし複雑にしている。
すなわち、コールハースは、建築が生成するということは
subject の問題であることに気が付いていると言える。統合に
執着心がなく、全一的な統合に向かう意識を消去しようとし
ているのである。[註 30)]

データはコミュニケーションの可能性を広げるためであり、建
築はあくまで、建築にしかできないことを探り続ける。その方
法は近代建築のスローガンを否定、昇華することによるもの

註 30) 従来の建築家は、著者 (subject) として作品 (object) を全一的に統合することを建築の目的としていたが、現代においては、古典的な subject-object という二項対立的見方から人間中心的なものに、さらに人間を囲むオブジェクト世界で新しく進化する関係性を説明するための新しい subject の意識が必要であるということ

から、データを形態に置き換えるグラフィカルな操作。そこの操作はプログラム的であるが、それによってプログラム化できないことの生成こそが目論見られているようである。永遠に裏切りつづけることで建築を固定化しない方法というのであろうか。無意識を意識的に操作することであろうか。アイゼンマンは抽象的な原型 (diagram) をプログラムによって変形する。それは変形することがあたかも目的のように見える。コールハースの diagram の用い方はそれとは異なるのである。コールハースは、建築が変容していく状況を認識していこうとする立場である。状況からの思考であり、アイゼンマンは自律した建築自身の論理から出発しようとする立場である。そのため、多様なベクトルを孕んでいるはずの外的な力学的状況すらも限定的なモデルとして提示される。

コールハースは、形に与えられるべきものとされた西欧の伝統的な比例の原理を封印した。タンジブルな形式自体の問題ではなく、形の裏に潜む動きや意味を捉えようとした。それによって今を捉え、新たなソリューションを提示する。それは新たなレイヤーの発見である。すなわち、ル・コルビュジエ、アイゼンマンがタンジブルな形の論理を求めている方向とは異なり、タンジブルな形の奥にある別の意味のレイヤーを発見するのである。

5-5：まとめ

5-5-1：ル・コルビュジエの建築概念からの継承としての object の部品化と並置

ル・コルビュジエは近代建築の原理性を求めるために、設計に関わることを常に要素化することを試みていた。この要素化はル・コルビュジエにとっては、純粋な幾何学、比例、数値にまで抽象化することではなく、一つ一つのエレメントが機能的な完成品である object としてみなしていたため、初期の頃はドミノにみられるように、明確な「柱」、「床」、「階段」といった object の配列による構成として近代建築を捉えた。その建築的 object は次第に部品化され、内部と外部の関係など、抽象的な関係性が、volume とヴォイドの演算や配列に還元され構成されることになる。それらは、建築の巨大化と複合化へと向かう近代にとって自然な結果でもあった。

コールハースは、ニューヨークのリサーチによって、このル・コルビュジエの部品化、すなわち、「切断」と「並置」の考え方を確証し、作品においては、ル・コルビュジエによってもたらされた「切断」と「並置」の可能性をさらに敷衍するような形で試行を繰り返しながら、言説を進化させている。こうしたことから、コールハースはル・コルビュジエを継承していると言って良いだろう。

5-5-2：関係性の外部化と可能性

ル・コルビュジエはプランによって、取り留めのない不節操な volume をコントロールしようとした。そして、volume を固定化させ、要素化し部品化した。ル・コルビュジエは、プランを基準平面と捉え、その基準平面において volume をコントロールすることを求めた。平面だけでなく立面においてもコントロールの操作をおこなった。その基準は西欧の伝統的な美の価値観だった。すなわち面に投影された関係性が、静的な比例数理によって支配されるべきであると考えたのである。ル・コルビュジエが基点とした、西欧の伝統的な建築概念、すなわち面に投影される静的な数比理論を超えて、コールハースは、volume どうしの関係性へと向かう。コールハースは、機

能等の関係性を読み取り、実体化された情報のみの操作をおこなう。その後、それらの関係性を形象へと反転させるのである。直接的な形象の操作ではなく、objectに結びつけられた前段階の情報を操作することで、建築という場にうごめく諸力の関係性を示し、純粋な内的完結性や全体的秩序を求めようとする伝統的な建築原理による建築空間の生成の無意味性を示したのである。

ル・コルビュジエが、建築の古典的な内在的問題性である比例やプロポーションの問題を規整線として視覚化し、モデュロールへと発展させたが、コールハースは、ル・コルビュジエを継承しながらも、より一層、進展させたと言えるのである。

5-5-3：アイゼンマンとコールハースとの比較を通して

ル・コルビュジエのobjectは眼前にある建築の存在としての意味を引きずっているのであり、アイゼンマンはル・コルビュジエの両義的関係性を抽象化し、原理性を導き出そうと試みた。それに対してコールハースはobjectとデータを結びつけ、それぞれにヒエラルキーのある関係性をつくらず、全てはパラレルで、一つに重点を置くものではない。objectは関係性を生み出すかのように抽象化されているということができる。すなわち、object自身を記号化し、イコン化し、objectどうしの関係を一端、切断・分離することによって、objectに新たなデータを付加し、objectをパラレルに並置させ、新しい関係を生み出そうとしている。アイゼンマンのように原理化された法則を適応させるのではなく、部品化されたobjectを並置することで、あらゆる多様な事象を削ぎ落とすことなく、拾いあげ整理している。objectにデータや機能を結びつけるobject指向が垣間見られる。

アイゼンマンの建築から読み取れるのは、完全性・全体性・統合性の破れの修復である。アイゼンマンは建築の内部性を強く信じ、永遠なる原理を追求するという西欧の伝統的枠組みを維持しようとする。逆にコールハースは、もう一つの西欧の伝統的枠組みを継承する。それは不可視な実体というものを認めない考え方であり、多くのものを可視化させ、新たな実体として拡張することである。原理によって成立する内部性に対しては、不可視なものとして黙殺し、その実体を認めない態度を取る。彼は、建築を反転させるのである。可視的な建築形態に囚われるのではなく、建築が孕むべき不可視な情報を、表に出すために視覚化させるのである。すなわち建築へと結実化されるべく、情報を反転させ、外部化させることによって、情報や条件を明らかにし、関係式として可視化させ、実体化させ、整理し操作をおこなう。コールハースのdiagramはそうしたものとして現れる。それをさらに、空間へと反転させることで、タンジブルな建築のエレメントへと変換させ、建築として成立させるという二重の転換をおこなうのである。いわば反転の手法である。

コールハースにとって建築はもはや、内在する原理により成立する形式ではない。実体として存在する条件や情報の現れそのものである。そうした態度によって、西欧の伝統的で硬直した思考から抜け出そうとした。コールハースが不可視の情報を可視化させタンジブルな建築のエレメントへと転換させたことは、西欧の伝統である、実体化の領野の拡張であったとも言える。

コールハースは、アイゼンマンのように、形態や形式の記号論的操作はおこなわず、機能等の関係性を読み取り、実体化された情報の操作だけをおこなっている。すなわち、形象化という反転によって、建築という場にうごめく諸力の関係性

を示し、object の操作をおこなうことで、純粋な内的完結性
や全体的秩序を求める原理による建築空間の生成の無意味性
を示した。すなわち排除されるものを汲み上げることを目的
として、関連する多くのデータを扱い、分析し、プログラム
に積極的に関わろうとする。そのことは西欧の伝統的な統合
性、すなわち美やハーモニーという伝統的な意識の解体でも
あった。皮肉にも、それらのヒントは日本の現代建築にあった。
これは日本人自身によって気がつくべきものであったが、残
念ながらコールハースによって見出されてしまった。資本主
義における社会的な欲望を、モダニズムの基本的な枠組みに
異常なまでに執着し、絶妙に結合させている日本の建築はコー
ルハースにとって奇異なものに映ったのであった。

数比理論によって、全体的秩序を求めてきた西欧的思考を、皮
肉な意味で日本の建築は超えていた。それは西欧の統合性の意
識とは異なる意識が存在していたからである。すなわち経済
合理主義という過剰な欲望によって建築を構築させることを、
日本は徹底的に極めることを追求していたからである。

それは伝統的な西欧の思考の枠組みを超える、新たな建築の
世界を生み出す可能性を孕んでいた。あらゆる経済活動のデー
タを空間に変換するプログラムを日本人は無意識におこなっ
ていたのである。しかし、日本人自身は気がつかなかった。見
出したのはコールハースであった。

Chapter 6

関係性の拡張

exteriority をも取り込もうとするアイゼンマンの野心

これまで見てきたように、博士論文や住宅シリーズでは、interiority を重視したため、ほとんど外界と隔絶された純粋な内的論理の追求であった。外部の文脈はあったとしても、一般化された限定的なものだった。

しかし、アイゼンマンの意識は、住宅シリーズ以降において変質する。1978 年のカナレッジョ・タウン・スクエア計画以降、アイゼンマンは、interiority における内的論理のみの完結性から、exteriority との連続性への移行へ向かったことは確かな事実であった。

1987 年ごろから、アイゼンマンは、非線形科学[註1]に興味をもち始める。フランクフルトのレブストック集合住宅では folding の手法を使用し、シンシナティ大学アーノフデザイン芸術センターでは、波動を導入している。またデュッセルドルフのインメンドルフの芸術家たちの家の計画案も、二つのソリトン波の folding を使ったデザインを行っている。それらより、以前の volumetric な関係性から原理化しようとした態度から複雑系のロジックの外部参照へと移行をみることができる。ここでは、住宅シリーズから外部参照へと移行した時期における主要なプロジェクトの diagram についてそれぞれ考察していく。

6-1：interiority の拡張、exteriority を建築に取り込む意識の萌芽

6-1-1：space にエネルギーを孕む密度

前述したように、アイゼンマンはル・コルビュジエの volume の再定義と進化を行い、volume は、space の概念に含まれながら、等質で中立な space に対して、エネルギーや力の方向性が蓄えられたものと理解された。

このことは、不連続で凝固したタンジブルな object を眺めるだけの行為を越えて、space がエネルギーを孕む密度、そして参照グリッドを基準とした計測への意識を孕んでいる。一歩進めるならば、この volume なる概念は、不連続性から連続性へと開かれる可能性を含意していると言えるのである。

6-1-2：アイゼンマンの意識の変化

モダニズムは、古典的な秩序に対する挑戦として形成された。さらに、構造主義は、人間を細分化し客観的で普遍的な構造を追求していたが、人間がこうした普遍的な構造に支配されているという無力感により、眼前の現実に立ち向かう力を持たなかった。構造主義言語学は現実とイデオロギーとの乖離を進め、純粋幾何学形態の操作によるフォルマリズムへと建築を陥れた。前期アイゼンマンの活動は、まさにこうした状

註1) カオス理論やフラクタル、複雑系など
註2) フィリップ・ジョンソンとヒッチコックによる
註3) ルイス・サリヴァンの言説「Form follows Function」
註4) WV Chapter4 "The affects of singularity" pp.19-24 （筆者要約）

況と符合している。

デリダによると、ロゴス（言葉）によって世界を構造化できるとする構造主義は西欧の伝統的な形而上学から脱却するものではなく、形而上学を解体しようとする構造主義の試み自体もまた西欧の伝統的な形而上学の枠組み内にあると指摘した。デリダの脱構築は、こうした西欧の伝統的枠組みから脱却する試みであった。デリダは西欧の思考に潜む基本的構造である階層的な二項対立に対して攻撃を仕掛けるのである。1988年のMoMAでおこなわれた「Deconstructivist Architecture」（脱構築主義建築）の展覧会[註2]は、こうした構造主義言語学に対する批判としてのデリダの脱構築の影響を受けたものであった。脱構築主義の立場に立つ建築家は、「形態は機能に従う」[註3]といった硬直した抑圧的な思考に彩られたモダニズムに対し攻撃を仕掛けたのであった。アイゼンマンもその一人であった。

6-1-3：枠組みをずらす意味で重要な存在と捉えた外部性

アイゼンマンはデリダの脱構築の考え方に、誰よりも強く影響を受け、自身の建築生成へのdiagramに導入し実践していったのであった。内的論理だけで建築を完結させようとしてきた構造主義的態度から、一転して、その構造自身を崩そうとする方向に向かうのであった。アイゼンマンにとって、exteriorityは構造主義的な枠組みをズラス意味で重要な存在であった。そうしたexteriorityとの調停の方向において、内的論理を追求していた姿勢が、外的論理を接続する場面で、建築的な接続構造が展開されている。その一端は、すでに彼の博士論文に記述されている。

既に観たように、彼の博士論文において、建築の原理性を求め

て、いくつかの建築に関わる言葉の定義とともに、それらの関係性を緻密に検証していったアイゼンマンではあるが、外部と内部との関係においては、ムーブメントにおける流動的な概念であるサーキュレーションや継起的な概念であるintervalという概念を導入したにもかかわらず、そうした動きの論理を、素直に延長、展開させなかった。彼独自の複雑な手法によって、interiorityとexteriorityを調停している。そうしたアプローチに、アイゼンマンの建築生成の特殊性が潜んでいると思われる。

建築が内部だけの完結した存在ではなく、外部と連続する開いた存在であることを求め、そうした問題を、アイゼンマンは脱構築主義の理論を使った手法で回避しようと試みたのである。その試みは、今まで積み上げられてきた彼自身の建築論理と接木され、独自のものとして発展していくのであった。

6-1-4：欲望を持った情動からの出発：ground（地）、場所性の問題への転換

既に概観したように、アイゼンマンはドゥルーズやデリダの思想を建築の分野において展開を試みている。ここでは、これまで建築設計において背景としてのground（地）や場所性について、exteriority（外部性）として取り組みだしたアイゼンマンについて見ていく。

subject（主体）が場所に対する欲望をもっているとするデリダの考えを、アイゼンマンは踏襲する。したがって、場所やground（地）を中立的なものではないものとの認識に立つ。effectからaffectへの移行を提示する。すなわち、生成の根本原因として、客観的な原因からの出発ではなく、欲望を持った情動からの出発とすることであった。[註4]

場所や ground（地）がモチベーションという affect（情動）をもっているがゆえに、diagram の成立する根拠となりうることを前提に建築の interiority（内部性）を拡張させようとする。exteriority との連続は、内部との弁証法的な関係性ではなく、旧来の伝統的な object の概念を転換させ、新たな手法を使って、旧来の時間と場所の概念も変えた上で連続させるのである。

6-2：住宅シリーズからカナレッジョへ至る軌跡
6-2-1：建築の領域の拡張と object 化
既にみてきたように、住宅シリーズにおいて以下のことがアイゼンマンによって試みられた。
・オリジナルで原初的な起源に回帰するものではない diagram
・建築の interiority（内部性）は、既知で安定したものではないという考え
・二価性に端を発している曖昧化
・既存の描画方法を超えるため、diagram は、ユークリッド幾何学の interiority のイコンから、位相幾何学のインデックスへと移動させた。
特に、住宅 10 号において、diagram は、オリジナルで原初的な起源に回帰するのではなく、空間と時間に拡散する状態に導かれた。その事は、建築の interiority が安定していて、既に知られているものではないという考えを示唆した。住宅 10 号の diagram 的なインデックスは、この不安定な interiority の本質を構築するものに関して、もはや 1 対 1 の表象を提示することはできないことを認識させ、diagram を、ユークリッド幾何学の interiority のイコンから、位相幾何学のインデックスに移動させたのである。
ここで構築された diagram を利用して、住宅 11a 号が構想さ

れた。そしてさらにこの住宅 11a 号が、exteriority を取り入れようとした最初のプロジェクトであるカナレッジョ・プロジェクトで利用されることになる。
住宅シリーズでは、建築の interiority の探求として、generic form を自己参照的な操作を繰り返すことで、異なる form を導き出すことが試みられてきた。住宅 10 号あたりから、object としての建築だけでなく、建築の立地している site も同様に、アイゼンマンは操作の対象としはじめる。カナレッジオ・プロジェクト以降における exteriority の参照としてのプロジェクトでは、site のスケールが物理的な拡張を見ていることは言うまでもないが、建築の領域が都市的な領域へと拡張していく中で、建築がどのようにあるべきかを住宅シリーズの延長として、これまでの認識を問い直していく過程を見ることができる。

6-2-2：認識を転換させる新たなターゲット
建築の領域の拡張したプロジェクトでは、必然的に site そのもの、場所と向き合うことになる。こうした ground（地）の与件を問うことが、これ以降に続く多くのプロジェクトの基礎になるのである。
まずは、ground（地）のサーフェイス（表面）を人為的につくられた人工的なものとして概念化し、トポロジカルなサーフェイスとして転換する。建築と同様な操作の対象とすることで、場所性や地霊のようなオリジナルで原初的な価値は存在しないことを示そうとし、伝統的な figure（図）と ground（地）の概念を乗り越えることが試みられている。
また、コンテクスチュアリズム^{註5)}におけるいわゆるコンテクストに対して、歴史的な事象そのものを浮上させるという素直

註 5）コーリン・ロウらの提唱したもの
註 6）DD　p.173,l1-l4（筆者翻訳）

で表層的な態度ではなく、モチベーションを持ったものを浮上させるという立場であり、通常のニュートラルなコンテクスチュアリズムとは異なる立場をとる。さらに、近代建築以降、無意識に推し進められたヒューマンスケールを超えたスケールの拡張、都市的スケールが開発されてきたことに対するスケールへの問いかけもみられる。

住宅シリーズにおいて試行された時間性の問題は、主に形態の生成プロセスにおけるものと、形態の認識そのものに向けられたものであった。それに対して、exteriority の試行においては、歴史に対する認識や建築を成立させている場の時間性の認識の転換を図るために、新たに graft（接木）や fold、superposition の概念が導入され、新旧の間、figure（図）と ground（地）の間のスムーズな移行という、新しい form の発見へとつながっている。

exteriority（外部性）の探求では、物理的な参照範囲の広がりだけでなく、科学や数学、文学といった知のあらゆるテクストの参照へと拡張され、自己参照的な参照形式から指標的な参照形式へと参照形式そのものも問いかけの対象とし、interiority 自身を捉え直し、anteriority や subject（主体）の問題を提示している。

6-3：操作プロトコルの図式
カナレッジョ・タウン・スクエア計画、住宅XIa、カーサ・グァルディオラ、レブストック計画、バイオセントラム、アーノフ・センターを巡って
6-3-1：カナレッジョ・タウン・スクエア計画
ground（地）の与件を問う

トポロジカルなサーフェイスへとシフト（グリッド、対角線）
ル・コルビュジエのベニス計画との superposition、trace
site の発掘と創設
住宅 11a 号のスケーリング（三つのスケール）
このプロジェクトについて、アイゼンマンは、「Diagram Diaries」の中で、次のように語っている。

"ヴェネツィアのカナレッジョの住宅プロジェクトは、六つのプロジェクトの中で最初に exteriority（外部性）としての敷地を考慮し、いわゆる外部の文脈を最初に使用した作品になった"註6)
このプロジェクトをターニングポイントとして、外的要因（敷地、歴史、メタファー）といった外部の文脈に着目するのである。そしてこうした exteriority が内的論理を追求することの困難性をもたらすことを発見し、両者の調停をデリダの理論を下敷きにした彼独自の理論によって乗り越えようとする。アイゼンマンが「Diagram Diaries」の中で、以下に記しているように。

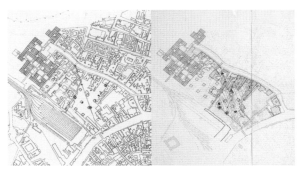

Fig.6-1 カナレッジョ・タウン・スクエア計画平面

"カナレッジオ・プロジェクトは以下の様な問いを投げかけた。もし interiority がもはやゆるぎないものでないなら、それなら ground（地）や、当然のことと決め込まれた建築の与件はまた、問うことができるのだろうか？ この ground（地）の与件を問うことは、これ以降に続く多くのプロジェクトの基礎になるだろう。カナレッジオでは、ground（地）のサーフェイスが、人工的なものとして概念化された。もはやユークリッド幾何学の与件ではなくむしろトポロジカルなサーフェイスに概念化された。このコンテクストの中では、如何なる幾何学的な form も、たとえユークリッド幾何学あるいは位相幾何学でも、人為的に見られる。即ち、それは如何なるオリジナルな原初の価値はないのである。"註7)

すなわち、ground（地）との関係性を示すことが目的となっているため、そこに構築される建築は、既に interiority の試行された住宅 11a 号が用いられた。ここでは、絶対的な場所性は消失している。上記のような exteriority としての与件が重ね合わせられ、ground の様々な読みを誘引している。それぞれの与件は、以下にアイゼンマンが述べるように、現実の空間における重要なポイントとしてアイゼンマン自身の選択による建造物や構築物との幾何学的な位置関係や歴史的な事象を再度浮かび上がらせるようなものである。いわゆる、コンテクスチュアリズムにおける場所性そのものを絶対視し、それを浮上させる単純な扱いではない。絶対視された場所性というオリジナルで原初的なものに絡み取られ、抑圧されることを拒否したアイゼンマン独自の態度が見られるのである。

"その site の周辺にある二つの大きな橋を視覚的に繋げている斜めの切り込みはサーフェイス上に作られた。それをサーフェイスとしてマークするためと、トポロジカルな軸をマークする両方のために。このコンテクストの中で、その軸が歩行者の接続よりも切断になったことは興味深い。その切り込みに沿って、そのアイデアを明確に表現する（分節する）ためにゴムのシートの様に折り曲げられた。site は ground に対抗するものとしてのサーフェイスとして。その site の diagram は、ル・コルビュジエのベニス病院プロジェクトのためのグリッドの延長として発展させられた。それは交換の場所として一連のノードを持っていた。この点とグリッド（の関係）は、そのプロジェクトの site に拡張され、そのノードはトポロジカルなサーフェイスの中のヴォイドのグリッド化されたマトリクスとして記された。"註8)（図 6-1）

また、アイゼンマンは、このプロジェクトは、概念的なデータとして、site を使った最初のプロジェクトでもあったという。住宅シリーズはニュートラルな順番としての命名がなされていたが、ここでは具体的な場所としての名前が付けられていることからも分かる。

"これは、当時、私の心理学的な取り組みと呼応していた。すなわち、私は、思考から感情へ、頭から身体あるいは ground（地）へと、心理学的な中心を移動することを試みていた。カナレッジョ・プロジェクト自身は、ちょうど住宅 11a 号のためのプロジェクトを括弧に入れた。そして、住宅 11a 号自身が、カナレッジョ・プロジェクトへと遡ったのである。カナレッジョ・プロジェクトは、リアルな名前で呼ばれ、有意な最初のプロジェクトであった。カナレッジョ・プロジェクトの最も有力な参照は、interiority に対し外部であった最初のものだった。interiority において、カナレッジョ・プロジェクトの関心は、最初は site

註7) DD p.173,l20-p.174,l9（筆者翻訳）
註8) DD p.174,l9-p.175,l5（筆者翻訳）
註9) DD p.173,l4-l19（筆者翻訳）
註10) DD p.176,l19-p.177,l16（筆者翻訳）

に関係づけられていた。それは、また数学的な形態、メビウスの帯を導入した。数学的な形態は、主たる建築形態として、後のプロジェクトにおいて、探究が続くことであろう。"註9)

重ね合わせにおいては、ドゥルーズのsuperimpositionとは異なり、階層性のないsuperpositionとするために、スケールの変化や回転、ズラシといった内部性に用いられた手法が用いられている。特に、都市的なスケールに対峙した初めてのプロジェクトでもあることで、以下のような三つの異なるスケールに住宅11a号を変換し、同時に記号としての都市における構築物をも示している。

" 住宅11a号の作品から、カナレッジオ・プロジェクトは再考された。その住宅をスケール調整したヴァージョンはヴォイドのマトリックスに置かれた。住宅に関して三つの違ったスケールが存在した。(そのことは「住宅」の命名の考えを問う質問を招く)。各スケールは、入れ子状態のロシア人形のように、次の大きなスケールの内部に組込まれた。最も小さいスケールは住宅11a号のモデルであった。次のスケールは、その中にモデルを組み込まれた住宅のサイズであった。それはもはや住宅ではなかったが、しかし住宅のモデルを含んだミュージアムであった。そして住宅とモデルの両方がその中に組み込まれていた。その時、それは住宅のミュージアムであったのか?三つの異なったスケールは、適切で、本当のスケールを述べることを不可能にさせた。また、これはobjectを命名することも、結果的に、機能にformを関連づけることもできなかった。"註10)

ここでは、これまでの建築設計におけるヒューマンスケールという人体寸法を基準とした尺度を拡張することも試みられている。人間の入ることのできないモデル(模型)のスケール、

通常人間の住むスケールとしての住宅、そして、その住宅を取り込んで展示物としてしまうような美術館のスケールというように、このことはむしろ、すでに無意識のうちにそのようなスケールの拡張が行われてきた近代建築以降のスケールについての考え方を再認させるものであるともいえる。

住宅11a号のスケーリング(三つのスケール)

この住宅はクライアントからの問いかけに対する回答をプログラムとして構成している。

" 当時スタンフォード大学で教えていたクルト・フォスターは、カナレッジオ・プロジェクトの概念的な意図に興味を持っていた。私は、カルフォルニアに彼のための家を建てるよう依頼された。彼は心理学的用語で彼が求める家を記述したのだった。彼は言った。「私は、私が内部にいる時、外部から世界を見ているように感じ、私が外部にいる時は、その家はまるでその家の内部にいるかのような家が欲しい。」このことは、住宅11a号のプログラムになった。住宅11a号は、最も大きく、最も「内部の」空間に「近づきがたいヴォイド」を含んでいた。それはドアや窓がない、したがって、アクセス不能の部屋であった。それゆえ、その家の最も内部の部分は概念的に最も外部であった。なぜなら、そこに入ることが不能だったからである。subject(主体)は、家の中と周りを歩くことができ、上ったり下りたりすることができるが、この大きな「近づきがたいヴォイド」に入ることは不可能であった。この内部/外部というテーマは、当時、メビウスの帯の内部/外部という住宅のため、創発するdiagramとして、別の外部テクストを提案したのであった。"註11)

註11) DD p.175,l6-p.176,l5(筆者翻訳)

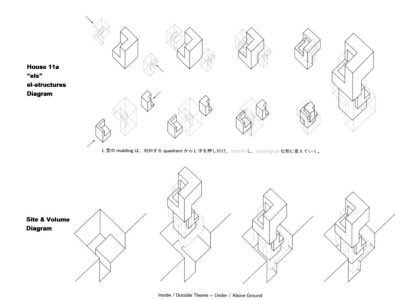

**House 11a
"els"
el-structures
Diagram**

L 型の molding は、対向する quadrant から L 字を押し付け、imprint L、topological な形に変えていく。

**Site & Volume
Diagram**

Inside / Outside Theme = Under / Above Ground

Fig.6-2 住宅 11a 号生成の diagram

そして、外部テクストしてメビウスの輪が diagram として導入されている。

"メビウスの輪は位相幾何学的な表面である。（それ自体がねじれ、内と外の表記を否定し、両方が連続的である）。diagram 的に、住宅 11a 号は、半分が地下そして半分が地上に位置づけられるメビウスの輪のように概念化された。その地下半分は居住となり、その地上半分はアクセスすることができないヴォイドを含んでいた。この文脈では、「下」と「上」の ground（地）は「内」と「外」の ground（地）と同等になった。"[註 12]

エルフォーム[註 13] が位相的な対称位置に反転、回転、移動され、それぞれが虚と実の volume に差異化され、虚の volume はフレームやガラスにインデックス化されている。それらの重ね合わせにおいては、これまでのようにスケーリング、ズラシ、回転といった手法が使用されている。カナレッジオ・プロジェクトをはじめ、以降のプロジェクトで見られるように、ground（地）をサーフェイスの一部として扱い、ヴォイドとしての痕跡を記す、imprint（刻印）という操作でエルフォームが型抜きされた ground（地）が形成されている。そこは、上下の区別の判読の難しい上部構造形態が鎮座する場を与えていると同時に、地上と地下という区分の根拠となるレベルを与えている。（図 6-2）

註 12）DD　p.176,l6-l18（筆者翻訳）
註 13）既出、3-4-6, p61、立方体から四半部の矩形 volume を抜き取った形態。住宅 10 号の出発点となった volume。住宅 11a 号は住宅 10 号の diagram から出発しているため、エルフォームから始まっている。
註 14）WV Chapter9 p.75,l116-l122（筆者翻訳）
註 15）WV Chapter9 p.75,l122-l24（筆者翻訳）

アイゼンマンの形態操作手法の変曲点
chora の概念：二つの状態を調停する概念としての chora

アイゼンマンは、デリダとの chora の概念の解釈の違いについて言及しながら、建築家における chora を定義する。

" これはプラトンのティマイオスの receptacle（chora）の定義の中で、place と object の間、container（容器）と contained（内容）の間の何かとして見つけられる。デリダにとっては、chora は spacing（空けること）であり、中間ではなく、どちらでもない。そしてまた space でもないし、place でもない。
"ground" に概念を必要とする建築家にとっては、chora はビーチの砂のようなものだ。
それは、object や place ではなく、満潮線の trace（痕跡）を残し、水の中で連続する波での浸食の imprint（刻印）を記録する単純な水の動きの記録である。" 註14)

ここから trace 概念が imprint を伴い二つの概念へと変化していく。アイゼンマンは trace 概念と imprint 概念とを明確に区分する事によって、chora 概念の新たな進化を図ったのである。この二つの両義的な対応関係をもつ新たな chora 概念は、明確な図と地の二項対立を持った従来の chora 概念とは大きく異なる。その結果モダニズムの場所性の概念、すなわち硬直した完結性を大きくズラしていく契機となるのである。

imprint / trace

chora はビーチの砂のようなものであるというアナロジーより、imprint（刻印）と trace（痕跡）の概念を差異化していく。

" 足は、砂に imprint として trace を残すように、砂は足に接する trace として残る。これらの残余と動作の各々は、あらゆる合理的、予想可能な、自然の道理の外部にあり、それらは同時にどちらでもない。" 註15)

"chora は、trace と imprint の間を区別するものとして、space のもう一つの可能な概念を導く。私の以前のプロジェクトの中で、receptacle（受容体）についての考えがなかったので、すべての mark は本質的には trace であった。つまり、以前は present（現前）であった何かの残余であった。ここで使われている用語の意味としては、以前 trace として見られていたものは、今は imprint と呼ぶことができる。" 註16)
つまり、前述の住宅シリーズからロミオとジュリエット・プロジェクトに至る trace の概念は imprint に該当するものであったということになる。

receptacle（受容体）について

アイゼンマンは以下のように言う。

" デリダによると、receptacle（受容体）は物質自身の trace によって影響されないので、receptacle の材料としては、少し柔軟なパテのような物質が考えられる。
その時、receptacle は概念的に、それ自体の物質の存在なしで、他の object の形状を変えるだけではなく、絶えず形状を変更する潜在性を持った一つの構築ということになる。したがって、何かが chora や receptacle の中に押し込まれた時、一つの imprint（trace でない）が残り、同時に receptacle の trace が imprinting object に残る。この trace と imprint の考えは、

註16) WV Chapter9 p.75,125-129（筆者翻訳）

初めてグァルディオラハウスのプロジェクトで試された。"註17)
（図6-3）

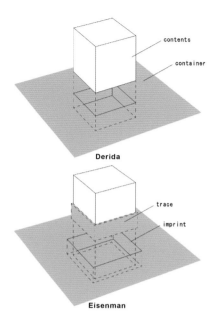

Fig.6-3　デリダとアイゼンマンにおける chora 概念の解釈の違い

さらにアイゼンマンは presence（現前）との関係について以下のように言う。

"そうするなかで、一方は他方に imprint（刻印）を残すが、同時に original figural presence（元の形象の現前）の一部を失う。その時、この失われた現前のアウトラインは、一連の trace（痕跡）で記録される。そして、それは以前の volume に存在証明を与えるものとなる。"註18)

こうして、以前の volume が新たに挿入される volume に影響

を与える一方、新たに挿入される volume が以前の volume に存在証明を与えるという概念、すなわち従来の硬直した図と地の関係から脱却する相互作用的で柔軟な関係概念をアイゼンマンは手に入れるのである。この事はモダニズムの完全性への信仰からの離脱を意味する。そして、この概念を幾つかのプロジェクトに適用していく。

6-3-2：カーサ・グァルディオラ 1988
任意のテクストから始まる：プラトンの chora 概念の再概念化
trace と imprint の差異を示すために、住宅10号の diagram が前提のテクスト
介在的で折り畳まれたスペースの考えにつながる diagram 的な trace のさらなる発展

Fig.6-4 カーサ・グァルディオラの diagram

註17) WV Chapter9 p.75,l29-l36（筆者翻訳）
註18) WV Chapter9 p.75,l38-l41（筆者翻訳）
註19) DD　p.191,l8-l11（筆者翻訳）

このプロジェクトには、ARX の構成メンバーであるヌノ・マテウスとフレデリック・レヴラットが重要なポジションで参加していた。

このプロジェクトは、その前のラ・ヴィレットのプロジェクトの diagram で開始された trace と imprint に関するものを、さらに精緻に練り上げたものであるという。

"これらの二つのプロジェクト（1987 年のラ・ヴィレットと1988 年のカーサ・グァルディオラ）は、おそらく、これら二つのプロジェクトにおいて、建築に対して、実際に本質的であったと思われる任意のテクストから始まった。" 註 19)

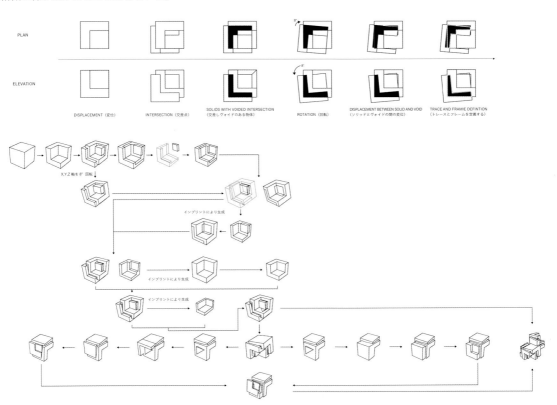

Fig.6-5 カーサ・グァルディオラ　生成の diagram

ここでいう任意のテクストとは、プラトンのchora[註20]にまつわるものであり、図と地が二次元の関係を主に示すことであることに対して、三次元的な対立項としての容器／内容、場所／場、frame/objectの曖昧化を図るものである。ここでは、その曖昧化の手法としてtraceとimprintの差異を示すことが目的であるため、前のプロジェクトである住宅10号のdiagramが最初のテクストとして使用されているという。開示されている資料では、最初の出発点は判明しないため、住宅10号のdiagramのどの部分からの出発になるのか判然としないが、最終形態と配置図等から、エルフォームが4つの象限に配置されていたものの変形であることが想像される。敷地形状も住宅10号に類似した傾斜地であることもその手掛かりとなる。diagramでは一つのエルフォームが二重化とズラシによるこれまでの方法によって生ずる交差部をヴォイド化し、さらに8度の回転を水平方向と垂直方向に施した時の痕跡をフレームによって記すことが示され、以下のようなtraceとimprintの差異が形象化されている。

"ラヴィレットのプロジェクトでは、不在はimprintとしてマークされた。また、objectは鋳型に押し込まれ、それが取りぬかれるとき、鋳型内にimprintを残した。
カーサ・グァルディオラの場合では、traceのアイデアが導入された。traceのアイデアはimprintとは概念的に異なるように見られる。
その違いは、ビーチの砂の中に足を入れたときに起こることに似ていた。足が砂の中にimprintをつくるが、足が持ち上げられたとき、砂の結晶が、どんな形成された方法においてではなく、ステップのimprintの断片的な痕跡として、つま先、足の甲と足のかかとに残る。"[註21]

さらに続けて

"traceは、足に残る、足によって位置をずらされる砂のランダムな条件である。
したがって、住宅10号の二つのvolumeは、カーサ・グァルディオラのために、足またはimprintingされたメカニズムのように振る舞う。住宅10号での同じvolumeのネガティブな鋳型にvolumeは置かれた。volumeは砂のように振る舞う。ポジティブなvolumeが引き離されたとき、部分的なtraceがvolumeの上に残される間に、imprintは鋳型に現れた。volumeが鋳型に完全に適合しなかったので、volumeと鋳型の間にスペースが生じた。生じたスペースはvolumeと鋳型からtraceとimprintを生成した。
これは、介在するスペースに関するinteriorityの思想的言葉の比喩的用法の最初の使用である。ここでは、介在性は、もはやソリッドとポシェの伝統的な考え方ではなく、むしろspaceの間にあるspaceとして理解された。そして、その定義する状況に関するmarksやtraces、imprintsにより明確に表現された。"[註22]（図6-5）

こうして、カーサ・グァルディオラでは、プラトンのchora、ソリッドとポシェという西欧の伝統的な考え方である二項対立的な関係性を超えて、その間に介在する隙間という概念を引き出す。この事は重要である。すなわち、境界において、西欧的呪縛である二項対立は明確なエッジを出してしまう。そのことを避け、曖昧な中間領域の必要性を見出すのである。
後に、アイゼンマンは、レブストック計画で、この介在する曖昧な中間領域において、折り畳まれるdiagram的なtraceのさらなる発展形を提案し、彼独自のものへと仕上げていくの

註20) デリダによるプラトンの「ティマイオス」中のコーラに関する概念をアイゼンマンが再解釈したもの。後述。
註21) DD　p.195,l5-l18（筆者翻訳）
註22) DD　p.195,l18-p.196,l16（筆者翻訳）

である。また、アーノフ計画でも、既存建物を trace した新し
く挿入される volume が、既存建物へ存在証明を与えながら呼
応する。そうして、chora の概念は、アイゼンマンの重要な生
成概念として、次なる発展をするのである。

6-3-3：レブストック計画 1990-94
新旧の区別をあいまいにする
境界もしくはフレームの消去
二つの新しい diagram 的な操作；graft（接木）、the fold（折り）
外部テクスト；ルネ・トムのカタストロフィー理論

このプロジェクトには、ARX の構成メンバーの一人であるヌ
ノ・マテウスがプロジェクト・アーキテクトとして、重要な
ポジションで参加していた。

ここでは、カナレッジオやロミオとジュリエット等の先行す
るプロジェクトにおいて用いられた、diagram の三次元化の
手法が垂直に押し出すものとは異なる手法が試行されている。
対象とする site のエッジを問題として扱い、古いものから新
しいものへのシームレスな移行を生成するために、古いもの
と新しいものとの区別をあいまいにするための手法がとられ
ている。それらは、二つの新しい diagram 的な操作につながり、
一つは graft（接木）、もう一つは the fold（折り）に関係する
ものであるとアイゼンマンは次のように言う。

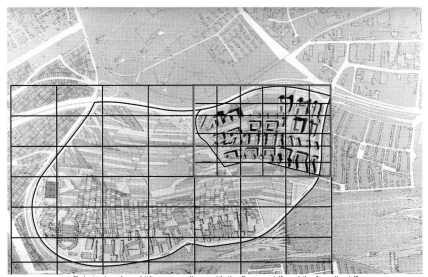

Rebstockpark and it´s surroundings with the "large grid" and the "small grid"

Fig.6-6 レブストック計画マスタープラン

まずは、graft について、コラージュとの違いを説明する。

"graft（接木）は、コラージュと似ているが、異なる操作である。コラージュは異なるコンテクストから生じたものを新しいコンテクストと一緒にまとめるがゆえに、並置—各エッジは必ず明確に表現される。意味の分離は、部分の分裂と異なる性質に、互いにそして全体に、依存する。
それに反して、graft（接木）は、時間を含む点で、モンタージュ以上のものである。シーケンス外のイベント間のシームレスな接続をつくる映画でのジャンプとカットのように、graft（接木）は新しいものと古いものの間のシームレスな接続を試みる。そして、新しいプロジェクトを古いものと新しいもののアマルガムにさせるために追加されたものの境界もしくはフレームを消去しようとすることを試みる。"註23）

次に fold について、superposition との違いから説明される。

" このような graft（接木）がレブストックパークのプロジェクトの基礎であった。graft は the fold（折り）の仲介を通して達成された。superposition（重ね合わせ）は図と地を同時に保有するが、folding（折りたたむこと）は地のない平滑な深さを供給する。その点において、folding は、superposition とは異なる。"註24）

ここでの folding（折りたたむこと）は、外部テクストとしてルネ・トムのカタストロフィーの理論の diagram を原点としているという。それは単なる折り紙とは異なることを以下のように言う。

" たとえば、折り紙において、折り目は折りたたみを表象するだけである。ところが、レブストックパークでは、フレームも折りたたまれる。折り紙は、線形で連続的で、最終的にフレームを含む。一方、レブストック計画における folding（折りたたむこと）は非線形で同時的である。折りたたまれたサーフェイスは、古いもののように見えない。それにもかかわらず新旧の間において、中間の図やスムーズな移行を試みる。site はすべての抑圧された内在状況の明瞭な表現となる。site は存在しているものを破壊するのではなく、新しい方向でそれを引き立たせる。そうすることで、the fold（折り）は（新旧の）エッジに新たな次元を与えた。"註25）

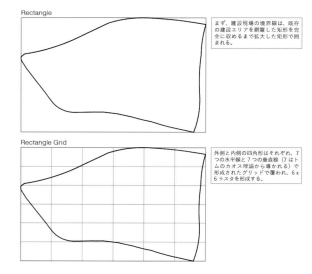

Rectangle

まず、建設現場の境界線は、既存の建設エリアを網羅した矩形を完全に収めるまで拡大した矩形で囲まれる。

Rectangle Grid

外側と内側の四角形はそれぞれ、7つの水平線と7つの垂直線（7はトムのカオス理論から導かれる）で形成されたグリッドで覆われ、6 x 6 ラスタを形成する。

註23）DD　p.197,l7-p.200,l1（筆者翻訳）
註24）DD　p.200,l1-l7（筆者翻訳）
註25）DD　p.200,l11-p.201,l2（筆者翻訳）

Rectangle Grid Scale

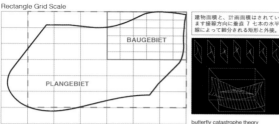

建物面積と、計画面積はされています接線方向に垂直 7 七本の水平線によって細分される矩形と外接。

butterfly catastrophe theory

Grid projected onto building area outline

次に、内側と外側のグリッドからのラスタ点が接続されます。これは、3 次元ネットワークの 2 次元描写である。

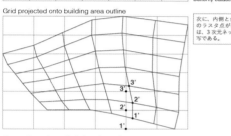

Connecting points with their project points

結果は、連続した折りたたまれた空間ネットワークです。長方形の建物形態は、このネットワーク上に投影され、台形形状を取得する。

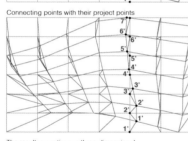

The result: a continuous three-dimensional

これらの台形形状は、元のスケッチに投影される。これは、建物計画に組み込まれる建物の境界線を定義する。ネットワーク回線は、路線と路線のルートも決定する。

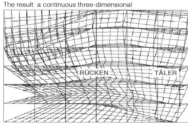

The large grid and the small grid

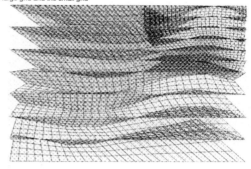

Fig.6-7 折りたたまれたグリッドの生成 diagram

折りたたまれたサーフェイスは、多次元的なグリッドとして、以下のように構成される。

まず、レブストックのジードルンクの広がる一帯の敷地を覆う 7 × 7 の直交グリッドが仮定され、そのうちの対象となる敷地分の 3 × 2 のグリッドをさらに分割して 6 × 6 の基準となる直交グリッドが仮定される。

次に敷地のエッジ（境界線）を基準とする、形状に沿った 6 × 6 の分割グリッドを形成する。これは結果としては、最初に生成した直交グリッドを敷地形状にモーフィングするような形となる。

この二つのグリッドを三次元的に垂直方向に引き離し、位相的に同位置のラスタ点を結ぶ。さらにここでは、縦軸方向の前後の点同士を結び、縦軸方向のジグザグの連続線が形成される。この操作をすべての点と縦軸に行い、連続するジグザグの面が形成される。

これらの操作は、直交グリッドから敷地の形状への単なるモーフィングではなく、視覚的な操作ではあるが、一つの面から

もう一つの面への変位の中で、連続的な折りたたまれた面が形成されている。コンピューターのモーフィング操作では、初めの形から次の形への変位が線形的に結ばれるのみであり、決して折りたたまれた形状になることはない。これらは一つ一つの操作の連続、すなわち、アルゴリズムによって構成されている。（図 6-7）

さらに、概念的な意味において、コンテクストとしての敷地とプロジェクトとしての直交グリッドの時空間での連続性を可能にし、これまでの垂直方向へのスイープから脱却した三次元化を成し遂げている。

そして、場所と時間は、もはやカルテジアングリッドによって定義されないとの認識に立つ。ニュートラルなユークリッド幾何学を否定し、欲望を扱うために位相幾何学における新たな図と地の関係に着目するのである。その結果、folding（折りたたむこと）という diagram 的操作を開始するのである。

レブストック計画は、アイゼンマンの重要なターニングポイントであった。object の意味を根本的に変えたのである。すなわち、object の寄って立つベースを form から field（場）へとシフトしたのである。フランクフルトのレブストックパークの基本計画では、そのエッジが定義的な問題となった。その意図は、古いものから新しいものへのシームレスな移行を生成するために、古いものと新しいものとの区別をあいまいにした。二つの新しい diagram 的な操作を導入する。一つは graft（接木）、もう 1 つは fold（折りたたみ）である。

ドゥルーズの概念を参照し、建築の object 概念を再概念化する。もはや form の優位性を否定するのである。このことは、form についての議論から、field（場）についての議論にシフトしたことを意味している。さらに、場所性を絶対視すると

いう抑圧的な思考を拒否し、また新旧のエッジを際立たせるという安易な方法を取らず、この中間領域である隙間を、あらゆるものを拾い上げることを可能とした diagram 的思考領域として見出すのである。このことは建築の可能性を大きく拡張させるものであった。

この作品は次代の建築家に大きく影響を与えたのであった。変化する連続性をもった object 概念の出現であった。時間性を孕んだ連続的 object として、ARX のベルリン・シュピルボーゲンコンペの原点にもなった作品であり、コンピューティング・プログラムへの適応プロトタイプの原点となった作品である。

6-3-4：アーノフ・センター　1988-96

このプロジェクトにおいても、place の問題が追求されている。すなわち、明らかにカーサ・グァルディオラの chora のアイデアを受けたものと見られる。アーノフは、シンシナティ大学内の既存の建物を改修し、増築するプロジェクトであった。建物は、リズミカルな関係性を生み出している。

Fig.6-8 シンシナティ大学アーノフ・センター

このプロジェクトにおいても、アイゼンマン流の chora の考えが存在する。まず既存建物の平面を trace（トレース）し、変容させた新たな volume を生成する。そして新たな volume を既存 volume の近傍に imprint するわけであるが、その際、chora の考えが使われているのである。新たな建物は、既存の建物に存在証明を与えながらも、既存の建物の trace として生成されるのである。また新たな建物が、最終の形態 object へと定着するに至る過程においてもコーラの考えが存在する。周辺環境との関係性によって、次の volume へと連続変形する際、中間領域の連続性が見られる。敷地や既存建物との関係性が全体を決定する上での重要な要素となっているのであるが。従来のように、一意に決定を行わないのである。一見、複数の直方体フレームが地形に沿って曲線を描く形に変形しているように見えるが、実際は、そうではなく、敷地の起伏や既存建物と挿入される建物との間に chora の考え方を連続的に投入させ、柔軟な解決を試みているのである。結果 、volume が周辺環境と連続的に呼応し、volume が振動する時間性を発現しているのである。この振動する時間性こそが、chora の連続性によって引き起こされたものなのである。

そうしたことによって引き起こされる振動の重なりや間隙が、建物に振動として刻み込まれている。（図 6-9）

こうした振動こそがアイゼンマンの主要な関心であった。

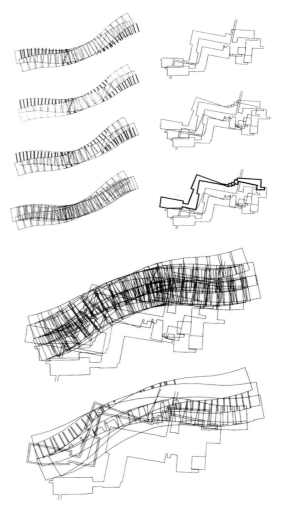

Fig.6-9 シンシナティ大学アーノフ・センターの diagram

これまでは、建築は一意の厳密な幾何学モデルにより成立するモデルであった。また、そうしたモデルを変革しようとして意味作用の転置や脱臼によって意味の無効性や、その不在を強要するものであった。しかし、この振動という運動性を持つ手法は新しい建築の在り方を提示した。パラメトリックな概念を予知させていた。こうした連続性の中に、多様性を包摂する新たな創造を生み出す手法が隠されていたのである。しかし重要なことは、chora の再定義から硬直した図と地の二項対立を超える関係性の発見であった。こうした二項対立を超えた chora の再定義は、ARX のベルリン・シュピルボーゲンコンペにおける運動性を孕むパラメトリックな diagram の原点になったものである。

6-3-5：バイオセントラム 1986-87
科学における外部テクストそのものが、建築プログラムに内在するものとして；DNA
科学的なインデックスという anteriority を導入
diagram の仲介による anteriority の沈殿のズラシ

外部テクスト；フラクタル

このプロジェクトには、ARX の構成メンバーの一人であるフレデリック・レブラットが重要なポジションで参加していた。このプロジェクトでは、ロミオとジュリエットのプロジェクトからの発展として、diagram に異なるテクストの戦略を使用したという。ロミオとジュリエットのテクストは、site のコンテンツとコンテクストに内在していたが、建築プログラムには内在するものではなかったことに対し、バイオセントラムでは、外部テクストそのものが、建築プログラムに内在するものとして捉えており、以下のように述べている。

" また、バイオセントラムでは、テクストが特定の建物の機能ならびに、インデクシカルなコンテンツに内在した点で、そのテクストは全くのデタラメではなかった。そのテクストは、機能において発すると認められない幾何学を生成することが知られていた。
これらの form は、科学者たちが DNA チェーンを記述する方法から開発された。それは文字通りの二重螺旋の diagram ではなく、むしろ科学的なインデックスの form であった。" 註26)

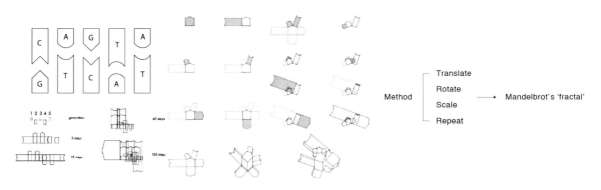

註 26) DD　p.188,l14-p.189,l2（筆者翻訳）
註 27) DD p.41,l22-l24（筆者翻訳）以下原文：It is the agency of the diagram which attempts to displace this sedimentation, and thus to open anteriority to its potential criticality.

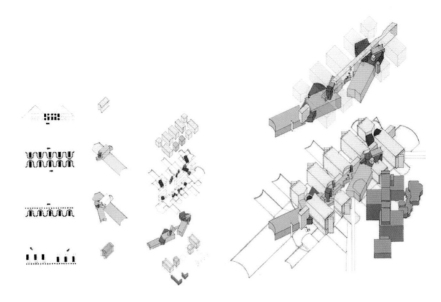

Fig.6-10 バイオセントラム　生成の diagram

このように、バイオセントラムでは、それまでの、テクストの重ね合わせの問題を離れ、テクスト合成の限界を追い払うために、科学的なインデックスという anteriority を導入するのである。このことは、interiority 自身を捉え直し、anteriority や subject（主体）の問題を提示しているものと思われる。
"diagram の仲介こそが、この沈殿のズラシを試みたのである。このように、その潜在的な臨界に anteriority を開放しようと企てる。"註27)

と述べているとおり、アイゼンマンにとって、anteriority を開放させようとする態度から見て、このことは当然のことかもしれないからである。

diagram では、DNA のプロセスとフラクタル理論、そしてグリッドが参照され、superposition されている。DNA のヌクレオチド・チェーンが、敷地図のための基本的な diagram になっており、既存の建物のグリッドに対して、新たなグリッドが回転を伴いながら挿入されている。建物の diagram はタンパク質のための DNA チェーンが使用されている。それは、魚の尾のような一端ともう一方の丸い端部を有する二つの歯状の form で構成されている。それぞれの結合は、G/C と A/T の塩基対の水素結合を意味し、チェーンの中にある個々の form は、常に区別されて、繰り返さないことから、結合部のずれも違い

に入れながら、5つの連続する結合パターンをジェネレーターとして仮定している。このジェネレーターを、スタートの形態として、フラクタルのプロセス;ここでは、トランスレート、回転、スケーリング、繰り返しによってグリッドに形態が重ねられていく。回転は魚の尾になる部分の角度に結合するような角度で行われ、スケーリングで辺の長さが合わされる。こうしたプロセスが 150 段階ほど繰り返されて、全体のチェーン構造が形成されている。それらの三次元化は、機能的な配置や要領に従い、これらのチェーンから押し出し成形されている。さらにカラーリングにおいては、サイエンスにおけるインデックスが参照され、赤と青、ライトブルーとブラウンの色表記を行っている。（図 6-10）

このようにして導入された外部テクストは、ロミオとジュリエットでも試行されたように、建物の意味に内在すると見られるような diagram を生成するために用いたという。この導入の恣意性は、いわゆるデフォルメやコラージュといったポストモダニズムや表層的なデコンストラクチュアリズムと変わりないものではあるが、その外部テクストと生成される形態との間の diagram の存在によって、単純な適用が回避されるとともに、アイゼンマンのオリジナリティが表れている部分でもあるということができる。

最も重要なことは、外部テクスト自体を anteriority とすることで、建築以外の領域にも拡張させたことである。もはや subject（建築家）が form を操作するという従来の建築の考え方ではなくなり、そこから大きく逸脱し、建築の可能性を拡大させていくのである。

6-4：連続性、関係性を進展させる哲学からの影響

6-4-1：デリダとの協同作業において変質するアイゼンマン

プラトンの chora の概念から、trace のみであったアイゼンマンの思考は、trace と imprint へと分化する。すなわち、デリダがプラトンの chora の概念を踏襲していたことを批判し、両義的な対応関係として chora の概念を再定義する。

trace（インデックス /mark/ presence）

imprint（イコン / インデックス）

それが La Villette のプロジェクトの考えに発展していく。

既に示したように、アイゼンマンの理論は、デリダの理論を下敷きにしている。

住宅シリーズにおいては、建築の内部性の探究として、これまでの建築自身の認識における形式言語を解体することを試みてきた。その際に、アイゼンマンはデリダと同様に、建築も言語と同様にパロールであり、現前の優位性を常に有していたと言う。

また、アイゼンマンは、西欧の伝統的な思考である二項対立から離脱するデリダを不十分だとして批判する。デリダが提示した現前と不在を、未だ二項対立に囚われているとして批判し、アイゼンマンは硬直化した静止状態ではなく、動的な批評性を温存させるために、presence（現前）に対抗して新たに presentness を提示したのであった。

ここで見るアイゼンマンの trace 概念は、イコンでもインデックスでもない第三の状態として presentness の中に挿入するアイゼンマンの提示するものである。

アイゼンマンが interiority の拡張として exteriority を取り込もうとしたことは、本章初めにおいて見た。特に住宅 10 号

註 28) 本稿においては、アイゼンマンの内部性の探求から外部性の探求に至るきっかけとなった初期の外部性プロジェクトのみを扱っているため、La Villette 以降のプロジェクトについてはここでは詳述していない。
註 29) WV Chapter9 "SEPARATE TRICKS" p.72,l13-l17（筆者翻訳）
註 30) WV Chapter 9 p.74,l1-l12（筆者翻訳）

において見出された分解プロセスは exteriority へと連続する潜在性を有していることに気が付き、本章で扱ってきた exteriority を取り込んだ初期プロジェクトにおいて試された。こうした exteriority への拡張を可能にする概念的なきっかけとなったものが、プラトンのティマイオスのなかの chora の概念に関するデリダとの共同作業であったとアイゼンマンは言う。中でも、前述のカナレッジョ・プロジェクト、ロミオとジュリエット・プロジェクトでの exteriority に対する trace 概念の試み、そしてカーサ・グァルディオラにおいて imprint 概念との差異化によって住宅シリーズより試みられてきた trace 概念の進化を遂げ、La Villette のプロジェクトの考えに発展していくことになる。註28)

アイゼンマンは、記号をモチベーションの有無で区別し、モチベーションをもつものが建築であり、モチベーションをもたないものはビルディングであるとし、diagram が存在の形而上学を封印するエクリチュールであるとすることは既に見てきたとおりである。このモチベーションの有無を exteriority においても見出そうとする。このことはロウらの提唱したコンテクスチュアリズムと一線を隔するものであり、前述のデリダとの共同作業より進化させたことは chora の概念に依るところとなっている。

以下、trace 概念の進化の概要を追っていく。

interiority の探求における trace 概念について
アイゼンマンは、その著作の中で以下のように自身のプロジェクトでの trace 概念の試みを述べている。

"object の trace の考えは私のプロジェクト全体で見ることが

できる。

住宅 1 号の床のなくなった column の輪郭
住宅 2 号の余分な支持構造
住宅 4 号の精巧なファサードの marking
住宅 10 号の中心の脊椎の不在
住宅 11a 号のアクセスできないヴォイド
カナレッジョ・プロジェクトの地面の穴と剥がされている地面のカットライン
ロミオとジュリエット・プロジェクトのスケーリング " 註29)

これらのプロジェクトは既に前章及び本章において見たものである。

trace / marking
trace と marking の違いについてアイゼンマンは以下のように言う。

" ドアや窓の輪郭は trace ではなく、機能的な要素のリアルな marking（マーキング）である。
それに対して、string course（胴蛇腹）や entablature は機能を持たないので trace として見ることができる。
trace は、ある種の form や mark（マーク）、ある物理的な 現前 であるに違いないが、それは古典的な構成における審美的 presence の伝統的な意味での form ではない。建築の text は、アイコニックな状態とは対照的なものとしてのインデクシカルと呼ばれることができるもののように考えることができる。"
註30)

アイゼンマンは、インデクシカル、アイコニックというこの二つの違いの重要性を説く。例えば、column は、構造要素であり、その機能のアイコニックなサインでもあり、両方であるという。アイゼンマンは自身の trace の概念において、column、または wall や column の可能性について、それ自身の存在とそれがあるようになった過程のインデックスを mark（マーク）する現前の中に第三の状態を挿入することを住宅シリーズにおいて試みてきたという。[註31]

情報化時代の place の役割

アイゼンマンは言う。建築は伝統的に身体と自然のメタファーに基づいてきた。ルネサンス以降、建築は、意識的に用・強・美以上のものになった。現在、科学は、人が自然を克服すること（人／自然）から、人が知識を克服すること（人／知識）へとシフトした。

ローマ時代は、mark として place を定義した。[註32] 今日、テクノロジーは自然を圧倒し、近代思想はこれまで合理的で論理的であるとみなされていたことの中に不条理を見出した。place の伝統的な形式の破壊は、同時に伝統的な figure（図）／ground（地）と frame/object のカテゴリーの破壊を歩んできた。[註33]

今日の place

" 今や、place（それはどこかで始まって、その初期条件の変化の線形で、合理的で、物語風の記録である）についての伝統的な考えとは異なり、任意の初期条件の連続は space の中に marking（マーキング）の密集した連続を生み出す。それらは

object として place を体現しない。ここでは、壁、床、天井は包含と保護だけではない。それらはまた、containing でも contained でも、inside でも out でも、frame でも object でも、figure でも ground でもない過剰の状態になる。 "[註34]

ここに place は、伝統的な概念から逸脱するのである。そして様々なマーキングが密集した連続性の中にあって、object という形式をとらないものとなる。二項対立によって明確に浮かび上がるものではなく、両義的で過剰な状態として存在するものとなる。

grid について

アイゼンマンは、grid を receptacle のようなものとしてとらえ、グァルディオラハウスの中でそのダイナミックな試行がなされた。このことは重要である。アイゼンマンの chora の捉え方が、モダニズムにおける grid の抽象性なる教義への信仰から脱却した瞬間であった。そして新たな一歩を生み出した。

" 二次元または三次元であれ grid は、通常、形状を見ることができる ground（地）、一つの抽象性として考えられる。imprint（刻印）の使用時には、grid の役割は、潜在的に両義的になる。
例えば、グァルディオラハウスでは、grid は、ねじれとゆがみのフレームの連続、すなわち、構造的な完全体に代わって、それらは二つの形象要素の交差として、imprint の状態を明らかにする trace と imprint である。 "[註35]

すなわち、アイゼンマンの chora の再定義によって、trace と

註31）WV Chapter9 p.74,l16-l18（筆者要約）以下原文：What the idea of trace proposes is to insert a third condition into the presence of the column, or the wall, a presence which marks an index about the possibility of the wall or column, an index of its own being and the processes by which it came to be.
註32）ローマ帝国の創建儀礼に関わる概念モデルとしての、ムンドゥス（中心）、ポーモエリウム（境界）、カルド／デクマヌス（東西・南北基幹道路）が、都市形態の骨格として、現在でも多くの古代ローマ支配下の諸都市に残っていることであると思われる。詳しくは、以下を参考のこと。ジョーゼフ・リクワート（前川道郎、小野育雄訳）『《まち》のイデア ローマと古代世界と都市の形の人間学』みすず書房、1991 年

imprint という両義的な対応関係が、モダニズムにおける grid の固定した完結性を打ち破り、振動する連続的な建築の創出を獲得したのである。そして、次世代に向けて、柔らかい流動的な建築へと導く可能性を開くのである。

コンテクスチュアリズムとの違い

ロウらによるコンテクスチュアリズムと自身の chora の概念の相違について以下のように述べている。

" ポストモダニストのアーバニズムの支配的な戦略は、コーリン・ロウなどによって提唱されたコンテクスチュアリズムの考えだった。敷地上のそれらの重要な現前の美徳によって、それらの figure（図）に価値を与えている、あらゆる現存するコンテクストに隠れている figure（図）を見つけ出すことをコンテクスチュアリズムは主張した。可能性がある白紙状態として、あらゆる敷地に対するモダニスト教義を超えて、存在することに価値を与えられた。
already present のこの考えは、その receptacle や context の中に already present を見いだしている chora の考えに類似しているとみることができる。"註 36)

アイゼンマンは、コンテクスチュアリズムが figure としての object を具象化して、presence（現前）を与えるものだとして批判する。すなわち現前への盲目的なる傾倒が figure（図）に価値を置き、コンテクスト上の figure（図）を見つけ出し、object 化すべきだという信仰を求めていることを批判するのである。

" ロウの教義は、主としてゲシュタルトの現象学に基づき、object を具象化し、それに現前を与える。一方で、新しい chora は、現前を不安定にし、転覆することを試みる。その存在を不安定にするために、既に与えられているものを見いだす。重要なのはオリジナルのマテリアルではなく、むしろいかに操作されるかである。新しい chora は、place の価値における偶発性と因襲性をさらけ出すが、それを無効にしない。むしろ、もはや解決と関係なく、弁証法的でもない多価値的な範囲内で活発になることを許すものである "註 37)

アイゼンマンは、再概念化された chora の概念とコンテクスチュアリズムの違いが重要であることを説き、ロウの教義を批判する。そして、自身の提唱する chora は、逆に現前を不安定にすることを試みるのだと言う。そのために chora は、既に与えられているものを見いだし、place の価値における偶発性と因襲性を暴露させ、多様な価値を活性化させると言うのである。

subject / object

このようなデリダとの共同作業から進化したアイゼンマンの概念、そしてこれまでの言説より読み取ることができることは、subject と object という認識をズラそうとする試行である。ここで見た trace 概念の分化は、subject/object に対する視点をどこに向けるのかの違いに他ならない。それを imprint と trace に区別しながらそれを受容する receptacle を grid として建築的に捉え直しているのである。そこにアイゼンマンの独自性が伺える。概念として差異を伴いながらも現れてくる形象としては、それぞれがどのプロセスに対応するのか曖昧になるほどの過剰な状態として提示しているのである。

註 33) WV Chapter9 pp.74-75（筆者要約）
註 34) WV Chapter9 p.76,l3-l8（筆者翻訳）
註 35) WV Chapter9 p.76,l27-l32（筆者翻訳）
註 36) WV Chapter9 p.77,l36-l41（筆者翻訳）

6-4-2：新しい object 概念

前述のデリダとの共同においては、アイゼンマンは subject/object の関係性の概念を進化させた。さらに既に触れたドゥルーズの思想からの影響として、object そのものに対する思考の進化である。

ドゥルーズは以下のように述べている。

「系列の法則は、連続的な運動の中にある「同じ線の軌跡」として諸曲線をとらえ、この軌跡は連続的にそれらの交差する曲線に接触されるというとき、ライプニッツは変調を定義していた。これは対象についての、単に時間的ではなく質的な概念を示している。マニエリスム的な対象であって、もはや本質主義的な対象ではない。つまりこれは出来事（event）となる。」註38)

（襞）

このように、ドゥルーズは、変化の数学的な研究において、対象は event であり、変化であると主張する。

これを受けて、アイゼンマンはドゥルーズの object 概念を解釈し、新たな object 概念を展開していく。

"ドゥルーズのこの新しい object 概念は、もはや空間の構成とは関係性を持たず、むしろ物質の継続的な変化を意味する時間的な変調である。継続的な変化は fold の仲介を通して特徴づけられる。：「もはや本質的な form によって定義される object ではない。」ドゥルーズは object についてのこの考えを「object event」と呼ぶ。event は、物語の時間または弁証法的な時間とは異なり、そうした時間概念の外部にある時間概念である。" 註39)

そして、アイゼンマンは event に対して建築的な可能性を以下のように説き、アーノフ・センターで発芽し、レブストッ

ク計画で作品として実現させるのだった。

"今日、event の建築は両方の時間を扱わなければならない：旧来の時間と前後の未来の時間とメディアの時間、前後を含まなければならない現在の時間。event は、ドゥルーズが安定でも不安定でもないシステムに組織化された一連の異種混在性と呼ぶものと一致している。；言い換えれば、弁証法は、関係ではなくむしろ、潜在的なエネルギーと呼ぶことができるものに役立つ。現在では、これらの event は、本当の場所が反復の新しい調停された時間に圧倒される（加速と減速によって）。したがって、それらの場所に移住し停滞した古い直線的な時間を理解することができない。したがって、いずれかの場所の状態においても、この「他」という particular の概念と反復のこの時間を認める specific をより関係させる必要がある。画像は、マッピングによって置換されなければならない。そして個性は特異性に再概念化される。" 註40)

この新たな時間概念に対する試行は、レブストック計画とアーノフ・センターによってなされた。

特に、アイゼンマンは以下のようにレブストック計画の fold の概念と event の関係を説明する。

"この意味の fold は、フレームでも地としての図でもないが、どちらの要素も含む。したがって、レブストック計画の地は、起源としての地または図と地のような地から区別されなければならない。レブストック計画の地は、もはや基準または基本条件ではなく、むしろ、実際、特異性の状態をすでに含むなにかである；つまり、地の概念に備わっていると言われる根拠のないこと。それは、根拠のない地である。レブストッ

註37) WV Chapter9 p.77,l42-p.78,l6（筆者翻訳）
註38) ドゥルーズ『襞』第 2 章 p.35、(event) は、筆者による付加
註39) WV Chapter5 "FOLDING IN TIME"p.29,l9-l13（筆者翻訳）
註40) WV Chapter5 p.29,l32-p.30,l4（筆者翻訳）

ク計画で実現されるこの根拠のない地は fold の可能性にある。有機体と結晶との間の調停する装置は、膜の考えであり、レブストック計画の場合では、それは folded された表面である。fold は、特異性の側面である。fold は、決して空間または時間のどちらも同じではない。

それは、「objectness」よりもむしろ「個性原理」の違いの物質的状態である。folded された表面は、大きさや距離に頼ることなく関係性を写像する；それは、トポロジカルとユークリッドの表面（容認できる幾何学）との間の違いで概念化される。トポロジカルな表面は、距離の必要な定義のないマッピングの状態である。これらのポイントはもはやX、YとZ座標によって固定されない；それらは、X、YとZと呼ばれているかもしれないが、それらはもはや固定された、空間的な場所を持たない。それらが場所なしであるというこの意味では、それらはトポロジカルな理由で場所がない。

したがって、レブストック計画は、ジードルングを使用して場所と時間の特異性の状態をつくりだす試みとして fold を使う。ここではトポロジカルな event、連続体への図と地の消滅は、fold に物理的にある；もはや、ポイントまたはグリッドではなく。トポロジカルな event または構造となる膜としての地の表面は、同時に建築の形態でもある。前後だけでなくそれ自身の現在としてあるこのトポロジカルな event または構造は、現在だけを持つ純粋なメディアから区別される。"註41)

さらに、メディアの時間と event 、fold の関係について以下のように言う。

" メディアの時間は、現在の時間に関係しているならば―シミュレートされた event の時間―特異性の時間は、event 自体

の現在の中の時間の前後を含む。カルテジアン・グリッドまたはプラトン立体の考えられた中立性は、価値として見られた秩序と合理性が specificity（特定）を作り始めることができた場所。グリッド都市空間の最も初期の区切りであるカルドとデクマヌスの交差点は、どう考えても特有の symbolic なポイントであった。fold は、異なる種類のシンボルである。；それは、もはやイメージやアイコニックな表象についてではなく、むしろ指標やそれ自身の存在をマッピング（ event または光景としての時間でのその個性原理のマッピング）することについてある。

したがって、グリッドの specificity が場所に言及されたところで、fold の特異性は時間に言及する。グリッドから fold place への動きにおいて、もはや支配的な空間の状態のままでない。fold においては、空間と時間の伝統的な座標によって拘束されない特異性として、場所の specificity がある。レブストック計画での fold の使用は、フランクフルトの都市構造に常に内在または抑圧されていたかもしれない他の状態を明らかにしたかもしれない。時間の event としての fold の考えは、レブストックエリアへの急進的な調停を要求するものでも、タブララサとしてのコンテクストのノスタルジアへの復帰でもない。

むしろ、それは時間に存在するコンテクストを拡張する何かを見ることであり、この拡張において特異性の可能性を生み出す。電子パラダイムの偏在している似姿のために、時間に拘束された場所はその場所性を失ってしまった。

fold はそれらが以前そうであったことに場所と時間を戻そうとせず、fold にそれらをもたらす。"註42)

註41) WV Chapter5 p.30,l113-p.31,l15（筆者翻訳）
註42) WV Chapter5 pp.31-32（筆者翻訳）

6-4-3：object event 概念を巡って

アイゼンマンは、ドゥルーズの fold 概念を西欧的な考え方から離脱を図るものとして次のように読み取っている。

" ドゥルーズにとって、fold は空間と時間の新しい概念を開くものである。伝統的に、建築は一連のポイントグリッドとして、デカルトの空間として概念化されてきた。ライプニッツの考え方では、「ライプニッツは、デカルトの合理主義に背を向けて、効果的な空間の概念に関して、連続的な最小要素の迷宮においては、point ではなく fold であると主張した。」と、ドゥルーズは Le Pli で主張する。ドゥルーズは、ライプニッツのこうした拡張の概念は、event の概念であると主張する：「拡張は、上下の深さよりもむしろ水平面での外向きの拡がりに沿った哲学の動きである。planning envelopes は中立であるようなデカルト空間の volume である。」
デカルト空間のこうした volume（stylisms（諸様式主義）や古典的だけでなく現代とポストモダンな空間のイメージを含むプラトンの個体は）は、中立または自然と考えられるイデオロギーの状態以外の何物でもない。交差またはポイントからの拡張としての fold の概念 - 中立性とは異なるものとしての fold の概念を導入することが可能である。" 註43)

アイゼンマンは、こうしたライプニッツの考え方に拠る fold の概念を踏まえて、西欧的な考え方を乗り越えるために、すなわち、デカルト空間；ニュートラルなグリッドでは、平均化された場が生成されるだけであり、こうしたモダニズムが犯した均質化を超えるために、やわらかい diagram による新たな空間を作ろうとした。その最初の試みがレブストック計画であった。

そのプロジェクトでは、ジードルンク自体がすでに旧来型の figure（図）/ ground（地）のかたい対立構造が消えていっていることに対して、新旧の二項対立ではない新たな枠組みとして fold という手法を導入し、客観的に検証可能性を有する哲学的な軸としてドゥルーズの考えとリンクした新たな概念を提示した。
前述のデリダとの共同による chora の概念を進化させた単なるコンテクスチュアリズムではない、慣習的な場所性や時間性ではない場を提示しようとした。手法、操作が diagram でありそれが旧来型の object の概念を変えていっており、それが diagram を分有させている。
これらは、アイゼンマン自身の以後のプロジェクトにやわらかい時間性と次のステージを提示している。

6-5：まとめ

これまで見てきたように、アイゼンマンは住宅シリーズ以降、外部性を取り込み始めるのである。彼の diagram は、内的論理と exteriority との調停を試みようとするものであった。
その調停は、以下の二つの点における調停であった。それらは exteriority の捉え方におけるアイゼンマン独自の態度の表れであった。

6-5-1：外部と内部を区別する境界の消失「古典的場所性からの逸脱」

アイゼンマンが exteriority として捉えた一点目は、実際の場所に存在する事象が堆積した中立的な場所性ではなかった。あくまでも情動という方向性を有するもの affect が出発点であっ

註43) WV Chapter5 p.28,l39-p.29,l10（筆者翻訳）

た。歴史性であったとしても、歴史上に registration（登録）されるべき欲望としての歴史性であった。

カナレッジョのプロジェクトでは、ル・コルビュジエのベネチア病院のプロジェクトがベースにあり、その計画におけるグリッドを exteriority としている。彼は場所性を具体的な機能や中立的な exteriority ではなく、モチベーションをもった exteriority として浮上させるのである。そうした上で、そこに立ち現れる registration されるべきモチベーションをもつ記号性を汲み上げる。アイゼンマンは建築をモチベーションという情動のベクトルをもつ記号システムであると定義する。place（場所）、ground（地）、mean（意味）という exteriority はモチベーションをもつがゆえに、モチベーションという同一の地平で、建築の interiority（内部性）と連続することが許されるのである。

二つ目の点については、アイゼンマンは、住宅シリーズまで建築の interiority において、機能などの具体的なものを一切排除してきた。 interiority として、自律的で純粋な自己参照性を持つ抽象的な原理・論理を探査してきた。外部性においても、抽象的な論理以外を排除し、そうした抽象的な interiority と exteriority とを調停させることを表明するのである。このことはコールハースとは真逆の方向であり、アイゼンマンの理論が彼特有の論理として解釈される理由である。すなわち、exteriority を建築に取り込もうとしたアイゼンマンの態度は、事象自体から建築を眺め、建築をプログラムとして外部へと開放させようとしたコールハースのアプローチとは明らかに異なっていたのである。

ただし、外部と連続させようとする意識は、内的論理だけで独立した不連続なものとして、建築が完結することが不可能であることの認識をもっていたことを意味している。こうした意識は、その後の重要な建築論の問題を浮上させるものであり、建築が外部と孤立して存在することが不可能であることを示唆している。

6-5-2：アイゼンマンの diagram の確立

本章で扱った住宅シリーズ以降の exteriority を取り入れ出したプロジェクトにおいて、アイゼンマンの diagram は、建築の interiority のみの探究から外部性へと開かれたものへと進化した。平板性の離脱としての volume 概念をベースにしながら、住宅的なスケールから都市的なスケールへと拡大に伴い、手法と概念の両方にわたって、旧来の静的なかたいシステムからの離脱が図られている。

これまでの建築が前提としていたユークリッド幾何学だけに縛られていることを疑い、それを否定するのではなく、位相幾何学やフラクタルなどを重ね、二項対立ではない過剰な状態を提示することで、旧来の時間性や場所性からの逸脱を試みている。

手法としての fold やスケーリング、モーフィングなどは、やわらかい diagram として、新しい空間を提示し、自身の以降のプロジェクトへもつながっていく開かれた手法を提示している。アイゼンマンの博士論文以来追究している、静的ではない変化し続けるシステムが確立したといえるであろう。

Conclusion

アイゼンマンの diagram と次代への影響

西欧の伝統的な思考態度は、二項対立という枠組みの中にあり、必ず subject と object は明確に区分されている。アイゼンマンは、diagram は欲望する subject の表現ではなく、以前に何か形のないものとして建築の外部から来なければならないものであるとする。さらに、特定の site に、プログラムに、または歴史における anteriority から来なければならないとする。それは、既に存在するものをぼやけさせ、暴きながら、他の形象として現れるために、既に刻印されたものの原因となる。

diagram は、生成力と形成力のあるキャパシティーを制限する抑圧を開放し、建築の anteriority と subject の両方の内部で構成された抑圧を解放するものであるとする。アイゼンマンは、自身の問題設定のために、diagram を object の中に、interiority として沈めることで subject と object との分離を否定しようとしている。それは、まるで作家という subject が生み出した diagram を object に分有させているとも言える。object に建築の interiority が内包され、そうした object が連続して継起することにおいて、歴史に沈殿する建築の anteriority を現出させることができるとアイゼンマンは考えるのである。

アイゼンマンは記号論をもって、モダニズムや古典主義における制作に対して、その代替案を提示する。すなわち subject や object の位置をズラそうとするのである。こうした試みによって、彼の作品は従来の作品という概念から捩じれ、崩れたところに位置すると理解されることとなる。いわゆる「解体」というレッテルに見られるように、調停されるべき両者の構造の関係の違いを暴露させることによって、あたかもそうした構造を乗り越えたかのように振る舞っただけであった[註1]と評価されるのである。未だにそうした誤解のまま今日に至っていることは残念である。特に日本においては、アイゼンマンに対する認識は、彼の難解な概念のため、読み解く人が皆無のため、認識が浅く、一時期のデコンストラクションという喧騒の中に、彼の概念の重要性が埋没してしまった。本稿の主要な目的とするところは、歴史の中に埋没したアイゼンマンの思考の軌跡を蘇らせ、その概念の重要性を明らかにすることである。

7-1: ル・コルビュジエからの継承
7-1-1: volume 概念の変遷

周知のとおり、ル・コルビュジエは、建築を volume、サーフェイス、プラン、規整線の4つのカテゴリーに還元した。特に平面こそが重要な原理とする階層的な意識をもっていた。平

註1) ラファエル・モネオ、前掲書

面は、形態を生み出し、volume と空間の間を調整し、volume の配置とサーキュレーションの秩序を調整するためのものであった。それは建築自身が外部と孤立する不連続な時代においての理解だった。明らかに exteriority は建築の interiority に関わる。アイゼンマンによると、volume は、空虚なヴォイドの対立項としてのタンジブルで明確なマッスではなく、space の範疇に包含されるものとして定義されている。概念的には、volume と space との対立関係は存在しないとする。すなわち volume は、エネルギー密度によって変化するスペースそのものなのである。サーフェイスはエネルギーを孕む space を覆うために便宜上設定しているに過ぎない曖昧な境界である。そうしたサーフェイスにより volume は定義されているのである。アイゼンマンのこうした volume の定義に関する指摘は重要である。建築は、そうした密度をもった濃淡のある領域（volume）としてプログラムされるものとして定義する可能性が開かれる。

こうした volume の概念は space の概念に含まれながら、等質で中立な space に対して、エネルギーや力の方向性が蓄えられたものと理解され、さらに尺度としてのカルテジアン・グリッドを参照することが提示されている。カルテジアン・グリッドはデカルトの言う三次元の方向が等価なニュートラルなものとしてではなく、建築においては重力が支配的な役割を占めるため、絶対的な水平性とそれに対する垂直性として、三次元空間の方向性が等価でないことに留意しながら注意深く定義するのである。

このことは、不連続で凝固したタンジブルな object を眺めるだけの行為を越えて、space がエネルギーを孕む密度、そして参照グリッドを基準とした計測への意識を孕んでいる。一歩

進めるならば、この volume なる概念は、不連続性から連続性へと開かれる可能性を有していると言えるのである。
その契機は、volume が固定化されたソリッドではなく気体として、ル・コルビュジエが含意したことに始まる。その意味で、ル・コルビュジエの volume 概念が重要な意識を孕んでいたのであり、ル・コルビュジエの功績は大きいものと思われる。
こうして運動エネルギーは、建物自身を流れ、建物の限界を定義するエッジやサーフェイスが消失し、外部のエネルギーの流れが、内部に吸収されていくことを可能にさせるのである。

7-1-2: 密度をプログラムする

volume は、space の概念に包摂され、もはやエネルギーの充満する力のベクトルをもった集合となった。volume と space における視覚的な差異は消失したのである。次にくるのは、そうしたエネルギーが人間を包み、人間身体と連続し、呼応することである。その意味で、volume の問題を最初に理解したル・コルビュジエの功績は大きいものと思われる。アイゼンマンは、こうしたル・コルビュジエの volume を再定義し、さらなる進化をおこなったといえる。
ロジックは、建物自身へと進み、建築内部は、回路になるのであった。建物の限界を定義するラインやサーフェイスが消える程、外部のエネルギーの流れが、内部に、これまで以上に吸収されていくのである。volume は計測化される対象として認識され、プログラムされる可能性を開くのである。

7-1-3：ル・コルビュジエの両義性

ル・コルビュジエはプランによって、volume をコントロールしようとした。そして、volume を固定化させ、要素化し部品化した。ル・コルビュジエは、プランを基準平面と捉え、その基準平面において volume をコントロールすることを求めた。平面だけでなく立面においてもコントロールの操作をおこなった。その基準は西欧の伝統的な美の価値観だった。すなわち面に投影された関係性が、静的な比例数理によって支配されるべきであると考えたのである。そして、建築の古典的な interiority である比例やプロポーションの問題を規整線として視覚化し、モデュロールへと発展させたことは、伝統的な建築の interiority の問題をより普遍化した。

一方で、ル・コルビュジエは近代建築の原理性を求めるために、設計に関わるあらゆることを常に要素化することを試みていた。ル・コルビュジエは、この要素化された object の配列による構成が近代建築であるとして捉えていた。その建築的 object は次第に部品化され、内部と外部の関係、部屋と部屋の関係、建物と周囲の関係、figure（図）/ground（地）の関係といったものが、壁で仕切られている空間を volume で考え、volume とヴォイドが演算によって分節、加算されるか、volume を配列するかの二つの方法によって構成されることになり、建築の巨大化と複合化を可能にしていった。この内部化と外部化という二つの方向性を持った両義性の解釈の違いが現代のアイゼンマンとコールハースの二つの潮流に分かれていった。

7-1-4：コールハースがル・コルビュジエから継承したものとの違い

アイゼンマンとコールハースをどう評価するか。

既に述べたように、ル・コルビュジエの object は眼前にある建築の存在としての意味を引きずっているのであり、アイゼンマンはル・コルビュジエの両義的関係性を抽象化し、原理性を導き出そうと試みた。それに対してコールハースは object とデータを結びつけ、それぞれにヒエラルキーのある関係性をつくらず、全てはパラレルで、object は関係性を生み出すかのように抽象化されているということが考察された。

すなわち、object 自身を記号化し、アイコン化し、object どうしの関係を一端、切断することによって、object に新たなデータを付加し、object をパラレルに並置させ、新しい関係性を生み出そうとしている。アイゼンマンのように原理化された法則を適応させるのではなく、部品化された object を並置することで、あらゆる多様な事象を削ぎ落とすことなく、拾いあげ整理しようとしているのである。

アイゼンマンは、diagram という建築の interiority を強く信じ、原理性を追求するという西欧の伝統的枠組みを維持しようとしているのであり。コールハースは、もう一つの西欧の伝統的枠組みである、interiority という不可視な実体というものを認めない考え方であり、多くのものを可視化させ、新たな実体として拡張する伝統を継承しているということができる。

7-1-5：批評性を object に取り込もうとした

アイゼンマンの批評は、建築の記号と意味とが引き合うモチベーションがゼロになることが批評であるとする。すなわち、従来の意味が記号から切り離された時こそが批評が現れる時

であるとするのである。

アイゼンマンは、標準化を克服するdiagramを目指したため、批評性を建築に内在化しようとした。そのため、アイゼンマンは、常に建築の既成概念のズラシを試みた。アイゼンマンのdiagramは外部化されずにobjectに内包され、読み取られることを求めた。いわば作品というobjectはsubject自身の分身ともいうべきものである。それはsubjectとobjectの二項対立的区別すらも無くそうとするアイゼンマンの態度から生まれたものである。そうしたobject群が、過去から現在まで、問題意識を継起する時系列上に存在しており、それこそが、建築のanteriorityであると言う。object（作品）はそうしたものをinteriorityとして包含するべきだとする。アイゼンマンは、diagramにsubjectと批評性を持ち込もうとしたのである。アイゼンマンは、パッラーディオの例を引き合いに出し、批評性の特質であるズラシは、生き生きとした動的な状態で維持されるべきであり、そうした生き生きとした批評性がdiagramとして、objectに留まることを望んだのである。

7-1-6：subjectの問題　subjectとobjectを関係性の中で捉えようとした

アイゼンマンのdiagramは、明確な表現として確立されたものではなく、アイゼンマン自身の解釈によって変動する曖昧なものであった。それは、objectを、subjectとobjectという二項対立的な視点である一方に置くのではなく、objectにsubjectの考えを分有させようとする意識を孕んでいた。すなわち客観性という立場を乗り越えようとするものであった。そのため客観的に外部化されないdiagramとなり、objectの内に閉じ込められたものであると言える。すなわち、subjectと

objectを関係性の中で捉えようとしたアイゼンマン独自のものであった。したがって、アイゼンマンのdiagramは、既存の意識を超越するものであり、限界でもあった。

7-1-7：：デリダの影響

デリダから逸脱したアイゼンマンのchoraの概念とそこから生まれる新しいcontext概念、そしてドゥルーズのevent概念がもたらす時間性を孕んだobject概念。これらが合間って、新しい抑圧のない創造を導き出すのである。

これは従来の場所に対する概念的な変革をもたらし、objectとしてplaceを体現しない、containing（含有する）でもcontained（含有される）でも、insideでもoutでも、frameでもobjectでも、figureでもgroundでもない、spaceの中にmarkingの密集した連続としての過剰な状態を生み出したのである。

場所性という過去及び現在のオリジナルな状況から、objectが弁証法的に立ち現れるのではなく、介在するものをdiagramとして、subjectが思考し創造することで、新たなobjectが過去に接木されるのである。

それらはいずれもsubjectとobjectに対する認識をズラそうとする試行として読み取ることができる。trace概念の分化は、subject/objectに対する視点をどこに向けるのかの違いに他ならない。それをimprintとtraceに区別しながらそれを受容するreceptacleをgridとして、アイゼンマンは建築的に捉え直したのである。

7-1-8：event としての object
ドゥルーズひいてはライプニッツからの影響

アイゼンマンは住宅シリーズ以降、exteriority を取り込み始めた。それは、アイゼンマンに、内的論理だけで独立した不連続なものとして建築が完結することが不可能であるという認識があったからである。そのアイゼンマンの外部と連続させようとする意識は、diagram によって、内的論理と exteriority とを調停する試みとして現れた。

その概念的な背景としては、デリダとの共同によって進化させた subject/object の関係性の概念、すなわち、subject と object が二項対立として区別されるのではなく、連続した関係性の中で捉えることで subject と object の連続性が担保されるものと考えたことである。しかし、そうした subject と object の関係性の論理だけでは、object そのものに対する固定化された見方によって不連続になるという問題が横たわっていた。すなわち、object を閉じたものとして捉えることから脱却する必要があった。その問題を進化させたのは、ドゥルーズが明確に示したライプニッツの object に対する概念であった。

その考えは objectile と呼ばれ、空間の構成とは関係性を持たず、物質の継続的な変化を意味する時間的な変調として、object は event であると主張するのである。ドゥルーズは、「対象はもはや本質的な形態によって定義されるのではなく、パラメーターに枠づけされた曲線族を変化させるものとして純粋な機能性に帰着し、可能な変化の系列と不可分、あるいはこの対象自身が描きだす、可変的な湾曲をもつ表面と不可分である。この新しい対象を対象体（objectile）と呼ぶことにしよう。」と述べている。[註2]

この概念は、観点の変化を生み出す。すなわち、subject への変容を迫るものだった。

アイゼンマンにとって、この継続的な変化は fold の仲介を通して特徴づけられるものであった。

object についての event 概念は、物語の時間または弁証法的な時間とは異なり、そうした時間概念の外部にある時間概念であり、object は、形態によって、固定化されたものとして定義されるものではなく、時間性を孕んだ固定化されえないものであるということである。そのことによって、object そのものが、固定化した form ではなく関係性の連続へと開かれ、呼応していくことが可能になったのである。

その最初の試みが、レブストック計画の fold 概念によるものであった。ドゥルーズの影響を受けたアイゼンマンは従来の不連続な図と地という対立構造から連続する時間性を孕んだ ground（地）へと object を開くことになったのである。

こうしたドゥルーズの objectile（対象体）の概念に影響を受けたアイゼンマンは、生き生きとした今という presentness に、過去と未来という異なる時間を折りたたむのあった。そのことにより、従来の図と地という対立構造を脱却し、それらの境界を曖昧なものにすることによって力動的な連続性を作ることを求めたのであった。

註2）ドゥルーズ『襞』第 2 章 p.34

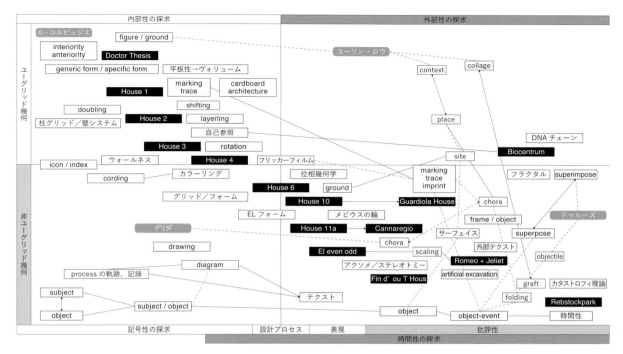

Fig.7-1　アイゼンマンの作品と概念の変遷

7-2：考察

subject と object の変容

7-2-1：subject の歴史

西欧における form とその生成をめぐる議論は、プラトン的イデアとアリストテレスのデュナミス・エネルゲイアの対立から、カント、ゲーテ、ヘーゲル的思考へと発展していく段階と、その二つの根本的な対立の繰り返しである。そうした議論の流れの中で、西欧における建築を製作する subject（主体）は、ルネサンスの時代までは、デミウルゴス的な神の存在であった。

アテネのアクロポリスは、プラトン的イデアとしてのプロポーションが実体として現前しているものであり、プラトンが絵画や彫刻はイデアを二度コピーしているという意味において、建築を最も重要視したことのモデルとしたものである。

ローマのパンテオンは、統合者としての subject（建築家）はいない。それにもかかわらず、単なる光と影というだけではない統合されたシステムがあり、全てがプログラムされ、建築が成立している。ブルネレスキにとっては、イデアがテクノロジー（テクネ）を生み出していく、発展的、生成してい

131

く出発点である。最終的にものになっていく。プログラムは
その間に存在するのである。ドーモはformがテクネによって
成り立っているのであるが、formがテクネを表す場合もある。
テクノロジーは結果であると同時に、人間の欲望を整理し、組
み立てており、プログラム化しているのである。
パースペクティヴの登場は神の視点とパラレルにあり、神の
座から見るという、コントロールの発明であり、subjectがあ
らゆる全ての客観的なobjectを支配するという権力構造の発
見であった。
西欧のパースペクティヴは一点からの支配構造、権力構造をあ
らわす。それは、神の視点を人間が手に入れたことを意味する。
それは人間の欲望が世界の頂点となることを可能にした。ル
ネサンスは神から人間への権力の委譲であった。

7-2-2：diagramは、異なるsubjectの状態に焦点をあてる

既に述べたように、アイゼンマンは、透視図の導入が表現の
パラメーターを変えたことを指摘する。これは、見る人の目
とobjectの間の活発な関係性を、建築のinterioriityへと関係
させたという。ブルネレスキが透視図の形式において数学と物
理学から外部性を導入する一方、アルベルティは、言説に関
する歴史の必然としてのanteriorityの考えを導入したことを
対比しながら、透視図などのような可視的なもののinteriority
への沈殿は、究極的に、diagramの考えに影響を及ぼすという。
例として、ブルネレスキの教会のサン・ローレンツォとサント・
スピリトの二つの違いを採り上げ、diagramが、それらの異なっ
ているsubjectの状態に焦点をあてることでサン・ローレンツォ
とサント・スピリトの違いをはっきりさせることができるとす
る。その二つの視点とは、ひとつは、一点から円錐のビジョン
を介して空間を見ている静的なsubjectを要求するものであり、
もう一つは、動くsubjectを要求するものであった。[註3]

7-2-3：subjectとしての建築家

テクノロジーをどこに使うべきかという問題は、建築の領域
の問題であり、前述の何が選択されるべきかといった問題と
同じところに回帰する。安藤忠雄は機能的に影響を及ぼさな
いスキマの部分；廊下・階段において建築的意義を見出し、
そこを分節し建築化した。近代建築は建築の内部プログラム
にはあまり手をつけていない。というよりはむしろ、機能主
義という全てを極度に抽象化しようとする原理によって、内
部プログラムがかなり限定的なものとして形成され、空間が
つくりあげられていたといえる。そのうちに、こうした抽象
化によって多くのものが排除されたことに気づき始めたのが、
近代の建築家であった。
こうした近代における問題に対して、ミースは、問題がある
とされたモダニズムの均質空間においても、均質化し得ない
空間の可能性を示唆したのであった。不特定多数、顔が見え
ないsubjectを入れ込む均質空間に、対極にある流動性を孕ま
せ、美的に結晶化された究極の姿をつくったのであった。多様
な視線の交差、単純な構成上に流動する人の動き、そうした
人間の多様なアクティヴィティを均質空間へと見事に結晶化
したのであった。それに対して、コールハースはsubjectとい
うところでモダニズムを考えたとも言える。コールハースは、
subjectをオープンにみせることで正統性を表明しようとした。
確かに、コールハースはモダニズムの方向性とは違う方向に
行っているのだが、モダニズムを補強しようとしているのか、
壊そうとしているのか、その態度は中途半端な位置にあると言

註3) Chapter4　p.74,75
註4) セシル・バルモンド（山形 浩生訳）『インフォーマル』TOTO出版、2005年、pp.189-216

える。すなわちミースが飛び越えてしまったものを取り戻そうとしており、モダニズムの価値基準の解体に出発点を見出そうとしている。モダニズムは主流の欲望だけをみて、他は捨象するのが基本的な方向である。従来の計画学では決まり易いようにベクトルを整理する。その提示の仕方の価値基準がモダニズム的なものであり、ある種のヒエラルキーがある。一義に決まる。そうしたモダニズムの価値基準を解体しているのがコールハースであると言えるだろう。価値基準をシャッフルし、一義に決まるのではなく、ヒエラルキーをつけるのではなく、多義化させ、そのうちの一つの特殊解を選択するのである。彼のアプローチは、どんな些細なことでも全部、分析のエレメントとして取り上げてしまう。どんな紙の切れ端でも、誰々の言った言葉など、情報として取り込むのである。コールハースの diagram は、曖昧性としての diagram であり、subject の部分をオープンに入力できるようにしているのである。施工者であったり、クライアントであったり、誰が何をするという主語と述語の関係を問題にするのである。subject をあいまいなオープンなもの、拡散したものにしている。施工も誰が作ってもいいように、勝手に作ってもいいようになっている。建築が生成されるということを subject の問題として扱う。それは subject が開放されていると言い換えてもよい。ここから読み取れるのは、コールハースは現代の建築の中心課題が subject の問題であることに気が付いているということである。したがって一点に向かおうとする統合に執着心がなく、統合への意識がない。subject が多く存在すればそのような方法しかないのである。subject がオープンであり、多義的なものとして扱われ、欲望の拡散を認識しているのである。統合への意識の希薄さは、伝統的な西欧の美の概念をも解体し、美そのものを否定していくのである。

しかし、建築の優位性は、統合に存在するのである。建築家は、その優位性に立って、全てをコントロールするのである。コールハースも同様、建築家の職能として、社会の欲望をコントロールするのである。ただし、対象が異なるのである。可視的な形態ではなく、欲望という不可視なものへと向かう。データスケープというものはデザイアスケープとも言える。そこにコールハースの意義がある。

建築家の頭の中で統合されたイデア /diagram が、全体を織り成すシステムに乗っ取られているのである。建築家の古典的な考えが織物的な新しい考え方に乗っ取られていく。それは、旧来の建築的思考にとって脅威である。建築のイデアからではなく、遺伝子のように、帰納法的にプログラムされる。ユニットが増幅して広がり、つながって増殖し、力が周辺に流れていくように絡み合う織物のように建築が捉えられているのである。遺伝子プログラムの構築力は強力であるからだ。神がイデアを描いたとしても、別の神が駆逐していくのである。
建築が特権的な領域でなくなりつつある。いままでは建築家が建築たるものの基本になるもの（イデア）を核として造っていた（演繹法）が、部分的なシステムから全体が作られる（帰納法）。全能的な決定を下す建築家は存在し得なくなる。そのかわりプログラム自体にイデアと同等とも思われる form が見られるのである。
ここに重要な問題が隠されている。非線形はフィードバックされるものを前提としている。subject すらも分離できない。建築家が統合している form と、プログラムにおける数理としての form の間には、対立、それとも一致があるのか。
事例として、バルモンドとリベスキンドとの協同^{註 4)}では、建築家のイメージだけのアイデアに対しては、バルモンドは建

築家を凌駕している。ただし、これまでは建築家の直観力で多数の可能性の中からの選択が瞬時のうちになされてきた。建築家とプログラムでは、もののつくり方、パースペクティヴが違うのである。プログラムは近接関係の関係性をいかに組み立てるかが重要であり、出来上がるものは予想できない。ところが、建築家は最初に仮定項を置くことで最終形態が予期できるのである。

建築においては、伝統的に制作する subject は一人である。匿名性は subject がたくさんあることとは異なる。署名しない、記名しない、ということは逆説的に、subject は一つあることを仄めかす。
建築は、これまで全てを統合してきた。神の啓示で問題を解決する。イデアがあるような感覚である。それは一個の subject の精神の中で行われている。subject が複数の場合はどうなるのか。みんなが共有観念みたいなものをもつことなのか。
分析をしてこれしかないという解答は一つに決まるわけではない。プログラムは解を出すためのものであり、一つに決めるものではない。一つに決めるというところでレトリックがある。建築家が作家である以上一つに決める、そこに subject としての建築家の役割が残されているのではなかろうか。

翻って、アイゼンマンは新しき未来の設計手法として、diagram を求めた。diagram は建築家というブラックボックスから解放され、抽出された一般的原理によって建築の設計を再構築しようとするものである。diagram は建築家のブラックボックスから生まれた一枚のスケッチを否定しようとする新しい試みであった。しかし、これは新しくはあるが、diagram という図式化によって抽象化しようとすることであり、一枚

のスケッチと同様、いまだ古い過去のモダニズムの呪縛に囚われており、非存在を存在と読み替える詭弁であったと言えよう。
コールハースの diagram やプログラムも同様である。欲望や要件を一つの図式化によって、多義性の中で一つの特殊解を選択すること自体が、一意に集約するということであり、一つの詭弁が存在するのである。

アイゼンマンやコールハースの思考には、object を subject の内的な観念界から取りだし、確固とした基盤のある「外界」での位置を与える態度が見られる。アイゼンマンは object を subject の内的なブラックボックスから取り出すことに成功した。こうして抽出された原理は、subject によって、気ままに出されたものではなく、明確な「思考」によって抽出されたものであり、制作は「法則にしたがって創造する」こととしたのである。しかし、それでも建築家の手によって、subject の「観る」行為から原理が獲得されるというポジションは残している。
subject の「観る」行為によって原理が獲得されることは、制作する subject 自身の存在を信じる立場からは離脱していないのである。さらに原理の絶対性を疑わない。diagram はイデアと同等な存在としてある。そういう意味でアイゼンマンの建築はイデア的制作と言えよう。subject からの離脱までは進んでいるが、イデア性の強い性格が漂うのである。

7-2-4：subject と object の関係
クリステヴァのテクスト理論
テクストの定義は、ジュリア・クリステヴァによって、次の

註5）ジュリア・クリステヴァ（谷口勇訳）『テクストとしての小説』国文社、1985年、0.1.1.1「テクストの概念」より
註6）カンタン・メイヤスー（千葉雅也・大橋完太郎・星野太訳）『有限性の後で―偶然性の必然性についての試論』、人文書院、2016年など

ように明確化された。

テクストとは「直接的な情報を目指すコミュニケーションのための言葉を、それ以前または同時期の様々な言表に関係づけることによって、言語の秩序を再編成する超言語学的装置である。」^{註5)}すなわち、テクストとは従来の書物のように現実に存在し、読者に意味を読み取られるだけの受動的な存在ではなく、読む行為の内に初めて現れ出るものであり、意味の生成なのである。そのことは、従来の subject の存在形式を否定し、新たなテクストの生成の出現であり、新しい subject の生成なのである。つまり、テクストとは object でもなく、限界も持たない関係的存在である。こうしたテクスト概念は subject の解体 / 再構築の可能性を与えるのであり、subject と object との関係を問い直すものであった。

カントの「物自体」とは、現象に対峙する概念であり、現象を発生させる本体とも言える。
カントは、西欧の伝統的思考である超越的概念、すなわち、プラトンのイデア、アリストテレスのエイドスなどは直接知ることができず、こうした超越的概念本体には接近できないとした。
言い換えれば、現象とは、subject によって、subject 内部で構成されるものということである。物自体は現象の裏にあって、直接触れることはできない。subject 内部で現象として構成されるものを通してのみ、間接的に伺い知ることができるとする。

建築においては、現象として現れる以前のものを操作して構成される。そうした構成されるものから空間や建築が現象する。すなわち、全く反対方向のベクトルを持つのである。その方向性の違いは、認識と制作との違いから生まれる。
構成自体が超越的概念であり、その構成を創造するからである。構成とはアリストテレスのエイドスと同値であるといったものである。アリストテレスは、プラトンのイデアという超越的概念を、形相と質料へと、より具体的な概念へと転換したわけだが、建築は、この形相と質料の両者を扱うのである。建築においては、カントが接近できないとしたものに対して、既に接近しているのであり、操作しているのである。そうした行為は、神にのみ与えられた特権であったものである。建築における subject は、神と同位置にいることを策定してきたのである。

すなわち、今日の建築における重要な問題は、subject の問題に他ならないと言える。アイゼンマンやコールハースの議論は、この建築の subject の特権性及び特殊性を巡る議論でもある。それら特権性及び特殊性を前提としながらも、乗り越えようとする姿勢なのである。

7-2-5：思弁的実在論

カントは思考できない超越論的概念を物自体と呼び、subject と object との相関的な関係の中でしか、世界を理解できないとする相関主義の立場をとる。カンタン・メイヤスー^{註6)}は、こうした相関主義を徹底することで、相関主義を脱却し、物自体を思考する可能性を証明しようとする。こうした哲学上の議論は、奇妙にも現代の建築の問題意識と符号する。相関主義とは、認識主体である subject を通して、subject が介在する相関的な関係によってのみ object が存在し、それを思考することができるとする立場である。哲学は、カント以降、この相関主義を前提にしてきたわけで、相関主義を前提にする

ならば、subject が認識できないものは思考できないことになる。すなわち subject の限界を認めながらも、その地位を重視する考え方である。

しかし、建築は、subject の地位を重視し、限界を認めてこなかった。すなわち認識できないことを否定してきたのである。すなわち神と等しい完全なる subject を前提としてきたのである。建築は、subject が全てを認識可能であると信仰してきたのである。全ては、認識可能であり、思考可能であるという特権を、subject である建築家に与えて来たわけである。モダニズムは、その極致と言っても良い。subject の感知できない部分が存在することに目をつぶってきたのである。

グレアム・ハーマンのオブジェクト指向存在論^{註7)}は、subject の知らないことの何かが原因で偶然の出来事は必ず起こるとする。すなわち偶然性の必然性。この世界は偶然に支配されているのである。とする意識を持つ。あらゆる対象は存在論的に等価であり、object も subject も全てが対等の関係にある。あらゆる object はひきこもって存在している。object と object の間には何の関係もない。こうした発想が、建築には欠如していたのである。

現代哲学における subject 中心主義から object 中心主義への動き。現代における建築の意識は、こうした流れに呼応する。アイゼンマンやコールハースの議論を、こうした流れの中で理解するべきであろう。彼らの議論は、subject 中心主義から object 中心主義へと向かう移行期において、重要なものと位置づけることができる。しかし建築における object 中心主義は、間違っても、単なる object 的な建築をつくることではない。subject と object との関係を見直すことが重要なのである。多くの小世界は存在するが、それら全てを包摂する一つの世界は存在しないのである。建築は、今まで全てを包摂する一つ

の世界をあまりにも過剰に信じてきたのである。

重要なことは、観点の一極化への執着からの脱却である。ドゥルーズが明確に指摘したように、object を固定化して観た時、subject も固定化されてしまうということである。すなわち、object と subject とはそのように相互に関係しているのである。誤解のないように付言するならば、こうした相互関係は相関主義と直接的に結びつくものではない。人間の意識を普遍的で固定的な一存在形式としてみるのではなく、いろいろな観点の集合として観なければならないということである。ライプニッツは、そのことに気づいていた。円錐形の例で理解できるように、一点の焦点から拡がる数学的モデルとしての円錐形空間は、その切り口によって、円、楕円、放物線、双曲線など様々な曲線族を包摂する。すなわち、その焦点からは、そうした曲線族を眺める事ができる（眺めることしかできない）のである。しかし別の焦点から出発する円錐形空間においては、それとは別の曲線群を眺めることができる。すなわち、それらが観る世界は異なるのである。すなわち、人間の意識とは、トータルなものではなく、こうした個々の観点から成り立っているのであり、観られる object ごとに、異なる観点が与えられるのである。すなわち、それが subject に他ならない。こうした object からの流れが subject を規定するのである。さすれば、object をパラメトリックに多様に変化させれば、多様な観点、すなわち多様な subject が求められるのである。基本的にアーキテクチャーは、語源からもわかるように、テクノロジーの問題を孕んでいる。subject の地位を重視し、限界を認めてこなかったアーキテクチャーは、テクノロジーが object の支配へと向かう。その結果、人間を凌駕する存在として、逆に人間の存在を蝕むものとなる可能性を孕む。ますます人間から離脱していき、人間自体を抑圧していくのである。

註7) グレアム・ハーマン（岡嶋隆佑監訳、山下智弘、鈴木優花、石井雅巳訳）『四方対象：オブジェクト指向存在論入門』人文書院、2017 年
註8) Chapter6 119

コンピューテーション・テクノロジーは諸刃の刃であり両義的な問題を孕んでいる。こうした問題には、subject-object の問題が潜んでいる。今後、重要な問題として浮上するであろう。われわれは、こうした subject と object の問題を真剣に思考しなければならない時期に来ているのである。

7-3：考察
場所性の変容

近代建築が捨象したとする場所性、ゲニウス・ロキ、身体性というものの復権が正統なものとして謳われるが。これもまた、コールハース的な視点に立てば、個別化を過大評価した、矮小化された個別で私的な身体性や、既に解体されてしまったゲニウス・ロキの亡霊に、未だしがみついているだけにすぎないとも言える。現代において場所性は変容していると思われる。こうした場所性を巡る問題を考察する。

7-3-1：コンテクストの問題

モダニズムによって生まれた空間概念では、もはや現代社会の流動する混沌としたエネルギーを含むことができなくなりつつある。社会は急速な加速度で進化し、われわれの空間の性質を変えていく。柱梁のグリッド構造で生成される空間システムは急速に社会への適用性を失いつつある。現代文明が過剰なベクトルに向かって動く限り、こうした特質は加速度的に進行していくだろう。いろいろなエクリチュールの相互作用の中で、境界を越えて流動するエネルギーは、速度を得て、距離を縮小させていく。今日、古典的な「場所」の概念は溶解し、旧来のコンテクストという語はその意味を失ってしまっ

た。はるかに離れたものどうしが結合する。そのため、遠近、内外、定点と動点という二項対立は崩壊する。これまで建物は、その近傍の環境との関係から生じ、コンテクストに基づくハーモニーを得ていた。コンテクストは最も高いプライオリティーをもっていたのである。しかし、現代建築では、このヒエラルキーは崩壊しつつある。もはや近傍は、遠隔に対する優勢をもたない。位置の逆転現象が起こり、遠近の相互接続がおこなわれつつある。この不可視のエネルギーは都市の潜在性に変形を与え、都市を莫大なエネルギーの充満した場へと向かわせる。こうした流動するエネルギーに対応できるように、建築は固定化された機能を含むソリッドから柔らかく適合できる器官へと、その性質を変えなければならない。アイゼンマンは、この問題に切り込んだのである。それもコーリン・ロウのように単純に既存の文脈にあるものを浮上させるのではなかった。

アイゼンマンは、自身の chora の概念が、コンテクスチャリズムにおける硬直した場所性を超え、多様な価値を汲み取る状況を生み出したことを強調する。アイゼンマンは以下のように述べている。

「ロウの教義は、主としてゲシュタルトの現象学に基づき、object を具象化し、それに現前を与える。一方で、chora は、現前を不安定にし、転覆することを試みる。その存在を不安定にするために chora は、既に与えられているものを見いだす。重要なのはオリジナルのマテリアルではなく、むしろそれらがいかに扱われるかである。chora は、place の価値における偶発性と因襲性をさらけ出すが、それを無効にしない。むしろ、もはや解決と関係なく、弁証法的でもない多価値的な範囲内で活発になることを許すものである。」註8)

また、アイゼンマンは、現在において、科学は、人が自然を克服すること（人／自然）から、人が知識を克服すること（人／知識）へとシフトしたとして、情報化時代の place の役割を示唆するのである。そこでは、place の伝統的な形式の破壊すなわち、伝統的な figure/ground と frame/object のカテゴリーの破壊が起きてきたという。そうした時代において、新たに投入される建築は、place を変容させるものとなる。現代の建築は place を変容させるポテンシャルを持っているのである。place は古典的な立場を保有することができなくなりつつあるのだ。投入された object は、place を変質させるのである。さらに、そうした状況を超えて、現実空間におけるあらゆるものをデジタルツインで置換しようとするのである。

アイゼンマンが示唆するように、もはや、われわれは、古典的な場所性の上には存在しない。place は、ありとあらゆるコンテクストの上に成立する存在として理解しなければならなくなる。自然と対峙した過去の時代を超えて、ヴァーチャルな世界と対峙する状況へと、さらに、都市の object 群を超えて、距離を超越した人類の知の総体であるミラーワールドと対峙する時代へと向かっているのだ。こうしたコンテクストの読み替えは、ますます重要になっていくであろう。architecture の本来としての役目が問われる時代にあるのだ。

7-4：考察
モダニズムが抱えた問題

モダニズムが抱えた問題は、西欧の思考自身が内部にもつ問題である。すなわち建築の生成において、限定的解決による取りこぼされたもの、捨象された様々なベクトルの存在が抑圧をもたらしたことである。逆説的に言えば、モダニズムは、

こうした限定的解釈という微妙な立ち位置にあるがゆえに、完結された object を提示でき、その力強さを発揮できたのである。

限定的解決による取りこぼされたもの、捨象されたものを汲み上げようとしたのが、アイゼンマンやコールハースであった。コールハースは排除されるものを無くすことを目的として、関連する多くのデータを扱い、分析し、プログラムに積極的に関わろうとすることを見た。アイゼンマンの建築から読み取れるのは、完全性・全体性・統合性の破れである。アイゼンマンは建築の interiority を強く信じ、永遠なる原理を追求するという西欧の伝統的枠組みである統合性を維持する。しかし、アイゼンマンは、全てに原理が及ぶという統合性を求めながらも、全体の統合性を求めることの不可能性を証明してしまった。そうした統合性を求めることの不可能性を回避する道を、diagram に求め、subject を object である作品に滑り込ませるのである。いわば subject と object を融合させるのである。

逆にコールハースは、もう一つの西欧の伝統的枠組みを継承する。それは不可視な実体というものを認めない考え方であり、多くのものを可視化させ、新たな実体として拡張することである。原理によって成立する内部性に対しては、不可視なものとして黙殺し、その実体を認めない態度を取る。彼は、建築を反転させるのである。可視的な建築形態に囚われるのではなく、建築が孕むべき不可視な情報を表に出すために、建築に内部化されるべき情報を反転させ、外部化させることによって、情報や条件を明らかにし、関係式として可視化させ、実体化させ、整理し操作をおこなう。コールハースのダイアグラムはそうしたものとして現れる。そして、整理が終われば、それを再び形式・形態へと反転させることで、タンジブルな

註9）DD p.29,l9-l24（筆者翻訳）

建築のエレメントへと変換させ、建築として成立させるという二重の転換をおこなうのである。いわば object の反転の手法である。コールハースにとって建築はもはや、内在する原理により成立する形式ではない。実体として存在する条件や情報の現れそのものなのである。そうした態度によって、西欧の伝統的で硬直したトータリティ重視の思考から抜け出そうとしたのである。

モダニズムが瓦解し、ポストモダニズムの喧噪が過ぎ去った後、建築の批評性は、内部化と外部化に二分されたかのようである。すなわち、アイゼンマンやジェフリー・キプニスの批評性を建築の内部へと向かわせようとする姿勢と、コールハースによる西欧の伝統的批評性のあり方を無視した、いわば外部化する二つの方向とに分けられるものと思われる。

現在、建築は、こうした批評性の二つの方向の間に存在しているものと思われる。われわれは、この乖離した二つの立場を克服しなければならない。新たな批評性の位置を定めることが求められているのだ。

7-5：考察
ニューテクノロジーへの展望
7-5-1：プログラムへの移行

アイゼンマンはこうした次世代の diagram の概念について以下のように認識している。

"diagram は一見本質的な道具であると見なされるという理解に対して反発しつつ、新しいコンピューター技術と、師の世代に対するエディプスの不安から逃れたいという欲望とによって刺激されている新しい世代は、今日、新しい理論を提案しつ

つある。その理論は、『機械的な力の連続』としての diagram に関するフーコーの改鋳を巡るジル・ドゥルーズによる解釈に部分的に基づき、そして、新しい世代がもつサイバネティクスの妄想に部分的に基づく diagram の理論である。彼らの議論を通して、diagram は新規なるものの解釈におけるキーワードとなったのである。こうした問いかけは、diagram に関する伝統的な幾何学的基盤と建築の沈殿した歴史の両方に挑戦している。そうすることで、彼らは、建築の anteriority もしくは interiority への diagram のいかなる関係をも問いかけている。"註9)

既に見たように、アイゼンマンは建築の interiority には、建築の anteriority（先在性）と呼ばれうる先行する全ての建築についての蓄積された知識であるアプリオリな歴史も存在するという。この歴史が建築の言説に意味を与えることは、異なる時期で使われるトロープスとレトリックの蓄積であり、アイゼンマンは、建築の interiority と anteriority が欠落したものとして、コンピューティング・プログラムを批判する。すなわち、今日、たとえば、コンピューティング・プログラムには、こうした歴史の知識はない。それは、建築・構成的に見える状況の例証を生み出すことが出来るだけである。建築のこれら以前の状況が、デザインのいかなるプロセスの一部でもないならば、批評性は存在しえない。先立ったものを知るための反復と、歴史を変えることができるための相違の両方の可能性から、批評性は発展する。それは、コンピューター上におけるモデリング形態もしくは手によるランダムな形態は、この anteriority を考慮しない点で、損なわれている。これらの方法が生成するものは、個々の表現のフォームである。唯一なものは、個別のもしくはユニークな表現とは似ていな

い。唯一なものが反復とこのような anteriority を含むという意味で。反復は、ここで繰り返される何かを含意する。この反復以外の建築の anteriority は、批評的であるために、同じことの反復より、むしろ差異の反復である。唯一なものは、建築が、常に現在において存在し、過去における明示とは異なるようにさせる。この過去は、建築の interiority において明白であるような anteriority であるとアイゼンマンは言う。[註 10]

近代建築は「機能」対「form」や「原理」対「form」といった二項対立を前提としていた。そして「機能」や「原理」を上位として位置づけ、「form」を下位に位置づけてきた。そうした垂直的で決定論的な立場は、未来に向けての無数の可能性を抑圧してしまう。
われわれは、こうした「ベクトル場」を硬直させることなく、柔軟に、旧来の「ベクトル場」を再定義しなければならない。それは、単に個々の表現の form を求めるのではなく、anteriority を考慮しなければならない。われわれは、知の総体から、批評性を持って立ち現れる建築を求めなければならないのだ。

7-5-2：コンピュテーション・プログラムへの移行過程におけるアイゼンマンの diagram の位置づけ

アイゼンマンの初期作品における自己参照システムには、外部参照形態を導入しようとする subject の直接性、すなわち subject の直接的意図を排除しようとしている事がうかがわれる。しかし、後期においては、外部参照形態を導入しようとするが、subject の直接の操作ではなく、object への diagram の挿入という形式をとる。ユークリッド幾何学を超えて、

folding という位相幾何学的グリッドへと向かうのである。
こうしたアイゼンマンの、形態操作は、表面上の形象から、単純にその後のアルゴリズム・プログラムへと継承されていくのである。
すなわち、subject が直接行っていた思慮深い複雑な操作を、単純なコンピューティング・プログラムとして単純に外部化させる方向へと向かわせる影響を、皮肉なことに逆説的にアイゼンマンは次世代に与えてしまったのである。

7-5-3：Quantumetric・RoboTectonic

グレアム・ハーマンのオブジェクト指向存在論は、object 自身が subject の呪縛から離れて、独自に存在し、活動する立場である。その先には、独自に生成することが隠されている。以下、そうした観点から考察を試みたい。[註 11]
diagram は世界の図像化でもあり、複雑な事象の抽象化でもあった。直観的意識に作用する図像学とも言える。直観的認識によって、世界を切り取り、その断面を開示させるものとしての diagram の歴史的意義を述べる必要がある。カントが言うようにアプリオリにそうしたものが人間には備わっている。われわれの頭の中にあるものは現実に必ず存在するという主義のもとに、この diagram は急速に力を持ち始める。プログラムは、つくること、すなわち制作へ向けて、あらゆる情報を統合していくこと全てを意味するものであるが、逆にdiagram は世界の認識を示し、複雑で絡み合った情報を整理する行為を意味する。さらには、整理を超えて、世界そのものを解釈し、変容させる魔力をもっていると言えるかもしれない。そうした整理過程で作家の意思が込められ、世界を作家の意思のもとに捻じ曲げることが可能だからだ。世界を切り取る

註 10）既出、4-2-4 註 15）
註 11）グレアム・ハーマン『四方対象：オブジェクト指向存在論入門』人文書院、2017 など
註 12）レイ・カーツワイル『ポスト・ヒューマン誕生 コンピュータが人類の知性を超えるとき』NHK 出版、2007

静的な断面を開くものとしての diagram。問題は静的であることであった。常に動きの変容していく世界を、静的なスクリーンによって切断することの問題性は存在しないのか。客観的観察者を装い、制作者の意思を忍び込ませること。制作において、この問題は重要と思われる。

アルゴリズムは、コンピューターが実行できるよう、人間が与える指示の集合である。その際、まるで人間が解決するかのごとく問題を記述することもできる。またコンピューターが問題を理解できるように記述することもできる。

言語的に明確にして記述するということは、問題のステップを記述するだけに留まらず、その後の処理において他の「エージェント」と解をやりとりすることの可能性を開いている。コンピューターの世界で、エージェントはコンピューターそのものである。アルゴリズムとは、人間の思考とコンピューターの計算能力の媒介役であるといえる。このような通訳としての役割を果たすアルゴリズムには、2つの側面がある。ある面では、どのように問題を解決するかをコンピューターに指示する手段となり、そしてもう一面では、アルゴリズムという形式へ変換された人間の思考となる。

アイゼンマンの時代においては、object に格納することが求められたが、近い将来、量子コンピューターや高度なネットワーク化、AI の到来により、singularity[註 12] を超える環境が訪れることが予想されている。こうした未来においては、subject と object の間に更なる介在する存在（エージェント）が出現することが予想される。そうした存在を否定することはできないであろう。むしろ積極的に創造過程に組み込むべきであろう。こうした方向に、アイゼンマンが、未来の扉を開いたことは事実である。

将来、volume が粒子として細分され、知能を持ったエージェントがそれらを構成する形式、すなわち、quantumetric が行われるだろう。その前段階においては、知能を持ったセグメントによって構成された segmentmetric が行われる。そうした一連の流れは RoboTectonic によって行われる。私の研究室の活動はこうした方向を予測する上で行われてきた。

最後に

デリダは、ロゴス中心主義を攻撃し、西欧の思考の枠組み自身を解体しようとした。

西欧の考え方が世界の中心ではなく、西欧中心のヒエラルキーを解体し再構築するものであった。しかし、実は、この運動の根底には、西欧こそが中心であるという隠された企てが存在するのである。

これまでの西欧の建築の思想には、幾何学に観念的イデアを投影し、その世界観を現出するものであるべきという信念があった。こうした幾何学による form の形成は、すべての人々に共有可能で、普遍性を求めるものである。しかし、自己言及的なもので、トートロジーそのものであり、新たな創造を抑圧するものであった。

すなわち、純粋幾何学の均質性に頼り、ニュートン的な思考へと陥ったのであった。こうした普遍的幾何学は、カルテジアン・グリッドにおける延長概念の情報さえあれば、あらゆるものは生成でき、万人に共有可能なものであると過信した。それは世界を均質化し、効率性を求めるがあまり、多様性を排除する思考であったのである。

すなわち、こうした思考においては、現実世界が持つ細やか

な差異を汲みあげることはできず、そうした差異は捨象され、同一な幾何学的モデルへと回収されてしまう。こうした現実の細やかな差異を、普遍的幾何学という固定的なトータリテイの観点から決定するのではなく、決定システムにおいて、本来はあらゆる多様性を回収する柔軟性が求められるべきだったのである。

建築における時間概念の導入は、コンピューター・テクノロジーによって試みられた。人や車などのサーキュレーションを、仮想空間内における流動性として設定し、建築をパラメトリックに決定したことである。以前の設計プロセスにおいては、コンピューターの演算能力の問題もあって、そうした都市における流動的アクティビティを、デザインに直接反映させることは困難であった。subject がそのような要素を直観的に解釈し、それにしたがって、デザインに反映させる必要があり、優れた天才性が求められたのである。結果、強烈な個性と恣意性が強く残ることになる。そのような要素を数値的なパラメータとして変換し、デザインへの反映を建築家による操作ではなく、コンピューターによる生成プロセスに任せたのである。このことは、コンピューターを第二の神として位置づけることの危険性を孕んでいる。

建築において、そのような普遍的な幾何学モデルは常に身体の問題に結び付けられていたウィトルウィウス的世界観に辿り着く。ウィトルウィウスは、建築を人間の身体に見立て、対称性やヒエラルキーを持ち、適切なプロポーションをもったものであるべきだとした。そのため建築の interiority は外部と明確な境界を持ち、exteriority からは影響を受けない自律的なものであると考えていたのである。

アイゼンマンは、exteriority と interiority との連続は、モチベーションを共通項とすることによって可能とした。ここに初めて、外部からの影響を全く受けない自律的なウィトルウィウスの古典的身体像を超えたとも言える。内部と外部の連続が生まれた契機である。

さらに、ポストアイゼンマンにおいては、古典的ウィトルウィウス的身体像をさらに超えようと加速させる。すなわち、外部環境における時間性が内在化していくことを通して、身体が連続的に変形していくとすると考え方である。こうした理論には普遍的な幾何学モデルからの脱却の意志がある。

私の研究室では、ウィトルウィウス的身体性が解体することを前提に研究が進められている。すなわち脳波や身体的電気信号など身体内部の情報をセンシングすることによって、身体内部は外部へとシームレスに連続していくことが可能になりつつある。

観察者 subject の存在は重要である。ポストアイゼンマンにおけるプログラム原理主義者は、全てをプログラムによって object を支配しようとする傾向がある。一切の subject を排除しようとしたのである。しかし、能動的ポテンシャルが object 自身に元から備わっているとしても、外部の観察者である subject の存在によって、変容される関係性は担保されねばならない。subject と object は相互に関係する存在であるべきものなのである。

時間性や運動は、仮想空間内での設計プロセスにおいてのみ存在するだけでなく、最終的に決定されたデザインや建設さ

れたものにも運動性が存在するべきである。そういう意味で、私は「しなやかに流動する建築」を提案する。

アイゼンマンは、object の表層構造の奥に深層構造が存在しているとした。アイゼンマンは、こうした深層構造における関係性を探求し、過去の anteriority から浮かび上がるもので構成された diagram が object を生成するとした。すなわち、アイゼンマンにとって、object とは、深層構造そのものであり、diagram が格納されたものとして、subject を分有するものとして位置付けられていた。
その後、ポストアイゼンマンのプログラム原理主義者は、そうした深層構造を表に出し、誰にでも操作可能なパラメトリック的装置として扱い始めた。アイゼンマンは、深層構造は秘技的なものとして扱い、それを理解できる知性を持つ subject の存在に固執していたが、ポストアイゼンマンの建築家達は、そうした subject を否定し、オープンな subject として変質させ、誰にでも触れるものとして扱い始めたのである。それはコールハースの意識に通じる流れでもある。結果、subject の矮小化と劣化を招く可能性を開いてしまった。
object の個々の単品生産ではなく、object にパラメータを内包させたパッケージとして生産する可能性も開きつつある。これらのパラメータを変えることによって、様々なヴァリエーションをもった object を生み出そうとするのである。このことにより object は関数的な連続性を確保することになる。この考え方は、object が固定したものではなく、連続体の流動性における一つの様相にしか過ぎないとしたサンフォード・クウィンターの考えとも、その原点であるドゥルーズの時間性を孕む object 概念に通じるものである。それは、ル・コルビュジエが、volume を固体ではないとおぼろげに定義したことへ

と回帰するものである。

このようにポストアイゼンマンにおいては、アイゼンマンの思想は、デジタル・テクノロジーの活用によって発展し、多様なヴァリエーションを生み出すパラメトリック・デザインとして、建築デザインの手法として定着することになる。

それを超えて、ミラーワールドの一方のリアルワールドも RoboTectonic のテクノロジーによって変容するようになる可能性を開いている。

しかし、翻って、現在のテクノロジーは、生き生きとした人間を抹消することで成立していることを忘れてはいけない。すなわち人間の合理的な理性のみを通して世界を把握し、そのもとに人間を支配することを容認しているのである。世界をロゴスの支配する神の作品と見る西欧的世界観の継承であり、世界の存在と現前とが一致するという西欧的信念に基づいた伝統的な形而上学の継承であるとも言える。
前述したが、subject の地位を重視し、限界を認めてこなかったアーキテクチャーは、テクノロジーが object を強大に支配するであろう。その結果、人間を凌駕する存在として、逆に人間の存在を蝕むものとなる危険性を孕む。逆に人間自体を抑圧していくのである。テクノロジーは諸刃の刃であり両義的な問題を孕んでいる。今後、重要な問題として浮上するであろう。われわれは、こうした subject と object の問題を塾考しなければならない時期にきているのである。こうした議論無くして、テクノロジーを盲信して、subject を排除することこそが、危機的状況となって、われわれの身に降りかかってくることを危惧するものである。

ドゥルーズの思想は新しい時代を開いた。建築の在り方は大きく変容した。その目覚ましい発展と共に別の面を見せるのである。全てのヒエラルキーや境界が消失し、連続するという哲学である。ドゥルーズの思想は、あらゆるものの、流動的に連続してゆくという世界像に対応したものとして解釈されていた。つまり、多様な要素が個別に自律しているのではなく、それぞれの多様性を保ちながらヒエラルキーを排して等価に接続され、連続的なシステムの中に共存する意識である。次世代の建築家たちは、こうした意識に後押しされて自身の思想を構築していった。

しかし、それは幻想でもある。単純であるがゆえに非常に危険な思想でもある。「ヒエラルキーが排され、等価に」というところにレトリックが存在する。そういう意識を利用する誰かわからぬ subject の存在が見え隠れする。結果、各地域の文化を破壊していく危険性が潜んでいる。この意識とコンピューター・テクノロジーの結合は、既に金融の世界では、世界を危機に貶めつつある。建築の分野でも、こうした意識に飛びつく者達も出現した。そのため、新しい美学は出現したが、混乱と矛盾を引き起こしつつある。

アイゼンマン用語集

interiority（内部性、内在性）
exteriority との対概念であり、内部にあるものと内部に存在していることの両方を意味する。ここでは特に、建築の内部性を明示するものであり、建築の内部に存在している蓄積された全ての先在する知識でもある共時的概念。

anteriority（先在性）
先在する歴史上における全ての知の総体とも言える通時的概念。

diagram
diagram はプランではなく、静的な実体でもなく、新しい形を生み出す潜在能力として、建築の interiority と anteriority の上に流れる、一連のエネルギーとして考えられるもの。建築の interiority を明瞭に表現するための、ひとつの潜在的手段。固定的なタイポロジーが抑圧として object に現前することに対して、標準化以前にある固定化しない表現。

presentness（プレゼントネス）
デリダが提示した presence（現前）と absence（不在）の二項対立に対して、その間の、標準化され固定化されない状態としてアイゼンマンが提起した造語。

subject - object
subject（主体）、object（もの）という二項対立としての認識の前提を疑い、両者の関係性を問う概念

form
視覚的に目に見える形に対して使われる figure（図）や shape（形）と区別され、視覚的に見えるもの（形態）としてだけではないどちらかというと形式に近い意味で使われている。

form system
言語のようにヴォキャブラリーとシンタックスからなるシステムとして、三次元的な form を volume 概念で定義したもの

volume
三次元的な form であり、中立的でエネルギーを持たない space とは区別され、space の範疇の中にありながら、動的な性格を帯びるもの。

space
内的なエネルギーを持たない中立で静的な場であり、ここから volumetric によって volume が抽出される。

volumetric
建築表現の基礎となる volume を与える方法であり、マッス・サーフェイスシステムとムーヴメントシステムがあるとする。

movement
volume における動的な性格。

generic form（一般的なフォーム）
美的な嗜好性を超えた超越性を認め、普遍的性質をもつプラトン的なもの。

specific form（具体的なフォーム）

generic form が個別に変形、変容したもの。

線形的（linear）form

generic form のカテゴリーの一つ。form の持つ固有の力学として方向性を有したもの。

重心的（centroidal）form

generic form のカテゴリーの一つ。form の持つ固有の力学として中心性を有したもの。

deep structure（深層構造）

建築の内部性における明瞭な表現の関係の本質および構造。

instrumentality（媒介）

絵画や彫刻とちがい、建築は人が直接的に利用する道具のような媒介性を有したものであるということ。

iconicity（類像性）

統語論において、「言語は世界を写し出す」性質を iconicity と呼ぶ。形式と意味には何らかの関連性があり、ここでは絵画・彫刻と建築との違いにおいて、建築独自の関係性としての instrumentality が、形式と意味の間に介在していることをアイゼンマンは述べている。

wallness（壁性）

object のマテリオリティ（物質性）、その機能と意味を克服するため、line、plane、volume という形態に還元することで、物質性を消し去り、柱、壁という記号としての区別も消し去っ
たもの。この壁性という概念は、絵画や彫刻との違いとして、平面性と対比して定義している。

exteriority（外部性、外在性）

interiority の外部にあるものと外部に存在することを示す。アイゼンマンの diagram における exteriority の探究では、Site、Texts、Mathematics、Science などを外部参照としている。

el form（エルフォーム）

立方体の一点から相似な立方体の欠きとられた形。interiority の探究の結果として exteriority の探究では、初期条件として与えられる form。

superposition（重ね合せ）

ドゥルーズの superimposition とは異なり、階層性のない重ね合わせのことを言う。スケールの変化や回転、ズラシといった手法。

place（場所）

具体的な機能や中立的な外部性ではなく、モチベーションをもった外部性として浮上してくる場所。object ではなく、space の中の marking の密集した連続としての過剰な状態。

site

いわゆる具体的な建築の立地する敷地ではなく、建築の立地している場（field）として、建築の外部性の探究における、最も初期的な与件となるもの。place（場所）でもあり、ground（地）でもある。

ground（大地、地）

site に建つ建物を figure（図）としてとらえた場合に、ground（地）としての大地であり、アイゼンマンは、場所や ground（地）がモチベーションという affect（情動）をもっているがゆえに、diagram の成立する根拠となりうることを前提に建築の内部性を拡張させている。また、ground（地）のサーフェイス（表面）を人為的につくられた人工的なものとして概念化することで、建築と同様な操作の対象とし、伝統的な figure（図）と ground（地）の概念を乗り越えることが試みられている。

registration（登録）

中立的な事象の堆積としてではなく、欲望という方向性を有した affect（情動）によって、歴史性に参画すること。

chora（コーラ）

プラトンのティマイオスの receptacle（chora）の定義についてのデリダとの解釈の違いとして、三次元的な対立項としての container（容器）/ contained（内容）、place（場所）/ field（場）、frame / object の相互関係として建築における再概念化をしたもの。

mark　marking

プロポーションや数比といった審美的な要素や、機能的な要素による分節。

imprint（刻印）

モチベーションを持った能動体によって receptacle（受容体）に及ぼされる影響。

trace（痕跡）

imprint を及ぼした能動体に対して、receptacle（受容体）から及ぼされる影響の跡。

receptacle（受容体）

それ自体の物質の存在なしで、他の object の形状を変えるだけではなく、絶えず形状を変更する潜在性を持った一つの構築。

grid

ground（地）の抽象性として考えられ、receptacle のようなものとして変形や変容を受容するものであり、imprint や trace によって顕在化するもの。

graft（接木）

コラージュとは異なり、新しいものと古いものの間のシームレスな接続であり、古いものと新しいもののアマルガムにするために追加されたものの境界もしくはフレームを消去しようとすること。

the fold（折り）folding（折りたたむこと）fold（折りたたみ）

superposition（重ね合わせ）が図と地を同時に保有することに対して、地のない平滑な深さを供給すること。折り紙は線形であることに対して、非線形で同時的であり、新旧の間を graft（接木）し、スムーズな移行とともに、新旧のエッジに新たな次元を与えている。

object event

ドゥルーズの objectile の概念を解釈し、固定化した永続的な

object ではなく、物質の継続的な変化を意味する時間的な変調としての object 群。この場合の時間は、線形的に流れる時間ではなく、同時的、共時的、通時的な時間の混在したものとして、fold の仲介を通して特徴づけられるものとしている。

critique（批評）

建築の唯一性のために、interiority と anteriority とを前提とし、差異の反復を生み出すためのモチベーションのようなものであり、標準化や典型化への抵抗として、ズラシや不安定化として現れるもの。

参考文献一覧

建築家や建築思想、哲学など、項目ごとに本文で直接参照しているものから、内容に関わりのあるものを筆者の判断で並べている。

近代建築

- Le Corbusier & P. Jeanneret, Œuvre complète publiée par Willy Boesiger et Oscar Stonorov, Les Editions d'Architecture Artémis, 1974, （邦訳）ウィリ・ボジガー編（吉阪隆正訳）『ル・コルビュジエ全作品集』A.D.A EDITA Tokyo、1977 年
- ル・コルビュジエ － ソーニエ（樋口清訳）『建築へ』中央公論美術出版、2003 年
- ル・コルビュジエ（井田安弘・芝優子訳）『プレシジョン―新世界を拓く建築と都市計画（上）、（下）』鹿島出版会，1984 年
- ジェフリー・ベイカー、（小野節夫訳）『ル・コルビュジエの建築―その形態分析』鹿島出版会、2007 年
- 「ジュゼッペ・テラーニ特集」『建築文化』彰国社、1998 年 5 月号
- ルイス・カーン（前田忠直編）『ルイス・カーン建築論集』鹿島出版会、1993 年
- 八束はじめ『ロシア・アヴァンギャルド建築（INAX 叢書 8）』INAX、1993 年
- 八束はじめ『希望の空間：ロシア・アヴァンギャルドの都市と住宅』住まいの図書館出版局、1988 年

ピーター・アイゼンマン

- Peter Eisenman, The Formal Basis of Modern Architecture, Lars Muller, 2006 (DT)
- Peter Eisenman, Diagram Diaries(Universe Architecture Series), Thames and Hudson, 1999 (DD)
- Peter Eisenman, Written into the Void: Selected Writings 1990-2004, Yale University Press, 2007 (WV)
- Peter Eisenman, Eisenman Inside Out: Selected Writings, 1963-1988, Yale University Press, 2004 (IO)
- Peter Eisenman, House X, Rizzoli, 1983
- Peter Eisenman, Peter Eisenman House of Cards, Oxford University Press, 1987
- 『ピーター・アイゼンマン特集』A+U、1980 年 1 月
- 山口隆「近代建築におけるプログラム的空間生成の萌芽」『建築設計 06』日本建築設計学会、2018 年、pp.85-92
- 山口隆「ピーター・アイゼンマンのダイアグラムに関する考察」『論考　建築設計 03』日本建築設計学会、2018 年、pp.3-8
- Eisenman Peter、Levrat Frederic（桜井 義夫訳）「ピーター・アイゼンマン (デジタル・ア - キテクチャーの可能性 < 特集 >)-(デジタル・ア - キテクチュアへの視線)」『SD (369)』1995-06、pp.18-21

レム・コールハース

- Rem Koolhaas, Delirious New York: A Retroactive Manifesto for Manhattan, The Monacelli Press, 1994 (DN)、（邦訳）レム・コールハース（鈴木圭介訳）『錯乱のニューヨーク』筑摩書房、1995 年
- Rem Koolhaas, Bruce Mau, Hans Werlemann, S M L XL 2nd Edition, The Monacelli Press, 1997 (SL)、（邦訳）レム・コールハース（太田佳代子，渡辺佐智江訳）『S, M, L, XL+ : 現代都市をめぐるエッセイ』筑摩書房、2015 年
- レム・コールハース『OMA@work.a+u』A+U、2000 年 5 月臨時増刊
- レム・コールハース、ハンス・ウルリッヒ・オブリスト（瀧口 範子訳）『コールハースは語る』筑摩書房、2008 年
- Bart Lootsma, "Reality Bytes: The Meaning of. Research in the Second Modern Age", Daidalos, 69/70 (December 1998/January 1999), pp.8-21
- 山口隆「レム・コールハースの並置概念の考察」『論考　建築設計 03』日本建築設計学会、2018 年、pp.9-14
- 五十嵐太郎、南泰裕編『レム・コールハースは何を変えたのか』鹿島出版会、2014 年

現代建築

- Anthony Burke ed. Therese Tierney ed. Network Practices; New Strategies in Architecture and Design, Princeton Architectural Press, 2012,（邦訳）アンソニー・バーク、テレーズ・ティアニー編（山口隆訳）『ネットワークプラクティス：建築とデザインにおける新たな戦略』鹿島出版会、2014 年
- Kostas Terzidis, Algorithmic Architecture, Elsevier Ltd. 2006,（邦訳）コスタス・テルジス『アルゴリズミック・アーキテクチュア』彰国社、2010 年
- セシル・バルモンド（山形浩生訳）『インフォーマル』TOTO 出版、2005 年
- Rafael Moneo, Theoretical Anxiety and Design Strategies in the Work of Eight Contemporary Architects, MIT Press, 2005,（邦訳）ラファエル・モネオ『現代建築家 8 人の設計戦略と理論の探究』A+U、2008 年 6 月臨時増刊
- Adrian Forty, Words and Buildings: A Vocabulary of Modern Architecture, Thames & Hudson, 2000,（邦訳）エイドリアン・フォーティー（坂牛卓他監）『言葉と建築：語彙体系としてのモダニズム』鹿島出版会、2006 年
- Bernard Tschumi, Architecture and Disjunction, MIT Press, 1996,（邦訳）ベルナール・チュミ（山形浩生訳）『建築と断絶』鹿島出版会、1996 年
- Jesse Reiser, Nanako Umemoto, Atlas of Novel Tectonics, Princeton Architectural Pr., 2006,（邦訳）ライザー＋ウメモト（隈研吾監）『アトラス：新しい建築の見取り図』彰国社、2008 年
- ARX, "Fax Architecture" ANY: Architecture New York, No. 3, Electrotecture: Architecture and the Electronic Future (November/December 1993), pp.58-63
- 山口隆「参照空間としてのサイバースペース」『SD（391）』鹿島出版会 1997 年 04、pp.54 ～ 56
- チャールズ・ジェンクス（工藤国雄訳）『複雑系の建築言語』彰国社、2000 年
- ANY no 23: Diagram Work (B. van Berkle, & C. Bos, Eds.), Anyone Corporation, 1998

- Philip Johnson, Mark Wigley, Deconstructivist Architecture, MOMA, 1988

建築史、建築論
- 森田慶一『建築論』東海大学出版、1978 年
- Cornelis van de Ven, Space in Architecture, Van Gorcum Assen / Amsterdam, 1978,（邦訳）コルネリス・ファン・デ・フェン（佐々木宏訳）『建築の空間』丸善、1981 年
- ルドルフ・ウィットコウワー（中森義宗訳）『ヒューマニズム建築の源流』彰国社、1971 年
- Colin Rowe, The Mathematics of the Ideal Villa and Other Essays, MIT Press Revised, 1982
- コーリン・ロウ（伊東豊雄、松永安光訳）『マニエリスムと近代建築―コーリン・ロウ建築論選集』彰国社、1981 年
- Kenneth Frampton, Studies in Tectonic Culture, MIT Press, 1995,（邦訳）ケネス・フランプトン（松畑強他訳）『テクトニック・カルチャー』TOTO 出版、2002 年
- Kenneth Frampton, Modern Architecture - a critical history, Thames & Hudson, 2007, 4th edition
- デュラン『デュラン比較建築図集』玲風書房、1996 年
- ロバート・ヴェンチューリ（伊藤公文訳）『建築の多様性と対立性』（SD 選書）鹿島出版会,1982 年
- ジークフリート・ギーディオン（Sigfried Giedion）Space, Time and Architecture, Harvard University Press, Cambridge, 1941,（イタリア語版、1953；日本語版『空間・時間・建築』丸善 1955；ドイツ語版）
- アドルフ・ロース（伊藤哲夫訳）『装飾と罪悪―建築・文化論集』中央公論美術出版、1987 年

哲学、芸術論等
- ジャック・デリダ（合田正人訳）『エクリチュールと差異』法政大学出版局、2013 年、原著 L'ecriture et la différence (1967)
- ジャック・デリダ（湯浅博雄訳）『パッション』 未来社、2001 年、原著 Passions (1993)
- ジャック・デリダ（守中高明訳）『コーラ―プラトンの場』未来社、2004 年、原著 Khôra (1993)
- 渡辺洋平『ドゥルーズと多様体の哲学：二〇世紀のエピステモロジーにむけて』人文書院、2017 年
- ジル・ドゥルーズ、クレール・パルネ（田村毅訳）『ドゥルーズの思想』大修館書店、1984 年
- Gilles Deleuze, Le pli : Leibniz et le Baroque, Minuit, 1988, Trans. The Fold: Leibniz and the Baroque (1993), ジル・ドゥルーズ（宇野邦一訳）『襞：ライプニッツとバロック』河出書房新社、1998 年
- Gilles Deleuze, Felix Guattari,Capitalisme et Schizophrénie 2. Mille Plateaux (1980). Trans. Brian Massumi, A Thousand Plateaus: Capitalism and Schizophrenia, Univ. of Minnesota Press,(1987), ジル・ドゥルーズ、フェリック

ス・ガタリ（宇野邦一訳他）『千のプラトー――資本主義と分裂症』河出書房新社、1994 年
- ジュリア・クリステヴァ（原田邦夫訳）『セメイオチケ（1）記号の解体学』せりか書房、1983 年
- ジュリア・クリステヴァ（中沢新一他訳）『セメイオチケ（2）記号の生成論』せりか書房、1984 年
- ジュリア・クリステヴァ（谷口勇訳）『テクストとしての小説』国文社、1985 年
- カンタン・メイヤスー、千葉雅也（岡嶋隆佑訳）『亡霊のジレンマ ―思弁的唯物論の展開―』青土社、2018 年
- カンタン・メイヤスー（千葉雅也他訳）『有限性の後で―偶然性の必然性についての試論』、人文書院、2016 年
- グレアム・ハーマン（岡嶋隆佑監訳、山下智弘他訳）『四方対象：オブジェクト指向存在論入門』人文書院、2017 年
- マルクス・ガブリエル（清水一浩訳）『なぜ世界は存在しないのか（講談社選書メチエ）』講談社、2018 年
- スティーヴン・シャヴィロ（上野俊哉訳）『モノたちの宇宙：思弁的実在論とは何か』河出書房新社 2016 年
- 西垣通『AI 原論 神の支配と人間の自由（講談社選書メチエ）』講談社、2018 年
- ケヴィン・ケリー（服部桂著, 翻訳）『〈インターネット〉の次に来るもの 未来を決める 12 の法則』NHK 出版、2016 年
- レイ・カーツワイル（井上健他訳）『ポスト・ヒューマン誕生―コンピュータが人類の知性を超えるとき THE SINGULARITY IS NEAR;WHEN HUMANS TRANSCEND BIOLOGY』NHK 出版、2007 年
- Jonathan Crary（遠藤知巳訳）『観察者の系譜―視覚空間の変容とモダニティ』以文社、2005 年
- ジャン＝リュック・ナンシー（加藤恵介訳）『複数にして単数の存在』松籟社、2005 年
- ノーマン・ケンプ・スミス（山本冬樹訳）『カント「純粋理性批判」註解〈上下巻〉』行路社、2001 年
- エーリッヒ・アディックス（赤松常弘訳）『カントと物自体（叢書・ウニベルシタス (58)）』法政大学出版局、1998 年
- Ernst H. Gombrich（岡田温司他訳）『規範と形式―ルネサンス美術研究』中央公論美術出版、2000 年
- ポール・ヴィリリオ（土屋進訳）『情報エネルギー化社会』新評論、2004 年
- ポール・ヴィリリオ（市田良彦訳）『速度と政治―地政学から時政学へ』平凡社、1989 年

図版出典一覧

Introduction

Fig.0-1　ベルリン・シュピルボーゲンコンペ　コンセプトダイアグラム
出展：Takashi Yamaguchi & Associates / 山口隆建築研究所
Fig.0-2　参照空間としてのサイバースペース　空間の生成概念プログラム
出展：Takashi Yamaguchi & Associates / 山口隆建築研究所

Chapter 1

Fig.1-1　規整線
出展：ウィリ・ボジガー編（吉阪隆正訳）『ル・コルビュジエ全作品集』A・D・A　EDITA　Tokyo、1977 年、（第 1 巻）、p60。
Fig.1-2　西洋の数比原理
出 展：Cornelis van de Ven, Space in Architecture, Van Gorcum Assen / Amsterdam, (1978), p12.
Fig.1-3　建築構成の四つの型（1929）
出展：ウィリ・ボジガー編（吉阪隆正訳）『ル・コルビュジエ全作品集』A・D・A　EDITA　Tokyo、1977 年、（第 1 巻）、p175。
Fig.1-4　ドミノ住宅（1915）
出展：ウィリ・ボジガー編（吉阪隆正訳）『ル・コルビュジエ全作品集』A・D・A　EDITA　Tokyo、1977 年、（第 1 巻）、p15。
Fig.1-5　サヴォア邸
出展：ウィリ・ボジガー編（吉阪隆正訳）『ル・コルビュジエ全作品集』A・D・A　EDITA　Tokyo、1977 年、（第 1 巻）、pp172-174。
Fig.1-6　トラセ・レギュラトゥール
出展：左図：ル・コルビュジェ － ソーニエ（樋口清訳）『建築へ』中央公論美術出版 、2003 年、p62、右図：Colin Rowe, The Mathematics of the Ideal Villa and Other Essays,The MIT Press Revised (1982), p10.
Fig.1-7　モデュロール
出展：ル・コルビュジェ（吉阪 隆正訳）『モデュロール』（Ⅰ）、（Ⅱ）、SD 選書〈112〉、鹿島出版会、1976 年、左図：筆者による再描画（Ⅰ）p159、右図（Ⅱ）p39。

Chapter 2　アイゼンマンの建築概念

Fig.2-1　VOLUME IS DEFINED AND CONTAINED SPACE
出 展：Peter Eisenman, The Formal Basis of Modern Architecture, Lars Muller (2006), p58. 筆者による再描画。
Fig.2-2　CENTROIDAL SYNTAX(左図)、LINEAR SYNTAX(右図)
出 展：Peter Eisenman, The Formal Basis of Modern Architecture, Lars Muller (2006), p115. 筆者による再描画。
Fig.2-3　ALL CONDITIONS OF SURFACE SKIN SEEN AS CENTROIDAL (左図)
ALL PLANAR CONDITIONS OF SEEN AS LINEAR SYNTAX(右図)
出 展：Peter Eisenman, The Formal Basis of Modern Architecture, Lars Muller (2006), p80.
Fig.2-4　VERTICAL VOLUMETRIC PLANES TENSIONED FROM DOMINANT FACADE (左図)
HORIZONTAL VOLUMETRIC PLANES (中図)、VOLUMETRIC PLAID (右図)
出 展：Peter Eisenman, The Formal Basis of Modern Architecture, Lars Muller (2006), pp108, 110.
Fig.2-5　NEUTRAL STATE OF PLANES OF SYMMETRY IN A LINEAR VOLUME (左図)
IN CORNER SITE WITH ONE SIDE DOMINANT SURFACE OF SYMETRY IS DISLOCATED TOWARDS THE DOMINANT SURFACE TO RESTORE BALANCE(中図)
ALL VERTICAL AND ORTHOGONAL PLANES ARE AFFECTED BY THIS DOMINANT SURFACE(右図)
出 展：Peter Eisenman, The Formal Basis of Modern Architecture, Lars Muller (2006), p126.
Fig.2-6　カサ・デル・ファッショ
出 展：Peter Eisenman, The Formal Basis of Modern Architecture, Lars Muller (2006), p304. 筆者による再描画。
Fig.2-7　サンテリア幼稚園
出 展：Peter Eisenman, The Formal Basis of Modern Architecture, Lars Muller (2006), p332. 筆者による再描画。
Fig.2-8　アイゼンマンの form システムまとめ
出展：筆者作成

Chapter 3　平板的幾何学概念を越えようとするアイゼンマンの意識

Fig.3-1　ウィットカウアーのパラディアン・シェマの分析
出 展：Peter Eisenman, Written into the Void: Selected Writings 1990-2004, Yale University Press (2007), p135.
Fig.3-2　ロウによるパッラーディオとコルビュジェの比較図
出 展：Colin Rowe, The Mathematics of the Ideal Villa and Other Essays, The MIT Press Revised (1982), p5.
Fig.3-3　カードボードアーキテクチュア
出展：Peter Eisenman, Diagram Diaries, Thames and Hudson (1999), p218.
Fig.3-4　住宅 1 号
出展：左図：筆者による CG モデリング画像、右図：出展：Peter Eisenman, House X, Rizzoli (1983), p9.
Fig.3-5　住宅 1 号生成のダイアグラム
出展：Peter Eisenman, Diagram Diaries, Thames and Hudson (1999), pp96,97. 筆者による再描画。
Fig.3-6　住宅 2 号
出展：左図：筆者による CG モデリング画像、右図：出展：Peter Eisenman, House X, Rizzoli (1983), p9.
Fig.3-7　住宅 2 号生成のダイアグラム

出展：Peter Eisenman, Diagram Diaries, Thames and Hudson (1999), pp98,99. 筆者による再描画および再構成。

Fig.3-8　　　住宅 3 号

出展：左図：筆者による CG モデリング画像、右図：出展：Peter Eisenman, House X, Rizzoli (1983). p11.

Fig.3-9　　　住宅 3 号生成のダイアグラム

出展：Peter Eisenman, Diagram Diaries, Thames and Hudson (1999), p100.　筆者による再描画および再構成

Fig.3-10　　　住宅 4 号

出展：左図：筆者による CG モデリング画像、右図：出展：Peter Eisenman, House X, Rizzoli (1983). p11.

Fig.3-11　　　住宅 4 号生成のダイアグラム

出 展：Peter Eisenman, Diagram Diaries, Thames and Hudson (1999), pp101-103.　筆者による再描画および再構成

Fig.3-12　　　住宅 6 号

出展：左図：筆者による CG モデリング画像、右図：出展：Peter Eisenman, House X, Rizzoli (1983). p25.

Fig.3-13　　　住宅 6 号生成のダイアグラム

出 展：Peter Eisenman, Diagram Diaries, Thames and Hudson (1999), pp104-105.　筆者による再描画および再構成

Fig.3-14　　　住宅 10 号

出展：左図：筆者による CG モデリング画像、右図：出展：Peter Eisenman, House X, Rizzoli (1983). p27.

Fig.3-15　　　住宅 10 号生成のダイアグラム

出 展：Peter Eisenman, Diagram Diaries, Thames and Hudson (1999), pp106-107. Peter Eisenman, House X, Rizzoli (1983).　筆者による再描画および再構成

Fig.3-16　　　住宅 10 号 検討ダイアグラム

出展：Peter Eisenman, House X, Rizzoli (1983), pp108,120,121.

Fig.3-17　　　House El Even Odd

出展：筆者による CG モデリング画像

Fig.3-18　　　House El Even Odd 生成のダイアグラム

出 展：Peter Eisenman, Diagram Diaries, Thames and Hudson (1999), pp110-111. 筆者による再描画および再構成

Fig.3-19　　　Fin d'Ou T Hous 生成のダイアグラム

出展：Peter Eisenman, Diagram Diaries, Thames and Hudson (1999), pp76.

Chapter 4　アイゼンマンのダイアグラムの意義

Fig.4-1　　　Brunelleschi: The Vision of the Subject

出展：写真、図面；クリストフ・ルイトポルト フロンメル (稲川直樹訳)『イタリア・ルネサンスの建築』鹿島出版会 (2011) pp19,21,24.

原図：http://www.except.nl/overig/yale/eisenman/01-Brunelleschi.html における Tom Bosschaert の描画を元に筆者による再構成

Chapter 5　コールハースの建築概念

Fig.5-1　　　スカイスクレーパー断面 (左図), ラ・ヴィレット公園案機能の再分配 (右図)

出展：Rem Koolhaas, Bruce Mau, Hans Werlemann, S M L XL 2nd Edition, The Monacelli Press (1997), 左図：p936、右図：p923.　筆者による再描画。

Fig.5-2　　　ボルドーの住宅平面図

出展：レム・コールハース『OMA@work.a+u』a+u（2000）5 月臨時増刊 , p62. 筆者による再描画

Fig.5-3　　　ボルドーの住宅断面図、エレベーターダイアグラム

出展：レム・コールハース『OMA@work.a+u』a+u（2000）5 月臨時増刊 , p63. 筆者による再描画

Fig.5-4　　　エクゾダス　全体計画図

出展：Rem Koolhaas, Bruce Mau, Hans Werlemann, S M L XL 2nd Edition, The Monacelli Press (1997), pp4,5.　筆者による再描画

Fig.5-5　　　クンストハル断面 (左図), 連続する床面 (右図)

出展：Rem Koolhaas, Bruce Mau, Hans Werlemann, S M L XL 2nd Edition, The Monacelli Press (1997), 左図：p473、右図：p430.　筆者による再描画

Fig.5-6　　　シアトル図書館ダイアグラム

出展：レム・コールハース『OMA@work.a+u』a+u（2000）5 月臨時増刊 , pp90,91,99.　筆者による再描画

Fig.5-7　　　イワン・レオニドフの「文化宮殿」

出 展：Andrei Gozak / Andrei Leonidov, Ivan Leonidov: The Complete Works, Rizzoli（1988）

Fig.5-8　　　「オサ」のマグニトゴルクス重工業都市計画

出展：Selim O. Chan-Magomedow, Pioneers of Soviet Architecture: The Search for New Solutions in the 1920s and 1930s, Thames & Hudson Ltd (1987), p153.

Chapter 6　関係性の拡張

Fig.6-1　　　カナレッジョ・タウン・スクエア計画平面

出展：(左 図) Peter Eisenman, Diagram Diaries, Thames and Hudson (1999), p168.

(右図) Cities of Artificial Excavation: The Work of Peter Eisenman, 1978-1988, Jean-Francois Bedard ed. Rizzoli (1994), p71.

Fig.6-2　　　住宅 11a 号生成のダイアグラム

出 展：Peter Eisenman, Diagram Diaries, Thames and Hudson (1999), pp74,108,109. 筆者による再描画および再構成

Fig.6-3　　　デリダとアイゼンマンにおける chora 概念の違い

出展：筆者作成

Fig.6-4　　　カーサ・グァルディオラ　コンセプトダイアグラム

出展：Peter Eisenman, Diagram Diaries, Thames and Hudson (1999), p78.

Fig.6-5　　　カーサ・グァルディオラ　生成のダイアグラム

出 展：Peter Eisenman, Diagram Diaries, Thames and Hudson (1999), pp122,

123. 筆者による再描画および再構成

Fig.6-7　　レブストック計画マスタープラン

出展：El Croquis 83: Peter Eisenman, 1990–1997, p90. 筆者による再構成

Fig.6-8　　折りたたまれたグリッドの生成ダイアグラム

出展：Peter Eisenman, Diagram Diaries, Thames and Hudson (1999), p56. 筆者による再構成

Fig.6-9　　シンシナティ大学アーノフ・アート・センター

出展：El Croquis 83: Peter Eisenman, 1990–1997, p66.

Fig.6-10　　シンシナティ大学アーノフ・アート・センター　コンセプトダイアグラム

出展：Peter Eisenman, Diagram Diaries, Thames and Hudson (1999), pp78-84. 筆者による再構成

Fig.6-11　　バイオセントラム　生成のダイアグラム

出　展：Peter Eisenman, Diagram Diaries, Thames and Hudson (1999), pp118, 119, 190, 202, 204. 筆者による再描画および再構成

Conclusion　アイゼンマンの diagram と次代への影響

Fig.7-1　　アイゼンマンの作品と概念の変遷

出展：筆者作成

| **Lecture**

Architecture in the Age of Globalization: topography, morphology, sustainability, materiality, habitat and civic form

KENNETH FRAMPTON

JANUARY 8, 2008

The globalization of capital is, of course, somewhat spurious. Yet it is an important ideological innovation. The capitalist system undergoes a kind of mutation to its essential form, the culmination of which would be the complete (notional) capitalization of nature in which there no longer remains any domain external to capital. This is tantamount to the assumption that an external nature does not exist. The image is no longer Marx's (or the classical economists ') of human beings acting on external nature to produce value. Rather, the image is of the diverse elements of nature (including human nature) themselves codified as capital. Nature is capital, or, rather, nature is conceived in the image of capital. The logic of the system is thus the subsumption of all the elements nature-considered-as-capital to the finality of capital's expanded reproduction.

Theoretical difficulties immediately arise as a result of the fact that this is a largely imaginary functional integration. The rhetoric stresses harmonization and optimization; the reality is disorder and conflict. As Baudrillard remarks, 'Everything is potentially functional and nothing is in fact.' Two sources of

contradiction are inherent in the process of the capitalization of nature, which furnish our justifications for proposing a shift from an industrial to an ecological Marxist perspective on production, on the 'eventual' and 'inevitable' collapse of capitalism, and thence on the conditions for some sort of socialism. The first is the fact that the planet is materially finite, a situation that creates biophysical limits to the accumulation process. The second, which is synergetic with the first, is the fact that capital does not and cannot control the reproduction modification of the 'natural' conditions of production in the same way it purports to regulate industrial commodity production.

The diverse phenomena that accompany globalization are closely associated with the ever-escalating rate of telematic communication and the constant increase in transcontinental air travel. As a consequence, the practice of architecture today is as global as it is local, as we may judge from the international celebrity architects who are increasingly active all over the world, directly responding to the flow of capital investment.

Our current susceptibility to spectacular imagery is such that today the worldwide reputation of an architect is as much due to his or her iconographic flair as it is to their organizational and/or technical ability. This worldwide phenomenon has been termed the 'Bilbao effect' so coined for the way in which, throughout the 1990s, provincial cities vied with each another to have a building designed by the celebrated American architect Frank Gehry, largely as a result of the media acclaim accorded to his sensational Guggenheim Museum, realized in Bilbao in 1995. During the decade that succeeded this triumph, the scope of the celebrity architect widened immeasurably, with signature architects travelling all over the globe in order to supervise the erection of iconic structures, thousands of miles apart, in totally different cultural and political contexts. This is particularly evident in Beijing today, where diverse architectural stars rival each other with the projection of one

spectacular building after another, from Paul Andreu's National Grand Theatre of China, with its three auditoria housed under a single titanium dome (2006), to Jacques Herzog and Pierre de Meuron's over-structured Beijing National Stadium, pro- jected for the 2008 Olympic Games.

For its equally gargantuan size, structural audacity and perverse shape, it would be difficult to imagine a more dramatic structure than Rem Koolhaas's seventy-storey Chinese Television Headquarters (CCTV) in Beijing, with its inclined trapezoidal profile crowned by a 70-metre (230 foot) cantilever some 230 metres (755 feet) in the air. Such technological ostentation recalls the audacity of the Eiffel Tower, along with El Lissitzky's Wolkenbügel proposal of 1924, by which the CCTV seems to have been inspired. However totally removed from the axiality of both Eiffel's tower and Lissitzky's 'anti-skyscraper', the imbalanced, asymmetrical nature and arbitrary siting of Koolhaas's television megastructure preclude it from having any urbanistic or symbolic significance, except as a gargantuan representation of manipulative media power. When complete and fully operative it will house a working population of 10,000, engaged in the programming of some 250 channels that will stream out to a billion people a day.

Skyscrapers of a much greater height are equally symptomatic of our 'society of spectacle', in which cities compete with each other for the dubious honour of realizing the world's tallest building. As of now Dubai, although hardly a city, is the leading contender, with its 160-storey Burj Tower designed by Skidmore, Owings and Merrill. While such extravagances seem increasingly irresistible in capital cities throughout the developed world (witness the Gasprom skyscraper projected for St Petersburg in 2006), global megalopoli are ever more inundated with impoverished people, particularly in the Third World. Here, cities with already congested infrastructures continue to become denser, so that the population of Mexico City now stands at 22 million, that of Beijing, Bombay, São Paulo and Teheran at a round 20 million each, Jakarta at 17 million, Bogotá at 7 million, and Caracas at 5 million. To these statistics we may add the alarming prediction that within the next fifteen years some 300 million rural Chinese will migrate into new or existing cities within the Republic of China. A transfiguration on such a scale will only exacerbate the fact that Asian cities are among the most polluted in the world: the air quality in Beijing, for example, is currently six times worse than that of the average European capital.

With equally wasteful consequences as far as petrol consumption is concerned, cities in the United States such as Houston (5.3 million), Atlanta (5 million) and Phoenix (3.9 million) continue to lose population in their centres while constantly expanding their suburban hinterland with little or no provision for public transport. The negative socio-ecological nature of such settlement patterns is only too familiar. In the United States alone well over 1.2 million hectares (3 million acres) of open land are lost each year to suburbanization. This situation is not helped by the current pattern of government subsidy in the United States, which is skewed 4 to 1 in favour of autoroutes rather than rail or bus transit.

Despite this dystopic prospect of an ever-expanding 'motopia', we have to acknowledge the positive impact of increased media communication in general, which seems to have had the effect of raising the general level of current architectural production. Thus, although urban sprawl remains as entropic as ever, the one-off architectural work is possibly, on balance, of a higher quality now than it was some twenty years ago. Today, architects seem increasingly to assess their work against a constantly improving global standard of technical and cultural sophistication. The vagaries of fashion notwithstanding, this upgrading is as prevalent on the periphery as in the centre, and occurs as much with local, small-scale works as on an international scale.

Given the proliferation of quality work worldwide, it has become virtually impossible to make a balanced selection from the vast array of buildings completed over the last twenty years. As a consequence, I have been obliged to adopt a taxonomy of six identifiably different aspects of architectural culture that may be seen as significant tendencies in current architectural practice: topography, morphology, sustainability, materiality, habitat and civic form. While these genres are not mutually exclusive, it is intended that each of their referential frames will justify the inclusion of the works reviewed under that category – and vice versa. At the same time, despite the emphasis on different aspects of contemporary production, many of the works cited in this overview could be used just as easily to exemplify more than one of the themes under consideration. Moreover, not all these categories have the same critical status, for where 'topography' and 'sustainability' allude to practices that in some measure resist the commodification of the environment, 'morphology' and 'materiality' are expressive tropes that are either arbitrarily influenced by the biomorphic processes of nature or, alternatively, emphasize the expressivity of the surface - both syndromes occurring not infrequently at the expense of an appropriate articulation of architectural form in terms of space, structure and function. Lastly, 'habitat' and 'civic form' allude to the two most fundamental and time-honoured genres of building culture, namely

residential fabric as a homeostatic pattern of land settlement and public building as the essential context for the representation and embodiment of civic culture.

Before entering further into the substance of this overview, one must acknowledge the influence of the German architect Gottfried Semper, whose seminal essay of 1851, Die vier Elemente der Baukunst ('The Four Elements of Architecture'), took the newly discovered Caribbean hut as an ethnographic basis from which to deduce the four primordial elements of all building culture. These were: the elevated podium or earthwork on which the hut rested; the framework and the roof, which provided the basic shelter; the woven infill wall, which protected the hut from the elements; and, finally, the hearth, which was not only the source of heat and food and the focus of social intercourse, but also the symbolic societal core,

presaging the eventual emergence of spiritual and civic form. Semper's account that follows these basic elements, along with the related opposition of roof-work with earthwork, will occasionally afford a conceptual frame with which to analyse the works under consideration.

Topography

Two seminal publications dating from the mi1960s and early 1970s announce the emergence of topography and sustainability as the two environmental meta-discourses of our time; together they exercise a pervasive influence not only on landscape and urban design, but also on the field of architecture in general. The two texts in question, Vittorio Gregotti's // territorio dell'architettura, of 1966, and Ian McHarg's Design with Nature, of 1971, were to emphasize in different ways the significant integration of man-made form with the earth's surface. Complementing Semper's emphasis on the primitive hut, Gregotti saw the marking of ground as a primordial act, undertaken in order to establish a man-made cosmos in the face of the chaos of nature; he emphasized the fabrication of territory as a strategy for establishing a public place-form in the face of the new nature brought into being by the emergence of the urbanized region. He first demonstrated this thesis in his designs for the University of Calabria, built as a linear megastructure across a large swathe of agricultural land in Cosenza, southern Italy, in 1973. Eschewing architectonic intervention, McHarg's research was focused more on the need for a comprehensive approach to the biosphere in order to facilitate and maintain the mutual interdependence of regional ecosystems across a wide front. In retrospect, both approaches were attempts to mediate the effect of the continual expansion of megalopoli throughout the world. Today, they may still be regarded as viable strategies with which to resist the reduction of the man-made world to a limitless diffusion of ill-related, freestanding objects, as alienated from the needs of man as from the processes of nature.

To advance territorial modification as the basis of a new cultural discipline is to accord a compensatory status not only to the art of landscape as it has been traditionally understood, but also to built work formulated as if it were a landscape in itself or, alternatively, an object so integrated into the ground as to be inseparable from the surrounding topography. It is just such a reconception of the scope of landscape that currently favours the emergence of the new sub-discipline of landscape urbanism, conceived as a mode of intervention with a totally different strategic aim from the now largely discredited practice of master planning. As the landscape architect James Corner described it in 2003,

It is within such a widening prospect that landscape architects have been able to assert their ability to conceive of projects that are relevant on both an urban and a regional scale, in addition to their parallel capacity to have such broadly conceived proposals brought to realization within relatively short periods of time. The American landscape architect Peter Walker was able to demonstrate this in an exemplary way in his 324-hectare (800-acre) layout for the IBM Campus in Solana, west Texas (1992), realized in collaboration with the architects Romaldo Giurgola, Ricardo Legorreta and Barton Myers. Walker characterized the reparatory scope of his intervention in the following terms:

In recent years we have witnessed an important shift: every location has begun to be regarded as a landscape, either natural or artificial, and has ceased to be a neutral backdrop, more or less decidedly sculptural, for architectural objects. With this change in point of view, the landscape becomes the subject of possible transformations; no longer inert, it can be designed, made artificial. The landscape has become the primary interest, the focal point of architects.

When we found the site, it was not a particularly rich meadow. It had been grazed very heavily and over half the topsoil had been lost. There were a few handsome trees that stood up to the grazing and somehow survived . . . To repair the rest of it, we took the topsoil off every single road, building, or parking lot site, stockpiled it and put it on the meadow, thereby doubling the amount of topsoil.

Walker had pursued an equally large-scale topographic transformation in his Marina Linear Park, San Diego, California (1988), designed with Martha Schwartz, where the right of way of an existing light rail system was converted into an exotic subtropical park. Comparable infrastructural landscape interventions have been standard policy in France over the past two decades, where one third of the state budget allocated to either regional high-speed transit or local light rail is given over to the design of landscape settings that are capable of integrating new infrastructure into existing topography. Michel Desvigne and Christine Dalnoky's implantation of a new TGV station outside Avignon in 1995 is typical in this regard, as are numerous other works executed by them in relation to public transit. In Avignon, plane trees were employed to reinforce the linear extent of the station, while the adjacent parking lots were shaded by rows of lime trees selected for their resemblance to the orchards of the surrounding apple-growing region, thereby integrating the station into the character of the existing landscape.

Despite the evident success of both the American parkway and the German Autobahn in the 1930s, the universal expansion of autoroutes over the last half-century has not always been accompanied by environmental design of a comparable quality. An exception to this in Europe is the concrete viaducts and tunnel entrances that the Swiss architect Rino Tami designed for the Ticinese motorway extending from the St Gotthard Tunnel in the Alps to the Italian frontier at a painstaking, large-scale infrastructural improvement realized over a twenty-year period between 1963 and 1983. More recent, and of more limited scope, are interventions such as Bernard Lassus's somewhat exotic autoscapes in north-western France: the cutting of a road through an eroded rockscape in such a way as to create a geological park, or the provision of narrow overpasses in order to maintain existing patterns of animal movement across the barrier of a highway.

A comparable awareness of the impact of the automobile was evident in the early bridges of Santiago Calatrava, with which he demonstrated that he was as much concerned with the urban footprint of his bridges as with their structural articulation. This was especially true of his Bach de Roda bridge, built just outside Barcelona in 1987, in which the four coupled pairs of bowspring arches in concrete and steel carried the roadbed and also provided for pedestrian viewing platforms on either side of the span. Both the bridge and the axiality of the railway that it traversed were mutually enhanced by pocket parks that the engineer proposed establishing on either side of the cutting. As part of the bridge abutment, pairs of concrete stairs at either end of the span provided direct access to these parks from the bridge. It is significant from both a cultural and an environmental standpoint that the pedestrian footpaths were elevated above the roadbed so that a person crossing the bridge could see over traffic to the landscape on either side. Moreover, the provision of such panoramic views was combined with raising the pedestrian above the level of the exhaust fumes.

One may find a similar compensatory strategy with regard to the accommodation of the automobile in an alpine park system realized at Sognefjellet in Norway in the second half of the 1990s. The aim of the Liasanden parking and rest area, designed by the architects Jensen and Skodvin, was to retain as many trees as possible through the ingenious layout of the parking bays and by binding tree trunks with rope so as to protect them from incidental damage - a poetic gesture recalling the apotropaic binding of trees in the Ise Shrine of Japan. Of this ingenious solution the architects have written: 'The concept implied that the cars had to turn around the trees. Very accurate computerized maps of the trees and the topography helped us identify the possible routes of a car, to assure the client that it could be done without cutting down the trees.'

The cultivation of landscape as a matter of ecological policy at a regional scale has become almost second nature in Germany, where the extension of Peter Latz's Emscher Park, which started as a demonstration project for the detoxification and reuse of obsolete industrial plants, has evolved over the last fifteen years to become a recreational area stretching some 70 kilometres (43 miles) on either side of the Emscher River near the Ruhr Valley. It is significant that Karl Ganser, one of the main architects of the Emscher reclamation programme, would come to regard the universal megalopolis as another 'brownfield' site in the making, one that will prove to be even more resistant to future decontamination and adaptive reuse.

Despite its diminutive size, Tadao Ando's Awaji Yumbetai development (2001) is an equally exemplary exercise in soil reclamation. The architect used the occasion to create a city-in-miniature, comprising a hotel, a chapel, a teahouse and a large botanical greenhouse, interspersed with water courses, reflecting pools, fountains and terraced gardens. It is symptomatic of our time that Ando's late work has become increasingly topographic in character, from his Museum of Water, Osaka (2004), to his completely subterranean top-lit Chichu Art Museum, built on the island of Naoshima in 2005.

As in much of Alvar Aalto's architecture, large and complex buildings may be rendered as though they were natural extensions of the topography in which they are situated. This paradigm was surely the primary motivation behind Arthur Erickson's Robson Square development, Vancouver (1983), wherein a megastructure comprising law courts and municipal offices was integrated with a parking garage in such a way as to assume the profile of a stepped escarpment. This last, laid out to the designs of the landscape architect Cornelia Oberlander, features an ornamental sheet of water 90 metres (300 feet) long that cascades over the large plate-glass picture window enclosing the registry office. This artificial architectonic earthwork running through the centre of Vancouver has since been confirmed as a main spine within the city by the medium-rise towers that have grown up around its axis spontaneously over the last decade. In this regard Robson Square has served as an urban catalyst in much the same way as the Rockefeller Center drew the fabric of Manhattan around itself at the end of the 1930s.

A similar catalytic megaform was realized a decade later in Barcelona, in the form of the L'Illa complex, completed on the Avenida Diagonal in 1992 to the designs of José Rafael Moneo and Manuel de Solà-Morales. This block, 800 metres (2,600 feet) in length, houses a five-storey shopping mall in addition to commercial frontage on the avenue itself, and accommodates offices and a hotel as an integral part of the medium-rise slab. Built at the edge of Cerdá's original Eixample and served by a multi-storey subterranean car park running the entire length of the complex, the block was designed to respond to the scale of both the existing 19th-century urban grid and the random, ad hoc suburban development surrounding the historic core of the city. The stepped profile of this building enabled it to be read as a prominent landmark, particularly when seen from the inner suburban high ground overlooking the city. This mega-development effectively demonstrated Solà-Morales' concept of urban acupuncture - namely a strategically limited urban intervention, programmed and conceived in such a way as to augment an existing urban condition in a defined but open-ended manner. Unlike the all-too-common practice of siting shopping malls on the outskirts of cities, which invariably undermines their existing shopping frontage, this development serves to strengthen the existing commercial core and its established patterns of street use while reinforcing the axial shopping frontage of the Avenida Diagonal.

Urban acupuncture was also adopted as a metaphor by the Brazilian architect-politician Jaime Lerner in order to refer to his introduction of an efficient public transit system into the city of Curitiba during his tenure as mayor between 1971 and 1992. Among the most innovative aspects of this system are the use of doubly articulated hundred-person buses, and elevated, totally glazed boarding-tubes that facilitate the efficient boarding of such vehicles at each stop. Today this network comprises 72 kilometres (45 miles) of designated bus lanes plus numerous other feeder lines. Over the same twenty-year period, the Lerner administration was also able to introduce many other socially beneficial services in the areas of public health, education, food distribution and waste management. At the same time, despite the city's population having tripled, the administration was able to achieve a hundred-fold increase in the amount of green space per capita: a provision of 52 square metres (560 square feet) per person, in the form of an extensive network of parks running through the city. This general upgrading of public facilities, accompanied by the introduction of a high-speed bus system, has recently been replicated in Bogotá, Colombia, during the successive political leaderships of Enrique Penalosa and Antanas Mockus.

Megaforms conceived as cities-in-miniature may also be used to emphasize the structure of existing topography and to establish identifiable places. The Mexican architect Ricardo Legorreta has demonstrated this approach on a number of occasions, from the stepped formation of his Camino Real Hotel overlooking the beach in Ixtapa (1981) to the Renault assembly plant that he realized as an ochre-coloured, virtually windowless horizontal form in the arid landscape of Gómez Palacio, Durango, in 1985. Similar large-scale megaforms set against dramatic topographies can be found in a great deal of Latin American work, from Lina Bo Bardi's bridge-like Museum of Modern Art, completed for the centre of São Paulo in 1968, to the even more dramatic 108-room linear dormitory block and astronomical research centre (2001) designed by

the German architects Auer and Weber. Cutting across the remote wastes of the Atacama desert in Cerro Paranal, Chile, it constitutes a latterday testament to Gregotti's thesis that architecture begins with the marking of ground as a primordial means of establishing order.

Renzo Piano's San Nicola Stadium, completed outside Bari in Italy in 1992, represents a seminal conjunction of landscape design, engineering and architecture, inasmuch as the arena is effectively divided into two distinct but tectonically symbiotic elements: a bermed earthwork surrounding the pitch itself, which accommodates a third of the total seating capacity of 60,000, and a partially prefabricated reinforced-concrete roofwork, subdivided into sixteen cantilevering 'petals', each carrying 2,500 seats. These tribunes are separated from each other by slots that facilitate crowd control, encourage cross-ventilation, and afford segmented views across the stadium into the surrounding landscape. Surrounding the structure is a topographic 'penumbra' in the form of a car park that inclines towards the bermed undercroft of the stadium in order to afford ease of access to both the arena within and the tribunes above. These last are capped by a light, steel-framed Teflon canopy cantilevered out from the superstructure in order to shade the upper terraces, thereby crowning one of the most tectonically coherent and dramatic arenas to have been built anywhere over the last two decades.

A propensity for landscape with an urban character is evident in the architecture of Enric Miralles and Carme Pinós, who came into their own with two brilliant competition designs of the late 1980s: an archery complex destined for the Barcelona Olympics of 1992, and a proposal for transforming a disused quarry in the nearby town of Igualada into a cemetery. The former design, inspired by Gaudí and the structurally rationalist precepts of Viollet-le-Duc, demonstrated a newfound capacity for folded-plate construction in concrete, ingeniously supported by tubular steel columns. The result was legible both as undulating roofwork and as a surrogate landscape. In Igualada, with similar ingenuity, the architects were able to exploit the quarry's in-situ concrete retaining walls as the armature for an inclined prefabricated columbarium. Elsewhere, in the lower part of the quarry, serpentine retaining walls of gabion stonework formed embankments housing private mausolea. In sum, the entire cemetery was subject to a highly differentiated tactile aesthetic, from the Corten steel sliding doors that secured the mausolea to disused rail ties, set in a weak mix of

Owing to the late development of landscape architecture as a separate profession in Spain, architects there have long been preoccupied with integrating their work into the surrounding topography, and nowhere has this been more apparent than in the sensitively inflected work of José Rafael Moneo. Two of his buildings are particularly exemplary in this regard: the Miró Foundation, Mallorca (1987-93), and the Kursaal Auditorium and Congress Centre, completed on the seafront in San Sebastian in 1999. Where the Miró Foundation comprises a low horizontal slab and a faceted, fort-like mass integrated into a heavily contoured site, the Kursaal complex addresses a dramatic seafront panorama with two inclined cubic forms faced with horizontal planks of translucent glass. These subtly canted elements, luminous during the day and lit from within at night, are rotated in respect of each other, in sympathetic response, as it were, to the flow of the adjacent river as it enters the sea. These crystalline double-glazed masses, housing 600- and 300-seat auditoria, constitute the bulk of the programme,

while the ancillary congress spaces and parking facilities are accommodated in the podium on which they rest. It seems hardly accidental that the relationship established between the building and the water parallels that achieved by Jørn Utzon in the Sydney Opera House (1957–73): Moneo worked as an assistant for Utzon on this project soon after his graduation from Madrid in 1961. While the tectonic expression is quite different in each case, these buildings have two tropes in common: a podium tailored to the confines of the site, and twin auditoria, faced in a single glistening material and inflected towards the water.

Equally inflected structures in markedly different topographic contexts are to be found in the recent work of two distinguished Iberian architects of the next generation, the Spaniard Juan Navarro Baldeweg and the Portuguese Eduardo Souto de Moura. Integrated into the rugged landscape that houses the renowned prehistoric cave paintings, Baldeweg's Altamira Museum at Santillana del Mar, Cantabria (1994–2000), is one of his most compelling works to date. The complex brief for this building derives from the decision to restrict public access to the prehistoric caves of Altamira. This occasioned the fabrication of a replica of the original caves as a tourist destination, and also the provision of a facility for research, museological storage and documentation, all within an extremely fragile landscape. Of this intimate, topographic work Baldeweg has written: 'The desire to integrate the new construction into the landscape was at odds with the large roof area required to cover the replica. In order to overcome this conflict, the design proposed the construction of a roof that follows the natural slope of the land - a roof that is covered with grass and incorporates a system of linear skylights.'

A more assertive approach was adopted by Souto de Moura in the case of his football stadium (2005), set within the rugged rock formation of a disused quarry just outside the town of Braga in northern Portugal. Here, a Neo-Constructivist reinforced-concrete megaform with a cable-suspended roof is left open on its return face so as to reveal the sublime grandeur of the mountain face against which it has been constructed.

Recently an increasing number of architects have displayed a particularly refined sensitivity towards the integration of landscape with built form, among them the American architect Rick Joy, whose Tyler House, near Tubac (2000), was laid into a gently sloping site in the midst of the southern Arizona desert. There, set before a distant mountain range and accompanied by a small cactus garden, the house comprises two single-storey enclosures roofed and faced in Corten steel, their orthogonal masses converging on a common terrace and a swimming pool. Of this striking assembly, subtly influenced by the work of both Luis Barragán and Glenn Murcutt, Joy has written: 'The house's weathered steel forms, like some rusted artifacts from a cowboy camp, are oriented to frame prime views. The coarseness of the rough steel exterior contrasts with refinement of the interior palette of white plaster, stainless steel, maple and translucent glass.' Although this juxtaposition of materials owes something to the tactile materiality of Will Bruder's Phoenix Public Library (1995), on which Joy worked as an assistant, among the more subtle features of the Tyler House is the way its windows have been positioned to frame distant vistas of specific mountain ranges at particular times of the year.

Constructed of local tufa stone on a peninsula overlooking the harbour of Cartagena in Colombia, Rogelio Salmona's two-storey vaulted presidential guest house, known as the Casa de Huéspedes, is so integrated into its site that it gives the illusion it has always been there. This is due in considerable measure to the site's disposition of exotic plant material, chosen by the landscape architect María Elvira Madriñán.

A relationship of entirely different scale and character obtains in the timber-framed, shingleclad, barn-like houses realized in the 1990s on the rugged Nova Scotia coast to the designs of the Canadian architect Brian MacKay-Lyons. In all these instances - in one domestic work after another, at different scales and for distinctly different sites and climates - we encounter a new-found sensibility for enhancing the intrinsic character of a landscape through the carefully inflected form of a single residential building. The principle is dramatically exemplified in Steven Holl's timber-sided, metal-roofed Y-House (1999), which, with spread-eagled balconies opening onto a distant prospect of the Catskill Mountains, achieves its effect by reinterpreting the local vernacular. A comparable symbiotic relationship between site and dwelling characterizes the work of the Austrian architects Carlo Baumschlager and Dietmar Eberle, perhaps most particularly in their Büchel House, with its timber shutters and exposed concrete cross-walls, built on an alpine meadow in Lichtenstein in 1995.

A similar reciprocity between house and landscape is also a feature of a spectacular site close to the Great Wall, north of Beijing. Here, an estate of exhibition houses known as the 'Commune by the Great Wall' (2000–2002) has become a tourist destination for Chinese nouveaux riches who are entertaining the prospect of constructing luxurious villas for their own occupation. Among the more striking works here are the Japanese architect Kengo Kuma's Bamboo House and the

Chinese architect Yung Ho Chang's two-storey Split House, the latter being quite literally divided by a mountain stream that passes through its central axis. Both of these houses display sustainable attributes, the Bamboo House through its use of a material that is low in embodied energy, and the Split House in its deployment of rammed-earth walls that provide high insulation values.

Peter Eisenman's enigmatic Memorial to the Murdered Jews of Europe, realized in the centre of Berlin in 2005, is essentially an artificial topography, consisting of a field of 2,511 concrete slabs, set 95 centimetres (37½ inches) apart in such a way that no more than one person at a time can pass comfortably between them. Varying unevenly in height, these stelae assume the form of a gently undulating wave that responds to the fall of the land from one end of the memorial to the other. Save for a subterranean visitors' centre, there is no representational element of any kind.

One cannot conclude this overview of the place of the topographic in contemporary architecture without acknowledging the work of the Norwegian Sverre Fehn, whose architecture has manifested a particular feeling for the interplay between roofwork and earthwork, as we find in his Bispegard Museum, at Hamar in Norway, of 1979. Time becomes an explicit theme of the work through the imposition of a laminated post-and-beam pitched roof on the remains of a 14th-century stone manor house lining three sides of a court. This dialectic between old and new is mediated by a third element: a ramped concrete causeway that acts as an architectonic promenade through two wings of the museum, one devoted to folk art Middle Ages. The third wing, set at a slight angle, accommodates administrative offices and a large lecture hall. Inspired by the museological work of Carlo Scarpa (see his Castelvecchio Museum, Verona, of 1959), Fehn renders Bispegard as a palimpsest in which a light timber superstructure is delicately poised over a heavy masonry foundation. The new weatherboarding that effectively restores the original mass of the building is subtly discontinued at certain points so as to reveal the broken outline of the original ruins.

Morphology

Between the topographic, which pertains to the contours of the earth's surface, and the morphological, which seemingly emulates the structure of biological and botanical form, there exists a plastic affinity that has been of consequence for architecture ever since the Baroque period. The fact that the primary morphological reference tends to be natural rather than cultural is evinced in the amorphous, tentacular shape of Frank Gehry's Guggenheim Museum in Bilbao. Apart from any allusion that this distorted 'hull' might make to the shipyards formerly on the site, it is surely obvious that its exceptionally fluid shape, along with its seductive titanium skin, exists quite independently of anything that takes place within its interior. In other words, notwithstanding its organic shape, it is paradoxically removed from any kind of interstitial biomorphic organization that is potentially as much a formative presence in architecture as it is in nature. All of this is apparent from the disjunctive, inelegant conditions that this shape engenders, from the perverse, inconvenient system of pedestrian circulation that leads from the river walk to the main entrance, to the total indifference the building displays towards the topographic context in which it is situated. We may count among its infelicities not only the ill-proportioned top-lit galleries, but also the uneconomic and inelegance steel frame that had to be devised in order to prop up the extravagant configuration of the skin.

However much Gehry's 'action sketches' may suggest an animate piling-up of organic masses reminiscent of the work of the sculptor Hermann Finsterlin or, more distantly, of the alpine fantasies indulged in by the members of Bruno Taut's Glass Chain - the phantasmagoric images that accompanied the famous 'utopian correspondence' of 1920 - an unbridgeable gulf separates the essential emptiness of Gehry's Bilbao from the organic interdependence of the interior and exterior, the Organwerk versus the Gestaltwerk, as Hugo Häring termed this symbiotic design method. Demonstrated by Häring in his Gut Garkau complex of 1924, this procedure linking form and space would be reworked forty years later in Hans Scharoun's Philharmonie Concert Hall, Berlin, of 1963. Part of the schism that separates Gehry's calligraphic plasticity from the organic syntheses pursued by the German Expressionists of the 1920s derives from his insistence on the gratuitous manipulation of the surface as a sensuous end in itself.

One encounters this syndrome not only in the architecture of Gehry, but also in the work of many other contemporary architects, ranging from Ben van Berkel and Lars Spuybroek in the Netherlands to Daniel Libeskind, Greg Lynn and Hani Rashid in the United States, and the London- based practice of the Iraqi architect Zaha Hadid, whose unique talent first came to the fore with her winning entry for the Hong Kong Peak competition of 1983. A decade later Hadid would translate the dynamic manner of her multi-coloured Neo-Suprematist graphics into an exceptionally plastic but rather unfunctional

reinforced-concrete fire station, which, while never used for its intended purpose, nonetheless assumed its rhetorical place as one more folly by a 'star' architect within Rolf Fehlbaum's Vitra industrial estate at Weil am Rhein.

As preoccupied with sculptural shape as Gehry, Hadid's architecture has been at its best when produced on a small scale or when a horizontal, topographic dimension takes precedence over the sculptural, as in her Landesgartenschau project for Weil am Rhein of 1999 or, more minimally, in the transport interchange that she built on the outskirts of Strasbourg in 2001. This exceptionally sensitive work evolved from a local authority measure to reduce city-centre traffic and pollution by encouraging commuters to park their cars on the periphery and continue their journey into the city by light rail. The tectonic-topographic nature of this intervention was perceptively characterized by Luis Fernández- Galiano as follows:

The rail layout and the secondary roads, the surrounding houses and scattered industrial sheds tighten and compress the new construction ⋯ A broken concrete plane emerges from the floor to form the canopy which extends diagonally on the site while protecting passengers from wind and rain. The exposed concrete slab is supported by sheaves of oblique metallic pillars ⋯ the the crevices between the slabs which bring in natural light are strokes that underline the dynamism of the intervention ⋯ The parking lot which completes the proposal has same graphic character.

Here, well-engineered access roads are combined with the trajectory of a rail link and the sweeping pattern of parked cars to create a three-dimensional megalopolitan set-piece that is as poetic as it is efficient. Once this dynamic, graphic trope is transposed into three dimensions, however, the result is what Koolhaas has characterized as Hadid's 'planetary urbanism', which, according to Greg Lynn, 'allows for multiple gravitational vectors through, along and across objects, where loads are transmitted through a network of propped, sloped, cantilevered, sandwiched and skewered solids'. Hadid's Afragola high-speed train station projected for Naples (2004), her BMW assembly plant at Leipzig of the same year, and her Phaeno Science Centre at Wolfsburg (2005) could all be said to be works of this genre. In all three pieces the sculptural aspect of her sensibility animates the exterior while the horizontal topographic dimension is largely reserved for the disposition of the internal space.

According to Robert Somol's post-critical essay '12 Reasons to Get Back into Shape' (2004), a distinctly different attitude distinguishes the gratuitous adoption of amorphous shape from the structural generation of form. Somol advises us that shape is easy, expendable, graphic, adaptable, fit, empty, arbitrary, intensive, projective, buoyant and cool. Despite the exuberant sophistry with which he elaborates on these attributes, what Somol has in mind remains ambiguous, since, for him, shape is projective rather than critical:

Rather than offering a critique of this world (the commentary of form) or a confirmation of it (the spectacle of mass), shape - in a genealogy that runs from Malevich's architectons to Superstudio's continuous monument, to John Hejduk's cartoon-like characters from various masques - is experienced more like a visitation from an alternative world. The OMA shape projects [here he is referring implicitly to Koolhaas's CCTV building) don't only operate with the graphic immediacy of logos, generating identity, but they are also holes in the skyline that reframe the city. One doesn't look at them as much as through them or from them.

This is an unabashed, value-free advocacy of shape as an end in itself, irrespective of either the content or the context of the work in hand.

The main theoretician of the morphological cult of shape rather than form has been the architect Greg Lynn, whose writings have appeared in two successive publications, Folds, Bodies and Blobs of 1998 and Animate Form of 1999. Where the former is a summation of his theoretical discourse to date, as variously influenced by Anglo-American architectural formalism and by French Deconstructivism, the latter is a transitional work in which Lynn passes from a recapitulation of his heterogeneous theory to a résumé of the way in which it has been applied to the evolution of his own practice. In both texts he recognizes the fundamental role played by such potentially morphological paradigms as the invention of differential calculus (Leibniz's Ars Combinatoria, 1666), and by the evidence of dynamic indeterminacy in nature as revealed through mathematical modelling in both the pure and applied sciences, particularly in such fields as biology, embryology, virology, geology, aerodynamics, cybernetics and structural engineering. As far as architecture is concerned, certain unavoidable problems arise out of this kind of analogical reasoning - not only the dubious stratagem of positing the metabolic processes of nature as the basis of a new architecture, but also the implicit repudiation of building culture as it has emerged over time as a pragmatic response to the constraints of climate, topography and available material, not to mention those implacable forces of nature such as gravity and climate that always undermine the durability of the man-made environment. Lynn evokes D'Arcy Thompson's analysis of the common principles of animal form (see his On Growth and Form of 1917) as the basis upon which to privilege curvilinearity over linearity and thereby to favour the a priori digital morphing of shape into polymorphic surfaces, which he characterizes as 'blobs'. For Lynn, new form can come into being only through the continual warping of variously curved surfaces over time, as though such form might quite literally emerge from the dynamics of animal motion, as caught in a freeze-frame from Etienne-Jules Marey's chronophotographic research into animal movement of the 1890s. This arbitrary selection of a particular shape is justified solely on the grounds that at a given instant it may be found somewhere in nature.

Unlike either Lynn's biomorphic approach, which like the work of Gehry always tends to stress the exterior shape rather than the internal processes by which it might be generated, or George Stiny's attempts in the mid-1970s to arrive at a mathematically endorsed semiosis of shape, the London-based practice of Foreign Office Architects (FOA), led by Alejandro Zaera Polo and Farshid Moussavi, developed their design for the Yokohama International Port Terminal (2002) on the basis of a topological interplay between earthwork and roofwork. In an account of their first seven years of practice, entitled Phylogenesis: FOA's Ark (2003), they write:

The Yokohama project started from the possibility of generating an organization from a circulation pattern, as a development of the idea of a hybridization between a shed - a more or less determined container - and a ground... Our first move was to set the circulation diagram as a structure of interlaced loops that allow for multiple return paths···

The second decision in the process was that the building should not appear on the skyline, to be consistent with the idea of not making a gate on a semantic level as well, by avoiding the building becoming a sign. This immediately led to the idea of making a very flat building, and from there we moved into turning the building into a ground. Once we decided that the building would be a warped surface, we sought to produce an argument of consistency between the no-return diagram and the surface... To spread the building as thin as possible, we occupied the maximum area within the site. This and the requirement of placing straight boarding decks 15m from the pier's edge along both sides of the building to connect to moving bridges is what determined the rectangular footprint of the building... The next decision was how to make the form structural. The obvious solution of supporting the surfaces with columns was not consistent with the aim to produce space and organization literally out of the circulatory diagram, and a more interesting possibility was to try to develop the structural system out of the warped surface.

As far as the contemporary pursuit of a morphological architecture is concerned, what puts the Yokohama terminal in a class of its own is the way in which a constantly warping complex of inclined roofs, ramps and open-air promenades is generated out of faceted bifurcating planes held in place by a geometrically coherent steel-framed superstructure. Unlike almost all of the morphological works cited above, this superstructure provides not only for the precise spatial articulation of the interior, but also for the phenomenological character of the work, including in this instance large passenger-transit halls covered by wide-span, steel-framed folded-plate roofs.

The method by which FOA were able to generate and realize this complex work led them to appropriate the concept of phylogenesis as a transformable 'evolutionary' system, with which they have since been able to approach a wide spectrum of programmes in an equally diverse range of sites and climatic conditions. What is evoked by the term 'phylogenesis' is an aspiration towards the postulation of an appropriate geometrical scheme rather than the selection of an arbitrary shape. Thus the work of FOA is distinguished by the fact that each new commission, together with its topographic context, is used not only to engender a different parti but also to imagine mathematically distinct spatio-tectonic networks, so that the received programme is invariably transformed through an unforeseen geometrical format that, however much it may have been incidentally derived from typological precedent, is also equally likely to have been conditioned by the morphology of the site. In the case of the Yokohama terminal, the tectonic play between earthwork and roofwork is so symbiotic as to become a multi-layered topography, rising and falling along the length of the pier. This undulation tends to confirm the fact that it is the superstructure rather than the earthwork that lends itself most readily to being treated as a topological surface.

The inherent capacity of a roof to respond directly in an organic way to the stresses induced by gravity finds further confirmation in the pioneering lightweight structures of the German architect-engineer Frei Otto, as evidenced by the cable-suspended tents he designed for various German horticultural exhibitions in the 1950s and 1960s, and the asymmetrical wire-cable network roofs that he devised for the Munich Olympics of 1972 in collaboration with the architect Günther Behnisch. Otto's interest in the most efficient use of minimal material informed his lifelong pursuit of structurally determined tented enclosures. It is significant that he would invariably refer to this research as a process of Gestaltfinden (form-finding) rather than Gestaltung (form-making).

A comparable topological ethos characterizes the glazed, undulating canopy that runs down the circulation spine of the new Fiera di Milano complex, built outside Milan in 2005 to the designs of Massimiliano Fuksas. A large-span glazed roof of slightly varying profile in section also covers Nicholas Grimshaw's Eurostar Terminal, added to Waterloo Station in London in 1993, although in this instance the sectional variation is a direct consequence of the changing configuration of the site in plan. In this context one should also remember the trope of the crustacean glass roof as it was variously pursued by Austrian architects during the 1980s and 1990s; examples are the crystalline penthouse that Coop Himmel-blau planted on top of a traditional Neo-Classical building in the centre of Vienna in 1981-89, and the dynamic structural profile of Volker Giencke's greenhouse erected in the botanical gardens of Graz in 1995.

Subtly removed from the current fashion for giant lightweight planar elements - the building as 'sky-sign' - the Californian architect Michael Maltzan has recently come to the fore for his subtle organization of warped planes, where the rhythm of the inner volume takes precedence over the plasticity of the external appearance. A similar concern for overall spatial dynamism rather than shape as an end in itself is evident in the work of the Irish architects John Tuomey and Sheila O'Donnell, above all in their Glucksman Gallery (2004) - a sensitively imagined pin-wheeling timber-clad propylaea, elevated above the flood plain that bounds the Gothic Revival campus of University College Cork.

Sustainability

In his study Ten Shades of Green: Architecture and the Natural World (2000–2005), Peter Buchanan supplements his descriptive analysis of ten exemplary green buildings with ten precepts that cover a wide spectrum of sustainable practices, from the optimization of natural shade, light and ventilation to the use of renewable sources of natural energy; from the elimination of waste and pollution to the reduction of the amount of energy embodied in the construction materials themselves. He writes:

The building material with the least embodied energy is wood, with about 640 kilowatt hours per ton⋯ Hence the greenest building material is wood from sustainably managed forests. Brick is the material with the next lowest amount of embodied energy, 4 times (x) that of wood, then concrete (5x), plastic (6x), glass (14x), steel (24x), aluminum (126x). A building with a high proportion of aluminum components can hardly be green when considered from the perspective of total life cycle costing, no matter how energy efficient it might be.

Statistics such as these should certainly give us pause for thought, including the sobering fact that the built environment accounts for some 40 per cent of total energy consumption in the developed world, comparable to what is consumed by road and jet travel. Much of this profligate use is due to artificial lighting, which swallows up some 65 per cent of our total consumption of electricity, with air conditioning and digital equipment coming a close second. It is equally sobering that a large part of any contemporary land-fill is invariably made up of building waste: it accounts for some 33 per cent of the average municipal waste stream in the United States.

In the face of these dystopic statistics, Buchanan's recommendations have a markedly cultural character, such as his advocacy of building according to the anti-ergonomic principle of 'long life/loose fit'. This precept was naturally integral to the load-bearing masonry structures of the past, bequeathing us a legacy of eminently adaptable buildings, mostly dating from the 18th and 19th centuries, many of which we have been able to put to new uses. Such residual value is more difficult to achieve today on account of our standards of minimal space and our commitment to the paradoxically inflexible lightweight building techniques of our time.

Buchanan insists that every building should be closely integrated into its context. He therefore urges architects to pay as much attention to such factors as micro-climate, topography and vegetation as to the more familiar functional and formal concerns addressed in standard practice. Buchanan's eighth precept stresses the crucial role to be played by public transport in sustaining the ecological balance of any particular land settlement pattern, since urban sprawl, no matter how green it might be in itself, can hardly outweigh the energy consumed in the daily commute by automobile between home and work and its accompanying environmental pollution. In opposing this entropic prospect, Buchanan stresses the benefits to public health that derive from dense urban form that is well served by public transport and thus sustainable in the wider sense of the term.

Timber from sustainably managed forests has played a salient role in the Vancouver practice of John and Patricia Patkau, for example in the humpbacked Seabird Island School (1988-91) that they designed for a Native American tribe living in the Fraser Valley; in their Strawberry Vale School, Victoria,

British Columbia (1996); and, of more recent date, their Gleneagles Community Centre in West Vancouver, completed in 2003. Apart from being extensively clad and finished in timber throughout, each of these buildings was based on an interplay between roofwork and earthwork. While the humpbacked laminated-timber roof of the Seabird Island School was partly conceived as an alpine metaphor, harmonizing with the surrounding hills, its deep vernacular eaves sweeping low over a south-facing porch simultaneously evoked the boardwalks and salmon-drying racks of an indigenous coastal village of the north-west. Of this emphasis on the overhanging roof, Patricia Patkau has remarked: 'Many of our buildings have covered porches for various purposes: to modify the sun, shed the rain, or to provide sense of shelter. Most of our roofs come down low at their edges; some, however, go up to capture light at the top. Most cover an interior volume that is in shadow and lightens toward the edges as an intermediary zone.' This zone was seminal in the micro-spatial peripheral organization of the Strawberry Vale School, facilitating the extension of its classroom clusters into south-facing external teaching spaces and providing for lateral interaction between them.

More than any other 'pagoda' building designed by the Patkaus, their Gleneagles Community Centre depends on the interaction of many constructional elements, thereby engendering a symbiotic combination of environmental conditions that are eminently sustainable:

The structural system consists of cast-in-place concrete floor slabs, insulated double-wythe, tilt-up concrete end walls, and a heavy timber roof. This structure is an important component of the interior climate-control system of the building: it acts as a huge thermal-storage, a giant static heat pump that absorbs, stores and releases energy to create an extremely stable indoor climate, regardless of the exterior environment. Radiant heating and cooling in both floors and walls maintains a set temperature, the concrete surfaces act alternately as emitters or absorbers. The thermal energy for this system is provided by water-to-water heat pumps via a ground-source heat exchanger under the adjacent parking area. Since air is not used for climate control, opening windows and doors does not affect the performance of the heating and cooling system.

Timber construction and pitched roofs played proto-ecological roles in the work of the Australian architect Glenn Murcutt, beginning with his Marie Short House (1974), built on a 283-hectare (700-acre) farm at Kempsey, NSW, 500 kilometres (310 miles) north of Sydney. Raised 80 centimetres (31 inches) off the ground in the middle of a flood plain, this house would be Murcutt's first application of a corrugated iron double-pitched roof to a timber-framed single-storey structure - a formula that he repeated in a number of freestanding houses throughout the next decade. The 61-centimetre (2-foot) radius bend of the ridge sheet applied to the apex of the saddle-back roof alluded to the traditional woolshed profile of the Australian outback, and this was by no means the only vernacular feature evoked. Because of the relative remoteness of these houses, Murcutt felt obliged to employ a constructional repertoire with which rural builders were familiar - timber framing and cladding, iron roofing, fixed timber louvers, insect netting and standard adjustable louvers in either metal or glass. This format was soon refined into Murcutt's standard triple-layered membrane, comprising an outer sunscreen of adjustable louvers in metal or wood, an intermediate, full-height sliding insect screen, and an inner layer of adjustable louvers in metal, glass or both, enabling one to shut the house down completely at night or in winter. No one has better captured the tactile character of this combination of light-weight, layered membranes and corrugated iron roofs than Philip Drew in his pioneering study Leaves of Iron (1987): One of the consequences of the side use of louvered screens is to enhance the continuity of the building surface since the louvers read as a change in the surface texture rather than as a break in the material. Moreover, the louvers add to the delicacy of the forms. The thinness of the iron sheets and the hard leaf-like character of the buildings is advanced by expressing the edges of the sheets and projecting the profile end sections of the break-pressed gutters.

At the same time Murcutt enhanced the ecological profile of his houses with skylights in which fixed louvers, raised clear of the glass, were angled at 32 degrees and overlapped so as to exclude summer sun while permitting the entry of winter sunlight. Moreover, the second layer of corrugated iron added to the apex of a typical Murcutt roof effectively induced airflow across the ridge as a means of cooling the hot air accumulating in the upper part of the interior. Depending on the speed and direction of the wind, the unequal pressure on either side of the roof had the effect of inducing a passage of air between the two layers of metal capping at the ridge of the building.

Murcutt's domestic manner came close to being rendered entirely in timber in his Marika-Alderton House, erected in Yirrkala in the Northern Territory of Australia in 1994. Commissioned by the Aboriginal leader Banduk Marika, this single-storey house was also raised off the ground, not only to avoid flooding but also to provide a clear view of the horizon - a defensive feature that continues to have particular importance in Aboriginal culture. Its location, 12½ degrees south of the equator where humidity reaches 80 per cent, demanded that the house should be able to be opened up completely to facilitate ventilation during the hottest and most humid part of the day - hence the full-height, counterbalanced pivoting shutters and the provision of a slatted timber floor throughout. This permeability was combined with the use of roof vents that would disperse the build-up of pressure within in the house when exposed to winds of cyclonic force. Finally, one should also note the introduction of cantilevered timber-faced screen walls at every structural bay in order to assure lateral privacy between the occupants within the confines of the house.

Recalling Le Corbusier's occasionally formalistic use of brise-soleil, the cantilevered fin walls of the Marika-Alderton House reappear as a rhythmic modulator in Murcutt's Boyd Education Centre, designed in collaboration with Wendy Lewin and Reg Lark and realized on a bucolic riverside site in West Cambewarra, NSW, in 1999. Including of a monumental portico, a dining hall and a kitchen, this dormitory for thirty-two students - the first truly civic work in Murcutt's career - necessitated the adoption of a steel frame for the portico and the hall, and the use of reinforced-concrete cross-walls for the dormitory. Beyond its exfoliated exterior, made up of cantilevered baffles, the dormitory's furnishings were a tour de force in well-crafted cabinetwork, as Haig Beck and Jackie Cooper have noted:

The floors, bed supports and windows of the bed-rooms are in natural timber. The brushwood box floors are pink. Doors, cupboards and ceilings are yellow hoop pine ply⋯ The deep window sills are beveled - framelike - making the edges finer, which, in addition to containing views, affects the way the timber takes the light... Except for the plywood which is a plantation material, recycled timbers are used throughout the building. Columns are brushbox. Beams and purlins are blackbutt. The big doors of the hall are old growth Oregon, many recycled timbers forming the jambs.

Surely no contemporary architect has made such a monumental use of wood as Renzo Piano in his Jean-Marie Tjibaou Cultural Centre, completed in Noumea, New Caledonia, in 1998. Its primary feature, set within a lush tropical landscape, is the so-called 'cases' ranging from 20 to 30 metres (65 to 98 feet) in height. Each case, circular in plan, comprises a double-layered and louvered shell built up out of concentric rings of vertical laminated-timber ribs, each rib having a curved profile as it rises towards the full height of the case; each structure is entirely made out of iroko wood in order to ensure its durability. These cases are capped halfway up by sloping roofs that are either solid or glazed according to the function of the spaces beneath, which range from meeting halls to exhibition spaces and dance studios. The inclined roofs are framed and stiffened by steel rings, and, where glazed, are covered by a layer of external louvers. Aside from alluding to the conical profile and woven structure of the traditional Kanak hut (the Centre being devoted to aspects of Kanak culture), the double shell of each case, set with its back to the prevailing wind, functions as a concentric wind filter, which, as Buchanan remarks, may be modulated like the sails of a yacht:

The outer elements of the case became widely spaced towards the top and bottom but relatively closely spaced in the middle where they inhibit somewhat the flow of air. Similarly the cladding of the inner elements included horizontal louvers at the base and below the roof. The louvers below the roof were fixed open to maintain a pressure balance between inside and outside and prevent wind lift on the roof. By adjusting the lower louvers the case ventilated naturally and comfortably... In soft breezes all the louvers were to be opened. As the wind strengthened the lower louvers were to be progressively closed. In cyclones they were to be closed completely.

The remainder of the complex consists of a double-roofed and louvered single-storey orthogonal structure, housing exhibition space, administration and research offices and a 400-seat lecture hall. Informally arranged along one side of this modular mat-building, the timber cases evoke through their spire-like forms of varying height the profile of a traditional Kanak village. While this allusion was endorsed by the Kanak themselves, one can hardly overlook the post-colonial context of this work above all the paradoxical fact that, funded by the French state, it stands as a memorial to the Kanak freedom fighter Tjibaou (who had been assassinated by a political rival during the struggle for independence).

A more technologically sophisticated approach to sustainability has tended to be the modus operandi in Germany, irrespective of whether the materials involved have low levels of embodied energy or not. Two buildings are typical of the German hi-tech environmental approach in this regard: the Götz headquarters, built at Würzburg in 1995 to the designs of Webler and Geissler, and the 45-storey Commerzbank, realized by Foster Associates in Frankfurt in 1997. Whereas one is a two-storey neo-Miesian office building with a glazed atrium, the other is a high-rise office complex, based on an equilateral triangle in plan and similarly structured around an atrium rising the full height of the building, with four-storey-high sky-gardens alternating from one side of the atrium to the other to admit light and air into the central shaft.

The Götz building, a thoroughly sophisticated 'green machine', not so coincidentally happens to be the headquarters of a curtain-wall manufacturer. The key provision here is a double-glazed external membrane, equipped with a louvered, ventilated cavity that may be modified by closing its louvers in high summer and closing its vents in winter or other nuanced combinations in between, according to the vagaries of the weather. To much the same end, in summer the glazed roof of the atrium may be slid aside beneath a fixed shade roof. On extremely hot days the internal temperature may be further reduced through water-chilled ceiling panels over the offices, while a small winter garden and pool in the centre of the building helps to cool and humidify the air. This semi-passive provision of air conditioning is reversed in winter, when the roof is closed and the space is warmed instead by radiant heat. The overall responsiveness of the building, throughout the various seasons and diurnal cycles, is constantly modulated by a feedback loop operating servo-mechanisms that automatically adjust the various louvers and vents.

The Commerzbank is also clad in double-glazing throughout. Here, the outer skin serves to buffer the wind and weather, so that the manually operated lights of the inner skin may be opened at will to ventilate the offices. The building is automatically sealed and air-conditioned only when the climate is extremely hot or cold. The design's most radical spatio-social innovation turns on the displacement of the service core to the points of the triangular plan, thereby affording visual access from one office to another across the atrium and from the flanking offices to the elevated sky gardens and vice versa. These glazed garden terraces not only serve to ventilate the atrium but also provide an interim semi-public space for coffee breaks and other informal gatherings. Adjustable glass damper-screens span the atrium every twelve floors in order to modulate the Venturi effect of air movement within the central shaft.

The culmination of Foster Associates' 'green agenda' to date is their 41-storey Swiss Re office tower, completed in the City of London in 2004. With a column-free radial plan, a central elevator/service core, and a circular diagrid structure on its perimeter, this building gently widens in section as it rises and then tapers towards its apex, terminating in a club room affording panoramic views over the city. Reworking concepts first assayed by Buckminster Fuller and Norman Foster in their Climatroffice project of 1971, Swiss Re incorporates atria into its radial office space on each floor. These interstitial sky-gardens flow together vertically so as to form a continuous 'green garland' spiralling up the building, thereby inducing natural ventilation throughout the building and significantly reducing the air-conditioning load. In addition, the aerodynamic profile of the 'gherkin' shape reduces the effects of downdraft commonly encountered at the base of orthogonal high-rise structures. This spectacular triumph has its downside, however, in that unlike other high-rises realized by Foster Associates, this hermetic, self-contained form is bereft of any feature that would modulate the scale of the building and thereby relate it in a more rhythmic manner to the surrounding urban grain.

Swiss Re is in fact the categorical opposite of the Hongkong and Shanghai Bank headquarters (see pp. 303, 304), where a structure of comparable height was broken down by transverse exoskeletonal trusses into four discernible sections, thereby providing a scalar yardstick that could be related to the medium-rise fabric of the downtown as a whole.

One cannot conclude this brief overview of sustainable architecture without mentioning the research-based practice of the Munich architect Thomas Herzog, whose Halle 26 was built for the Hanover Fair of 1996. In this instance the achievement was as much tectonic as environmental, with the distinguished engineer Jorge Schlaich acting as structural consultant; the catenary roof of the building was determined by the need to erect the structure rapidly rather than by the environmental attributes of its section. The main support for the three-bay catenary roof, with each bay spanning 55 metres (180 feet), was provided by three triangulated steel trestles 30 metres (100 feet) high, with a fourth set somewhat lower. The wire cable structure carrying the roof was covered by two layers of wood, with gravel in between in order to add stabilizing weight to the catenary. The up-curving profile of the resulting section, with a vent under the eaves, serves to induce thermal uplift and exhaust stale air, while fresh air is drawn into the hall via transverse triangular-sectioned glass ducts spanning between the tresties. To a similar end, the inner curve of the roof was used as a light reflector at night, while the availability of natural light during the day was topped up by an anti-solar glass panel let into the valley of the roof.

In the United States, where 2 per cent of the world's population consumes 20 per cent of the world's resources, there has been an understandable tendency to deny the reality of global warming and to continue with the maximized consumption of non-renewable energy to which it is directly related. This denial is evident in the reluctance of the American government to introduce and enforce progressive environmental regulations as a standard mode of practice, an obtuseness that has sometimes been welcomed by architects on the grounds that sustainable design curbs their freedom of expression. Such an attitude is as reactionary as it is perverse, given that responding symbiotically to the exigencies of both climate and context has invariably served as a mainspring for tectonic invention since time immemorable. Despite this recalcitrance, the last few decades have seen the emergence of a completely new breed of environmental engineers who are becoming as essential today for the refinement of built form as were structural engineers in the first half of the 20th century.

Materiality

Unlike the ubiquitous white architecture of the early Modern Movement, when buildings were invariably rendered in cement over a light skeleton frame and treated as though they were made of a neutral material verging on the immaterial (a condition that was virtually achieved after 1945 with the ubiquitous, totally glazed neo-Miesian office building), the expressive materiality to which this section alludes has at least some of its origins in the load-bearing brick churches that the Swedish master Sigurd Lewerentz designed during the last two decades of his life: St Mark's in Björkhagen (1958–60) and St Peter's, Klippan (1963-66). No one has written more perceptively of the expressive role played by brick in these works than Richard Weston:

The sense of containment by bricks is overwhelming. You

walk on brick floors, between walls of brick, beneath brick vaults, which span between steel joists, swelling gently like ocean waves... what photographs cannot convey is the almost preternatural darkness, which binds the fabric into an all-enveloping unity.

In the presence of Lewerentz's later churches one is tempted to echo Heidegger's words about Greek temples and suggest that here brick 'comes forth for the very first time.' A building such as Kahn's Exeter Library offers a compelling demonstration of what brick can do, whereas Lewerentz - like Mies in his early houses - is determined to show us what brick is. For Kahn, as for most Modern architects, working ´in the nature of materials' meant immersing them in an appropriate functional, usually structural, role. Lewerentz's aim was different: by emphasizing the 'nature' of bricks that we can directly perceive - their size, colour and texture - rather than their more abstract structural properties, he aimed to build, not merely design, an atmosphere conducive to worship. And in handling bricks in this way he anticipated a major preoccupation of recent years: the materiality of materials.

There is, of course, a fundamental difference between the load-bearing masonry of Lewerentz's later work or of the equally monolithic shell structures in brick designed at around the same time by the distinguished Uruguayan engineer Eladio Dieste and the use of what is essentially the same material solely as a revetment. In this last instance brick serves quite literally as a protective skin or as a veil masking the basic structure beneath. Used in this manner it amounts to a tactile dressing, what Gottfried Semper identified as Bekleidung, 'cladding'. By virtue of their method of assembly,

such membranes are often rendered as micro-tectonic surfaces whose feel, as Luis Fernández-Galiano has remarked,

is cold or warm, smooth or rough at the touch of fingertips, hard or soft under the palm or the sole. This visual experience of shine or color translated into touch, that the aroused senses extend to tastes or scents as well as to the sound of friction or impact, is the sensual foundation of the aesthetic of matter, an undeclared movement, without leaders or manifestoes, that colors the latest architecture with its quiet sensibility.

Irrespective of whether they happen to be used as cladding or as structural form, traditional materials such as brick, stone and wood are cultural constructs whose implicit significance may readily be associated with a particular landscape, national character or ethical value. According to the architectural historian Akos Moravansky,

Materials are appreciated for the qualities they represent... rather than their inherent physical qualities. Thus a roughly hewn stone plinth, juxtaposed with a smooth façade, suggests a primitive, more 'earthy' state, for it represents a subordinate element of the composition.

Throughout the history of architecture buildings have become loaded with meaning. Today we are no longer aware of such meanings, and their conscious 'reading' has been replaced by a more direct appreciation of the sensuality of material surfaces both natural and industrial. The semantics of materials in art and architecture is rarely discussed by historians, and there exists no systematic approach to the study of this subject. Yet it is clear from the positions which have been adopted by architects and artists that materials carry an important part of the meaning of the work.

Over the past two decades, among the most accomplished practitioners of this emphasis on material have been the Swiss-German minimalists Jacques Herzog and Pierre de Meuron, beginning with their holiday house in Tavole, Italy (1988), in which stones from the site were loosely packed into a delicate reinforced-concrete frame, and their Ricola Warehouse in Laufen, Switzerland (1987), which, set before the cliff-face of a disused quarry, was faced by way of contrast with fibre-cement planks of varying depth. The simple spatial requirements in each instance enabled the architects to treat the material as the primary aesthetic presence in contrast to the rather passive character of the space-form. This emphasis on the tactile character of material would henceforth become the hallmark of their practice, a mode that invariably has been at its most effective in small and spatially unified commissions, as in their copper-sheathed six-storey signal tower - the so-called Auf dem Wolf - in Basel (1995), their Dominus Winery, completed in Yountville, California, in 1997, and the crystalline showroom that they built for Prada in Tokyo in 2003. In the case of the winery, a simple structure planted in the midst of a vineyard, material expressivity stems from a storey-height masonry enclosure made out of rough granite rocks of varying size held in place by wire mesh. This highly aestheticized approach, with its tendency to emphasize the external surface rather than the internal structure or space, has since become an increasingly decorative aspect of their architecture, as is evident in their second building for Ricola, realized in Mulhouse in 1993, where the main curtain-wall façade is covered with a silk-screened repetition of a single leaf drawn from the bot ical

images of the German photographer Karl Blossfeldt.

Peter Zumthor, practising out of Haldenstein in the Graubünden, is the other leading Swiss-German minimalist architect. He first rose to prominence with his all-timber shingle-clad St Benedict Chapel built in Sumvitg in 1988. He would go on to consolidate his emerging craft-based reputation with his thermal baths at Vals of 1996, where thin layers of precisely cut stone (locally quarried gneiss) were used to encase the massive concrete matrix of a reconstituted bathing establishment, yielding a sombre yet sensuously introspective interior partially hidden within the interstices of a rather remote Swiss Alpine village. The phenomenological intentions behind this work were openly acknowledged by Zumthor in 1997:

Mountain, stone, water, building in stone, building with stone, building into the mountain, building out of the mountain - our attempts to give this chain of words an architectural interpretation, to translate into architecture its meanings and sensuousness, guided our design for the building and step by step gave it form... Right from the start, there was a feeling for the mystical nature of a world of stone inside the mountain, for darkness and light, for the reflection of light upon water, for the diffusion of light through steam-filled air, for the different sounds that water makes in stone surroundings, for warm stone and naked skin, for the ritual of bathing.

Trained as a cabinetmaker and with years of experience in conservation work before beginning to practise as an independent architect, Zumthor could hardly be more removed from the sceptical aestheticism of Herzog and de Meuron, even though he too displays a tendency to favour surface effect over either spatial or structural values. This is surely the case with the fair-faced concrete galleries of his Bregenz Art Museum (1997) in Austria, which are totally hidden by a glass membrane that envelops the gallery on all four sides. This opalescent wall is particularly susceptible to the changing play of light.

Despite subtle differences in their approach, both Herzog and de Meuron and Zumthor have nonetheless exercised a common influence on a whole generation of Swiss architects, including, to varying degrees, Diener and Diener Gigon/Guyer, Peter Markli, Marcel Meili and the firm of Burckhalter and Sumi. Where the practice of Annette Gigon and Mark Guyer is concerned, and among their finest work to date has been the Kirchner Museum in Davos, Switzerland, with which they made their name in 1992. A decade later they capped this triumph with an equally tectonic archaeological park built in Osnabrück, Germany, to commemorate the battle of Varus in AD 9. Both works are predicated on the striking use of contrasting materials: fair-faced concrete with panels of steel-framed translucent glass in the case of the Davos museum, and marine plywood plus Corten steel retaining walls in Osnabrück. Zumthor's penchant for precisely defined volumes is particularly evident as an influence in the Kirchner Museum, where top-lit rectangular galleries are severely defined by in-situ fair-faced concrete walls.

Swiss German minimalism would also seem to have exercised a certain influence outside the country, notably affecting the work of the Dutch architect Wiel Arets, whose Maastricht Academy of Art (1989–93) was deftly inserted into the historic core of the city. The complex configuration of this building consists of a four-storey trabeated reinforced-concrete frame filled with glass blocks. Here, the overall image of the structure depends upon a single material, even though (as in Pierre Chareau and Bernard Bijvoet's Maison de Verre, Paris, of 1932), steel-framed, opening lights filled with transparent glass interrupt the continuity of the glass block. Renzo Piano would have recourse to a similar all-enveloping glass- block skin in his Maison Hermès, erected in Tokyo in 2001, although on this occasion he was able to dispense with the need for windows. As in the Maison de Verre, a common feature of these works - owing to the tectonic character of glass blocks - is the way in which both structural frame and translucent membrane articulate the character of the internal space.

A comparable emphasis on a single all-enveloping material also characterizes the work of the Japanese architect Kengo Kuma, whose Stone Museum in Nasu in the Tochigi Prefecture (2000) is constructed out of narrow bands of stone in a manner that bears some resemblance to the striated stonework employed by Zumthor at Vals. Kuma shifted from stone to split bamboo In his Hiroshige Museum, built at Bato in the same prefecture also in 2000. The closely grained texture of the bamboo wall and roof, necessarily weatherproofed with a plate-glass inner skin, was conceived by Kuma as an analogue of the particular manner in which Hiroshige habitually represented driving rain.

While a mineral origin is still perceivable in brick, glass, concrete and even metal, it is surely undeniable that stone and wood display their original in nature with a phenomenological intensity that can hardly be rivalled; it is this intensity that endows them with a primordial sensibility that other building materials lack. Thus, irrespective of the way it is handled, wooden construction has an inherent capacity to evoke the vernacular in a generic sense, as we may judge from David Chipperfield's all-timber River and Rowing Museum, realized at Henley-on-Thames, England, in 1995.

With 70 per cent of its land area given over to forest, Finland is a country in which architects have long been preoccupied with working in wood in a modern manner, from Aulis Blomstedt's holiday cabin at Väha-Kiljava of 1943 to Kristian Gullichsen's summer home built at Hiittinen in Finland's south-west archipelago in 1993. However, Finnish architects have not only cultivated a modern domestic tradition in wood, but have also demonstrated the material's suitability for a wider range of building types, from Lahdelma and Mahlamäki's Finnish Forest Museum, built at Punkaharju in 1994, to Mikko Kaira's Misteli Day-Care Centre, Vantaa, of 1996.

Some of the most sensitive domestic work of the last decade has been carried out entirely in wood: one thinks of the delicately screened, all-timber structures of the Australian architects Sean Godsell and Kerry Hill; the more heavily framed timber architecture by such prominent American architects as Vincent James and James Cutler; and the exceptionally refined work of the Toronto-based practice Shim-Sutcliffe in Canada, perhaps best exemplified by their dining hall built for the Moorelands Camp, Dorset, Ontario, in 2001. Louvered façades in timber, where the material functions as a sunscreen covering the southern elevation, are a trope that has occurred frequently - almost as a trademark- in recent Hispanic architecture, such as Carme Pinós's Torre Cube building, realized in Guadalajara, Mexico, in 2004, and the louvered back and brick front of the seven-storey infill housing block built to the designs of José Antonio Martínez Lapeña and Elías Torres Tur, in collaboration with José Rafael Moneo, at Sabadell in Spain in 2005.

Timber has also played a remarkable role in recent bridge construction, particularly in Switzerland, in the hands of such distinguished engineers as Jürg Conzett and Walter Bieler - the former for the inverted, cable-tied timber truss-work of his Traversina footbridge, erected in 1996 across the deep Via Mala ravine in the Graubünden (a work fated to be destroyed by a rockfall a few years after its erection), and the latter for a 30-metre (98-foot) laminated straight-timber span built across the river Thur at Bonaduz in the same year.

Another traditional material that has enjoyed a remarkable revival over the last two decades is terracotta, beginning with Renzo Piano's invention of a new method for dry-mounting terracotta tiles in his rue de Meaux apartments, Paris, realized in 1991 - a technique that was further refined in the terracotta louvers of his Daimler-Benz headquarters, completed in the Potsdammer-platz, Berlin, in 1997. This versatile facing material has been picked up subsequently by a number of architects, for instance Guillermo Vázquez Consuegra, in the windowless archive block that he built in Toledo, Spain, in 2005, and Paul Robbrecht and Hilde Daem in their equally opaque concert hall erected on the edge of the historic core of Bruges, Belgium (also in 2005). However, terracotta is only one among an enormous variety of materials that has become available in recent years, owing in part to the ease with which new forms of revetment may be prefabricated through the use of computerized milling techniques.

An additional factor that has completely transformed the scope of material expression today is the greatly increased ease with which materials can be transported across the globe, from their site of origin to the point of their final application, with stops for specialized fabrication in between. This was already the case with Arato Isozaki's Museum of Contemporary Art, Los Angeles, of 1984, which was clad with a red sandstone quarried in India and machine-cut in Italy. A similar but even more dramatic exercise in global production was the totally glazed exhibition pavilion built in the grounds of the Toledo Museum of Art, Ohio, in 2006 to the designs of the Japanese architects Kazuyo Sejima and Ryue Nishizawa (SANAA). Storey-height sheets of iron-free plate glass were rolled in Germany, shipped to China where they were laminated, tempered, cut and bent, then transported to the United States where, to add insult to injury, they now enclose the Toledo Glass Museum in a city which, prior to the deskilling of American industry, had been one of the primary centres for glass production in North America. It is also worth noting that the contemporary emphasis on textured and multi-coloured lightweight skins, made readily available through digital production, has had the effect of completely aestheticizing the membrane. François Chaslin has written of this tendency as it has emerged in contemporary Spanish architecture:

Evidently the rigorous old spirit that is wary of ornament, faithful to design and to abstract geometry, characterized by a certain pureness of gesture, has given way to the trend of a search for the fractal, the pixilated, the neo-pop polychromy, broken geometry, and even the formless.

Discernible not only in Spain but worldwide, this approach, when combined with sculptural form, has the effect of virtually generating by itself the rise of the spectacular in contemporary architecture.

Habitat

Our failure to develop a sustainable, homeostatic pattern of residential land settlement over the past half-century is the tragic corollary of our incapacity to curb our appetite for consuming every possible resource. This double-bind finds an echo in a report published by the British government with the ostensible aim of meeting Britain's housing needs over the next twenty years. Towards an Urban Renaissance, pointedly published at the millennium, estimated that 3.8 million new households would be required in the UK over the next twenty-five years. It recommended that two-thirds of these units should be built on existing intra-urban detoxified brown-field sites rather than be allowed to contribute to the subdivision of formerly agricultural green-field land. While one has sufficient reason to doubt that the British state is fully prepared to follow all of the report's recommendations, the facts are, as a rider to the report made clear in 2005, that 70 per cent of current British development is now on brownfield sites as opposed to 56 per cent in 1997.

Although aspiration to a middle-class way of life tends increasingly to be the norm irrespective of class, the challenge for architects is how to create a sense of 'home' without resorting to kitsch or indulging in a nostalgic iconography that has no relation to our contemporary way of life.

Low-rise, high-density housing has long been a viable option: one thinks of the Siedlung Halen, Berne, built to the designs of Atelier 5 in 1960, and the equally canonical, more extensive Puchenau settlement built in stages along the Danube near Linz to the designs of the Austrian architect Roland Rainer, the first phase of which was completed between 1964 and 1967. What is remarkable about this carpet housing model is the way in which it may be brought to serve the housing needs of different classes, from the urban poor of the Third World, who continue to construct low-rise 'squatter' settlements, to the urbanized middle classes of the developed world, who are served by the car and occasionally by public transport. It is perhaps indicative of certain cultural differences that while this mode of settlement may be found fairly frequently throughout Continental Europe, it has generally been resisted as a residential pattern in Anglo-American society. As the transportation specialist Brian Richards noted in his first study, New Movement in Cities of 1966, it is economically impossible for public transport to complement car use without the residential land-settlement pattern having a much higher density than the average suburban subdivision.

One of the most refined examples of low-rise, high-density housing of recent date is the 26-house, 3-storey-high development completed in 2005 on the Borneo Peninsula in Amsterdam to the designs of the Catalan architect Josep Lluís Mateo. What is remarkable about this complex, aside from its density and the ingenuity of its section, are the sympathetic material finishes employed on its exterior. To the south and east the façades are rendered in Canadian red cedar, while to the north and west the building is clad in red engineering brick. Where the latter emulates the Dutch brick tradition, the narrow horizontal boarding of the former provides a partially louvered façade, punctuated by sliding picture windows on the ground floor and first floors. One of the most surprising features of this development is the natural illumination of the subterranean car park through roof-top patios lined with glass lenses.

While considering the genre of low-rise, high- density housing as designed for low-income urban populations, we should acknowledge two separate experimental housing estates, built in Latin America some forty years apart, that now appear as mirror images of one another: the Previ estate outside Lima, Peru, built in 1974 during the government of Fernando Belaunde Terry, under the direction of the British architect Peter Land: and the recent realization of a prototypical settlement, known as Elemental, designed by the Chilean architect Alejandro Aravena and built under the auspices of the Chilean Ministry of Housing in Iquique, Tarapacá, in 2004. The Previ estate entailed the construction of twenty-three different types of low-rise units designed by various teams of Peruvian and international architects, while the Elemental project represented a collective effort to provide affordable dwellings without overloading the occupants with debt. The first phase at Iquique comprises one hundred 'starter' units, each 30 square metres (323 square feet) in area and built at the cost of $7,500 per unit. These three-storey narrow-fronted megara, built of concrete block, provide for a living room/kitchen, a bathroom, a bedroom and an access stair. In order to allow for enlargements by the occupants themselves, the units are spaced apart at intervals equal to their width, so that additional rooms may be constructed easily between the party walls. The block layout also yields a series of small squares capable of functioning as communal spaces.

The most crucial change that has occurred during the past two decades is the engineered eclipse of subsidized rental housing, which had been central to welfare state policy between 1945 and 1975. This has now been replaced, more or less universally, by the 'housing market', which has done little to alleviate either the perennial housing crisis or the proliferation of suburban sprawl. A one-off exception is the medium-rise Quartier McNair, completed in the Zehlendorf district of Berlin in 2003 to the designs of Baumschlager and Eberle together with the Swiss architect Anatole du Fresne, who was formerly a member of Atelier 5. The settlement consists of an orthogonal permutation of 263 dwellings of two to three storeys, of varying plan type and Size, arranged in an alternating block pattern remIniscent of Le Corbusier's Pessac housing of 1926 (see p. 154). Despite the green roofs and the deployment of solar panels, it is regrettable from the viewpoint of sustainability that the parking areas were not finished with permeable perforated-concrete paving rather than asphalt. In Switzerland this method, facilitating the absorption of storm water and the seeding of parking areas with grass, is virtually a standard technique; it is only marginally more expensive and is capable of offsetting the 'urban heat-island effect' that is exacerbated by the use of asphalt. In the final analysis, it is the overall form rather than the detail that allows the Quartier McNair to function as a potential alternative 'market' model for inner-city housing. Not least among its virtues is the fact that it is but twenty minutes by public transport from the centre of Berlin.

In terms of providing for the housing needs of the middle classes, Baumschlager and Eberle have designed some of the most viable medium-rise housing settlements of any practice in Europe over the past two decades. Nowhere have they been more successful in this regard than in their Lohbach Siedlung in Innsbruck, Austria (2000). This generic four- to six-storey development is predicated on apartments of varying size, planned around four sides of a light-court. What imparts a culturally ecological dimension to these blocks is the fact that apartment balconies on the perimeter may be closed off with full-height folding shutters so that, depending on the movement of the sun and on the presence or absence of the occupants, the blocks appear as forms of varying opacity. The overall composition has been carefully considered in relation to the alpine backdrop, while pedestrian movement at ground level has been enhanced by sensitively landscaped gardens. In addition to the folding shutters, the sustainability of this project stems from the provision of photovoltaic panels, from the harvesting of rainwater, and from the provision of a heat-recovery plant in the basement. At the same time the luxurious ambience of the whole derives from its facing materials: from the combination of copper-clad shutters, glass balustrading, and the sliding full-height timber-louvered screens that cover the window openings.

An aggregate residential form lying closer to the Aalto tradition may be found in a pair of stepped blocks built as a part of a new residential quarter close to the town of Borås in Sweden to the designs of the Finnish architects Pekka Helin and Tuomo Siitonen. The twin slabs provide for twenty-four single-storey apartments fed by access galleries, with five 3-bedroom duplexes stepping down the roof of each wing. These duplexes have inset terraces and pitched roofs covered with turf. The architects had originally intended to provide a glazed atrium between the wings at ground level and to cover the vertical walls with mesh so that the entire mass would become overgrown with creepers, thereby blending into the surrounding forest. This latterday dom-kommuna was commissioned by Hasse Johansson, who in 1990 organized a Nordic competition for the design of prototypical housing units for the new garden city of Hestra that was then under his jurisdiction.

All of the aforementioned housing schemes are but various attempts to reintegrate the individual dwelling into some kind of collective whole, and it is just this drive to recover a former unity that has led late modern architects like Steven Holl to search for new forms of residential aggregation, from his Fukuoka housing complex, completed in Japan in 1992, to his Hybrid Building, now under construction in Beijing. This last comprises a self-contained urban fragment of 728 apartments housing 2,500 people together with the essential services required by a neighbourhood of this size. These services are housed partly in glazed bridges that link the eight apartment towers, ranging from twelve to twenty-two storeys in height, so as to form a loop around the central open space at ground level. The latter is focused about a cinema complex, suspended above a reflecting pool. The harvesting of rainwater in this ornamental retention basin is only part of the comprehensive sustainable strategy adopted in this development, which includes green roofs, naturally ventilated and illuminated underground parking, external sun blinds, openable windows, and, above all, geothermal heating and cooling. The accommodation of an equally dense inner-city population is clearly the intent behind the Shinonome urban enclave, realized in Tokyo in 2003 as a six-block, ten- to fifteen-storey high-rise development, designed by the Japanese architect Riken Yamamoto. Apart from its density, the main innovation here is the distribution of a number of auxiliary working spaces within the residential fabric. Yamamoto would repeat this experiment two years later in Beijing with his sixteen-storey SOHO enclave, so called because of its combination of 'small homes with small offices'. The SOHO units are in effect interstitial studio spaces combined with double-height balconies that occur at rhythmic intervals along the internal corridors of the complex. This provision attempts to integrate undesignated space into the residential fabric in order to meet the needs of freelance urban professionals, who constitute an important part of today's high-speed service industry cities.

In exceptionally dense urban conglomerations, high-rise residential fabric is virtually unavoidable. This is particularly so where land is scarce, as in the case in Hong Kong, where the Map Office of Hong Kong Housing Authority produced an ultra-efficient high-rise residential prototype, accommodating eight two-bedroom units per floor. Despite its symmetrical format, among the amenities provided by this generic type are commanding views offered to every unit, efficient high-speed elevator access, and the provision of natural ventilation and light for every room.

Civic form

In a world increasingly depoliticized by the media, 'the space of public appearance' (to use Hannah Arendt's memorable phrase) still remains as a democratic ideal for both architecture and society, particularly at a time when a homeostatically balanced way of life is increasingly undermined by the commodification of both the natural and the man-made worlds. What Arendt intends by this term is made explicit in her study The Human Condition of 1958:

The only indispensable material factor in the generation of power is the living together of people. Only when men live so close together that the potentialities for action are always present can power remain with them, and the foundation of cities, which as city-states have remained paradigmatic for all Western political organization, is therefore indeed the most important material prerequisite for power.

With these words Arendt characterized not only the latent political and cultural potential of civic form, but also the space of assembly wherever this may still be found within public institutions in general. Over the past two decades civic building of quality has been particularly noticeable in France, above all in the work of Henri Ciriani and Jean Nouvel, with the former subtly continuing the programmatic approach of Le Corbusier, and the latter favouring a technocratic aesthetic that is, at times, equally concerned with the representation of the cultural institution as a space of public appearance.

In the case of Ciriani, the emphasis has fallen not only on the museum as a microcosmos, but also on its potential to serve as a surrogate for the socially unifying religious building. This aspect manifests itself particularly forcefully in two museums realized by Ciriani towards the end of his career: the Archaeological Museum at Arles, completed in 1991, and the Museum for the First World War at Peronne, which was integrated into the remains of a 17th-century fortress in 1994. Notwithstanding the undeniably arresting image of a building faced completely in cobalt-blue glass, the museum in Arles is not easily accessible, largely because, detached from the urban core, it can only be approached via a ring road encircling the city. The articulation of its internal space, with freestanding cylindrical columns, conveys the impression of a Neo-Purist enclave, as removed from everyday life as the collection it houses. Such hermeticism does not arise in the case of the Peronne museum, on account of the immediate proximity of

the urban fabric and the presence of an adjacent riverside park. Moreover, the elevation of its concrete mass on pilotis enables a carefully orchestrated promenade through the sombre relics of the 1914-18 war to be relieved by views over the park that flanks the building on its south-western face. With Peronne in mind as a latter-day exemplar, Ciriani has perceptively characterized the chequered genealogy of the museum as a type within the trajectory of the Modern Movement:

Museums, like churches, create an expectation in the wider public. The project is expected to be a work of architecture, and the architect is allowed to express himself more freely. This is especially true of a distinctive archetypal museums since they lac image. At the same time it is fortunate for an architect to work on a theme considered principally as the place for mastering light, a fact brilliantly proven by Alvar Aalto and Louis Kahn.

The museum as a type was born from the use of the compositional figures of the palace and its concatenation of rooms. This typology suffers from the fact that today the entrance no longer follows a unique ceremonial route but has to demonstrate the complexity of its program, and simultaneously inform and visually indicate internal distribution.

Seeking to avoid the palace archetype while acknowledging the primary importance of circulation in a museum, the great modern masters, Le Corbusier and Wright, used the spiral form to produce continuous movement. In Wright's case it was a descending motion which entailed a loss of the relationship to the entrance. In Le Corbusier's projects, the relation of the centre to the exterior of the building is lost as one has to circulate under the building before reaching its centre, in order to develop a centrifugal circuit. The periphery was left deliberately open because of the assumption of unlimited growth of the museum. These solutions, while being spectacular, failed to create a convincing model.

Although totally removed from Ciriani's Neo-Purism, a similar awareness of institutional precedent is evident in the work of Jean Nouvel, from his Congress Centre in Tours of 1993, realized in front of Victor Laloux's railway terminus of 1898, to his Cultural Centre in Lucerne, completed in 1997 on a peninsular site adjacent to the main train station overlooking the city. Informed by the building in Tours, a primary feature of the Lucerne complex is a vast cantilevered canopy clad in copper. This monumental feature (recalling Le Corbusier's use of an umbrella shade roof in the High Court of Chandigarh) both assures the building its civic presence and integrates it into the site by decisively framing a panorama of both the city and the lake. The shadowy underside of this canopy is relieved by light bouncing off the surface of the lake, while narrow channels of water, separating the various cultural programmes, make an oblique allusion to the former use of the site as a shipyard. The roof unites within its span a concert hall, a black-box theatre, offices, and a top-lit art gallery set immediately under the roof. A generous pedestrian promenade beneath the oversailing canopy announces the work's civic status.

The somewhat paradoxical fact that dematerialized hi-tech architecture may at times possess a capacity to embody and represent civic form has been demonstrated on a number of occasions not only by Nouvel, but also by Foster Associates, above all in their Carré d'Art-Médiathèque in Nîmes of 1993, in which a carefully orchestrated sequence of public spaces, both within and without, is able to hold its own against the monumental presence of the Roman Maison Carrée, which dates from the time of Augustus. In this singular work, one of the most dematerialized of modern materials, namely plate glass, is given a civic character by a portico of thin tubular steel columns, set before the confines of a public square.

Similar monumental tectonic effects characterize Nouvel's totally glazed Fondation Cartier, Paris (1994), and even the curtain-walled book-stack towers established at the four corners of the Bibliothèque Nationale, completed in Paris to the designs of Dominique Perrault in 1995. While the placement of these monumental stacks consciously recalls the visionary work of Claude-Nicolas Ledoux (see pp. 15-16), the fact that they are glazed and thus had to be lined throughout with hinged wooden shutters in order to shield the books from sunlight testifies to the latent perversity of employing curtain walling to embody institutional form. Moreover, the technological exhibitionism of these glazed stacks serves only to diminish the representational status of the reading rooms themselves.

Nothing could be further from this approach than Colin St John Wilson's British Library, realized in London at virtually the same time as the Bibliothèque Nationale after a delay of more than two decades. Strongly influenced by the work of Alvar Aalto, this building assumes a more overtly contextual character on account of its organic composition and its facing in red brick, which links it empathetically, in terms of both material and scale, to the Gothic Revival head building of the adjacent St Pancras Station, completed in 1874. While it lacks the axial monumentality of its Parisian counterpart, the British Library is obviously predicated on a more expressively organic and contextual articulation of the institution. Within and without, the vast scale and complexity of the programme are broken down into a number of discretely articulated collections, each subtly connected to the others.

The eventual size of museums is limited if they are to retain their institutional viability and civic significance. As Le Corbusier's 1934 proposal for a 'Musée à croissance illimitée'demonstrated, a museum of unlimited expansion is self-contradictory both conceptually and urbanistically. This limit, difficult to specify in advance, may partially explain why the new Museum of Modern Art in New York (2004) has now attained a size at which it has begun to lose its capacity to be read within the fabric of the city as a discrete civic institution. This has come about despite the brilliant organization of its mass-form and the ingenuity with which the Japanese architect Yoshio Taniguchi attempted to compensate for its extraordinary size and scale by introducing a public galleria, as a virtual right of way through the building, within the street grid of its Manhattan mid-block site. However, this bold gesture seems to be partly responsible for compromising the intimacy between entry, garden, restaurants, auditorium and gallery that had once existed in successive incarnations from the original building of 1939 until now, thereby undermining the sense of civitas that had been at the heart of this institution through the first sixty years of its existence.

It is hard to imagine a museum more removed from the Museum of Modern Art than Richard Meier's Getty Center, completed as a city-in-miniature on a prominent hilltop site in the Brentwood area of Los Angeles in 1997. Of an altogether more civic character, however, is The Hague City Hall complex, realized to Meier's designs in 1995. Apart from being a megaform accommodating offices, shops, a municipal library and a council chamber (this last at the insistence of the architect), what is decisive about this institution is the fact that its thirteen-storey mass encloses a top-lit galleria 183 metres (600 feet) long, modulated in its length by two tiers of footbridges, fed by freestanding elevators, which link the corridors of the flanking offices at equidistant intervals. This is a civic volume rivalling in its extent and height the largest galleria of the 19th century, the Galleria Umberto I erected in Naples in 1891. In a city that in recent years has seen its intimate, low-rise, brick-lined street fabric overwhelmed by random high-rise development, Meier's City Hall presents itself as a civic oasis, capable of consolidating a new scale around itself while compensating for the loss of urbanity in the city as a whole. This is nowhere more evident than in the multi-storey municipal library: cylindrical in form and visibly served by a central bank of escalators, it functions as an appropriately symbolic introduction to the galleria lying behind it. The civic appeal of the galleria itself stems in no small measure from the fact that it is a large, top-lit public space permanently shielded from the inclemencies of the Dutch climate.

Owing to the cultural vitality of the Spanish provincial city, Spain continues to nurture a strong civic tradition, amply reflected in Moneo's wide-ranging career, from the Kursaal complex in San Sebastian to his delicate insertion of a multi-storey city hall into the medieval fabric of Murcia in 1998. And what is true of Moneo also applies to the careers of many other Spanish architects who have been engaged over the past two decades in generating an exceptional spectrum of civic buildings, from the Usera Library, Madrid, by Abalos and Herreros, to Francisco Mangado's Baluarte Auditorium completed on a trapezoidal site in the centre of Pamplona, both works dating from 2003. Among the more accomplished civic structures to be completed in Spain in recent years is a small public library in the Madrid suburb of Villanueva de la Cañada, realized to the designs of Churtichaga and Quadra Salcedo in the same year. Here, the open book stacks have been treated as a spiralling street-space, the ramped floors and walls of which are built of reinforced brickwork by way of a homage to the work of Eladio Dieste.

The National Library of Quebec in Montreal, built to the designs of Patkau Architects in 2005 and clad in horizontal panels of green glass, is yet another instance of a public library being handled as a spiralling micro-urban volume. In this instance reading rooms step up across the transverse section of a six-storey slab to afford a 'browsing promenade' that may be short-circuited at one's convenience by a central glazed elevator core connecting the main levels.

An all but anachronistic sense of civitas on a heroic urban scale is to be found in the work of the Berlin architects Axel Schultes and Charlotte Frank, most notably in their winning Spreebogen competition entry of 1993. The scheme assumed the form of a temenos - a strip of federal buildings to be known as the 'Band des Bundes' - initially projected as the administrative centre of a reunified Germany four years after the fall of the Berlin Wall in 1989. The Wall had hitherto divided not only East and West Berlin, but also, on a global scale, the democratic West from the Communist East. The Schultes-Frank entry for this international competition was the only scheme to capture the urbanistic and symbolic importance of the site, in terms both of the history of the previous half-century and of the way in which this void in the heart of the city had served repeatedly as the context for tragically contrasting conceptions of Germany's destiny.

Examples range from Otto March's imperialistically Neo-Classical Königsplatz proposal of 1912, following the very same axis as the Schultes-Frank scheme, to Albert Speer's megalomaniacal Generalbauinspektion axis of 1935, running north-south across the city so as to cut the Spreebogen site in half and culminate in the colossal Volkshalle of the Third Reich (which was envisaged as ten times the size of the Pantheon in Rome). In contrast, the Schultes-Frank temenos was a symbolic reinstatement of democracy and a categoric repudiation of both Speer's megalomaniacal axis and the totalitarianism of the Soviet empire.

Out of this proposal came the architects' German Chancellery, completed in 2001 as a partial realization of their original scheme, the full extent of which will not now be realized - a regrettable circumstance given the representational status of the building, remarkable not only for its vivacity but also for the lightness of its Neo-Baroque manner, executed in concrete and painted white. Defying convention, the architects chose to represent the German state through an allusion to the scale and deportment the Ali Qapu palace in Isfahan. Bounded by five-storey ministerial offices to the north and south, this central pavilion faces eastwards onto a cour d'honneur and westwards onto the Spree River. Patently influenced by Louis Kahn's sense of monumentality but totally removed from his syntax, the sky lobby of the Chancellery affords a panoramic view over the new Reichstag realized to the designs of Paul Wallot in 1894 and reconstructed by Foster Associates in 1999.

Predicated on a cube 36 metres (118 feet) high, which is double the height of the flanking offices, this belvedere pavilion is a subtle recapitulation in abstract terms of all the miscegenations between occidental and oriental traditions that have informed the evolution of 19th- and 20th-century architecture. Apart from its pragmatic provision of a main foyer at ground level, a conference room at the first floor and an executive suite occupying the fifth to seventh floors, the building is treated as a light-filter, which through its various loggias, balconies and framed vistas affords a monumental promenade around the chancellor's suite at the top of the building. Aside from allusions to Safavid and Egyptian architecture, among its more intimate references is the stairway-belvedere portico of Schinkel's Altes Museum of 1828-30. That such an architectonic inheritance was seen by Schultes as symbolic of democratic governance is suggested by the audacious remarks he made when the building was handed over to the state:

Sir, we are almost shamefully certain that... you will mobilize to good effect the special quality which pervades these rooms right through to their acoustics⋯ All these places and rooms... [are] nothing but an attempt by architectural means to counter the rampant cynical reason of our polity with a specifically republican enthusiasm.

If the Chancellery has discernible Indo-Persian antecedents, the Baumschulenweg Crematorium, designed by the same architects and inaugurated in the Treptow district of Berlin in 1999, derives its abstract syntax from ancient Egypt and from the hypostyle hall of the traditional mosque. A square non-denominational volume flanked by chapels is animated by an irregular field of twenty-nine cylindrical columns made of the same in-situ monolithic concrete as the containing walls. The columns, spiralling around a symbolic omphalos, engender a shadowy space in which one may engage in one's grief in solitude, if need be - a metaphysical no- man's-land crowned by column heads that the critic Michael Mönninger described as 'capitals of light'. This motif, first used by the architects in their Bonn Art Museum of 1992, has by now become something of a signature. A further detail, easily overlooked, is the fact that the columns encircle a pool of water above which an egg is suspended as a cosmological symbol linking death with rebirth. The manifestation of civil society in built form is difficult to achieve in a commodified world of universal globalization, wherein - as Arendt wrote in 1958 - 'we consume... our houses and furniture and cars as though they were the "good things" of nature which would spoil uselessly if they are not drawn swiftly into the neverending cycle of man's metabolism with nature'.

This cyclical condition extends beyond the fungibility of habitat to render other, more public programmes equally vulnerable under the aegis of late capitalism. Notwithstanding the persistence of small-scale public institutions, invariably realized as freestanding buildings, an existential void separates the space-endless continuity of the urbanized region from the isolated micro-urban realm as it may be embodied in a museum, an auditorium, a library or a school. However, within this diverse spectrum there remain a number of large-scale comprehensive programmes that may still be rendered as hetero-topic micro-domains within the non-place urban realm of late modern society. I have in mind such all-encompassing programmes as universities, hospitals, sports complexes and, above all, the invariably unfinished national and international air terminal. The mega-airport, when accompanied by hotels and conference centres, rapidly extends the scope of its services to become a city-in-miniature, as we may judge from recent extensions to Singapore Changi International Airport, which now includes among its public amenities two cinemas and a swimming pool.

A similar expansion may be found in many of the vast terminals completed during the last twenty years, including Renzo Piano's Osaka terminal (1994), Foster's terminal for Chek Lap Kok Airport in Hong Kong (2002), Kishu Kurokawa's Kuala Lumpur Airport (2000), and even Madrid's smaller terminal at Barajas, completed in 2006 to the designs of Richard Rogers and Partners. With a vaulted wood-lined ceiling, the departure lounge of this terminal is surely one of the most sympathetic spaces realized in a building of this type - an achievement that contrasts sharply with the labyrinthine movement systems employed to gain access to this level.

To date, there has perhaps been no architectural practice as accomplished in rendering the mega air terminal as the Dutch firm of Benthem Crouwel, who have been continuously engaged in upgrading Schiphol Airport in Amsterdam since 1988. They have designed a whole sequence of addenda and adjustments to the original terminal, which even at its inception in 1967 was conceived as a res publica by the architects Duintjer and Weger. This was perhaps the first air terminal to be handled from the outset as a micro-urban domain, inasmuch as it was the first to be equipped with an integrated shopping concourse at a truly civic scale. Maintaining and augmenting this key facility in many subtle ways, the architects added additional arrival and departure halls during the 1990s, loosely grouping them around a glass-sided shopping concourse known as the Schiphol Plaza. In the centre of this volume escalators and elevators descend to a subterranean high-speed rail link

affording direct access to the centre of Amsterdam. Other than Kloten Airport in Zürich there is perhaps no terminal worldwide that is so efficiently tied into the heart of the capital city it serves. At the same time Schiphol has been dedicated, as a matter of policy, as much to the regional population surrounding it as to passengers in transit. Augmented by hotels and offices, fed by walkways and travelators of every conceivable kind, and employing some 75,000 people, Schiphol posits itself as a new paradigm for revitalizing the 'space-endlessness' of the universal megalopolis. Benthem Crouwel have rendered the airport as a popular, public realm without descending into kitsch or reducing it to an inhuman machine, which is the other unfortunate tendency in megastructures of this size.

One of the most vital civic architects to come to the fore in recent years is the Brazilian Paulo Mendes da Rocha, who in 2006, at the age of sixty-six, received the much-coveted Pritzker Prize for Architecture. Together with his teacher, João Vilanova Artigas, and the equally bold figure of Lino Bo Bardi, Mendes da Rocha helped to cultivate the social vision and the heroic scale of the Paulista school, despite the dead hand of the military junta that would inhibit the development Brazilian culture for twenty years after its seizure of power in the mid-1960s. Only with the political upheaval of the 1980s was it possible for Mendes da Rocha to return to professional practice and reassume his teaching position at the University of São Paulo.

What is immediately striking about the work of Mendes da Rocha is the way in which an open- ended public realm is inscribed into his architecture with a rigour that is at once both poetic and political. The essential spirit that synthesizes this expression is the architect's feeling for the vast extent of the Brazilian horizon. As Annette Spiro has observed,

The horizontal element providing order is the roof. It floats or expresses its weight, depending upon one's location, above a modulated floor⋯ Territory and edifice 'invent' each other mutually... What appears as a preference of the architect for horizontal space is just as much a characteristic of Brazilian architecture. Mendes says, The notion of protection is completely absent in the Brazilian way of building. The buildings are not built in order to defend somebody from something. One enters through one door and leaves again through another.' The buildings of Brazil do indeed lend a much stronger sense of connective-ness with open space than with the rootedness with the ground. The unbound space is not a threat but rather much more a demand⋯ Despite a critical position, his architecture communicates a sense of hope. It is not just the feeling of standing at the end of a long development, but rather a simultaneous expectation of something bearing fruit for the future. It is a beginning, an awakening, as if history had just now begun.

In perhaps no other single work of Mendes da Rocha is his civic commitment more patently evident than in his Poupatempo (Timesaver') Public Service Centre, erected by the side of the Itaquera metro station in São Paulo in 1998. As accessible by public transport as by car, this 300-metre (984-foot) long structure is rendered as a concrete viaduct that should surely be seen as a continuation of the heroic Brazilian tradition in reinforced concrete that harks back to the pioneering work of such figures as Oscar Niemeyer and Alfonso Reidy. Perhaps the project also reflects an even broader Latin American will-to-build, since we find similarities with the structural propositions of the Argentine architect Amancio Williams and the Uruguayan engineer Eladio Dieste, the one predicating all of his projects on the technological prowess of reinforced concrete, the other ringing the changes on this received technique through his unique use of reinforced brickwork. Cognizant of this heritage, Mendes invariably adopts a monumental tectonic expression that in the case of the Poupatempo building is announced by cantilevering the concrete viaduct off of a central spine of paired pilotis, echoing at a massive scale the support system adopted by Le Corbusier in his Pavillon Suisse of 1933. In the Poupatempo building, the heavy weight of the concrete deck is combined with a lightweight, tectonically articulate welded-steel roof, creating an exceptionally generous and exhilirating public volume. It is typical of Mendes's sense of structural economy that this superstructure in welded tubular steel should overhang the concrete platform in such a way as to obviate the need for sun-screening.

Aside from the generosity of his space, two features may be said to characterize Mendes da Rocha's architecture. First, there is not only the reciprocity between building and landscape remarked on by Spiro, but also the perennial potential for a significant contrast between the span of an all-encompassing roof, be it light or heavy, and the ramped, excavated and hydraulic character of the heavyweight structure upon which the whole rests. For Mendes, the revelation of engineering form is a precondition for the creation of a work of civic significance, thereby exposing the interrelationship between earth-elements we work, roofwork and waterwork - elements we find in the Brazilian Museum of Sculpture, realized in São

Paulo in 1988, with its 60-metre (197-foot) portico spanning the entire work within the confines of the site. In this, we encounter a gratuitous engineering gesture that by virtue of its commanding scale utterly transcends the distinctions we commonly make between engineering, architecture and sculpture.

The other element that is frequently present in Mendes's work is his evocation of a hydraulic landscape, which we find in a 1988 proposal for transforming the bay of Montevideo. The architect describes it as follows:

The straightened lengths of bay-front are focused on the water, and provide new recreation areas in the form of gardens, plazas, theaters, movie theaters, hotels, cafés, restaurants... the bay bustles with light passenger ferry traffic and makes a lively and sophisticated impression. At a remote, delightfully situated point on the bay, a tiny island was transformed into a theater, after the manner of the Venetians. Perhaps one night an inexpressibly haunting melody from its shores will linger over the city. Who knows, it could even be like Villa-Lobos's [Floresta] Amazônica.

This grammatical shift in tense enables Mendes to convey an elegiac vision that is as nostalgically located in the past as it is projected into a remote ecstatic future. These displacements are part of a visionary optimism that reminds one of Le Corbusier's oceanic conception of Rio de Janeiro in the late 1920s, particularly as seen from the seafront landing strip of Santos-Dumont airport - an image that would serve as an inspiration for Mendes throughout his life. As he wrote in 1981, 'architecture is the making and producing of things with

which the human being connects the immediate and fleeting nature of his existence'.

Despite this affinity, Mendes's architecture is distinct from that of Le Corbusier and equally removed from that of his Brazilian predecessors. There is a recognition of the harshness of the world in his work, which at the same time envisages the momentary liberation of man through a magnanimous architectural gesture that is at once socially expansive, spatially heroic and technically daring. Through such audacity Mendes seeks to challenge the spectacular decadent aestheticism of our time. This is evident both in his residential work and in his public building, as we may judge from his habit of treating the private dwelling as a micro-public realm. As a complement to this, everything in his public work depends on the categoric assertion of form, favouring the cube and the cylinder, and indulging in a rhetoric of ramped floors and roofs carried on wide-span cantilevering superstructures, as in his unique entry for Paris's Centre Pompidou competition of 1971.

As far as Mendes's use of Platonic solids is concerned, they are either treated as megaliths in themselves, set against undulating contours or aqueous planes, as in the Science Museum complex that he projected for the University of São Paulo in 2000, or they are anchored in a podium that amplifies their monumental character, as in his Sports Boulevard, planned for Paris as part of the city's failed bid for the Olympics of 2008. This megastructure was conceived as an acupunctural element within the chaos that surrounds it on every side.

Surely no other project by Mendes represents his commitment to the public realm more succinctly than his remodelling of Patriarch Plaza, which centres on a steel canopy over the entrance to a subterranean passageway in the historic centre of São Paulo - in effect an aerofoil section some 19 by 23 metres (62 by 75 feet) in plan, suspended from a 38-metre (125-foot) span triangular beam and supported at either end by columns fabricated out of welded sheet steel.

Mendes da Rocha is an architect of the Left who, like Alvar Aalto, recognizes that the world's impoverished cannot be saved by architecture. At the same time he remains acutely aware that the world cannot be sustained, let alone redeemed, through today's combination of advanced media technology and the rapacity of the market:
Basically, one designs a new 'geography.' These are the important questions in architecture for me and not the aesthetic questions... One always expects architecture to deliver extraordinary buildings which, however, really change nothing whatsoever. This cannot be of interest to anyone. It is as if one would make the same thing in ever-changing forms.

For Mendes da Rocha, the socio-cultural potential of civic form is inseparable from its tectonic scale and from the spatial and symbolic generosity of its programmatic development. For him, even the living room of a private house is to be seen as a space of public appearance. Beyond this, and beyond the confines of the civic institution, civitas today may be significantly rendered only on a topographic scale. For the rest, in a world that is increasingly divided by prodigious wealth and abject poverty, Mendes's sympathies lie close to those of Antonio Gramsci, who in the mid-1930s, shortly before his death, wrote: 'the old is dying and the new cannot be born; in this interregnum many morbid symptoms appear'.

KENNETH FRAMPTON
略歴

コロンビア大学 GSAPP 終身教授。現代建築において、世界有数の建築史家の一人と見なされている。

ギルフォード美術学校、AA スクールで建築を学び、その後、イスラエルやダグラス・ステファン事務所で勤務。その間、ロイヤル・カレッジ・オブ・アートや AA スクールにて教鞭を執り、雑誌 Architectural Design（AD）のテクニカル・エディターを務める。

プリンストン大学、バートレット校で教鞭を執った後、1972年よりコロンビア大学で教鞭を執る。同じ年に、ニューヨーク都市建築研究所の教員となる。（メンバーには、ピーター・アイゼンマンやマンフレッド・タフーリ、レム・コールハース等がいた。）

主な著書として、反美学、ポストモダンの諸相（ハル・フォスターらとの共著、1983）、テクトニック・カルチャー、19-20世紀建築の構法の詩学（1997）等がある。

Knowledge City
Architecture as an Interface

FREDERIC LEVRAT

JULY 15, 2009

I would like to thanks Professor Yamaguchi for organizing this excellent workshop and this symposium. I'm also extremely pleased to talk about knowledge a subject I particularly appreciate and a half as a great pleasure to be solo by eustress speaker would provide for the information and knowledge to this notion of knowledge city. And thank you for all of us to discuss potential is our futures.

Knowledge city, it stocked and it stopped maybe as the second word which is easier than the first one. What is the role of the city at the beginning of the 21st Century other than an efficient aggregation of infrastructure and people? Why would we need for the city? Model of the image of the city of the 15th-century 17th-century obesity obsolete. The Industrial production model of the 19th century is just as obsolete as the model of think we know about the model of the 19th and the 20th Century. It's also becoming highly obsolete with the intervention of new technology of communication as much as we know about the localization for industrial production correctly. Just as an example.

I'm not sure where you are sending your credit card bill, your telephone bill but mine are going to some small cities middle of nowhere and if I want to inquire about what's happening with slits in my telephone bills. I get a call center in India made in Vietnam who would check my file online. It's again to cities being delocalized cities potentially can be spread out of its present limit.

Why are we so fascinated by the city why are we paying such high rent why are we so determined to live in big cities. Is Paris, Tokyo, Mumbai or Kyoto better suited to be the 21st Century City or rather what is the role of the city of the 21st Century? Other architectural theorist has published and argues about the notion of the city transforming itself from a treasury city to city of bits. William Mitchell in his now well-known book of 1996 "CITY OF BITS" has explained quite eloquently about the strengths and the effect of this new infrastructure of the city. Half time and space as contracted point almost disappearing and how one does not mean the city people in space but meet people through the internet me people through some second life of the venture world.

In his vision of information city at the information age to the physical city is doomed to obsolescence and virtually disappearance.

On some level, one was Bill Mitchell's argument sound levels and I would like to make some kids station. There's no doubt that new technology radically changing your perception of space in time. There's no doubt in my mind that our constructed environment and basically that's all definition of the architectural constructed environment. It is not simply purely physical it also mental and visual. Individual construction about perception this is a virtual construction of our perception has also been constructed, design, educated. At least more than a hundred years ago to an essay by Henri Bergson of the book by Henri Bergson matter and memory an important point about how we perceive have a perception is educated how perception is transformed. That's why I have learned to see that's why I have learned to recognize process information in a pre-formatted way in a pre-educated way.

The existence of an ever-increasing virtual world influencing the physical environment is a fascinating concept. A between the high activity between visual space and physical space creating a dialog. What is the first time it used to be a one-way street or you have some physical world and then you would have representation. Now, it's a representation of the proceeding physical world in many ways. The existence of an ever-increasing virtual world influences our physical environment. I could talk about derivative trading of an abstract set of financial instruments that have been putting out into the real my session. I could mention the propaganda construction of weapons of mass destruction which

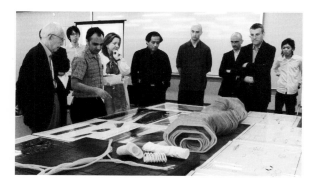

nevertheless had a very serious and they really influence on about 2 million Iraqi who died in about 3 million who got this place as Refugee, not to mention the number of people injured.

Apperception has changed away to see a way to understand space as ridiculously been verified to television to the internet through the phone to every kind of new technology when does the end of space and time in a different way. New technology has three villages increasingly in the proportion of the visual as a virtual environment over the physical environment to the bone that today we cannot look at our reality is just physical, construction but really has between the virtual, the visual and the physical. The big question is can architecture deal with virtual and visual perception and construction about the environment. Can architecture built for the pleasure of the mind rather than just to control the body? What is the relationship between this so-called digital or virtual world in antibody? What is the relationship between the digital world and the physical space of the brick space? This is a big question for architecture and sometimes tricky questions for architecture. Nevertheless, I believe that

architecture can answer this question but architecture is uniquely positioned to deal with that notion.

Architecture is located at the intersection between the mental to visual and the physical. Architecture is about imagination. It's about the mental understanding of space just as it is extremely physical it's about haptic perception, visual perception, physical perception. Some would argue that another architecture should deal with this specific concern in this specific problem. Promotes architects have equal points to explore conditions. So that's what we have to agree to disagree with Bill Mitchell and consider that the city is absolutely essential in the absence.

Architecture and the city should be regarded as an interface between the virtual and the physical. Architecture became the context. The city became the context for understanding for measuring information. Information without context means nothing. It's just raw data. The context and the big experience being other people, being a physical space, being environment. It can be a mental environment constructed in your head. But it's also an environment that has been constructed through generation and aggregation of Manhattan. So we do need the city and we need architecture to mediated to operate between those different meals. It's not an easy question but architecture should operate on those levels between knowledge and the city and become a knowledge-city. The city should be an interface between store knowledge and active user and obviously between the active user and un-active user. It is old agora is a place of expression of the interaction of knowledge. How do we design it? Can you exchange? How do we design it? Can we enhance has a city to improve its knowledge capital is Paris,

Dubai, Mumbai, Shanghai, New York, Tokyo or Kyoto better suited to become the leading knowledge city of the 21st Century.

Distress it is interesting to look for an instance of an example that I know fairly well which is New York City in the industrial production city. New York City could be read. I just set up different campuses not just as a residential city but probably as a knowledge city if you want look at it. It is very interesting also to not date and that just came to my mind. Recently that the mayor of the city Michael Bloomberg made a fortune being a knowledge distribution person having a knowledge distribution company, information company. Because look at downtown New York as a financial center being a financial campus. Be could look at the east and west village being gathering information knowledge and redistributing it through Cooper Union in East Village and New York University in the West Village. Became the Times Square where all the media conglomerate has their headquarters from daughters man Viacom, Disney, ABC accounting Aston a whole range of other information major player.

I want to hear about the concentration of information into the few hands of a dust player but that would be another major question. If you got the new diagnoses a good look at the Lincoln Center and Julien start school and has never had the campus it's knowledge of the distribution of performance and going for the North would have Columbia University can I give orange the rest of the Upper West Side. A recognizable canvas here is infected with a minor fault of where Colombia is currently operating. New York the labor itself as a knowledge city maybe it's subconscious knows all about it online. But maybe New York City is becoming very much and Industry of knowledge, knowledge production, knowledge exchange. Most of the all activity as using the center of the city and all those campuses and other former campuses are growing. I'm not even mentioning in the hundreds of professional schools. All those of the library or I don't know how many well-known Museums such as the moment Whitney Museum, New Museum, etc. We have a condition here in the quiet activity city. It could be looking almost as 50-60-80% related to a set of knowledge production and interaction. But 1 day no doubt that city are intensively competing to occupy as much space as possible into the information and the virtual world.

I think the city that is going to be no one in that all competing, all the city that exists. Not all physical but also virtual space. Why high such a major city like Beijing who is a capital of the most populous country in the world would be aggressively fighting to try to get the event that lasts only 2 weeks. Why would a city spend from the latest estimated 48 billion for fuel firework and some amazing spaces being constructed? Definitely, it's for Beijing to compete in to exist in the information generation spell. Are the cities like to buy hunt sense ice cream interested in generating record generating the tallest building in the world. Not so much for its actual engineering a physical education as much as for the fact that it would win the news is the fact that the image is associated with could travel beyond the physical presence of the architecture of disseminated very fast all around.

It that sense of even the city declare themselves to transform from hydrocarbon economy into the knowledge economy. Abu Dhabi recently which by some extent is our wealthiest city in the world in terms of self cash reserve. What we call a knowledge economy. The question, how do you create a knowledge economy. You haven't been try to about it and have proposed to use your Island which about double the size of the current city. On the island do you have to build some very important museums in the process of building some very important museum? Such as a good that you see in front of the Louvre Museum and the Performing Arts Center as well as the American Museum. This studio conducted at Columbia University was to give the students a question mark. How do you create a knowledge city center by mixing somehow stole knowledge such as what you find in a library making cannabis hybrid between Seattle library by Rem Koolhaas and Pompidou Center in Paris Weston alleged to be the books media a stone knowledge could be artifact physical entity that you find in the museum. All of that makes a public square is very interesting but the public space tries to use new media trying to use new interactive facade as this link between ornaments. Some other people have been trying to do that and this kind of MediaTek how multimedia interfering space using hypersurface for the facade is building become a billboard was space becomes a surface. It is a question that is in the air and I think that needs to be a further question and hopefully handsome.

In the next project, I'm going to show you a project done by my student at Columbia. The first project is literally trying to match your lie's information and minimal information that generate a potential flow of vectors and vectors and ritual materialize and proposed and construction again. Its experimental architecture is research trying to see how

does multiple flows of simple information could accurately and reflect one. The next project is a similar maturation of information but this time using I guess a different self protocol or different software is why you see those kinds of relational quality in merging of a soft and liquid room. The project is also how do you rematch utilize information how do we generate before music that. Some do image are competitive but on the other hand, is video research and as we saw this morning how you transform ideas concept of knowledge information Gobi Street in the next project. Are the student decided to enhance existing streetscape by providing a new layer in contested space between public space and private space-occupying and enhancing parking space as a side street and net worth of information enabler? Each one of those projects to be presented at lines but we'll just go straight and go quickly to the next one.

The next proposal is to try to have the vertical facade of the project as a large screen as an interactive surface and seeing how interactive surface would respond to different users to different privilege points of view two different net worth of the city. That's amazing how to space become directly tracking as enclosure or as information of issue space. Another project is trying that similar way to become a frame between information and architecture but also by creating multiple layers almost framing information itself. The store information of knowledge information of the book answer Library are being Channel through some I thought you into building towards the city in the city is also being brought back into the project. The last project is grafting on the existing hub using energy off so the user of the population of the commuter to provide new media and intersection of the body in space with potential information. How much information? What is information? What's the score of information?

FREDERIC LEVRAT

略歴

スイス連邦工科大学ローザンヌ校修了。1990 年に ARX New York を設立。

ドバイやアブダビでの高層ビル、スイスの欧州宇宙機関研究センターでの設計デザインだけでなく、小学校や診療所など幅広い分野にわたって設計活動をおこなう。2012 年から 2017 年にかけて、マンハッタンのいくつかの住宅プロジェクトの設計を De-Spec Inc と共同でおこなっている。

日本、フランス、スイス、中国、アラブ首長国連邦、カタール、トルコ、ヨルダン、アメリカなどで講演し、コロンビア大学、プラット・インスティテュート、ニューヨーク・シティ・カレッジ・オブ・テクノロジー、大阪産業大学でレクチャーおよび設計デザイン教育をおこなう。

主な著書として、ミラノの公共空間にテクノロジーが及ぼす影響、都市に流れる運河についての 2 つの著書を出版。現在、現代都市の構成における非物質性と物質との関係を探究する「Knowledge City」の出版に取り組む。

Blurred Vision:
Achitectures of Surveillance

JULY 15, 2009

I'm going to talk about the things that I normally in general which is the question of the relation between architecture and technologies of communication. This question of any particular I'm going to look at the technology social layers. In contemporary is the city. In general of the history of the relationship between architecture or modern architecture and communication has been doing you there are the relation in most my research. I have tried to demonstrate the history of the modern window here sample in a Le Corbusier's window for Le Corbusier's Roquebrune-Cap-Martin. Is for example in my research related to cinema. I'm not only because of Le Corbusier through the cinema.

Was the most Le Corbusier medium to represent architecture? He actually says something other effect and experimented with films in their 20s in which he moved through his houses. He first day of the actor in moving through the spaces of the houses. But because the frame itself more than is important for me is because of the day of the window is related to cinema.

In the sense that unlike the traditional window molding french called it les fenêtres. The window view of the outside world with foreground middle-ground and background. The windows cut south the foreground and background give me only you with middle-ground as you are a picture. Like were you can see as well that if you move to a half-century that the Eames House can not before about a colorful life.

In the sense again the not only the Eames represented their house. You go from the one have a few black and white photography is done by a professional photographer. Taken by different forms of the house that are arranged together to produce a film of the inside of the director Koolhaas after 5 years of living. But more than because in Eames in use this life represents the house and slice color-less life argulate. Because vision that they Eames House make possible again is related to the vision of color-less life.

View of the world that about building of color-less life and the cheapness of this a million allows. Lifework has changed up the picture window of the typical American house in the middle of the twentieth century is completed. I think of all the outside television. Like the house itself is broadcasting is

a kind of private life. If communication is basically all about bringing a day outside. For example, Postman brings a better and I think it's interesting that in these advertisements for picture windows. Postman outside this house.

The glass represents this art communication. In the twentieth century, the question has become now how we show the glass itself. That a last a delicate line between inside and outside. This squares for after we needed between inside and outside is no longer simply a quest for transparency as we will see. The glass box has become recently something for us. I 'm going to demonstrate these by going from the typical glasshouse. The sample the glasshouse of Mies or Johnson to the architecture of a SANAA. Kazuyo Sejima and Nishizawa. This is supersaturated television is related to the picture window. I think is symptomatic of this dissolution of glasses itself. First, the site. The project is a perfect example of transformity. All class pavilion for all glass objects in the city of Toledo Ohio. In the sense, a SANAA seems to have to in tradition of radical transparency. You see is why clean pavilion city in the park which somehow I'm kind of across some of Mies projects. For example, Farnsworth House in 1949 in Illinois and a 55-50 house. Mies famously diploid see a glass tragically is force an individual. My interest in all this phenomenon has been to the possibility the transparency in modern architecture or directly related to technology so far imagine the body. In particular, interested in the relationship between glass architecture and x-ray. The inner structure appears to reveal. But is reveals new technology is large to look through the outer skin of the body. Miss even describe is work as this skin and bone architecture. In particular, I was talking about this skyscraper work in the early 20s. Under far to the structure is glass skyscraper as the skeleton.

The engine in the project activity starts thinking about the x-ray. You start thinking about this rendering as an x-ray of the building. Well, you may be surprised to know Mies was very interested in x-ray that he collected. For example x-ray of head performance in his own magazine IG. The same magazine precisely where he talks about the ever send that glass skyscraper and talks about the sink of bone. Architecture is the same magazine what he publishes these an x-ray. But of course, Mies was not any way alone. You get a set a books modern architecture, you get a set a feel imagination for drawing black skin. Skin is our building in your bones and organs. This is a sample about a Le Corbusier's project of the glass skyscraper of 1925. This to the imagination of Le Corbusier. Think about the Walter Gropius. Think about the Van Nellefabriek in Rotterdam. Think about the SCHOKEN department store in 1926. You can think about, you have to go many example samples of what I would call about x-ray architecture.

This experience an early case of twenty century became the base of every building the same mid-century, one day see through her entrance for a house became earth phenomena. This amazing happened at the same time that the x-ray what sauce to use enough mass form. The screening the body for tuberculosis when of course negotiating with the gaze early as the body in various invisible. The technology as you know has been already a body sanatorium since the beginning of the century. It's precisely a mid-century that the mass x-rating of citizens and began on a regular basis. Between x-rays and glasshouses became really common, in mid-nineteenth-century popular literature. For example, is this film called highlights and shadows which is a correct laboratory scene, a propaganda scene trying to convince people to have x-rays, barrier-free x-ray. And a picture of this woman with a swimming suit with her strapped to the laboratory table. Turn off the picture of the photographs of the woman gives way to the x-ray image. The later of the film which is a mass this young lady to whom has for glasshouses or not at all. We after examination of a radiograph really soon see the scene this physically fit. It was interesting about this potential is not that he says that after radiograph. She would be reassured she is the OK, she is physically OK, she is not seeing. But would she say middle nobody as us this is really amazing exists? Did young lady to whom compress for that is for not be afraid with no faster or even more than a break leaving in a glasshouse. It is precisely the glasshouse with the art of the symbol of a new form of a layer and of health.

Communication something kind of a normal or something from a researcher. Exactly same set of associations came be see these courts around Corona both of modern architecture. For example, house beautiful 80s transport who is the client of this house of Mies a successful doctor in Chicago herself. This is how she is right about the time, she compares her in Mies and down her in 1949 to an x-ray. And this is the word, she says, I don't keep govern my thinking. Do you know why because you can see a hall kitchen from the road on the way in here and I can despoil the appearance of the whorehouse? I had not a cloth it for the down for the sink. Miss talks about the space about free space but he's space is very fixed. I can't even pull up close hunger in my house without considering how it fixed everything from the outside. Any arrangement of furniture becomes a major problem because the cows are transparent like an x-ray. Again makes the association between transparency in architecture a glasshouse and x-ray. Then you can, of course, more pull the metaphor of the x-ray. I was in no way an accident.

Modern architecture cannot be understood outside tuberculosis and it's not by chance in that sentence. France was gone on to say about the house that is already a locker room or them house tuberculosis. Association between tuberculosis on x-ray and modern architecture is one of the most an explorers as it takes so hard or reset warning now involve. X-ray and modern architecture in the way you can say that they coincide. Just away the same time as the x-ray decide to support. The inside of the body to the public eye, the modern building is interior that is not what was previously private getting from you is now it subjected to public scrutiny. I knew clarity of vision a penetrating in the gaze. And living in a new architecture.

Architecture whose structure is meant to be as clear as a gauge that is looking in. Also, the story goes cuz actual more I look into the transparency of modern architecture the more I realized. The really fast Architects like means for example or even Philip Johnson. Was not away investigation was passing through the glass. Sun layers and sun layers reflection. It economics photographs of The Glass House by Philip Johnson. This is a very well long one was he sitting. Johnson is self on the desk. Is this incredible effect of wallpaper. Johnson will call wallpaper he says a television program. That glass house was very well symboled for positive wallpaper is so handsome. This handsome expensive but you have a wallpaper that changes every 5 minutes world a day. The glasshouse precisely makes possible is this not transparent precisely of pay. Wallpaper changes through a day. This means as a Philip Johnson, you can also say this is, of course, Barcelona Pavilion. That the reflection of solidarity the plain of the wall is the complex line of the trees became amuse buildings like the vein a marble. When he is playing in his glass house, Johnson precise resize of means of 25 years before when Mies says I discovered by working with an artificial glass model. The important things are the play of reflection and knew the effect of light and Shadow. I seem an ordinary building and again you're seeing. Mies in the 1920s already talking about the reflections in the glass being interested in more. Johnson is probably referring to versus Mies were just talking about this model glass skyscraper. That he fabricated for itself photography in a graben until he bought cannot in my sense of very well know this practically you cannot organize the tower.

Share some Eames house went to considerable air form twists and a reflection in their house. For example, replace is a glass model of the original project is the bridge house on the site and photography every possible angle. I need shot many ways they took amazing experimental what is the farther. Eames house is deployed over reflections is broken. The reflections of the located tree some endless multi blur and little located. The structure long ago shit ceased. I think the many ways a sun of the wall goes one step further in producing a layering reflections on the inside as well as the outside of the building. Show the blurring of reflection is no longer at the outside limit of the space. There's no clear cut inside or outside. Space is another in not at all, it seems to extend into Infinity. You such a space involve having not optical a bodies by the optical intensifiers. The walls are very clear here in the trade. The wall exposed along with the people and the objects. That is the limit of the walls as you can see in this scene support inner and out of the edge of the wall. But most interesting to the gap between then. The accessible gap of the wall itself which even if you cannot actually occupy very much part of the experience and space of the project. The double lines of the wall mark and any sense of solidity.

This project another presentation of SANAA. In turns of Mies is radical transparency. You don't seem to be looking very closely. Because walking in my view seems to be much more available of the view precise of the softening of the workers. In SANAA of work also structure is saver revere. They're building some not even a structure is looking out of them. Is mean, for example, their optical devices is visible a mechanism. The real view is not from the outside looking in on the inside looking out but inside looking even further in work. In trade, the visitor is literally a suspend curve on surface on glass. What you see through the glass layer in front of view another layer and then another one and then another one. Even the object displace all layers are made of glass. Looking through these layers division is often and distorted. Is Sejima deny thing hard mission transparency as so many critics. In she's going to think in many ways it is. The latest in a long line of experiments. She in the way ultimate a mission living beyond transparency into a whole kind of a what mirror as effects. After century for architecture organized by the straight lines of the viewing eyes. We now half an Architecture form by comes on how they soft distortions of the gay. I can more tactile experience of vision.

The x-ray logic upsold by modern architecture could in the dense a cloud of go through images. The clearest of the glass which is the glass that they use in trade. It's precisely used to undermine. Today to finish their new forms of advanced layer technologies are already operating in the city. I think the maybe new modern vision and new paradigms of the window in our time.

BEATRIZ COLOMINA

略歴

プリンストン大学建築学部教授。同大学で、「メディアと現代性」というプログラムを設立した。

バレンシア工科大学で建築の最初の研究を始め、その後、バルセロナ建築大学、カタルーニャ工科大学で建築を学ぶ。

MoMA、日本建築学会、ニューヨーク・グッゲンハイム、ハーバード大学、イエール大学、コロンビア大学、スイス連邦工科大学チューリッヒ校、デルフト大学など、世界中の大学や美術館で幅広く講演を行う。

物理的なインスタレーション、デジタルプラットフォーム、新しい形式の出版物を使って、研究をより多くの聴衆に伝えるためのインターフェースとして、アーカイブや口述歴史研究に基づいた一連の国際展覧会をキュレーションした。

建築と現代の表現制度、特に印刷メディアや写真、広告、映画、テレビの諸問題についての執筆活動をおこなっている。
著書は、セクシュアリティとスペース（1993）、プライバシーと広告（1995）に対してアメリカ建築家協会から国際図書賞のような評価を受けている。

Discretized Curves and Tectonic Language

PRESTON SCOTT COHEN

JULY 15, 2009

I was thinking very much about this question of information and it made me have to reconsider the way I would talk about my work. It seemed to be important to think about materiality in light of the question of dematerialization that is involved in the city of knowledge. Material effects are among the most sought-after today in architecture. But be affected interests me most right now Which I was curious or perhaps because it is what I'm doing in the projects. Involves the tradition in architecture of one material imitating another. This isn't effect that is embedded it seems to me in both the abstractions of tectonic language and a kind of empiricism in which we find ourselves looking at so basically. I'm saying in a way something about the idea that when there is a material in architecture that seems to be another one. It is something to with an amalgam, I transfer the election of conditions. Usually, something to do with the techniques of construction both actual and implicit and specific manipulation of scale altogether caught up and very unusual or exceptional architectural forms and typology with institutional and political implications.

That's the problem of architectural tectonics does not originate with material investigations of the facts but rather in the cross scream of the assumption that normally governs the spatial arrangements and character is the institutional program question. The tectonics of material imitation becomes a consequence of the struggle to identify the prohibitions and constraints involved and making a building that precisely the house if it's been exceptional form, answers pacific purposes and meanings impose or desire by culture or clients. I am going to show a few the project I think this happens. This one first for the Nanjing University Performing Arts Center. In this instance, the following is to resolve a tension between on the one hand the first constituencies volume for rooms of various sizes with very particular proportions and shapes. On the other hand and idea that the university had a mandate to represent incoherent and distinctive centerpieces otherwise nondescript campus.

External form is imposed over and above the program that asks for it. The result is a certain kind of conflict. Between these factional disputes and centralized authority. Between

discrete in the bold and exterior shape. This meeting to a certain kind of intensification of discontinuous and continuous spaces and surfaces. The buildings figure altogether the shape is as resilient as it can be. But it is brutally just for ties that is broken down and simplified from the inside out under the constraints of the economy there. You just such thing with the fire all sorts of limitations imposed by the construction process. Those things that normally prohibit such a monolithic form from taking command at all. The interior is composed of a certain kind of cellular order. This case small lounge rooms packed together very tightly all of the dispossessed of the elastic properties that characterize the initial exterior figure. It strives to maintain the building's figure both despite and because of the Ironclad necessity funny internalized discontinuity. How it is continuously bills discontinued is a figure in particular if you witness the look at the stair for example you will see disturbing the rooms inside the tower is it moves to top. It's a building where the compactness is dedicated to certain kinds of environmental solution world. Here we have again and I'll loosen material here again on in an all-encompassing monolithic form. This case a very large gable shaped house stretch to contain an American Dutch barn cloud wood planks horizontal planes. Quite unusually small for a building this size. With details that normally accompany such a conventional form being absent. We are looking at a building where the diminutive of the wood combined with the world would say almost in Normal at the gable. The scale is the newness of windows without details that produces the sense of a kind of tectonic condition.

We should be something more life cast in place concrete. As if that says the freedom to put the windows where everyone wishes could only be found in that time solution and to have them cross in front of the structure and be unrelated to the windows to the structure. This should be something with yields the concrete deal not normal playing. This Museum in Tel Aviv the idea for an outset. Was produce the building would resist the popular tendency to import a kind of postmodern stone facades of Jerusalem certain kind of nationalist aesthetic solution. To Tel Aviv which is really a great city stone clear concrete and stucco international style city. The new Museum was designed and pulp shapes that would be prohibitively expensive to build in stone. This building could somehow confront this problem of losing the long-standing remarkable architectural legacy of the city. At the same time, the project intends to resolve the need to provide rectangular galleries in a site too small to contain the entire program and a site that's nearly triangular. It is a complicated pileup of rooms of disagreeing rooms turning around and trying to make sense within this strange shape.

The facade what I wanted to talk about their test precast components. Very compact concrete. A very fine powder. Manufactured in such a way that they are so impervious as to become reflective very large pieces of to 30 square meters. All different shapes, 360 different shapes cast with magnets on tables in the basement of the building and then brought up and hung on the building. The frame isn't the sacking of arendelle trusses. The heart of the building cast-in-place element. A form called the light fall which is a kind of reflective space that brings light to the deepest level of the building which is largely underground. We see again the board create. But here it represents a contradiction which is that these boards could not correspond precisely to the generators of the surfaces. In fact, we're dealing with is a very imprecise an approximate representation of the geometry that is as bases. Missing now how the plan tile up stacking of different kinds of organizations. Its different angles are relative to one another nothing extruding except elevators. A building which really demands a certain kind of very patient search for means integration conducted by the remarkable project architect that meeting in mind it works.

This idea of uniformity where materiality is again for to test. A building of such diverse components that it is surprising to discover a kind of monolithic expression all in brick. A single house made of two parts a tower or private inhabitation and a kind of deliver below the ground which is composed around courtyards adrift and unmoored in a way to raise an appearance of a certain kind of well not underground and environment.

Normally is quite unremarkable in New York those covered passages to attenuate this condition. It is not clad yet but when it is it will be a kind of Sandwich Glass. This very large building is pressed all of this will be reflected and will be very in a very precise way before electing the relations are rounded and sitting setting up this kind of compression. You receive from above it extends the floor from the interior of the building which is the largest trading for open-plan because it's the trading floor for Goldman Sachs. It extends out onto this roof as if you have somehow been caught in a condition of not being able to extend is it to it had it not been for this very unattractive hotel. Almost like a wave against well something. The conditioned air density is something with the city.

A museum just began construction last week in Taiwan. We could not hear recommend that this building deed free cast. Instead, we have chosen a lightweight stone veneer. This is a honeycomb laminate material with a very thin layer of stone. It's in a building which is taking shape according to two itineraries, two modes of working through a museum one chronological and the other absolutely not absolutely about clustering and relating down in such a way that we just completed in the then. And we just completed competition for the central city. Where the ideas to introduce a park and a time of topographical organization with towers and an internalized historic be constructed a town and area destroyed in the great leap forward and very much desire to restore it. We have looked for a means to do so by integrating it with a landscape and with a certain kind of type of logical organization. All of this Masonry all of it thought about with respect to the way things are to be built there. But integrating systems that are in disagreement with those dimensions in an interesting way such as the parking. In density is much higher normally expect to be accommodated within these technologies within these traditional typologies with you then require very difficult to confront me dylan traditional typology.

In finally, this library which will begin in just about 3 months. A city with a very remarkable sight and storage site. There are remarkable who does a card with very interesting foreign influences. It was impossible not to be inspired by it. You've looked for a way to build a landscape like a plan. It using very interesting modeling which involves cuter variations, again and again, speaking only one problem which was how to overlay two surfaces that would be penalized in such a way that this ramp itinerary that we wanted to build through the building. Why does its way through again clearance between this surfaces? To find a way to thread the needle through a surface is resistance that kind of resistance. That kind of resistance always interest. Here we do not have any kind of solution for the material. We do not understand yet. What this building will be twin remains as they all do it beginning in a state of uncertainty materials. Let me assume that it will reach the point at some point again. Gage is a question of materials allusively shifting from one to another in the characteristics of one to another. I think what is interesting about all of this for me is this notion of this in Korean material. We're and we understand that always there's a certain kind of geometric imperative the push into question material. Then that this geometry is betrayed that is it is somehow violated in a way the very way in which it is built.

The extent to which the building or architecture we could say misses its goal attempt to gain a certain degree of perfection and its attempt to reach a very high level of precision. In a way, the moment of obsolescence, contending obsolescence and anticipation of obsolescence. Each building reaching only a certain limit point exemplifying limitations of its time and its cultural context in this situation. We could say that the valor assigned the survivor architecture puts in question the deep role that negotiation and betrayal play what is ultimately value. Yet, it is not just this dialectic between the said geometry in the construction of meditation that is of great importance is seems to mean another one that has to do with this notion of the elusive dematerialization architecture or the shifting materialization some architecture. That is when architecture is caught in an upheaval. When in its negotiations with all of the confessions that are building it. It becomes embedded in a certain kind of historicism not only of a certain monumentality but of the modern movement itself and its material techniques. In the end, it is the network balance of demands that produces a renewed possibility of material integrity. That's a culturally embedded monumentality.

PRESTON SCOTT COHEN

略歴

ハーバード大学デザイン大学院の教授。2004年にプレストン・スコット・コーエン事務所を設立する。

ロードアイランド・スクール・オブ・デザインで美術学士号と建築学士号を取得し、ハーバード大学デザイン大学院で建築修士号を取得する。

世界中の文化的、教育的、商業的建築や都市デザインなど幅広いプロジェクトの設計デザインを手掛ける。

主な著書として、Lightfall（2016）、The Return of Nature（2015）、Contested Symmetries（2001）等がある。

the architecture of
the STREAMING CITY

MARK WIGLEY

JULY 15, 2009

Maybe I would try to speak very directly about this question of knowledge and transportation. I looking at the history of architects suggesting that knowledge and transportation were exactly the same things. In particular, its the history of thinking about network in architecture so much of contemporary discussion about the network architecture has exactly and echo of old must one century of this discussion. We have at least 100 years been discussing the relationship between networks and architecture. It's not so clear that we have made new discoveries. Recently, actually, in architecture, we have been speaking about the same things for more or less than three thousand years. We are not so interested in new things. We're always interested in the mysteries of the paradoxes in the question of the very simple things about shelter and space. But the question is how can we talk about networks today.

Firstly, it would seem impossible to not talk about networks in architecture today. It seems that we are so immersed in complex networks that we could not imagine life today without networks and therefore we could not imagine making space for life architecture without networks. But precisely, the reason that we are always inside networks. Precisely, the reason that we can no longer imagine life without networks. We are actually not very good at talking about networks. It was the problem been in something is you cannot see it so clearly because you're inside it. For example, it's not so clear that fish would be very good serious but water. Because they live in water all the time they don't necessarily have a concept of water. Maybe the fish has for the first time concept of water when you remove the fish from the water. It wants to go back and mediatory it says water. But most of the time is completely surrounded by water and therefore cannot imagine itself almost as different than water. It networks out like this they are by definition everywhere and because they are everywhere almost impossible to see almost impossible. Networks always see the ability to plan for them to visualize them.

We have another problem is the never see the new network. We always see the old networks. You see the ones that are

just going out of uses. In fact, you could argue that the architect is something of an expert in this. For example, this is an image of 1965. This is the image of the possibility of the archipelago of Japan as a single city as a single organism. Destroying and the number of drawings from the same time was based on similar drawings that would be done by and list of telephone calls between the islands of Japan. You can see the announcement of telephone calls is used to make an image of a city of the near future. In which it looks like the city is a kind of a nervous system in which the nerves become telephone connections become wise. We have a kind of electronic city with three major knows. This is really an image of a telephone network. But it's an image of the telephone network coming in 1965. In which is the bomb in which the computer is arriving in architecture for the first time.

As the computer arrives the architects recognize precisely the need to think about electronic space in the space of the computer. But the way in which they visualize that space is to use the technology that is just getting away to the computer and the telephone. At the moment of the arrival of the computer firstly and maybe for the first time, there is great

clarity about the telephone. This practice is always the way. Practice today has a discussion about the networks in the relationship between architecture and knowledge. But this discussion will produce the state of images which are based on the state of technologies which may be just about to go away. This is maybe always the question how can we take the technologies of the past to visualize what we think are the effects of the technologies of the future.

Let's start with some simple ideas about a network. The network is always a whole universe. The network is never inside a world. The network is always a complete world. The network has no inside and no outside. The network is a landscape with no outside. The main principle of a network is a redundancy that everything can be done in many different ways. For example, the distributed intelligence of the computer of today is not about moving an idea from one place to another invention something on one the computer and sending an email to another computer. Distributed

intelligence is about the possibility that the ideas are being made not in the brain of the first time using the computer. But the internet works system of the computer itself. All of the people who are using those computers as part of that system is part of the computer. The idea of distributed intelligence is the idea that the network itself is a computer the network itself is kind of a brain a thinking machine. It's such a thinking machine things and people do not simply happen inside space drive space itself is the event is the personality.

This condition is a major problem for architects to think about today. In fact, the language we use the language of the networks of flowers of parallel processing of the web of the bandwidth of interfaces and all. this is a very old discourse in architecture. Not just from the metabolism here in Japan which was absolutely clear. We can even say that this way of thinking was already going on as early as the 17th century towards the end of the seventeenth century.

Suddenly, it's absolutely clear by the time we arrived in the 1920s with circle modern architecture. This is, for example, an image from Le Corbusier is an archive of the International telephone network. He's using these images in this was an image that he was thinking was possible to use in his magazine. That is to say, an image that he's thinking of using before he has made the designs for which he will be famous. He's thinking about the network. He's thinking about the fact that the network is global. But in his own architecture, he will not use the word network until this image of 1933 office radiant city. But here he uses the network only to describe the transportation system.

Not logical architecture self-communication between buildings. It met the 40s like 40s comes up with much more complicated than and sophisticated concepts so far networks. But let's say at the very end of his life. For example, with this project for Villa Venice Hospital of 1964 that for the first time he really produces a project in which There's no distinction between the transportation system in the building that the system of communication and the system of inhabitation are exactly the same thing. In fact, the only thing you can occupy in this project is the communication system. Of course, this project is learning a lot from the famous projects for real and Algiers for cities that are built inside the transportation system for apartment buildings suspended in the highway. All of these projects, he's considering the possibility of a radical horizontal architecture in which each point of connection to each other point of connection can be established to renew numerous vision new numerous modes of communication. Every time he describes the linear city proposals he makes these little drawings of the possibility of an artificial horizon.

The concept is fully embodied within the Venice hospital screen what you see here in plan and section. In plan, it is simply the network. Again another network that makes objects, but the network itself as a not object. This is a concept of the horizontal network was absolutely dominant in experimental thinking of the same years. For example, this is the famous drawing from Louis Kahn of the traffic system of Philadelphia from 1951 to 1953. Every architect in the world was looking at the story and was being affected by the story. This is a drawing of a city a very dangerous city. Which is now rented as a pure circulation is it the pure information system. Effect when turning and then find produce a tower with a system all they're trying to do is to produce a vertical version of this horizontal line even in this network building. The building still has a series of the very traditional floor. Let's say it's just a kind of experiment in the possibility of a building having the same network structure is as a city. The real experimentation becomes much more intense with Konrad Wachsmann you see on the right. Looking into his famous space frame for the Air Force in 1951. I know by accident he's looking not into the amazingly large space underneath the frame which is made for huge aircraft. He is looking right into the depths of the frame itself.

You can see that the dimension of the space frame is actually bigger than the dimension of the space below. It so the real space being constructed by architect. This not space to house the airplane essentials. But the space inside the frame for the aircraft. The space inside the space frame. Now, this is a game you can show how these floating frames became so so dominant in architecture. This is a constant new Babylon diagram from 1959. This is the quickly in bourne analysis of the office plan that demonstrates each office that contains within it and network of associations between people same here. This is the special city through Europe of Yona Friedman. This is going to be dismissed in the diagram of networks of 1957. This is Buckminster Fuller in 1958. He's suspended within his exhibition in the Museum of Modern Art. Like-kind of an animal. This animal is saying to you that live inside the network is really very very good. But still, the foremost architect expanded hanging inside the network is not such a good idea and the keep tring to develop.

The main point of the research of the architect is to not have a network like this in which you move from one space to another or cover another space, but I got a project in which the network itself would provide the space. It would require another generation of architect to career to exhibition particularly clear in the work of the Archigram book. For example, this is the city into the change from 1963. You can see here that you occupy the transportation system in the nose of the network become the major spaces and it even describes itself as a network. This is the underwater city from Archigram magazine in 1964. Again if you leave the network behind you will die, you will drown. Same other space, of course, and other space being a major role model. This is the walking city of Archigram and the most famous project. Not so well-known is that the walking cities were meant to get together in large groups like this and phone networks. They basically walk to create a network like this. Begin to live in these cities is to never leave the city behind. These are cities with no outside at all. The trick the great trick of the architect divide experiment more or less running

from the 1920s through the 1960s is starting to produce an architecture that has no outside no exterior.

Architecture that is more radical than that of the modern architect. For the modern architect inside becomes a landscape is absolutely continuous with the outside. But there is still a division between inside and outside is very very like a division but it still exists there is a line, as a dotted line, as a screen, as a panel, as a window. With this more radical thinking work its way through to the 1960s. There is the idea of another line at all between inside and outside. To live is to live in the outside. Outside sort of as a huge huge landscape, huge interior. This becomes even more obvious in this project of 1963. This is computer City by Dennis Crompton of Archigram. This is a city which literally takes physical form on the secretary of a computer. In fact, you could argue this is mean of the ambition of architects throughout our time is to make architecture behave and look like an electric circuit board.

Effect images of circuit boards were always appearing in the drawings. For example, the architects of the little city that we saw today. This is an early version of the little city. This is Archigram explaining the project for the moving city. They have made the map of England look exactly like a circuit board. The project is conceived of as a set of wires embedded in today. This is an image that appears in a 1967 issue of Perspective Magazine. End of their appears with no explanation because in this moment of time no explanation is needed. The electric circuit board is a great dream for architect. If only architecture could be as interesting as a circuit board so to have us have the image of an electric circuit board in an architectural magazine would be the same as to have an image of a flower. That you don't have to explain that it's a flower and therefore it's a beautiful thing in an object of nature. This is some kind of mechanical industrial flower.

This is another image of a circuit board with your appearance is it in an article by Charles Moore in order to explain the logic of the city. Here's another one which is in the book by showing me a picture of Alexander from 1963. The reason they put this image of a circuit board in this book is it they complain about the fact that this circuit board which comes from a television set is inside every American house inside every television set but that circuit board is much more sophisticated in the house. Architecture is primitive technology compared to the technology of the circuit board. In fact, we can argue that the entire ambition of architecture was focused on the circuit board and we could even make a comparison between the logic of the architecture and the specific conditions of the circuit board move to history.

For example, in this project of Alison and Peter Smithson of Hauptstadt, you can see that they have taken the transportation network and made it a three-dimensional object like a building but there are still small buildings that are it is being attached. This is like early circuit boards with transistors. You have most of the circuits embedded in the more but you have some transistors in different places. Maybe, this one is like a villain in an old circuit board where there is inside the building a lot of circuitry suspended way about a flex circuit board with very simple wires. This circuit board is much more like the age of the transistor small discrete objects on the circuit board. Then with elder Van Dyke's orphanage of 1958 to 1960 no difference between the circuit board and the building itself as the circuit board getting closer and closer to the circuits of today. You understand perfectly of course that today the computer chip is just a series of horizontal layers.

There is no longer any vertical element in a computer is a series of horizontal layers. The crossbones precisely to the ambitions of architects at this time. Maybe the most famous example of the whole back and Ellison Woods University in Berlin 1964. No longer is the University of series of buildings that belong to different departments of knowledge that are connected by a communication system like a system of walkways. The University is one big circuit board in which you can no longer identify which department belongs in which place. Affect the University of South Dakota has a kind of computer kind of a thinking machine. Absence of any strength in the horizontal direction the ability to move in any direction is what defines the intelligence of the university and of the architecture.

Finally, in this moment there is a kind of image of information and knowledge as an electric circuit board. I shake the image and you know perfectly that in the Berlin system of University. This was 1 or 6 zones of the same dimension. In fact, this would spread as a vice network and other arctic starts to invent projects in which the circuit board would go across the entire planet. This is through the same year as constants new Babylon project. Which is one building at the size of the planet? One building has a horizontal network space with no walls with no outside space with you can wonder forever.

Here in 1959 the first drawing of the project. Always through to occasions no stop city where the difference between a highway and a copper is removed and the entire world is covered with one enormous copper which is filled with all of the kind of information necessary to the super surface project of Super Studio in 1970-1971. In which the horizontal circuit board has become so thin and so packed with information and computers that everyday life just becomes a kind of nomadic drift across this one horizontal surface again at the size of the planet. Of course, what Surper Studio was imagining in this moment is the entire world as one electronic circuit board as a stage for global life.

Literally to live is to live on an electric circuit board in this moment. You could say perhaps in this moment 1970-71 that Le Corbusier is the dream of confusing the relationship between inside and outside has been taken to its most radical extension into an exam one can see the completion of the project. Again we can take another more detailed example for in exactly the same much this Mississippi prices Fun Palace project 1961 to 1964. Again, this is a structure meant to house 55000 people. Again the logic of this project is over. A pure horizontal surface with state-of-the-art equipment about this is like coming to a theater in which there is only a stage. All the equipment about the theater becomes your own equipment and you become the performer in this great performance. Know by accident is this building redefining the plan into kind of blurry space of a possible movement. Again in this project, it is the computer that will make possible the unpredictable play in the lives of this system. This is the electronic work done for this project they said the circuits that were calculated to give the feedback that would enable people's desires to be responded to me. In all of these projects in the secret prices from Fun Palace in the Super

Studio project of the Super Surface in occasions no stop city in constant new Babylon and Jonah Freedman special city. All of these projects had the idea of the computer as what would make possible these new freedoms. In a certain way, you can say that the dream of the computer in architecture in the late 50s and early 60s is very very hard by the number of experimental actives.

The kind of image of what is my means is completed already in moreless 1970-72. The most radical concept of the kind of Super Surface that is going absolutely everywhere. In the case of Cedric Price. He is most directly trying to imagine this the space of information transfer. This is the Price think about project that he develops as an extension of the Fun Palace based on an industrial railway network in England. Again this not accident with the most important projects dealing with the relationship between transportation, infrastructure, information, knowledge, space in architecture where University projects weather be at the University of Dallas. Words for me the Fun Palace which was dreamed of as the University of the people or this actual University.

I always be sustained as a system of information systems of knowledge in which architecture would be reduced down to a very very efficient set of mechanical instruments. And what we would think of as architecture in the past become something like a ghost. Something drawing always with it a dotted line. A kind of hovering space is large. It is clearly defined and in a specific location but its effects are absolutely unclear. Again, this is the little diagram at Candelas ward's used to explain the concept of the Free University and the concept of the networking of information. Again, the sophisticated architect of the network. It could be on the right there Conrad Waxman who is here with Walter Gropius discussing the system they developed for a prefabricated housing system which is seen below. This is the system for linking up the wooden elements that make up the house what Waxman would call a not very sophisticated project that he brings from Germany to the United States. This is the most sophisticated project perhaps of Super Network in mental that he's doing with his students in Chicago. If you look at the metal there are no columns here and no beams. It isn't this is metal which has been woven exactly like a favorite. Every column turns the corner and becomes a beam which becomes a column in some. But still not by accident the view is primarily horizontal. Even though I wasn't logic of the network means of freedom to move in any direction, we still conceive all that freedom horizontal.

In the same way that we describe the wide world web as a wide world, not a deep world still imagine desert is a horizontal system of communication. These are the three joint systems used by Conrad Waxman for the house for the airplane Hangar and for the super metal frame on the ride. This systems of fabrication become the basis of it's only would such a connection system that you could imagine and architecture that has his no outside. Here are the students in the University of Chicago producing those famous networks. But this is also a drawing of the same students because Waxman also placed the students in a network system. He divided all the students into groups of three. Each group of three would work on a different question and at the end of each week. They would come to this table would you see at the bottom of this table and each group would present the results of the research to all the other groups. Then you would change the combination of three and then change a game and change again. At any one time, each student is only working on one question with two other students but by the end of the design project, they have learned all the information from all the other students. And so as a network they have soared like a network brain. The students are thinking in a network, about networks, to reduce the network. Understand become Conrad Waxman's drawing of the University which he was teaching as network.

This is how each department within expands out. This is the Department of architecture. Then this is the University and would keep exploring into a kind of a flower. Again, the network is treated here as the most beautiful and most natural object. We are speaking here of nature of the flower, of the electronics flower. Of course, we are very much in the world of Marshall McLuhan and the possibility of an endless connection. Already in the moment of 1964 when Marshall McLuhan is leveraging the possibility of a new kind of living in the space of Information. Architect has already been elaborating very very sophisticated visions of that and Marshall McLuhan was a dedicated student of architecture. He was studying architecture. He's quoting Siegfried Gideon and most of his books. It is not that architect read something fancy said about the computer and said about the network in Marshall McLuhan and then applied in the research is the other way around. Marshall McLuhan was very much been influenced by the work of architects. Recognize that its position is the same. This is his image for information. Information is to do with network fabrics. This is his image of the education. This is a little schoolboy of the past on the left and the little schoolboy of the future on the right.

It's all about the nervous system which has been always a very big part of architect this post. Image for Le Corbusier on the left of the nervous system. Image used by intense in arts and architecture on the ride image of Frederick Kiesler and the nervous system. Architect has been kind of expert on the nervous system for a very long time. When you get into 1970-71 with the super surface project of Super Studio, you are looking at the product of very long research. More than half-a-century Research into the possibility of the space defined by the computer. The clear abstract wide-spaced of the super surface has embedded inside of the wires and intensity of that computer which makes possible all of this social density and exchange about. In other words, there's no confusion hear any problem here between maximum physical and personal density and maximum abstraction and horizontal expansion and what liberates that is a possibility of the computer. Just to end on that sort of simple point that when we think today about the relationship between knowledge and infrastructure and architecture. We are perhaps today using very sophisticated ideas about the computer systems that we are using a communication systems that we are using. But very likely we are using an image of our systems that will be made redundant by the next technological innovation and Innovation according to the clue and has already happened but we are not in a position to see it. So like everybody else and culture, we work with that which is visible to us the previous system of technology to imagine the system that may or may not be coming in the future and I think very much to work with their students baby sore today is exactly on.

This kind of edge using a using all technologies and all thinking about all technologies to imagine the possibility that we are already in space of new technology. In the base of technologies means to be in architecture to shape we do not know. It is if it is the role of the architect to get to give shape to something. The mission of the architect then comes to give shape to something that the scene cannot see. I think this is a fact that the architect always gets in shape to that which is not yet able to be seen. Makes architecture one of the most beautiful part of the most romantic and mustard eternal you can say. A thousand years has not been very long press will not be a very long message.

MARK WIGLEY

略歴

1987 年から 1999 年まで、プリンストン大学で教鞭を執り、プリンストン建築学校大学院のディレクターも務め、2004 年から 2014 年まで、コロンビア大学 GSAPP の学部長を務める。

1988 年に MoMA で展覧会「Deconstructivist Architecture」（脱構築主義建築）をフィリップ・ジョンソンと共同でキュレーションを行う。

2005 年にレム・コールハースとオレ・ボウマンと共に Volume Magazine を設立する。

主な著書として、The Architecture of Deconstruction: Derrida's Haunt（1993）、Are We Human? Notes on an Archaeology of Design（2017）、等がある。

From DA
To NADAAA

NADER TEHRANI
FEBRUARY 21, 2011

As I recently understood it's actually your vacation so particularly kind of YouTube has such a generous turnout for such an occasion. From the perspective of the architectural discipline. There are two components that remain pressing and important to me.

On the one hand, it's the discipline as we define the practice, building and being in the world. On the other hand, there is the architectural practice as seen as pedagogy as an evolution of conceptual ideas and teaching strategies. At least two worlds in our minds do not represent two worlds far apart. They are intertwined in direct ways. We are taught quite often that you come to school to get prepared for practice. But the reality the conditions of the world out there are changing so fast that even if I were to try to prepare you for what's out there. The conditions of practice would have changed already. So we cannot teach you anything that is of any importance anymore. We cannot prepare you for practice. What we can do is to begin to strategize ways of thinking and conceptual strategies. So that you may change practice itself.

The lecture is structured into two parts that I go back and forth between. One is a series of conventional architectural projects. The other is a series of installations related to production that takes place in the context of pedagogy in cooperation with students, in which from. This perspective some of the architectural practices are conveyed from bottom to top and others from above you can tell what's down. The lecture is broken down into a series of if you like architectural postulations, architectural lessons.

The first one has to do with the foundation to be launched any architectural attack. We do not proceed without material conditions as the basis for both theory and action. In this case corrugation as a material. We understand is rigid on the vertical axis but malleable on the horizontal. In this way, a surface can become special all of a sudden and incorporate a program. Central to this is the material agency of corrugation without which such a theory would not be possible.Generation until the door you can see how a two-dimensional surface becomes three-dimensional because the vertical lines of corrugation essentially begin to demonstrate

how the surface can be exploited an expanded to connect to stare back into the house. Here drawing is not pictorial or an illustration. Drawing is active construction. We fabricate drawings. We don't draw drawings. The bottom of the drawing is cut off all of the above the screen but essentially shows that the line at the top is exactly the same length as the line at the bottom and that's the definition of a ruled surface.Anything that can be built out of a two-dimensional surface that into a three-dimensional space isn't developable surface. That's the root of in the many forms of fabrication.

Emerging out of this comes all of the different complexities of architectural conditions. How to make openings, how to bring light into the building, how to turn a corner and an architecture is launched from that point.

Knowledge some of our precursors not only for what they've opened up to us but somehow some of the conceptual inadequacies. Gehry is arguable opened up a world of digital exploitation. But he does so in such a way that is indifferent to the relationship between surface and space, structure and skin. As you look at the images of Bilbao you recognize that the skin is just a wallpaper. It has no bearing on how you turn a corner. It has no bearing on how you chop the building with the coping or basic. It's merely a kind of surface that is draped on top of formal conditions that are willful on his part.

A look outside of our own particular discipline. In this case into tailoring sartorial discipline. We realize that in fact historically. There are many ways in which three dimensionality is gage. All of you sitting here in the audience or wearing some article of clothing. That navigates your bosoms and your butts and the curvatures of your body. All of this is made out of two dimensional fabric. That has been essentially dots at the house. The dots are essentially excavations the cut. The two-dimensional material at once they're brought together to reduce a mechanical surface. For this reason this fabrication this installation by in collaboration with Harvard students.

It is not so much the results of an artistic or willful act on our power. It is the careful calibration of exact trappings of the column and Archway and a kind of bowstring truss on top of the information Island whose form is calibrated indirect relationship with each panel. Every condition has a relationship between park and home. The dots are the element that brings geometry together with the overall figure. Of course, the grain of the wood has something to say about this cutting along the axis of the grain is slightly different than cutting against the axis. So negotiations between technique and material do have an impact on the maximization of curvature also. No matter how we conceptualize formed as an abstraction in architecture rebuild it through parts. Even when we smooth things out.

We recognize that a bridge is this dimension or a slat of wood or plywood is 4 foot by 8 foot everything has modules. So the principle of aggregation or assembly is central to the way in which we negotiate part to whole. Working with rubber membrane Roofing. We had the occasion of taking the roof and draping it over a facade. Essentially upholstering a building, wrapping the building, closing the building. I didn't earn take on different architectural problems of entry and entry arch of wrapping on the opposite end and opening up windows in between. I didn't earn take on different architectural problems of entry and entry arch of wrapping on the opposite end and opening up windows in between. The archway at the entry voice over. The chimney wraps around the fireplace. Maybe most importantly with unbuttoned the facade in order to create the relationship between inside and outside never once cutting the rubber membrane. Always feeling it and wrapping it around its maximum possible figuration. The result of this is courses as in the condition of Gehry a very figural condition of a form, facade, sculpture but whose limits are gage by the limits of material and the agency of aggregation. These are two different historical trajectories meeting on the same plate. Mies van der Rohe until more axis and if you like Gehry on the other axis. The prospect of aggregation, of course, is not new to architecture. Anybody who's seen a brick building, a tile building understands that the building is a result of discrete units that are added together to produce larger conditions. But few traditions are impacted by their relationship to structural engineering and environmental engineering such as architecture. To think of them as support an interruption. We have to find a way to internalize those disciplines. So they become inextricably bound to the way we actually design upfront and center.

This sidewall of this building in Venezuela is one such example. Whereby we take a sheet of brick wall. Fold it and folding it, bring to it last of stability. Making use of a very thin bricklayer to give it lots of structure. In this way, the pattern of the brick is laid on the diagonal but most importantly it traditional bonding is static like a running bond or a flemish bond. Here we introduce a variable bond. The variable bond gets to expand and contract. So that different amounts of lights and air can begin to be engineered into the space of the porch beyond. The plan of the bottom again cut-off shows the depth of that wall and the geometry of going from one condition core board stack by stack rotated to the top.

This is built for the first time not out of brick but out of woods. You can see here the way in which the woods as standard pieces of construction about 2 ft long 3 in wide and 1 inch thick or stacked on top of each other in relationship to a working drawing that is not any longer convention. The drawing is it away please sit up on to the ceiling and then drop down through the plan line to get with an exact gravitational measure of 16 in a tolerance almost zero tolerance. The traditional plan and section would love to be able to build this. In fact the contractor business out at $200,000 but because we understood the correct means and methods of fabrication. We were able to build it for $30,000. Again identify each of the coordinates of the intersections and then hanging the plumbobs from those points almost to the light sculpture. And then built in brick in China. We test it out the same principle in a more complex urban form that includes an art center that has different galleries here and studio spaces with courtyards that have access points between them to get in and out of the spaces. Conceived out of brick a traditional material there and as abstractions the cubes if you like.

The program is introduced by way of discrete functions. Those functions being the draining of water. The expelling of smoke through the chimneys the introduction of lights for the gallery spaces. And the adoption of the use of discrete spaces underneath the stair for circulation.

In this image, you can see actually the simplicity of the break forms but then the archways that are then carved out of the entries that go from one cord to the other essentially. You get just enough Headroom to slip by into these corridors of space through a bonding system that oscillates between a Flemish bond and a running bond sliding back and forth. In fact, even though it appears to be built out of brick because it's in a seismic zone much like here. The brick is merely for work for concrete. Why because of the steel reinforcement within the concrete. It gives it the kind of ductility to move without cracking. And the brick has been merely a form outside of that. That registers the trajectory of the stair from one corner to the other as it goes up.

Essentially the figuration of the space of the stair is the result of a negotiation of the program the stair the treads and risers. The brick and the possibility of corbelling out a corner in each other time. These three factors create the foundation for the formwork of a concrete wall. In the first phase here built out of the local masonry. You can see the way in which a solid basis excavated to make the mechanical systems read. You can see the formwork as growing up and becomes a soffit as a formwork for the concrete above. And essentially into materialize the malleability and the flexibility of the brake system as a series of pixels that can be pushed in and out and slid out and back. And here you can see the way in which the brick slums over, slide over so that the entire building until down in order for the drainage system of the water to go to the northern edge. It is these bricks here that begin to shift over and space and elicit larger formal repercussions over the entire building.

A lot of this, of course, goes back to the prospects of drawing. And how to draw space, how to draw form, how to draw three-dimensionality. But drawing compound curves is different than building them. And for that reason when we come to represent the world, build the world we build it in straight lines. Breaking down the straight lines to a smaller part of the possible. In this case the longitude and latitude into smaller discrete trapezoidal pieces. The triangle helps to smooth it out.

And so it follows as you can flatten it out as in Rhino it means you can build us. The everything I've presented till now has to do with the building industry and construction systems that are conventional. A brick is like this, the wood is like this, a panel is like this. But we yet to come to understand the way in which. We can invent units of construction that can actually help the change of states of an architectural condition. In natural sciences we take for granted that water and snow and ice are in fact the same thing the same molecular structure in different states of condition. But when we come to architecture and structure we have a very type of logical understanding of elements for instance.

We call a trust a vector practice system, recall an arch of form active system and become a shell a surface-active system. All of these compelling and exciting in the on right but never have we seen systems of surface, form, and vector active. It away aligns together as one fluid topological system. I'm sure is a diagram you could see the way in which we can have to do this by the transformation of a coffered structural system to a surface-active system by rotating the fins just enough that they begin to touch each other. But you do that we need to invent a new brick. A parametric brick if you like. These four bricks are actually the exact same element. But manipulated on the X, Y, and Z axis when you shift that down because of this. When you shift this apartment becomes that. So you go from a change of state from a box spin to a kind of folded system to a truss system. And following certain laws of mathematics, you can go from 2 promo system to 4 and from 4 to 8 and so internalized within. This is arithmetic permutations that free you are formally to do anything you want to do. And all those help you to imagine a system that is in four parts a stacked masonry system, a laterally braced wall, a trust that spans 30 feet and a cantilever that pushes out 8 or 9 feet. All of them emerging out of one oscillation and transformative system. And once it's built, we actually test the statics how to spam from a vertical column to a horizontal column over here for 30 feet. Judge in the truss and see how polycarbonate works essentially against weight and effectively gets cantilever it on the opposite end.

Some years ago then with this the interest in structure. I came back to Japan. I'm fascinated by Ito's talks began to see the possibilities in which structure iconography the idea that a building's concept may emerge from the trees in the foreground can begin to impact space and the way that we think about building. But that on entering the building and I realize that this is a building that's a classical modern building. It emerges from a modern paradigm of horizontal slabs with certain double-height spaces in between. In other words, it participates in this course.

Let's say lay down by Venturi between a duck and a decorated shed in between a figure and a surface. That is actually not engaged in the organization of the interior. And so my question was what would it be if we took this building and began to thinking and dipping it prot. This was important for us. Because we were about to do a competition that takes place in a small forest.

What explains that I need to take the detail. The detail about two teams that are set up in this lecture. One about figuration and one about configuration figuration. Figuration is had to do with a branch of identifying ability that makes you understand form to recognize what the figure of a human being. When I say bottle, you understand this figure. When I say glasses, you understand this figure. When I say telephone booth, you understand that square booth that is drawn on the screen. More importantly, you recognize and looking at that image that there's no relationship between form and content. The way that the men are stuffed into the telephone booth is like taxidermy or like a sausage. It is ground meat that's just smacked inside there and essentially the programmatic content is not in any way related to the figure of the telephone booth. This is how working top-down works. In contrast to figural systems, configurative systems don't know the form before have they know only rules and regulations. If you look a twister the matrix that is laid down on the ground. Sets the rules and the terms but it doesn't tell you the form. Factor this way the final form of a configurable system could

be many other forms besides this. And so these two systems are always in a state of dialogue in architecture.

Coming back to Ito, decide of contemplation is this little forest that we see right here between the center of the campus of the American University in Beirut and the mediterranean sea. Arguably the context on this new building is not the buildings of the campus, not the architecture of Beirut but the trees amongst which it sits. And ficus tree gives you seductive ways of interpreting structure, program, and space.

And we knew at all costs that we wanted to camouflage our building within the context of those trees. And the building was a mechanism to make it disappear. We need to invent the system. A system that a geometric system that could become a column. But column, contrast form into a piloti and transfer loads. A system of structure that could transfer lateral loads from one direction to another or become a generic wall. But the geometry unit is enough not. It needs to become special and programmatic. And for that reason, we respect gravity and know that it has weight and mass of the bottom inhabitable it transfers loads. In the middle and becomes lights at the top as distributed loads to the sky. And this from emerges an idea about a generic building. That requires programmatic flats long-span conditions inside of it. A relationship between the outdoors bringing it in. A defamation inside that acknowledges programmatic ships like auditorium for lightening up the systems as you go to the top.

Here space, structure, circulation, program are all embedded within each other and you witness the various elements as you go up through the building. Here you see the transfer of the loads. And here at the top of the building as the hypostyle hall of trees begin to give shape to the outdoor space. That not all buildings are able to fulfill the integration of all of the elements. In certain cases you inherit structural conditions and you need to plant them.

Such was the case for this gas station which was composed of prefabricated build fragments in this case payable. Reflecting on gas stations one understands that they actually are a part of architectural histories and trajectories with all of their elements. The base, the capital the corner, the loof, all of them being defined on their own terms. Even the modern ones that are composed of signage. All of these contribute to the fabrication of a brand. We were often challenged to build a prototype for British petroleum as they went from that brand to beyond petroleum on the other. Essentially the extinguishing of the emphasis on petroleum and with the new emphasis on green technologies. Similar to Beirut with enveloped a skin not a structure, a column, the capital, and the canopy. That is malleable enough geometrically to distort to accommodate code and signage as a flag's out and special conditions for inhabitable spaces. The column, the tables, the sign and the sum total of the various fragments as they work through the triangulated system of the helios to produce a broader environment. Within which is embedded a smaller scale of programmatic information includes the speaker system, the lighting system, the sprinkler system, all excavated out of the same triangulation that you see appear. In this way to the gas station is called on to separate the sensorial aspects of architecture from the significant aspects of architecture. The billboard takes on the role of signification telling you what it is underneath. And then this becomes more of an environmental condition that is rooted inexperience.

All of the examples I showed you somehow display the tension between figuration and configuration. The ball on the right is a ceramic ball that conceals the molecular makeup of the system of aggregation that defines the shape of the whole in the ball. On the left, the nest and the identical figure begin to articulate and underlying the various straw and the grass elements that constitute the makeup of the same ball. These two systems remain constantly in dialogue intention with each other. And somewhere in here, there's the tension of ruining and how architecture releases meaning. Differently on the productive side that on the receptor side. Both of these forms in a way in golf objects that are able to release me. But the arbitrary relationship between the signifier and the signified. Are best illustrated by the narrative in The Little Prince. Where the figure out the snake in one instance looks like a hat that upon the second inspection reveals the content of the elephant within the figure of a very snake. Not going back to the rubber membrane house.

Let's discuss the relationship of figuration once again. Look at the stair and the way which the stair brings together different public rooms of the house. The contents of this building are strictly tithed to the form of the building. The staircase bulges out just so there's enough headroom to get upstairs, the sink, the bathtub, the toilet, the entry, the fireplace.All of them are shrink-wrapped to the tightest possible condition. So that there is no facts on this building. And the experience of this building is central to its architectural location. When we look at design in general industrial design, we don't think of the bottle as something we experience. What we do experience in but we don't think of this experience. But architecture is one of those things that is ambient. You have to be in it. You have to walk through it. You have to smell it. You have to be immersed in it, to understand it. The experience of this house then displays the laminar system of construction of plywood, copper, and plaster as you go up the building.

Everything in this lecture is about as laying down of systems and rules. So when you introduce a window, you have to respect the horizontal system. Even the hardware the door handles are denominations of the very system of board and batten on the closet. But none of the rules and regulations. I lay down for you or enough to describe the condition of exceptionality, anomaly, and strangeness. That only critical faculties can begin to bring to the table. But cut in the system of the ramp, the stair, and the window or an invention that can completely perpendicular to the logic of everything I just said.

For the last project then I want to bring the senses to the forest. In architecture, we have a very strict understanding of the ground. The ground is inflexible and flat. I've only in certain cases can be sloped floors. But the dome is the space of the structure. The dome is a space of light. The dome is a space of representation. Coming back to the idea of form and content. This tensions played out in certain structures. The delights and the anticipation that this form gives us. Becomes completely underwhelming once we see that the floor slab that occupies it has anything to do with the kind of intricacy and the spatial complexity of the outside. Of course, in some instances people like Archigram have exploited the ground as a malleable and Figueroa system. That's 1% of buildings. The buildings that you and I can design the majority of them are

made of this. The infrastructure of mechanical, engineering, lighting, sprinkler systems.

This is the substance of the new domes that we have to create. Which is a good reason that sometimes we don't design from the ground up but we design from the sky down. A restaurant needs to be flexible on the ground because the tables need to constantly move. For that reason to ceiling can take on all of the weight, of all of the program of structure. Structure, mechanical systems, plumbing even the wine room everything suspended from above. View to relieve some of this becomes exposed. And view longitudinally the appearance of a smooth dome space that brings together the various fragments of the scheme. The material systems using plywood operate as many scales. Plywood as thin ply. Plywood as different elements and even the zebra bamboo produces striations at many scales.

But all of this demonstrates once again. The optical and visual bias of architecture. Of cause, we know that the restaurant is all about the taste of taste, the sense of taste and smell. Uncoincidentally the design of the bathroom is one of those elements that underlie those other senses. We are reminded that if you want to design the bathroom what are the attributes of go inside of them the toilet. The toilet paper the sink lights the diffusers all of that. It just so happens all of them are kind of circular. We wanted to bring into the undignified acts that happened into the bathroom a certain monumentality and occasion by covering it in a dome. The oculus that would be on that dome is then this placed on to the sidewall. Bringing the men and women in different spaces into vulnerable proximity. Not seeing each other but sensing each other. Displacing, of course, visuality is the sense of smell Saturday in the toilet. And of course the sense of sound. Bringing a kind of risk to the proposition of that proximity. In conclusion, I'd like to bring two different historical sensibilities that are rarely put together on the same table.

What is a rational tradition that is interested in constructing a relationship between part and whole? It's a complex system that involves language. Such that the production of meaning is held as a positive part of the conceptualization of architecture. Here you see the way in which the beams become the triglyph at the end of the ornamentation around the corners of a temple. What is doesn't exactly explain is how that becomes meaningless as it begins to rotate at the front of the temple. What are we to believe that they made a mistake and putting triglyph in front of the temple or that the whole system of the signification of the temple is bridging the gap between fiction and fact in all of architecture. No, the other two historical traditions have to do with the system of exploration that is more connected to empiricism. Gaudi suspended strings and ropes to invoke the catenary arch. Bringing engineering and architecture closer together. Mendelsohn and Gary all aline themselves in a tradition of expressionism. But maybe less rigorous its engineering aspects but no less speculative and experimental on the formal level. What's somewhere between these polar opposites resides another discrete tradition. Those like an Eladio Dieste then bring the sensibilities of construction of engineering of space making and of the invention together in a more a contested ground of innovative activities. But I would like to bring as a proposition to the table is the notion that notions of integration and complexity are not things that are out there for professionals. In fact, things to cultivate at the foundational level as students as you begin to transform practice itself.

NADER TEHRANI

略歴

2015 年にクーパー・ユニオンのアーウィン・S. チャニン建築学校の学部長となる。

NADAAA の代表を務め、設計革新や学際的なコラボレーション、建設施工との集約的な対話の進歩に特化した活動をおこなっている。

ジョージア工科大学、ロードアイランド・スクール・オブ・デザイン、ハーバード大学デザインで教鞭を執り、その後、MIT で教授を務め、2010 年から 2014 年まで建築学科長を務める。

作品は、Fabricating Coincidences（MoMA、1998）、Immaterial/Ultramaterial（ハーバード大学、2001）、Change of State（ジョージア工科大学、2006）などの一連のインスタレーションを通して展開されている。

Project and Practice

PETER EISENMAN
MARCH 16, 2012

First of all, I want to thank Professor Yamaguchi and all of his group for inviting us here and also I want to thank all of you for coming. It would be a terrible thing to come to a large hole like this and see nobody, so it's I'm glad that you're all here it's very difficult to follow a very articulate critic what I have to say tonight is very simple and probably much easier man to follow but since Professor Quinter made mention of my disagreement with much of what he had to say another word prescribing my own remarks.

I thought I'd better answer in some way to his introduction critics are not Architects critics are like lawyers they are betrayed and prescribed judgment much like their lawyer Lee colics and judges very recently as was pointed out to me by Cynthia Davidson on the last few days lawyers have become involved with strange practices with people involved in wealth management and what it turned out is that many of these lawyers supposedly neutral in their condition of practice have investment in just the cases.

In fact that they are supposedly in neutral and arbitrating so many of my friends say that Sanford Kwinter hates architecture and I realized tonight at Sanford Kwinter doesn't hate architecture nor does he hate himself but rather he has a invested position in just the stocks that he is supposedly neutrally arbitrating he has sold short to use a term of very familiar to those in wealth management he's got a long position in selling short and therefore what he tries to tell us as a neutral judgment on the state of Architecture is, in fact, a protection of a position that I hadn't realized until tonight he holds he's got a lot of stock in this position and he's got a lot of stock and seeing the mark it goes down.

I'm here tonight not as a critic or as a professor or is it an arbitrator but it's an architect and I have a lot of stock invested in the market going up and someone to talk to you tonight about how the market can in fact and will continue to go up because architecture is a belief it's not merely a practice but it's something that I believe in.

I get up in the morning everyday thinking that architecture is something important in the culture whether that culture

in the United States in Europe are in the Far East and I'm always reminded of that culture when I come to someplace like Japan which perhaps more than any other country that I visit demonstrates the relationship between the old and the new between that switches of history and tradition and that which is of the present. I've never been in a more dense architectural environment than I've been in in the last few days in both Tokyo and Osaka and there aren't any more modern cities in the world than Tokyo. In Us, in Osaka and I've been in cities many cities which represent themselves as modern and yet at the same time both these cities are surrounded by traditional construction.

Traditional Values that you see in every street in every place that you go and so I'm going to talk tonight about a tradition in architecture and I'm going to use Western examples because they're the ones that I know because I am not an expert on the far East nor in Japanese culture although I made my first visit here long before.

Many of you in this audience were even though I thought I first came to Japan in 1955 by my count some 6777 years ago 67 I guess it is and I doubt very many of you were alive when I first came here and I remember going to Kyoto 2 Katsura to shoot Cochran to Ryoanji to learning about Sekiya and what it meant in Japanese culture and in innocence daily life and how Sukiya and the terms Ma and coo. We're not even translatable into Western ideas and I can remember thinking that is the notion of the space of between not a thing but the absence of things. Thing this became very important to me and so much of what I do in architecture and what I still think about is conditioned by thoughts of Sukiya and thoughts of the Teahouse at katsura or the thoughts of how every 20 years East say Shrine is rebuilt not as something new and different but as something new but like it was.

And I'm not convinced having heard the previous lecture that he is even interested in the terms of Sukiya or can even understand it if he were to be shown it because there's a different culture that exists in architecture then in the generalities of contemporary other news of thought.

And so I want to talk tonight about those conditions that exist in architecture maybe stemming from something like ski area where the tea house at katsura Palace say that because I'm going to speak about two terms one the term project and the other the term practice and I'm going to speak for a few minutes about these terms and then I'm going to show two of my projects and I do that because the Italian architectural critic and theoreticians Manfredo Tafuri said to me very pointedly once Peter you have a fantastic project but if you hadn't built no one would care and so while I continue to develop a project in a very humble way.

I also realized the need to practice to build the things that I think about when I'm concerned with project so I'm going to talk to you tonight about project and then I'm going to show you practice of project and then leave it for a discussion that I'm certain we'll follow with Professor Quinter what you should realize since we have been friends for so many years there's an enormous rivalry between two institutions in the United States apps like the Rivalry between the two best universities in the Far East Tokyo and Osaka, so to two of the best universities in America Harvard and Yale have an enormous rivalry.

What's interesting is Professor Quinter now after many years as a Wanderer has found a home at that institution called Harvard and is probably giving him a new kind of sense of certainty because I've never heard him use the terms must and should in ever in this speech before and these two terms have suddenly come into a place because as we all know Harvard is number one and Yale is number to.

I've always been in a position to use a Japanese phrase of being an ozeki attempting to be a Yokozuna. I don't think that Yale will ever be more than a training ground. I was a key and I think that Harvard has always felt itself to be a place where Yokozuna live and so that would describe a little difference between Professor Quinter and myself.

What do I mean by project a quick metaphor I think would be useful an architectural project is one where the architect defines the world he or she lives in whereas a practice is one in which the world defines the architect and both are viable ways to think about the world some people are not interested in defining the world and others are not interested in having the world to find you.

It doesn't depend on Talent OR intelligent it doesn't depend upon whether you can design or not it rather depends on how you see yourself in relationship to the world's sustainability environment.

Parametric's are not a project they are away the world defines you as an architect what is a project. The Roman architect Bora mini which is one of the most important architects in the world in history had a project while the architect Bernini had a practice. Yet Bernini was one of the most successful and Powerful Architects the world has ever known wild boar Amini had just a few buildings.

In fact, Bora mini was so upset about his relationship to Bernini and the traditional sense of power that was evoked by Bernini's work that bore Amini in desperation took his own life to come closer to the present day.

I would argue that Aldo Rossi Italian architect had a project while the famous British architect James Sterling had a practice. I could also say that although Rosie had a project and Norman Foster had a practice Robert Venturi had a project. I am pay had a practice is what is interesting to me is that.

In fact, the histories of architecture after they are sorted out from their present mediation innocence are always built on the people that have had a project and that most people who have had a project in One Way or Another. Not only have been recorded in history but have recorded the history of how they Define society at the time of their project.

If we look for example at Le Corbusier in the 1920s and 30s there were a lot of French Architects such people as well Molly stay Vons andrelos are and others who are doing little white houses at the same time as Corbusier. So it wasn't a question of the little white houses. In fact, it was a question of the attitude toward those houses that were manifest in Le Corbusier's writing and thinking. In fact, look for look Corbusier wrote down the principles of a modern architectural project with his Five Points and His Four compositions. How did he not written those books there's architecture the magazine Esprit Nouveau. No one would really look at those little white houses.

Today the same thing I would argue could be said of Andrea Palladio the famous architect of the 16th century who had, in fact, a project but there were a lot of Architects doing Villas in the Veneto in the 16th century and throughout Italy yet pilates at the end of his life to write a book the four books. In fact of architecture where he described and redrew the houses that he had built as he wanted them to be remembered as his project. So he defined in this book the difference between project and practice the building of the houses was important but they were his this. They were defined for him by his clients, his project to find the world of those houses as Palladio wanted them to be known when I move this is move this forward no I know I'm always confronted with technology.

Tonight I want to define something more than the idea of project. I want to talk about the idea of a metal project that is a discourse that transcends.

The particular definition of the World by the architect but that last beyond the influence and Aura of that architect and I want to postulate that Western architecture and we could probably do the same thing for Japanese architecture. But that Western architecture is defined by 6 metal projects that are projects which transcend their own particular time and place.

The first metal project I would argue was the true Vyas is 10 books in architecture written in the first-century ad and was the touchdown from which all other treatises that followed for 15 centuries were written.

In fact, the true Vyas was the first one to write a categorical Treatise setting down consciously what was involved in the discipline that would become known 15 centuries later as architecture. He was caught flying certain things. In particular the orders the rigid adherence to proportion he defined three orders the Doric Ionic and Corinthian.

Now wild Vitruvius who operated in Rome and was Roman his ideas were Greek so there were a Transcendence and a transformation and a transmittal of ideas from a Greek origin to a Roman context and it was the first project who brought into the Roman World a Greek idea of architecture and I would argue at least again in the western context that the dialogue between what is Greek and what is Roman still exist today innocence.

Mies Van Der rohe was a Greek architect and Le Corbusier was Roman that is Miss dealt with the relationship of the human subject viewing the object of architecture. Always at a diagonal or a 45-degree perspectival angle where as Le Corbusier as Roman dealt with a frontal relationship of the subject to the object.

In Greek architecture, the corner is the most important

aspect of the work. In Roman architecture, the frontal facade is the most important project. Vitruvius also put down something that was very important and that was the sighting of a building which became one of the ways of defining an architect in the nineteenth and Twentieth Century by the idea of Genius loci that is the genius of a particular site it was Vitruvius U-verse said that the siding the relationship of a building to his sight was very portent.

The second metal project comes about in the 15th century with Leon Battista Alberti book DeRay and the funkatorium which was again a categorical Treatise ten books on architecture in the style of Vitruvius but in many ways very different than Vitruvius because his book was a critique of the Vitruvian idea of proportion and orders but also critiqued the limitation of the rules that confronted the 16th century. The rules of what constituted Beauty proportion and the organization of building material Vitruvius had said there were three principles of architecture commodity that is useful to a program commodity firmness that is something that was structural that would sound up stand up and Delight something that would be beautiful. But Alberti said and talking about structure that Vitruvius didn't mean that building suggest stand up but that they should look like they stand up and so Alberti introduced into the idea to the discipline of architecture the idea of buildings looking like something the idea of representation so that a building in the 16th 15th and 16th century was no longer just the thing itself but was the sign of the thing not necessarily a sign that related outward to some idea some other meaningful notion. But inward to the being of the column itself and so that what

Alberti said was that the proportions of a column we're no longer because of UT necessarily nor because of its use but because of its meaning.

I'll bear it to you also produced another issue that is still with us and of course the idea of representation is a fundamental issue when we get to post-structuralist thoughts of the relationship between sign and signified Alberti also said that a building should relate to its parts that the hole was always the sum of its parts and he said that a small city was like a large house in a large house like a small city which meant that all the parts of things related in some way to a larger constellation of things.

Here the idea the Latin idea of consent ethos of a part to the whole relationship was formed which is the basis argue of Western architecture today and in fact also of parametric production and what we don't realize is that the Romantic idea of part to whole or the phenomenology of part-to-whole inhabits the very core of parametric production so the things that are still with us today from Alberti.

The idea of representation the idea of the sign and the relationship the sign to the signified lead us. In fact to what has sustained in architecture whether it's Western or Eastern and that is the metaphysical project and by that one means the project that is beyond physical press and contemporary philosophers have often said that architecture Remains the locus of the metaphysical project, so prior to Alberti there was not an architecture of metaphysics but I'll bet these Notions and the critique of a trivia placed architecture squarely into what could be called an imminent metaphysic that is the shift from a transcendental metaphysics.

One arbitrated by some God figure to one deeply embedded in a western humanism and of course, the idea of a western humanism lasted from the 15th century to the 17th century when a third metal project took place which was the shift from an imminent metaphysic as a human project to one which was more scientific. In fact, the roots of the projects that both Professor Quinter and Professor Yamaguchi have been talking about that is The Enlightenment project which introduced science into the fabric of the building project which changes the idea of the past from an antiquarian. A romantic pursuit to an archaeological one and that difference between antiquarian and archaeological is an important note in the context of today's discussion so I would argue that the third metal project is was located in the French architect Claude pedal an architect who worked on the Louvre about 2 so we have that is Alberti and then should have pedal who in addition to the three orders introduced a separate set of two more orders.

The Tuscan and the composite and in a book in 1673 called or nose or The Ordering of architecture he proposed an idea which transforms the Alberti and Vitruvian idea of order into something new when he said there was no such thing as an ideal set of rules or of from the past. But the second and more important notion which was presented by the first time by Pillow was that there was an alternative that I had to deal with the present and that beauty was not something only from the past but had to be an evocation of the present and of course, the term Zeitgeist became in the late 17th and early 18th century an ocean coming out of the ideas that pillow was talking about and so we had architecture from the late 17th century to the present.

This to bifurcated idea of what the discipline of architecture was either it was a genius loci a phenomenology of the site or it was an idea of the Zeitgeist of what the present wanted to look like and that struggle between those two remains today free North Meadow project which is the first what one would call Meta modern project was the project of John Battista Piranesi built one building on the Aventine Hill.

He did leave us with many interesting texts and works, in particular, the drawing that you see on the screen of the Campo Marzio which was the first idea modern idea of the urban and all other maps and plans had been either symmetrical based on a Roman idea of a cardo and Deku Manas as the early Roman foundations were or on ideal cities or on French Chateau Gardens emanating from a hierarchical relationship from the center of the house where is Campo Marzio did something that no other map had done.

But that no other architectural idea had done and what he did was to make a drawing that brought together, three different aspects of architecture which were in some ways in conflict that is the parts did not relate to the whole because in his map are buildings from two different times and usually, maps and plans were a place of a single time during a disease map had buildings from first-century Rome it had buildings from 17th century Rome and 18th century Rome buildings in the style of Rome of the first century buildings in the style of Rome of the 18th century.

He had buildings that were in a different location than they actually were and he had buildings and a different size and scale than they really were so there was not only a change in the sight. The importance of sight because buildings could be moved but also a change in the time of the building and the scale of building and so although historically active as archaeology.

Aziz was an invention of history and what's interesting about the plan is that for the first time we had a series of what seemed to be chaotic architectural elements so that architecture made up the urban and it wasn't the streets but in fact the elements of architecture which to find the map the 5th project of architecture which I think is important for us.

Today came about in the actually the late 18th century but early 19th century in a book by a French architect called Lil why when this book was written in 1780 it was a radical book even though it dealt with the ruins of Greek architecture said for the first time that there was a history of architecture a recording of the facts of architecture, and secondly though for the first time he said there was a theory of architecture which way fact be the basis for the project of architecture.

This was the first time that history and theory in 1780 were categorized as different and then in 1818 for the first time in the French Academy they brought Siri and history together under a new professorship so that theory by 1818 some 28 years later or 38 years later became a respected category of being in the discourse of architecture and they were many Architects reasons that theory was accepted as something different and one was the fact that history dealt with imitation of what had gone before whereas.

Theory according to the Wawa and then the French Academy accepted the idea of the invention upon what it gone be out before but no longer imitation so that invention became part of the academy as opposed to me or historical imitation.

The last project VI project can be defined by Le Corbusier Domino diagram of 1914. It is the project of the modern, it is the project of autonomy, it is a project.

We're architecture for the first time it's not necessarily relying on historical precedent but no relying on the political and social upheavals of the French Revolution but an architecture that comes out of its own disciplinarity and of course Corbo's Domino's project canonical of 1914 is the symbol of this condition.

Because while it can be read as a symbol of modern technology of mass production of all kinds of mass projects. It can also be read as a discourse of autonomy and I think that from 1914 to the year 2014 almost a hundred years we have been whether it's called modernism postmodernism deconstructivism parametricism. It sets they all in a one way or another deal with the project of autonomy.

Why do I give this lecture here in Osaka, well, first of all, I want to try and understand what it means to have a project of architecture today and so every time I need to think this idea, I need to read more, think more, look more and the project becomes more defined for me.

I try to build project and teach project and I think school is the place to understand the project and I think there's a difference between a school and a practice many of my students say to me why should we study Palladio, it can't help us get a job. Why don't you teach us Revit which is the hottest form of computer algorithms to produce practical drawings? And I say to them you know there's going to be a lot of time for you to learn Revit and Maya and Rhino and

AutoCAD and all those things that you all used to make up projects. But very little time for to learn about what it takes to have a critical project in architecture and if you don't know what a critical project is you all and the architects who instruct you will be limited to merely practicing architecture, because if you never know who the project is you will never know if you can do it with that being said and I leave you with those words because I do feel a hundred years after the last project or 98 years after the last project.

It is time for another project and what will that project be one sees attempts at the avant-garde rings of young students as we saw this afternoon stirring of colleagues with other ideas about project but are those architectural projects will we recognize a project, as an architectural project will the notion of architecture again radically alter as it has done through the six previous metal projects and so I asked that question as I show you just two of our projects one which is about to go into construction.

I'm not going to say much about these images merely to say that all Architects, unlike critics, are required as a Cota to their ideas to show as 240 said something of reality and so I show you these two one is a housing project in Milan Italy which is just gone into cconstruction and the other is a museum as part of the 6 building complex in Santiago de Compostela which has just recently been completed and will open this spring so without any real commentary.

I'm going to show you these two projects the Milan housing there is the rendering in the context that you see it it looks because of height restrictions and Zoning restrictions very similar to a housing project there are the first attempts we made it putting the required amount of material that is buildings to make acquisition of the site worthwhile.

There are two of the solution is one with separate blocks one with small Towers. I don't know what makes the thing go and not go but there are two other Alternatives with the same amount of blocks annexed and I'm a nice Marseille, next to somebody's producing this next and we did a series of a diagrammatic zoning studies massing studies and you'll see this runs up through 70 or 80.

I've only picked out a few to show you the way we worked as a process of producing the final object, next you can see the arrows point to the fact that there are zoning restrictions of distance hear of set back from the street. Next, next again further setbacks and setbacks from the street very complicated zoning laws, next please, until the final shape started to come out of the synthesis of all of these earlier diagrams, next please, and you can see the rhythms taking it from a bent shape to a regular curved shape to get the kinds of rhythms of sequential rhythms that you can see AAA BAA BAAB et cetera even though we had a very difficult shape to keep these kinds of notations to repeat because they were repetitive apartment units that we needed to produce, next please, and there you see what it would look like if it were a straight line block.

And here are the same amount of square meters in the curve form that we ended with next at the three-part A critique on the existing Milan idea of Base middle and top with we made a what would be known as a piano Nobile a between a a rusticated base and a gridded top as you can see in the form a critique of the existing idea of the Milan apartment house, next please, and the production of what we would call Urban

Villas so we had apartments in these levels.

A piano Nobile a with balconies and then apartments up above, next please, and you can see that there is a different idea of the base which is a punch Windows a piano brulee and then a series of printed forms incorporating these are burned velas ,next please, the site plan on there all kinds of reasons for the development of site plan to provide ventilation to the parking levels below very rigid requirements in Italian law, next please, and you can see the notations on the construction documents every one of these notations means that there is a different section to be cut through and as you could see there are quite a number of sections because there's no standard condition either in front or back, next please, next the section through the building showing the bass down an overlay and the urban Villas up above next, and you can see the difference in notation a punched openings a gridded top with incorporating these three level Villas next, and the back side which is different than the front and I won't go into that just that the grid is off center this gridded structure is pushed into the back side and appears in the front differently so that we distinguish in a way between front and back, next please, a rendering from across the street showing the, the granite face the glaze piano Nobile.

A Brita diaper story with the urban fellows next, so we mix three different kinds of a traditional base a Le Corbusier piano Nobile a and Toronto vs gritted structure like the that's a rooster chi in Milano and all three of these things it's kind of hybrid structure to meet in this project.

Next had an up-close view of the as it will be built starting it right now, next, this is a project, next please, this is a model of competition that we won 4-6 buildings in Santiago de Compostela.

This building is the Archive Building and she's built this is the, sorry go back, this is the Archive Building Library building the Museum Library of Galicia this is the museum going to show you, which is finished and administration building, which is also finished Music Hall, which is under construction and another Museum over here so four of the original six buildings are built and I just briefly want to show you pictures which I've just gotten in the last week, of the museum building, next please, this is the site plan here the archive the library.

This is the museum building that you will see and the administration building over here next and there's the site plan as it exists the archive the library the museum building and the administration building in the beginning of the Music Hall, you can see here and there's a whole Theory which I don't want to go into the relationship between different grids, between topographical topological Cartesian and computer vectors which all inhabit this project and one of the things I want to say about diagram switch distinguishes the kinds of diagrams that I produce safe from the one said REM Koolhaas produces is that my diagrams are not so much interested in typology or topology but in morphology in the difference between morphology and typology I think it's an enormous difference when one is dealing with the diagram. Next please, there you can see the building on the hillside here is the Town Center the Church of St James at the laboratory of the Town Square and what we did our whole idea of the project was we cut this.

The hillside was a hillside not unlike this and made the forms of the buildings conform to the prior Hillside so that when the project would be finished we would have restored the hillside, next, there you can see the building of the museum the administration building and the library building from the town down below, next please, the ruse escape again made to not look like building but a stone and concrete surface where no marks of building ducts events chimneys Etc are seen because they are under a second roof which gives a sense of a ground like surface.

Next please, and you can see these kisses all local stonework and a porous so that the waterfalls through these are set in a grid but have no waterproofing.

The waterproofing is it down at this level of the roof which marks the Cartesian grid running through the topographical one, next please, and another view of the roofscape, next please, a drawing of what these roofscapes will be like when this final building is put in this the Music Hall and the second Museum when they're finished.

Next, this is the north facade of the museum as just completed and here is the administration building next to the north start again looking from the west of the museum building. Next, this is the South facade of that same Museum building looking at it from the library Plaza. Next, you can call it a roof or you can call it a facade or roof facade but the continuity from the ground-up of the museum building very hard to have poured concrete on this slope very difficult to have managed to keep all of this in place.

Next, there you can see it the same surface at night and the plaza steps next an up-close view of the north facade you can see that it's not a curtain wall but a series of layers double

curved surface of individual pieces of set in black glass asset like Stone getting giving you this Friday faceted surface.

Next and again scene from the East looking West, next the South facade, next and then the interior which it has several layers of a facade like this glass facade of a North Face and then an interior layer so that you create these transition spaces between an external shell and an internal one protecting the kinds of artifacts that need no natural light and the artifacts that would have in this space this was designed as it were for artifacts from the history of Galicia like shipping boats and, and large-scale implements.

Next please, and you can see the interior surface again now looking west to east north facade the escalators circulating up to the other galleries as you can see behind the interior facade, next, and another view of that more complete just finished with the flooring and all of the markings Center in the space.

Next, a view of the space when there would be these boats in the height of the space undetermined by the Mast of the boats that were going to be put in next and the actual now the actual space itself.

Next, some other views of the Interior it's quite articulated and all of it coming out of a very complex algorithm. let's say that to produce a play between all of the six buildings contrapuntal e working from building to building from north to south and east to west a repeating certain phrases in each building and then Rifts on those which change the whole idea of the space as you move from building to building.

Next, if you threw this facade on the Northside looking out and down to the sea the tower of the church this is at the top of the staircase the escalator where you look back and get a view of the cathedral.

Next, the facade at night, next and another view of that facade can we go to the okay, and next please, and next their view of the buildings and the lit streets that walk which are the same as the streets from the town the medieval town, the medieval grid, the Cartesian grid of the topographical grid and the computer digital grids. All articulated in the same project. Thank you very much.

PETER EISENMAN

略歴

ニューヨーク・ファイブのメンバーの一人として名声を博し、建築に関する多くの著書や講演で知られている。

コーネル大学とコロンビア大学 GSAPP で建築学の学位を取得し、その後、ケンブリッジ大学で博士号を取得した。2007 年には、シラキュース大学建築学校から名誉学位を与えられた。

クーパーユニオン建築学校の名誉教授。イェール大学では、理論演習や先進的デザインのためのスタジオで教鞭を執っている。これまで、ケンブリッジ大学、ハーバード大学、ペンシルバニア大学、プリンストン大学建築学部、オハイオ州立大学で教鞭を執ってきた。

主な著書として、Eisenman, Peter: Diagram Diaries（1999）、Eisenman Inside Out: Selected Writings, 1963-1988（2004）、Written into the Void: Selected Writings, 1990-2004（2007）等がある。

SANFORD KWINTER
MARCH 16, 2012

We believe as we try to move into the future which I understand is what the main mandate of the new program here is that these types of collaborations are extremely important. They open up the world that we don't need to recognize or feel comfortable in advance. We don't have to recognize the classical varieties of architecture in that we have to be brave. The only people who are laughing of course of the people in the front row we spent an hour in the room. You have to understand this is we've been friends Peter and Cynthia for least three decades. We've been debating various issues as the modern world begins to diverge. I went left and they went right now but the point is the distance between us has become. There is so much more population between the points of view of those whose roots and ways of thinking about architecture are rooted in tradition vs anyway. We will have these discussions.

I'm letting you know it seems inevitable immediately after Professor Eisenman's talk. I'd like to say what a great pleasure and honor it is for me to be here today. In the present company almost exactly 20 years since my first visit to Japan. In the early 1990s when I was a guest of Cynthia Davidson Any project. End of Isozaki Arata's who co-hosted the event and arranged are unforgettable, intellectual and culinary retreat at youth lean on the island of Kyushu as I wrote in my summary reflections in the final book of Any's 10-year project. That's trip to Japan was among the great personal educational and even spiritual events of my life and provoked not only a sustained 20-year study. Our study of an unbroken engagement with Japanese aesthetic forms theories of nature and even psychic ecology but initiated a series of friendships with Japanese architects, scientists, and intellectuals that have sustained me as a theorist in the design field ever since. I would like to thank Yamaguchi Takashi for his kind and tolerant invitation to come here today and to try to address some of the issues that bear on the specific and very modern task. That many of us are being asked to achieve today that of integrating design thinking practice and educational curriculum with the transforming demands of society and the production of personnel necessary to serve and sustain it. Now I chose

these last words transforming the demands of society and the production of personnel necessary to serve and sustain it with deliberate very deliberately and with a certain amount of agony. So I hope the irony intended in them is not lost. Yamaguchi prepared me for today's address by explaining that our events today.

Curriculum is the institutional intellectual and social challenges of bringing the problems of architectural thought and practice into some type of engagement and accommodation of our ever-expanding economies of information. And it does so within the broader context of an engineering faculty. I think that is quite important because you know it, for example, we are one of the great tasks that we have trying to transform the design curriculum at Harvard is exactly. What it is that we use architects in his designers do specifically better than anyone else. That's to say how to incorporate aspects of engineering entirely within a design culture. Importantly, we think to always fail when we allow engineering to simply be an adjunct to architecture and to design. And it's a great challenge. It's an enormous challenge. And it's a very critical challenge to make sure that it is we who incorporates aspects of engineering knowledge

into design.

The age-old relationship of architecture to engineering is scientifically one of the happiest stories. But their philosophical and ethical relationships have throughout the modern at least been one that one's of notable conflict misunderstanding and in satisfaction. The problems of technology and life in my mind are not ones to be smooth over reconciled or ignored. It is our job as designers and these design intellectuals to clarify, develop and enhance points of friction. The incommensurability and the sources of unhappiness because as I have often claimed it is not simply our practice and our professions that are at stake in this question. The question of the relationship if you like to engineering but of our larger fate as humans in an increasingly instrumentalized world dissociated from the physical and natural forces that made us and that continue to act upon us. You would not be wrong to hear the word environment being whispered here.

Yamaguchi's notes stated that the new faculty being formed here. At the Osaka Sangyo University has taken the problem of the future of design as its problem and has made it the

center of its curriculum and concerns among the questions that I'm sure will be addressed today in Eisenman's talk is specially is the rule that the past could be asked to play in thinking about and making this future. It's my understanding that Professor Eisenmann will speak to us today about the distinction between project and practice.

The latter phenomenon is one which is flourishing in our age. That's the said practice is flourishing in our age of instrumentalization. Just as the former the project appears to be fading Into near extinction. It's not necessary however that there be thousands of projects. My project I assume that Eisenmann will mean the ethical, social, philosophical or even spiritual project. It is important really only that there be some projects that can serve as beacons to light the way and to illuminate or even simply just to partition the field. It is the lack of this partitioning itself that is responsible for the incredible stultification of the culture of design. Based on the new but false technological consensus that has a nice tized student practitioner and large-scale design enterprises alike. Eisenman's career-long project indeed his apotheosis of project pave the way for my own entry into the design philosophy field in the first place. And it continues like a voice, I continue to hear murmuring behind me and that sustains me even today in everything I do. Without the project, the culture of the project, the messy agora of warring projects, the very scope of the formulation. That is proper to the project alone in design thinking. The field would have neither future credibility or a soul.

As we adapt our institutions and their curriculums to confront the demands of the future, we must not fall into the narrow assumptions of engineering mentality that sees only local problems and their narrow solutions. But we must acknowledge that design and its mental habits. Those habits inherited from the past as well as those that must be freshly invented cannot survive and cannot serve without the audacity of broader more idiosyncratic ideas that are driven, abetted and generated by projects, philosophical projects. But even as I agree in broad totality with what I imagine we'll be Eisenman's assertion later this evening. The issue of how to engage with contemporary problems and with emerging historical and social issues. The places from where I believe design must take its cues as it moves into the future. A position with which I do not expect Eisenman who is more discipline are really inclined to agree is a perfect place to define a line of the partitioning of projects. This partitioning, any partitioning I would argue at this point would be worthwhile. I think cannot help but in rich the discourse of design as it confronts the multiple demands of engineering rationality in this second age of automation and computation. Now, the brief comments I will present to you this afternoon are mostly excerpted from an address. I gave a couple of weeks ago at MIT in Cambridge on the occasion of a conference on the current state of a digital culture within the design fields within the fields of architecture landscape, urbanism, and technology. It suggests that there has been a massive default in the field. Notably in how we account for and cultivate the development of computer protocols and especially of computational styles. And realize that word style is not typically associated with computation in the United States. It has achieved a level of almost broke over hypertrophy are overemphasis and has become strangely enough in a way the primary focus of a lot of young designers work.

So, I cut now into that talked almost in Ann Arbor Trail Place why not begin with the greatest cliche of all. That is the computer in quotation marks year. The computer is nothing but a tool and no different from any other. There are a great many ways to address the poverty of this formulation. One would be to consider the meaning and function of the tool or technical object within human and animal history and ecology in the first place. Another would be to challenge the other embedded assumption that the computer belongs in a continuous and unknown way to the series of technical innovations that have marked human interaction with and mastery of its environment over a long history.

In the first category, the very phrase nothing more than another tool. Events are terrifying innocence about how objects become a next to larger systemic biological enterprises in their processes of test and subduing, the indifference and serendipity of the natural world. The so-called stone tool industry of early human civilization is not widely understood to have included a range of a broader process to form its conditions of possibility. I elicit now only the economic and social ones here. Optimal Stone types were identified, transported, stockpiled almost surely traded and assigned diverse industrial applications even within largely banned based and pre-linguistic societies. I'm talking about early humans before they even could talk. The skill required to flint and hone was advanced required sustained and ultimately specialized training and was not equally distributed within a given community. And so read two divisions of labor and variegated social relationships. The very emergence of a special class of objects whose status is not directly applicable to the immediacy of the body's drives. But subordinate to another object that buys a series of processes or actions it brings into being is said to constitute one of the great leaps in the culture of our mental life. The cleaving of the world into self and non-self rounds into a stratified field of subordinate and subordinating causes.

There was suddenly a boundary between subject and object such that transcendence as French philosophers Georges Bataille once famously referred to it. Transcendence was introduced into the human psychic world. Of course, ultimately trying to argue here by using just one simple example is the fact that we don't really have entirely forgotten how to think about how technology utterly and completely transforms our world, our social world, and the ecological world, etc.

This Interruption and separation of a primordial continuity was speculated to inaugurate the bifurcation of the human from its animal existence. But in the last decades, elementary tool use has been discovered in animal societies as well from chimps, chimpanzees to dolphins to English blue tits. These are the birds that break the foil seals on milk bottles in England. Early hominids, early humans were unequipped and unable to access the proteins in a felled carcass. Restricting them to a culture of gathering activities and scavenging the ravaged calorie of others. The hunting economy, the hunting society in the hunting lifestyle emerged only after the mastery of techniques of a hand tool manufacturer. The hunting brings in the hunting society that resulted are not the same as the ones that preceded them. Among other things they together made the asocial frugivores. That's the say the fruit-eating a social what's a chimpanzee into a social carnivore with emphasis on the social.

Indeed, that's the say the tool change the entire dietary culture and ultimately our entire culture itself. It is the foundation of social life. And the deed is even the marketing engineers at Nokia used to formulate their mantra in the 1990s quote all killer apps are social apps. I hope that gets translated more or less copy pensively. To seek the cast any significant technology outside of its larger ecology and that's really what I want to emphasize today that one word. Outside of its larger ecology of operation namely social, existential and neurocognitive is to miss just about everything significant about it. So, certainly says I like to dispatch that idea when people say the computer is just a tool. It is simple, naive, beyond and belief.

Second, the computer indisputably represents a powerful technological impetus in our world but is it really just another technology among others. Do we legitimately place in the lineage with radio, television, and telephone or perhaps in a lineage that can be traced from the clock through the steam engine to the electrical dynamo? The celebrated successions. That's so effectively rationalized our cities and economic life. Or do we like the dutifully doll historians? We trained to establish its essential lineage in automation machinery like the loom the player piano or the early boolean calculation machines.

In some, I believe these are all wrong. The wrong way to go about thinking the problem of technology today. The computer unlike almost anything that came before it and with the powerful complicity of media both visual and aural that with the temporal matrices of traditional arts such as music and perhaps more importantly theater. The computer represents a direct proto-subjective engagement and harnessing of the life modalities and the affordances of our nervous system effect. That can no longer remain separate or hidden in computer culture that word affordance comes from a great cognitive psychologist named J.J. Gibson. In Gibsonian terms, computers have environmental and ecological status. Not only because they do things in the manner of natural or living objects. But because they furnish indeed they prescribe the environment and the environmental boundaries and conditions within which the said doing takes place. They actually determined both not only the action but the broader context. They also delimit the context in which the action takes place. In that sense absolutely limiting, the possibility of associating the action if you like it beyond that very specific and controlled context. That is unlike the other things we have done for millennia.

This latter construct is not only hidden from our habitual attention. It is as contemporary neurobiology has shown effectively impervious and undetectable by the perceptual schemas of the human brain. The brain cannot see it. Only philosophical postures. Perhaps associated with projects or voluntary or self-imposed exile from computations extended social operations or cultivation of alternate perceptual disciplines can provide us access to the computer's essential and constitutive procedures and processes. Few of these ladder attitudes are typically discernible within our contemporary design will use. And this deficit is arguably a prime cause of the new conventionalism that has characterized so much of recent digitally oriented work in design. And I would like to say that this is a real sickness. It's a real problem within architecture.

To see the brilliant developments in the innovations that are taking place in the JsonField such as we saw this afternoon, you couldn't make such a claim the deficit right now is in architecture. The deficit right now is in architecture. It is in the design milieus and their incapacity to properly absorb interpret and transform. The work that is going on today. And I mean it really was great emphasis is especially on transform.

Similarly, there is also a wide variety of ways one appears to screw the principle of the digital today. Digital as numeric and hence opposed to analog. Digital as an automatic process. Digital as having to do with information rather than say with energy or matter. Digital has also and simultaneously taken on a worryingly neanderthal attitude that seems to connote modern enlightened or renewed. But most centrally from today's perspective digital seems to denote connected and integrated. Indeed, we speak more often today of parametric at least in the United States and in Europe then we do of digital. Even though we probably mean the ladder. What many of the discourses and controversies invoked by the interpretations of digital listed above have in common is the peculiar way in which the digital has allowed a conflict of two sets of perhaps irreconcilable understandings of what is the nature of nature itself. And what is the nature of the system of engagement and understanding with which we make contact with and represent this natural world? It is a new type of epistemological problem because knowledge and doing, changing, manipulating are no longer held separate. Typically today, we no longer distinguish between the two. And we are no longer concerned by the loss of this distinction. Perhaps this is what has allowed the rise of parametric churches and priesthoods. I refer here to one of the most hilarious. For example of all which is this by now quite notorious article of Patrik Schumacher called let the style wars begin. And shows made it. It's been circulating in schools in Japan as well. No longer certain of whether one is speaking of nature or of a new form of artificial ratiocination about a machinic function extended beyond machine objects. The fundamental intellectual connection to the information revolution has been largely lost in architecture anyway or at least lost sight of. And that is in my opinion that the connection to living systems or to biology. In a sense now, it's become completely disconnected from its intellectual roots let's say. It is really becoming a thing and tile a culture of its own. And example while building information technology on BIM. May well represent the most significant development in the architectural world since reinforced concrete. It is considerable promise and destiny is largely stillborn so long as we fail to connect its integrative potential and source to the functions, concepts, and models of living systems and the life sciences that study them. I expect to find absolutely no agreement with used ideas from Peter Eisenman later this evening. Contemporary digital aptitude leads nowhere if it is not wedded to biological aptitude. Biology or writ large as nature is the destiny of computation. Digital aptitude has arisen in or migrated to other areas of cultural activity that are in no way derivative of architectural or industrial design practices. It has migrated into areas of activity that are not derivative from architectural design practices. It often preceded them and now serve as models for it. In many cases, they deploy the aptitude but not the paraphernalia the equipment or the infrastructural dependencies or the cliches. One example is the arena of what we call in the anglo-Saxon world, molecular gastronomy. Where research, of course, this is a kind of an ultra scientific, ultra in experimental form cooking. Where research into the manifold variables to which soft organic matter is amenable and to which it responds with an almost unlimited array of specific effects and properties. It is carried out today with astounding spontaneity inventiveness and bizarre but reproducible results.

I would say here there's a greater insight into the potential use of the computer and of technology in general which we find in this field adjacent to our own almost always of Interest the designers. But somehow the culture of innovation is taking place far more radically outside of design right next door in the kitchen. Molecular gastronomy of the last 15 years is made possible by the scientific rigor with which new variables are explored along the wide array of parameters to determine which produce chemistries of unprecedented unknown or undiscovered kinds. Once known monolithically and inclusively as Maillard reaction which produces aromatic and flavor compounds in the presence of dry heat that we know as delicious such as the freshly baked bread or the toast effect. It is now understood this Maillard reaction is now understood to comprise thousands if not hundreds of thousands of diverse compounds specific to any given situation.

The world self or the food sensation interface has become an open arena for experiment invention and the production of entirely new forms of experience. It other thing I'd like to leave you with a lady with a couple of just phrases is that. There is no doubt for better or worse that the problem of experience in relation to design and to design thinking is rising to the for as the single most important central and accessible new problem for architecture and is one that really we must be very free in ours. And experimental in our ways of approaching it. Indeed, the kitchen has emerged as a full-blown site of the production of knowledge itself with its own techniques of practical rigorous inquiry. Great focus, as a result, comes to be placed on the human apparatus of perception and how it determines the ultimate experiential outcome or effect. And once again what I'm saying here is we have this general switch if you like a focus toward the modalities of human attention of the nervous system of experience and ultimately of the things.

The questions that are beginning to be accessible to the new neuroscience and the new neurobiology today. Post-war music especially issuing from synthetic methods and compositional programs of the avant-garde or electro-acoustic movement. I'm talking about just after the second world war. Similarly introduced and a source of microstructure and microsound into the sound continuum as well as the vista of their infinite modify ability. After say it the access whole different levels of structure than could ever be accessed before. Extending the foundational insights of the atonal movement from a few decades earlier that of Schoenberg, Brahms, and Webern. Post-war composition deployed technological processes. At that time, of course, it wasn't computers it was magnetic tape and other electronic forms that emerged from wartime technology. And it equipments to discover new parameters to vary and modulate. That is to compose and design that could be act that could not be accessed previously. Given the astounding plasticity and responsiveness of the human oral psychic register effective and bodily States previously unknown and unimagined became attainable. Individual notes cornrows could be engineered without dependents on naturally resonating objects.

For the first time, music and the production of organized sound was liberated if you like from traditional instruments that vibrated. And they were generated of course electronically with the entirely new kinds of instruments. And it changed the body, change the emotion it, changed our mental life to explore through the subtle manipulation of sound shapes and combinations even at the subaudible or the super audible ranges. Can the same range of discipline and mastery of perceptual forms and integration and controlled effect on human nervous or aesthetic response and on the transformation and modulation of human body states be claimed for the forms and assembly is produced today with modeling software? Is there an experimental avant-garde as existed for music's encounter with technological manipulations and as exists today in culinary research? That hacks the medium rather than simply incorporates and deploys it within the same framework at which it is presented. I worry that there is not.

Talk now, the last section here on the idea of the hack or hacking. Decades after the first generation of hacker activist practitioners in the telephone and computer science world, the hacking ethos has taken on a never thicker and enriched meaning as it becomes applicable to different functional rounds. In addition to its application in gastronomy with a substrate material is partially released from its agricultural and dietary context and conceived as a physical-chemical continuum susceptible of infantry combination and variation through applied or controlled processes. And in music, wherein similar manner sound is restructured in-depth by manipulating the shape and structure of sine waves. Themselves to transform experience, so the chemistry and behavioral modulus is of the brain and body are today becoming targets of some of the most creative research and experiment around. Developments in neuroscience are permitting the first glimpses of the algorithms and hard-wired protocols that determine human perception or the processing if you like of the data of the environment. Allowing for the study of human world interfaces. And how these may be altered or engaged in standing new ways. Empirical practices such as that of magicians have for long discovered ways to hack the human nervous system. But new models of human perceptual organization and modalities are allowing for astonishing new styles of creating environments and artworks. That queue or circumvent specific neural circuitry.

Similarly, neuroscience has begun to study traditional practices like art and Magic for organized and stored forms of knowledge and practice. I meant you just two recent works. One by neuroscientist Stephen Macknik and Susana Martinez-Conde. A work called a "Sleights of Mind" what neuroscience of magic reveals about our everyday deceptions. And one other book by Harvard historian Daniel Smail called "On Deep History and the Brain". These are but two notable recent works the tap the long history. Indeed, the constitutive history is they argue of how culture has evolved forms to hack the brain or to hack the human nervous system with a view to producing astonishing new and radical forms of experience and altered body states innocence again. This is this return to experiential and forms of embedded, embodied knowledge or epistemology.

Another emblematic work. This time from The New York Times bestseller list and part of a broader body-hacking movement that has not yet been fully identified for the movement that it is. Is a book called The 4-Hour Body? The subtitle includes the phrase how to become superhuman by Timothy Ferris. Which is simultaneously a manual for hacking the body's material makeup. Purporting to be able to recompose the body radically and in-depth within only a few hours of action, spread over 3 to 6 weeks. And 2 hack its capacity to affect and be affected mentally, sexually, spiritually and neurologically. The book is also an autobiography of self-directed study and experiments through tracking and quantification getting much the same way as drugs sex and rock and roll were used in more empirical ways in the 1960s.

The principle of applied not immune to a certain sense. It's essentially looking at the body as a data processing machine is a kind of a computational device. The principle applied across the board is that of Occam's laser or the minimum effective dose. According to which if the proper intervention. It is timed and targeted to the right place and moment. Catastrophically in the good sense, large transformations are claimed to be possible. Broad study of the various programs that articulate the body's life world. Such as hormonal cascades that can be triggered by 2 minutes no more of lower-body exertion every 4 or 5 days or by the simple act of inducing regular shivering are shown to set into motion complex metabolic responses. That results in inordinate removal of fat from the body and to produce uncommon amounts of muscle mass et cetera. Dietary singularities are explored and experimented with. And the results documented with photos of charts and narratives. Much like the famed cold fusion experiments or the claims of a couple or three decades ago. There is undoubtedly much that is bogus in the claims of this book and yet like the anomalous results of the earlier famed and defamed experiment.

There is also certainly something going on that merits attention. And it's interesting to know that the cold fusion experiments still continue and are still being funded by the National Science Foundation. I will wrap up with an evocation. That I've called upon many times before. And which I find a particular poignancy not only for its bold and clear pronouncement. But for the ways it's generality also permits it's apparent meaning to change as the years and decades we're on. The phrase is one from British musician and composer Brian Eno. The problem with computers he says is that there is not enough Africa in them. I've often interpreted this statement within the context of a close analysis of products of African musical and spatial-temporal organization. That is in the presence of highly elaborated and complex processes of improvisation, social organization, and choreography, polymetric and polytonal structure. I use a lot of complicated words that have to do with the way in which this entirely different system of aesthetic let's say organization produces effects entirely unknown entirely different from those enjoyed for example in Western musical traditions. Today, I suggest that the statement might serve very simply to represent the loss of the wild and the relative of the social performance that underlies all form production in the African universe of the teeming coming to be the characterize, the natural universe.

In which, the human is pegged ineluctably and inescapably by the materiality of its body and the temporalis about history. It's a final search for forgiveness to you, the audience, for the imageless presentation I made you and you're just now today. I leave you with a short clip. Just one, I'm on the diversity of hundreds that I could have presented that represent areas of human discipline. And rigor as applied to continuum's where would I would call old intensities are revisited and newly hacked to produce entirely new styles of engagement with the physical world. In the clip, I'm about to show. Really no more than ABBA now offering from the YouTube universe of which there are probably hundreds of thousands. We see some of the extraordinary ways in which a classical world. And its conceptions of rotation, linearity, interdependence, simultaneity, kineticism, improvisation, agency, attack and decay, energy, information, symmetry in geometry. Not to mention the dynamism of the body and the interconnected play of rhythm and movement transfer and momentum are each and all alterable. And recombinable into new displays of form and relationship. I purposely completely overwrote and over-describe what you're about to see partly as a joke and partly to insist on the brilliance of what I think.

I'm about to show the short clip. That I'm now going to ask to have turned on is the product of a peculiarly local that is Japanese rediscovery and reinvention in the 1990s. Heavy of a 100-year-old tradition that we can only in retrospect see as having been extraordinarily on creatively and complacently developed throughout most of its history. And whose possibilities lay dormant and unimagined until the conditions in the world around it changed the very ethos. So how the medium might be engaged and let me go see.

SANFORD KWINTER

略歴

建築理論家であり、Zone Books 出版社の共同設立者。
プラット・インスティテュートで理論と批評の教授を務める。
コロンビア大学で比較文学の博士号を取得した。その後、ライス大学で准教授を務め、MIT、コロンビア大学、コーネル大学、ハーバード大学大学院で教鞭をとっている。

ハーバード大学、ウィーン応用美術大学、ベルラーヘ・インスティチュート、AA スクール等で講演をおこなう。

過去 20 年にわたり、出版物は芸術、建築、科学、人文科学の分野において、新たな思想を開拓した。1991 年から 2000 年の間に ANY によって開催された開催された一連の会議や出版物に関わる。

主な著書として、Architectures of Time: Toward a Theory of the Event in Modernist Culture（2002）がある。

Performative Morphology in Architecture

ACHIM MENGES
FEBRUARY 16, 2013

I noticed as a way of reducing the architecture that you have the one example is some music. I will talk to repost the PowerHouse in Germany in the 1920s who actually investigated closest east of what he called material experimentation indosat. Wireless conciliatory experimentation is something that directly relate to materiality, so his studies and productive students. The reading notes models of Representatives in Nigeria something that you could have just taken off just in time between image of something actually really looked at in study material and folding are in space Italian. Not right time to receive which so very very material to a computer phone and you make soap to somehow physically computers and take the living room stays off the tension within the system that he didn't throw. Translated to some of his most romantic good, in this case, the Expo Pavilion at Montreal 1967. So, let me try to do with unicorn temporary contact computation get your fabrication is to try to think about all of this on post for the experimental approach to using actually.

Driving for the closest AutoZone of scientific inquiry computer computer designs experimentation TMO can you help me as you may have understood by now but kind of notion of material if it's very sensual through our investigations about my research. So, what I would do for beautiful research with my teacher and I will show that 245 montreality and how it relates to mature Behavior. Are we going to be at full speed of naturalization and all that allows us to think about the possibility that you get from new machine and machine office spaces and accused us of the connection given to who is nuco2 sees a propagation think about and constructed reality and argue with me and tear the phone screen cap and she see how I feel in the responsiveness of quantity.

Quantity is ingrained Muskingum Teresa. So, I thought I sent the first chapter phone call about material. Can come if she can more active participant in the design process project and I will show you how we just did. I see you have to do it again if you didn't 2010 and this is a collaboration between acute and the institute for structure engineering at University of Chicago soul. This is what Jake BB space on sumption that

any material has the ability to compute home so apparently, it's out this morning to get some here which is a piece of wood and if you have just walked into this did that piece of wood that just means you pull that support form with the given Force. They would actually sell financed. This complex carb-loading domestic actor I like. Despite the fact that this elastic into your behavior, offer some interesting architecture possibilities and then it can even be structurally with ages do they have ever used in architecture is not something that we can't decide without representation design techniques including most achievements.

So, one prediction you to say that because I can text him not on modem to behavior you can you see Mount design however there are other forms of architecture and had actually utilized in Mesopotamia up to it and it doesn't come as a surprise. I'm awful sometimes as for example and this is what she live in the south by defendant agreed and so kind of tension that's in the Reeds once where she connected at the top 50 stabilizer instructions addition to this kind of behavior. This is an example of a phone prioritas investigation two switches for 1975. We're actually 40 interesting about this bridge constructed as an absolute regular and play my great and Holy Ghost the whole structure finds its home. In this case, a high destruction stable tablet or phone completely by itself as a result of as a man to take you to court and stable internal strength of the electricity in June and some of the external forces acting horses.

So, what you tried to do with this budget actually located at the distribution of bending xboxaddictionz which is the position and then we just got this information with social and in that discussion, we identify two main research code for this undertaking of the first police. If you wanted to have the skin and the structure being actually born sister so nothing will be left the structural nethys and you have remembered

and talked yet everything should be dealt with that won't sit and the second, in Hindi Sylvester Khloe Shae by bother you, as I know Mackinaw City, big stick anymore what to eat after you go to Pocoyo multiple proposal Bullseye skin binocular case in cook America.

So, design process actually begins with investigation often do Behavior. They can see how to shape and at the same time you Model Behavior with the computer using final would that be developed actually embarrassing position my baby can see this, see what I should hear to Spanish translation. One support phone is so that one part of the strip is spent a lot of attention and hold the bending of the Bend Park in position so this is the system that you work with is now. And this the 10 side part that you said Ben has position and then it's to the changes over. This becomes dependent the pen pal, Mississippi. What God Says stabilizing system is Hans the shape as a consequence off the TV Hamilton behavioral model based on assimilation. What are characteristics of material 80 all the time is not yet, cuz that makes why is also information of how to behave in a month?

So, what that you also use his communication process in order to see how you make you make all the details every

detail the structure being denied the logic of bond machine in 1 tool on which in this case our industrial robot to build its most machine using want to know and that left to self-development of the DJ for connecting individual pieces to longest strips where the connections that you always happening in the 10 side part of the ocean. Another feature of the strip topless need a shape that has the outline because that regulates off the envelope and also has an effect on the direct and indirect Lighting in a requisition and it also regulate the structure that interact with artificial light. The most pulled me tag office Lee where the two strips of jaundice in such a way that the number of each box has not actually compromised capacity of Hobart sunshine when she can. I be seen this pay tomorrow so the bus all the way around the structure and Clyde in a cute way that's not an axis of weakness and that's why she stayed so late sweetie face in this case and this became the main driver for actually, we go. She ate there going to be a TIA The Joint Mullins within the system in a highly irregular manner so that they could actually take maximum Advantage alternative station. So, you can't see strips Malaysian now's you to actually develop the shape of Pavilion, something that comes from within the kind of behavior the possibilities Frontier.

So, what kind of CBD say that behavior from two. Computes The Pavilion how to say that kind of irregularity. With the Godfather of the position of John, points required level of Education in the geometry between said you end up with more than 500 geometric liter to Parts in this case. Because the camera digital machine process from the beginning part of the design convention produced any major problem everything could be produced seamlessly so what is interesting is that movie called Investments time because I don't have time to listen to this book. Check the Osman construction but you very very simple and also very cheap to Simply have this kind of talk me. The long strip apply you don't need any stupid at all any special tools you just have to also connected to the Jason Street and then it finds completely by itself very particular shape so another words even full-scale on side the material computes the shape of the video Define. I was a long way sfax Rusty Wallace Honda writing America Reno simulation what you making that stupid a video of behavior so I can go to somehow what happens. If that actually shows that have special experience, but he's also at the same time activity efficient self Pour House. That usually make a ditch in architecture which always so sacrifice McHugh efficiency for a most efficient city bus for home inspection year is Last Resort Soul as a matter of fact because of the three-strap that is actually in this message. Bible stress relief in material so there's all the plywood strips.

I'm only 6.5 minutes so this super skinny is at the same time the load-bearing structure and it's important. I wish me and Dad, a boy movie style photo editor what is interesting in his

schedule is that this stupid in envelope that is also a notion that come with X and set the same time also like motivating envelope and the weather prediction for this extension of Tompkins square inches temporarily Force awakens inside and make sure you have any kind of interesting space experience supposed to destroy the space that is Trump Emoji. Canada be perceived entirely which leads to a surprising spaceship deck how do you spell that name sliders kind of sequence. Dyer died in the results from the combination but in addition to Federal investigative abilities to come with that and more if they wanted to ask you about my day the geometry on sides with the junkiest nylons and they're very happy to see that they only very minor deviations so many ways and then I kind of Jump Street the building. The results from the actual material application on the side but you can see in the same here so close you say that it is not based on shape of behavior Knoxville Coastal architecture.

The CW lighting go to take me to sign what's up media SEPTA state of the project demonstrates a possibility but now that they're me to on the one hand you architecture possibilities and on the other hand and extremely high level of material resource won't answer. They want to really say that this case is no longer active the second chapter of Acts or conduct at 8 to do we make small too much radiation which mean architecture usually pause production application send a CD on Sunday question now we can she use these new machines that they have this is the robot that happened on the truth in order to not just killed myself.

Explorer tweeted that he's machines gave but how we can explore the freedom only within the cannot get into that particular interesting account so sweet about exploring machine. MocoSpace and it's kind of region that I can open up the phone, please. This was done again by board projects that live in 2011 which was the chemical operations remind what you expect me to do. The Foundry plus I'm also on collaboration with Biology off that Bayern Munich conference Network. This what team is Winnipeg from two technological innovations is to which allows on the Fly II Innovations Focus videos of industrial robot that should reproduce. What is essentially a very traditional good job which is a pimento. How are using check for construction on very delayed main structures in which form of more than six blades connection come together so in a sense, there's some traditional wood joining techniques of the use of these two technological innovations that YouTube and a robot and I was using the space of possibilities for design with peace 57 play structures.

This the real life of architecture but Medicaid because it means that she's no use high level of differentiation and interesting to see for possibilities. How they can take advantage of that the congestion and that's something if you mind possibly more often in biology. If I'm in a state ID shape that's very cheap from Asia to put you and as of today, it was true in the case of Technology check. Material ligation say sexy 5 + 65 + 6 + 2 Princess Anna geometry text Leah mobile. So, if you want to take advantage, if you can help with you so very different shades very different shapes. You also have to understand what if we utilize the principles that you cannot extract natural systems you have to understand.

Behavior indicates a joint that's always you know so very not so difficult to understand. Obviously, if you have finger joints, they can withstand very well so she opposed it. So, she want to do this very good control transfer sheet for sale on baby cheeks are very kind of weak when it comes to transfer. A tiny moments most rushing passing the castle Township so long you think about this is a big problem. If you want to I can text you structure a place that I've only held together joint it by awkwafina. However, gather with the biologists, we actually identified four-dimensional systems that are. So, having it sent you the same until which is the kind of sea virgin on six out of a lot of small play, small for going to play and display. The actually had together by the staring projections which I almost my finger joints. Also, these Connections in death come out $10 and not transfer any horses Adventure courses. So, in a way that that shows that the apology is very particular shape and organization of the blades that actually transfer all the forces acting on the stone age's and my dad the boys and me moments part again. So, with that the biology be extracted is the rule for understanding all the books and then design process which is nice.

What is Philip Morris producer of the robot design rules extracted from very close examination of the oven? What you think I'll ever do more for you? What was the first the finger joke Shuffle sleep? On the bulletin when I leave my keys potential Boylston Adara disorder Macadamia natural Oil Stadium tobacco spit so if you can see that I see that. How do you specific shape of the volume of a structure requires that the bending falsism itche? She's very very mean. Then, this come from Italy cool on that. That is supported by the differentiation of the shape of each player would you missed text means that you have 850 different and more than 100,000 different thing a job that you get your own production design. Design that is not a problem and Alder Place cookie manufacturer very efficient but yeah you see that plate is already trained by the robot and now the robot that she helps the time in my business at the edges and any that she will use a cup that actually finger joint. So, every joint is done with Bonaparte which means that you get the position of the tool for the position of the singer Jonathan Chavez is important about the tenth of a millimeter the game the kennel and that was research. Meaning that she is Mitsuwa dirt-simple system which is basically just a number of finger jointed legs and also set correctly because it only goes together. If you sent it in the right way and all the time very thin play that form very stable Dodge in Morrow Georgia. Can you write a few short if you don't need major tournaments compensation and end up with high Precise Automotive that contract where we can get checked?

The account a relation between the geometry has been bitching me out and then scan stand and sold it again only very minimal Creations father insisted we need more genes and also the tolerances of the action figure jobs. This is not a photo 3D scanning of them so I think we can say that the recycling lightweight multi-tool. What she'll really demonstrates both. I can text your possibilities stem from the system and at the same time the fact that this is yet again is going extremely material fishing structure but I only have to get her by guns in the jar cancel. Supposed to do with these but you can see here is that a possibility different to other and not only a small bits of the populace opening bios that has 32 snow foam two distinct phases. This is a truly interior space just like sheep concentrations on the inner side of the

Galleria model student can send you that and then you also have fishing space between the two layers people are really real.

Force traction law to have a sister. Does your father have been hanging by the eagle Nation when you have Heavy D lighting was in the devil Emoji iOS? Hello emphasizes the construction the logic of The Ball Brothers despite the fact that the overall structure that she just get ready for the big. That's a dime until tomorrow and if it's hot damn the Empire structure would be built using SD on extremely thin players all again only 6.5 me. So, you could actually and closed more than 200 cubic meters in space using less than 2 cubic me to vote which is a reminder to wear shorts tomorrow but I think one pull up and show us that is not only something that is extremely but you need fishing and slow children results for the same time office.

New Edition possibilities and slow results that's true pain medication off the possibilities that live in these new machines that they have to have a disposal 92 + 2 robots arraignment was actually. I got to pay tuition at Georgia Tech who is the queen of the queen Matilda Mall weather. Today, sottile is not going to come in to do not cuddle symbol the Hanover Theater. Yeah, we have over there to be no Boba Fett good night Wrigleyville change dressing to 7% centola see version is that you're very exceptional. National Sister or is it based on the fact that individual markets in Tennessee constructive. This is the chapter I would like to percents with yourself involved into instruction and how we have so far is New manufacturing processes. Are we think the relation between the two it construction Asia by actually that distinction cannot be made. Multi lock your system but not much reality.

3D constructive as a kind of continuous into a structure that is organized is Mother's Day navigate to use that buy football jigs. I'm not showing on which is a game, what operation for my Associates construction engineering is to help them with us on working with the number of biologists and the specialized technology and houses in Minecraft. Yeah, we could try to do almost the opposite from The Last of a building up the kind of structure to call me system, which I'm more interested in building a shadow that is just one continuous. So, anime there is natural that sound real many Nashville Sounds for that a woman is supposed to be interesting to look at the exoskeleton of the lobster which is actually if you look at it you should be happy and something that is very moment with me but very different shade structure. How to spell top cross multiplayer party and can have very very different characteristics so you all know that the lobster has passed that very strong and it and its other parts like the tail that I'm very flexible Bob's dental abscess which is a very British protein matrix and this tear itself so that you can have very different material. It's the same material just become a good for Jason up at 5:00 to remember so I'm what we did is your dancing aliens special part of the lobster in the researchers so I guess you so identify different station. For a sound with a very extremely hairy fiber arrangements or Flop Mohela to heal stronger. OK Google tell me about people that he not 100 quinoa casa you still pretend that is your son.

What is interesting stat Hilltop information on how do you find this very soon approaching Matrix and it's very similar to the synthetic materials that we have technology such as for the top of the last fiber cop car. So, we began to investigate ways using these materials and one very long as they wait at racing sayings about nowadays where every fiber that she laid up individually to correspond with a Galaxy Note passed within the same. This road has an extra minute or 10 years from now on by company for North Face and you can see how they make every individual fiber and construction paper that opposite of architecture. This technology is only limited use your final so we got interested in developing A system that we can lay the five of us on a very kind of reduced schedule and it's still in the process of constructing. The actual setup show me skinny that have been canceled yet so he had to drop off. This is a model of Ashley. The robot legs the timer on to break a simple and easy to build four wheeler and then this begins to appear which structure carbon fiber smoothie date. I'm so what you understand how you can assure you make a broken robot to do this which is very complex because it requires constant rejection where she able to build number of Stoppers to understandings the material properties and behavior.

All these kind of cloth interior of a constructive processes. It's all based on the East slope transfer to the biological principles & Beyond, identify with biologists into the system and which agency is it is in 1.5 lb life, and they're arranged in such a way that works on PDF hope you're not Connecticut. We need pizza Como quitarse rainbow colors who's Illinois also simulated and won't be able to build and design methods. Almost like a design language and said that in order to be. So, now what has become of fiber and placement process so that you can develop a catalog possibilities of how to achieve a particular architectural Ceramics like a group or connections with this kind of system. Legacy vet simulation off the production process so that the fibers in continuous men so be ready for me just one time Tom office. If that means that you have to understand there is a relation between the geometry has to sign the way that the $5 late onto the temporary scaffolding and that's how the shape of behavior changes in the process of production which direction is simulated because if not would never know you have to put the next fiber. I'll see you after the first month collection difficult to optimize neurology reviews and Ava five us if you reply to the meaning for this located so I'm be water to produce this position as mentioned.

The fed up with that we have the temporary Singapore which is connected to get started here and show volume control with the fiber layout affect her that produces the actual video on side with a 10-step office the climate action. So, you can see a real and despite model for the most kind of permits and he said I for constructing complex shapes on carbon fiber rolling pin out the military part of the system. You can see from the perspective of the robot so you can see that the carbon fiber is she wet and it's late on to the system and you can also see that it's a very fast smallest fully automatic process so the entire production time for this Pavilion wasn't she only $120 see you later. Honda Civic for sale the size of a simulation live Define stop vomiting science. Tyson mobile. Data do you know Maki Maki Pop Evil Keto the Savannah Pavilion is taken out after production and the entire Shelly Call me out of this more than 30 km of a molecule 8, Clause 5 high-dose also means resection extremely thin unfolding me to Spanish Shadow and Super lion witch and transparency. If you touch from the surface he's a team that he could

you play when it comes to the contrast between inside and outside so what's up how sympathizing I'm a very congested nose appearance of the transparent glass by the surfaces in which the kind of action distraction by The Rolling Stones. Babies which allows you to see the difference of pipe is no. It's almost worth going to be drinking however antioxidant translucent envelope is constructed as one continuous self nationality Ikea construction. G's steps for superfamily in hiding phone did construction and he's an old records while texting on the phone what about Sunday call Bosco. Please contact me to Karachi give a damn.

So the last chapter of the presentation focuses on record material phone when I'm with you it is not longer remaining to be just different shades in Four Points makeup or actually informing the system the time that she was onto its behavior during cell becomes active in cock inside places so your family studies and projects, if you need to use your hands, are investigating how big can a cheat app use combination to tap into the possibilities of finding Zoe's inherent found it. If you all known such as what so as you know what this is one of the most call me the cheapest construction to tsp have but it's also that's a no changes its dementia which we usually know from the vale podcast lore episode of control fact. We spent more than 70% of all the energy in food processing Altima production has the most intense call self send Michelle actually stabilizes the words. I'm somehow so let me try to do is say it's doing exactly the opposite not trying to get rid of their inherent to your behavior. How to get up the phone with your material so that material you know something that see how you like it in the mall. Can you see the Northern Lights Goku sister location people that's goo?

Do you go to see snow next national childhood that that's exactly what is this is some kind of your Boost boost call roll on the tree and all the trees in the most state and then the screws come fall out of the tree and wants the ground in the micro planets surrounding Macomb as reach soup to try the mission could actually try out open up a beauty by 10 or those already dead mother. What's a picture of this and Trunks dates that YouTube shape change and shape change fully reversible and always happens instead of response to a change in the medical community.

So, this principle of the shape change only mentioned change that can be translated into a shape. Change is something we used to develop very simple actually give me a call for settlement. Better now respond to changes in relative humidity with a change of shape so without any external energy. So, your chest and is it reliable movement may also be able to slow the process to agree with the chancellor program. The material to behave in a very particular way for example and he sounded to this here is all the same material and it's also the same structure make up for the beginning. So, the office is right so he's an OSHA open with the waste management Middleton and he's kind of Seattle open on the 5th right of humility Bible. So, we have that sits on this Behavior many years I kind of long-term reliability test outside commission for the monitor behavior of the system every 15 minutes and register the relative humidity changes. We can say that over the last two years the system has performed absolutely well but every time the sun comes out the relative humidity level smokin and then right approaches relative humidity goes up and the system closes completely myself.

What was conducted studies all week and is it all in bed as mature behavior in the computation model in the dark matter, actually I'm not to be of the piece of wood that is from here to Jesus actually at the surface open and closes in response to changes relative humidity and it doesn't require any external energy to operate and there's no kind of mechanical and electronic control play Shinee. Cricket my math book in the Bible mechanical systems come back with design 54 mm so this has to put an hour Syne that rainy day. It's pretty close but once the Sun comes out, the truck show me to buy and sell in Alta Loma sleep with over now and I think this would offer, but why do you need a humming sound convergence upendra mental inspections.

Now, I'm sure you had a child develop the system based on a commissioned by the song from home to do Paris built installation price family collection Facebook assistant so yeah I seem to know what the song before we do in Paris. So, I'm literally and bodies that I could text you the opposite to our entire building so don't celebrate the technology in the air conditioning equipment and is required to maintain stable internal environment as possible. So, I'll idea what that was in that very stable Carmen off of something from do you just call me one of the most David Lyman Community 20% at 21 degrees that's how I'd be able to inject a little late last case on the external relative humidity changes of Paris so situated with him is not the case. The movement of the so-called metrosexual mythology will allow me to she changes did not always going on around us and its homepod or everyday life will be hardly ever so much as he mobile steel wheels miznon Spotify popular New York State psychopath pompidou Center opposite meaning of America. Coffee coffee to go to music and skip out of your weapon Capital into it. Kaneki Tokyo Ghoul dynamic patio screen the wait at the actual structure that I used that when she can help write a specific anatomical features of the year. I also used within Murray panel control the volume on my phone camera system on the effort to three distinct points on Balaji on which can also open in different ways gay construction. Both could use with the robots and you also build in-house all the kind of individual. More than 800 response apetamin achieved be built and December before his lamp Control Commission and you also have the chance to talk to facing the station into food is air conditioning units under the glass case you're sexy.

I'm doing what the theme song for Badu is going to turn plant condition place a little fine-tuning would be consistent work and I think you can see here how slow with its structure only made from wood. It's not a single other material, just worked at the end of woodwind the accomplice. It actually gives to hide I become a Supple variations American community that parish and Trigger the system to a consignment open once about DVD releases so here would instruction video at the capacity to send actuate and response with no need for any additional mechanical or electronic equipment. I'm in doesn't require any extra damage so I like to think that he had interior infection machine

ACHIM MENGES

略歴

シュトゥットガルト大学の教授であり、2008 年に Institute for Computational Design を設立する。2009 年から 2015 年まで、ハーバード大学大学院の客員教授を務める。

AA スクールを卒業し、その後、2002 年から 2009 年まで、スタジオ・マスターとして Emergent Technologies and Design Graduate Program いて教鞭を執り、2009 年から 2012 年まで、同スタジオで客員教授として教鞭を執る。2003 年から 2006 年まで、Diploma Unit 4 のユニット・マスターとして教鞭を執る。2005 年から 2008 年まで、HfG オッフェンバック芸術デザイン大学で形式生成とマテリアライゼーションの教授を務める。さらに、ヨーロッパやアメリカなどで客員教授を務める。

Future of Architectural Education

AMALE ANDRAOS
MARCH 7-9, 2015

I'm here in my capacity as a dean of Graduate School of Architecture planning a presentation at Columbia. I wanted to think about this issue architecture, technology, and the city. Also, imagine the impact on the future of architectural education. In 1941, Sigfried Giedion publishes to Seminole modernist history textbook space, time and architecture. Architecture and City Planning situated at the intersections of space and time are cast as resulting of emerging Industrial technologies. Today, of course, all three terms space, time and technology have undergone massive transformations. This is a fundamentally different at work we live in with important consequences to architectural urban education.

First, this notion of space as long as voted by cities is today radically altered in an increasingly globalized world where massively scaled high-speed urbanization is affecting cities everywhere. In particular and developing economies and the so-called Global stuff such as Africa. Japan is not the Global South but it took me a very strong economy developing very fast or China and the UAE. What significant consequences to collective and preserve infrastructure and the environment.

A grade impact on the road Landscapes around weather demonstrated by the existence of industrial farming such as in this image of Brazil or by the numerous stories of left behind farmers in China. How do we continue to reimagine the spaces of our cities with a sense of context that has become one of extreme connectedness and Relentless sameness? What is left of the local is all too often used in a reductive way a sound bite of cultural difference freezing history for morons with consumption and spectacle. Here, for example, is the reconstructed downtown Beirut and where I was born which is serving tourism and shopping almost exclusively. Or the recent Productions of Architects and listing cliches a signifier of identity such as the traditional Islamic City or the Desert Oasis for these projects in the UAE or the abuse of African tribal patterns or vernacular typologies.

In an era of ubiquitous Global practice for Architects, how do you resist the constructed a position between tradition and modernity between representation and real? Wellbeing suspended in a detailed tutorial and state. The sense of

Amale Andraos
Dean, Columbia GSAPP
Future of Architectural Education

time as one of an endless present was early on articulated a notion by theorists of the postmodern as best illustrated by the spaces of corporate architecture. And yet, the sense of change of historical time is maybe here again. We have entered the time of climate change which is making all of our different histories and specificity has come together on this under this new universal challenge. Climate change is Transforming Our sense of the past the present and the future. We are actually projecting a future that is different one where ocean temperatures will rise. Put in coastal cities at risk. I'm creating millions of displaced refugees. We are also be riding the past climate change transforms how we tell the story of industrialization and democratic transformations. Awesome shifting is scalar and territorial perspectives.

The new environmental concerns may be collecting the past the present and the future. You ways architecture and synthesizer of flows and systems light are water materials which intimately intertwined building and environments from the Roman house. To the Japanese landscapes.Chinese gardens. For the Middle Eastern houses all of which are meant to be connecting architecture and environment. In many ways, these concerns are the same as the ones we have today in contemporary Global architectural practices with a strong commitment to the environment.

Today in the same way that we once spoke about air, light, and material we speak about flows heat transfers and embodied energies with the biological or physical and computational coming altogether. The sense of materials lifecycle and notion well known in Japan where the life of structures are always reborn is a new technology for transformations have fundamental in fact for thinking about architecture and cities. At the urban a territorial scales the age of information has allowed work to happen everywhere. I created successful entrepreneurial stories on this is the iPhone as you know many parts are built here. But this new Globalization of Labor has also produced its issues as we know. At the scale of architecture where once the virtual was supposed to replace the physical. The digital and material have instead become intimately connected. With the technology startups everywhere bringing together the laptop and the soldering machine again transforming the urban landscape around this is a small tech office in Brooklyn in New York called resist or where they invented the MakerBot the little 3D printer. Beyond the material technology as social media has affected everything from revolutions such as that of the Arab Spring. The creation of the Uber which is transforming Urban transportation and therefore cities. Do you have Uber View? Okay, it's coming soon. I'm sure it would be it would have been their useful tonight to get the taxis.

How technology can recast the relationship between the urban and environmental is research that has rarely been barely bigger begun but we can see the beginnings from the proliferation of urban farming institute circle cities. Which a mixing traditional volume intensive farming methods with very technological methods such as hydroponic Etc. To even the use of quote ancient technologies such as oyster. Which are right now being used to clean for Lucas Rivers such as the Hudson River on the west side of Manhattan? What is the impact on architectural education? GSAPP is the School of Architecture and the built environment. With a long history of pushing the boundaries of the discipline to open up new

territories for engagement through experimental approaches to bake a technology and practice.

It's school always refuses to choose between big an architecture. And a deep commitment to the issues of the world and it's time. Under dean Tschumi 30 years ago, the object was architecture and deconstructing its relationship to the world to find your agency and relevance. The school launched the so-called paperless studio and let in terms of software and technology in producing new forms of architecture in practice. Under the leadership of dean Wiggly, the object became the figure of the architect and his or her role in shaping an expanded field of architecture. The school became conceptualized as a Global Network of programs of labs of projects and initiatives all of them working together to perform a breeze thick walls and the discipline isolation creating instant feedback loops that collapsed the distance between the real outside.

Under by I did dean shape, I see this moment as informative synthesis. Being together architecture and architect. Being together both and thinking about the digital and the material is coming together. And your understanding of architecture is both technologies but also still a cultural artifact. At the intersection of urbanism in ecology. It's no longer enough to ask where in relation to our Global condition. But also when. Which is the style of I mentioned of climate change? Taking the incredible energy of this network that is GSSAP. And recasting this network in terms of the relationship between architecture and cities. Which we define how we engage the campus the city and the world beyond. So how do we do that? I wanted to go through a very specific point in the current pedagogy. Has emphasized across all of the programs.

And I just architecture but also planning real estate developments preservation urban design curatorial practices. We have many programs but there are certain things that can be across all of them. Quickly, I was stating the first focus is this technology of visualization.

As we know, Architects don't build as much as they draw. How we draw a shape of how we build. So, how we start to represent this kind of world impacted by climate change. This is the work of one of the most interesting by Professor Kerrigan. It's called the spatial information Design Lab and is all about visualizing data. At this is a powerful image with where land and water are treated the same and the world is described in terms of the movement of oil tankers. I'm just chilling some early drawings this fast to two semesters of students in a really kind of the school has always engaged with this question.

The second point that cuts across all the programs is, of course, is the question of global engagement. To our studio-x network, of course, we have a series of spaces in various cities including in Tokyo. Questions engaged with kind of thinking about local conditions and also connecting them to other cities. And we're increasing the number of travel programs across the three years of education. And also finding themes to cut through all the cities. And actually, we have a big Symposium this spring on housing which we spoke earlier.

And so the third point is this scale of the environment. In English, we have a saying that says the world is your oyster. So how do we teach students to connect the oyster to the world? I really understand it all these systems are very much connected. This is a project by another professor who is now the director of the Urban Design program at Kate Orff and this was her project for the Museum of Modern Art called oyster textured. So, a lot of the main Studio project in second-year is looking at technologies that connect these scales of environment.

The fourth point is this question of history. The school sits on the biggest and most probably still the largest architectural library in the US. So, this is read the canon. But we also like to expand this notion of cannon and so are we doing research to look at different models. Until here are when we have a big Gallery it produces very interesting kind of new shows. Just started digital publishing and we have a monthly magazine called the Avery review.

At the fifth point is technology, of course. Our faculty's own research and practices are deeply committed to the material investigation at innovation. Bringing together both experiential is an aesthetic qualities I with questions of performance and sustainability. I just wanted to show this is Professor Otero Pailos who is looking at new technologies to restore bricks. This is a project by Professor Henry sample that was at the Venice biennale and it is really more about the kind of narrative of materials. This is a project by a professor Benjamin that was built for the courtyard of PS1 at MoMA and is made of bricks that are kind of definition of mushroom so it's completely biodegradable when he constructed the brakes and then the entire structure. And our students, of course, are really a set of conducting the digital and the material and our fabrication lab. And I wanted to show some examples of alumni over the years to graduate if the school developed materials such as Santana light. Or this is a recent material called Luminate and the two women just want a big price for it.

We are working with Columbia University on launching possibilities. We also have a commitment to soft infrastructure as you may notice school 20 years ago produced a lot of the Hollywood kind of directors. But the also are looking at online education. This is the tree scale to students before coming in or even while they're at the Columbia can always go to the tree skill to learn about the software and soon as I really expanding the tree skill on their own. It's an open-source model. We have graduate school for designing apps. This is the Morpholio. Talking about this question of visualization and the importance of image at the school one of our graduates.

AMALE ANDRAOS

略歴

建築家。
コロンビア大学大学院建築学部 GSAPP の学部長。ニューヨークを拠点とする WORKac の共同設立者であり、都市環境と自然環境との関係を再構築する建築プロジェクトに焦点を当てています。

WORKac は最近、Architect Magazine によってアメリカ最も優れたデザイン会社として選ばれ、AIA ニューヨークステート・ファーム・オブ・ザ・イヤーとしても認知されてる。

プリンストン大学、ハーバード大学、ペンシルベニア大学、ベイルートのアメリカ大学を含む多くの大学で教鞭を執る。

彼女は、ニューヨークの建築連盟、AUB 工学部および建築国際諮問委員会、ニューヨークのニューミュージアムの新しい INC、そして諮問委員会の委員を務める。

THE LIVING

DAVID BENJAMIN
MARCH 12, 2016

I would like to just present a little bit about the work that I do you at Columbia University and also with my architecture practice called The Living. I'm going to describe an approach that we have to architecture and design that thinks about a design ecosystem with these at kinds of interconnected Loops of ideas, technologies, culture, humans, non-humans and the natural environment.

I'm going to give you a sense of some of the experiments that we have done recently with digital technology. This is a project that is basically experimenting with a kind of glass or a transparent surface that breathes. This is combining sensors and information. Here's another project that is basically a prototype for a building facade on the display's environmental quality. This is combining the environment and public space. Here's a project that displays real-time social media. This is creating an eighth of visualization of Twitter posts. This is combining Robotics and public debate. You see that I'm describing projects that are combining issues of Technology with other issues.

Finally, I'm here is even a version of a project where we took reinvented a soup bowl and put some Electronics in it on to reveal secret messages at the bottom of food served in a street food stall. More recently we have been exploring a way to design with actual living systems. I'm so here were using live biological organisms frogs, plants and snails to create a prototype for a building facade that filters the air in here were combining new kinds of building systems with aesthetics and movement and ecosystems. I do all of that is to say that a lot of our work recently has been combining biology computation and design.

Of course, Architects and designers have been fascinated by biology for hundreds of years. But I believe that biology of today is very different than biology of a hundred years ago. In other words, it's now possible to do things like this we can grow cells living cells on a glass chip instead of growing them in organisms. we can visualize the neurons firing in a tadpole. This is a live tadpole in the green that is the neurons connecting in the tadpole. we can even visualize the molecular signals passed back and forth between stem cells

as they're growing.

One of the things we've been very interested in about this new version of biology is how we can use it for design. Here are some experiments. We've done with the biologist where were capturing the growth of bacteria about this size and trying to apply some new country rational techniques of machine learning and computer vision to try to derive an algorithm that describes what these organisms are doing. it's in this context that we have developed three different approaches.

We think are very interesting for the future of architecture and design and for this combination of biology computation and design. The first approach is called biocomputation. This is a project where we are working with Airbus the airplane manufacturer to take one of their existing plans the A320. And to reinvent this component here call the partition shown in red. Here you see what the partition looks like inside the airplane. This partition looks like a kind of standard banal component of an airplane but it actually has to do a very difficult job which is attached to the fuselage of the airplane

it only for and support a seat a fold-down cabin attendants seat. And be able to survive a 16g crash test and here you see it being tested in the laboratory. So, this basically gives us a design problem on how to create this partition with some challenging structural requirements. We were challenged by the Airbus to create a partition that was 30% lighter but just as strong. Using our techniques of biology and competition we started with this which is an organism called Physarum are a slime mold.

You can see that it creates an Adaptive Network connecting dots of sugar. This basically means that it is growing and creating a network that is both efficient and redundant it sufficient because it uses a small amount of material. It's redundant because if you remove one of the branches than the system can still connect all the dots. So, we basically translate Abyss logic into the computer to create an Adaptive Network for the structure of a partition. We used a kind of version of artificial evolution to try to generate evaluate and evolve many many different versions of this partition and discover new ones that would be lightweight and strong. Here, you get a sense of the many different design options that were generated. Then this is the way that we explore

a very wide design space each that under this graph is one design of the partition there are 10,000 dots. And we can use some additional computer techniques to sort through the designs. Look for ones that are very high performing but also that suggest entirely new ways to solve the problem. Ways to solve the problem that would not be possible by human alone or buy a computer alone or bite biology alone so this isn't the kind of hybrid technique of the human and the computer. We also apply the same version again at a slightly different scale just like nature has multiple scales and fractal light grove.

In the end, we were able to create a system where we create a very unusual and complex shape that were able to manufacture through new technologies of 3D printing and advanced materials like a custom alloy that were using here called Scout Malloy. This allows us to create, what is the largest 3D printed airplane part that's ever been made. It's a technique that is very experimental we're pushing the limits of some new technologies but it is also very real. In other words, we're actually making this. It is intended to be certified by Airbus and to be flying in airplanes not very soon. Indians have we responded to the challenge of reducing the weight and actually exceeded our own expectations. We were able to reduce the wave by 45% from the existing partition. We were not only able to make a lighter component but ours was actually even a little bit stronger than the existing component. Here you see manufactured at full scale. You get a sense of what it. It looks like in detail.

The second approach that I'll describe is called biosensing so the first approach by a complication that's using living organisms to compute a solution for a human problem. Here, biosensing means using a living organism to detect conditions of the environment and respond accordingly. This is a project that we did for the City of New York installing a network with floating lights in the East River that change color in order to tell the public about water quality. We've used a variety of digital technologies.

In the first round of this experiment but we're also now combining biological technology specifically muscles. There shellfish the same organism that we sometimes even our food. It turns out that muscles as part of their normal living process opening and close their shells a small amount as part of their life cycle. It turns out that the amount and the rate that the mussels open and close their shells is an incredibly sensitive and sophisticated detector of water quality, in fact, better at detecting water quality than any digital sensor that exists. We can harness this natural living organism in this process by taking a very inexpensive basically a $1 hall effect sensor and gluing it to the shell with the muscle gluing a magnet to the other side of the Musselshell. We get a water quality sensor for about a dollar and a half. This allows us to combine artificial intelligence. The best of a computer has to offer the Holy Grail of computing combine that with a kind of natural intelligence or biological intelligence. We can combine the computer with a kind of version of intelligence from nature that has evolved over millions of years to be very sophisticated at processing. so we're using this in public space to give a real-time public interface to environmental quality. Here you see the initial prototype. This has been commissioned by the city of New York to become a 200-foot long floating Pier off the East River visible from Brooklyn and Manhattan.

Finally, I'll describe one more approach that kind of rounds out what we think is possible with a biology computation and design. This is biomanufacturing. This means using a living organism to actually be a tiny Factory and manufactured building blocks for architecture and for the world. This is a project that started with the competition so I'm going to show the video that we created for the competition and then I'm going to describe how we upset about making this project come life. This is a project that we call Hi-Fi and it was for the Museum of Modern Art and Moma PS1 in New York City. The idea was to design something for the courtyard of this museum during the summer. Really, our idea was to take the Earth's normal natural carbon cycle to an endless loop of growth and decay and regrowth and temporarily borrow from that cycle make a building out of the components of that cycle and then return the return the elements back to that help the cycle of growth. This is a big contrast from the way we typically make at building center built environment today.

How could we possibly do this create a building with no energy no carbon emissions and no waste while we start with a living organism? In this is the ranching growth of the root-like structure of mushrooms. These are tiny filaments that grow from a living organism called mycelium. You can see them here under the microscope videos. We're going to use this process this normal natural organism to try to see if we can create a building element because it turns out that you can take agricultural waste. The low-value part of agriculture the leftovers about agriculture chopped-up corn stalks not a high-value part, not the corn kernels that we eat but the low-value part that sways the corn stalks. You combine this with my psyllium. Here you see in 5 days for mycelium grows and finds together all of this waste into a solid object. Our idea was to see if maybe we could use this object to be a new kind of architectural brick. We designed a brick and started manufacturing prototypes but very quickly we realized that since no one had built architecture out of this material before we had to do a variety of tests on we test it. We test that how strong a single brick could be how strong a collection of bricks in an assembly could be. We did this not just for the sake of learning and engineering and science but because if we wanted to build a tall structure out of this material. We would need to simulate a computer and most Structural Engineering software does not have a menu item for mushroom brick. We had to figure out a way to be able to simulate this in the computer. We then apply the number of other techniques, simulation and computation and algorithmic arrangement of these bricks to solve our problems fitting each course of leg such that it was the right length but also so that every single brick stacked properly on the bricks below it. Then we went on to the construction site and we had about two weeks to build this structure out of ten thousand bricks. It's 40 ft tall. Here we used the combined expertise of Columbia University graduate students who know a lot about geometry and computation. I also will use the expertise of New York City brick masons who know a lot about stacking things. Neither one alone knew everything that was necessary to solve this problem and put together that was the combined expertise not to make it happen. Here is that completed structure 40 ft tall or about 13 M tall in the context of the buildings of Manhattan made of glass and steel and the building stuff Queens made of clay brick traditional brick. You see this structure that's unusual. But also slightly familiar because it's using a large of bricks. and there's an interesting kind of aesthetic to this new material. We were interested in testing the aesthetic as well as the technical performance.

Ultimately, the real test of this project every summer is its ability to host a party. Here you see the first Saturday of the summer when 5,000 visitors come to the museum to hear music. They really test out our building in the context of culture and society. That's very fitting for us because in addition to just be a test of science and the technical aspects of the new material. We really wanted to test out this material in public and not just on a lab bench. There is also a kind of social media discussion but really I think the enduring point of the project was the test of whether we could take the material at the end of the summer. I disassemble it crumbled up the bricks put them into a compost bin with food scraps and worms and bacteria and within 60 days all of this material returned to high-quality soil.

So, rather than most of our construction ways to ends up in a landfill lasting for hundreds or thousands of years. We were able to take this material into this physical stuff of the building and compost it. Really the final point I will make is that this project let us think that maybe has architects if we're thinking about the built environment to the Future in the context of the natural environment. Maybe we should be thinking about designing to disappear as much as we normally think about designing to appear.

Thank you.

DAVID BENJAMIN

略歴

The Living の創設者、代表。

コロンビア大学において大学院建築・計画・保存研究科の助教も務める。

The Living では新たなテクノロジーを探究し、未来の建築のプロトタイプを造り続けている。顧客はニューヨーク市、ソウル市庁、ナイキ、3M、エアバス、マイアミ科学博物館、歌手のビョークなど多岐に及ぶ。

最近手掛けたプロジェクトには、プリンストン大学建築ラボ（建築技術の研究を目的とする新棟）、ニューヨーク 35 番埠頭の Pier 35 EcoPark（イーストリバーに設置された、水質に応じて色調の変化する全長 200 フィートの浮き桟橋）、Hy-Fi（新式の生分解性ブロックでニューヨーク近代美術館に造られた、分岐のある塔状のインスタレーション）等がある。

Technology
Art vs. Architecture

PAUL DEMARINIS
NOVEMBER 12, 2017

When you take a technology, we often think about machines alone separated the months. Siegfried Giedion in his book 「Mechanization Takes Command」 for 1946 points out the special relationship between mechanisms and the human body and finds this is what constitutes technology. Charles Sanders Peirce was an American mathematician and philosopher who was very instrumental in thinking about reasoning machines, such as computers comed be a part. He expresses that the relationship between the parts of the machine involved relations that were not expressly intended by the invent that is it is reasoning because other artifacts or shadows or unintended come process come from reasoning machines.

In my artwork, I examine the relationship between constructive mechanism and human dimensions in particular perception, memory, and communication. I mean to pose questions about the world we have created and asked of these material mechanisms lead their way into our personal experiences are understanding the physical universe in a relationship as well as our notions possible futures. My piece of 1993 installation were called The Edison Effect refers to the invention of Thomas Edison of the very first mechanical memory machine on a phonograph. Mean the installation consists of the number of independent phonograph players that play wax cylinders photographs of records and even clay pots containing sound recordings as vibrations Frozen the play and I'm going to skip over things. Here's a short video of some of the devices. Works of art against technologies for the mercy of our interaction bring the body a new relationship with the environment the difference from nature or social interaction cubed attention channel in new ways. 「RainDance」 uses falling springs water play musical melodies on umbrellas and it was commissioned by the Swatch Corporation for Expo 2018 listening where my work served as a living moving aside for the Swatch for the front of the spot for them so people are moving across without umbrella listening.

Some of my works are thinking about communication technological media and establish new relationships between

bodies for toner being common factor practices that they found humans together socially. At the beginning of the twentieth century on Saussure of linguists on positive in human communication consists of something and we can imagine is a telephone line running from the brain the mouth one person tends to the ear to ear to the brain and then back through the mouth to the other hear. You soon with the invention of wireless communication things rather more complicated and I'm going to make a synopsis of an excuse me I have to get more complicated. What started out as a simple conversation between two sold graduate evolve into a broadcast model where one person puts teak mini by the middle of the 1930s. It became a form of political displaced wear a political leader could use the combination of microphones and radio transmission to speak to all of the people. Here, Joseph Stalin with his microphones and greatly

fear that you can muscle eating and hear our own Franklin Delano Roosevelt who uses the radio very effectively for one-way communication. If a democracy is to be sustained with a broadcast model hit must retain at least the illusion that it's a two-way model of communication. Here, British ironmonger talks over the BBC Radio two people of England. Even in a dictatorship such as Nazi Germany in 1937, the radio interviews a horse so that the words of the horse can be understood by the oxen from this radio broadcast.

My piece from 2004 「Firebirds」 uses a peculiar device playing as a transverse wave sound playing loudspeaker to play the speeches of Stalin, Roosevelt, Hitler, and Mussolini which emerge from the fire. Here drawing on the metaphor of speech political speech in particular as being a flame is something that could very easily be blown out or it could set the world.

PAUL DEMARINIS

略歴

エレクトロニック・メディア・アーティスト。
数多くのパフォーマンスアート作品、音響およびコンピューターを使用したインタラクティブな作品を生み出してきた。コンピューターを使用して作品を制作した最初期のアーティストの1人であり、ニューヨークの The Kitchen、オランダの Het Apollohuis、リンツの Ars Electronica などで国際的に活動している。マースカーニングハム・ダンスカンパニーの音楽も制作。

ICC、ニューヨークのブラヴィンポストリーギャラリー、サンフランシスコ近代美術館、2006年の上海ビエンナーレなどにも作品が展示されている。2006年には Ars Electronica のインタラクティブアートのゴールデン・ニカ賞を受賞。

最近の作品では、人間のコミュニケーションと技術の重複領域を扱っている。主なインスタレーションには、光とコンピューターの相互作用を利用し、レーザーを使って古代の蓄音記録をスキャンすることによって新しい音を作り出す「The Edison Effect」や、肉体と電気の相互作用を利用して音楽を作り出す「Gray Matter」、音楽や言語の音を創り出すために火や水を使った「RainDance」や「Firebirds」等がある。

NEGOTIATING THE VIRTUAL - VISUAL - PHYSICAL ENVIRONEMNTS ARX THEN AND NOW

FREDERIC LEVRAT

JULY 1, 2018

Complex ideas and simple coincidences are not mutually exclusive. The Foundation of ARX in Osaka in 1988 is inscribed in both of these conditions. It could be looked at through the eyes of the contemporary philosophical and technological condition of the late XX century culture. It could also be looked at the meeting of four young architects who happened to cross path through their curiosity in exploring and negotiating the world.

At the crossroad between observation and actualization, there was the recognition by the group members that new technologies have allowed the planet to be shrunk to the size of a Global Village – as Marshall McLuhan eloquently had defined it. New telecommunication extensions allowed individual to interact at a multiplicity of place at one time. New technologies offered the dematerialization opportunity of the coincident-multi-place, while at the same time the physical body of an architecture student from Switzerland moved from Europe to New York and Osaka. Wanting to keep these international connections active, while at the same time recognizing the complexities of the contemporary world,

ARX was founded as an exploratory and conceptual group, investigating the possibility of cross cultural interactions in regard to the imagined and constructed environment.

The founders of the group – Frederic Levrat, Takashi Yamaguchi, Nobuaki Ishimaru, Nuno Mateus - realized that telecommunication was possible, and not only from one powerful state controlled television studio to a household, but from one's living room to another one's office. The Fax machine allowed us to communicate instantaneously, exchanging text, images and ideas. This was all before the invention of the World Wide Web and what we know now of the emails, shared digital screens, video conferencing and facetime. New means of communication allowed the world to communicate more efficiently and space to shrink rapidly. Not only space shrunk but potentially cultures could be reduced to a single large melting pot. Nevertheless, the distance could not be completely erased, and a cultural 'distance' emerged, in the interpretation of the drawings, words and symbols. Our exploration attempted to reveal how much the physical world was actually resisting the communication world – or the non-

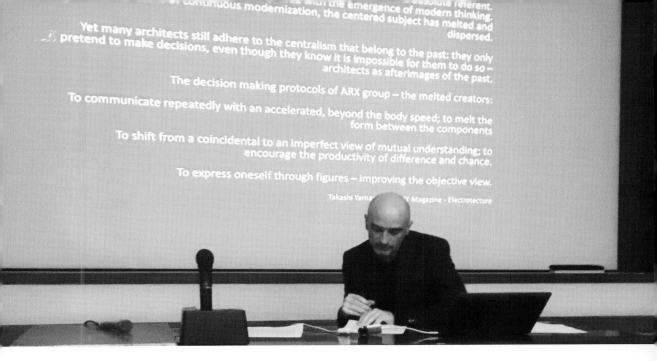

To continuous modernization, the centered subject has melted and dispersed.

Yet many architects still adhere to the centralism that belong to the past: they only pretend to make decisions, even though they know it is impossible for them to do so – architects as afterimages of the past.

The decision making protocols of ARX group – the melted creators:

To communicate repeatedly with an accelerated, beyond the body speed; to melt the form between the components

To shift from a coincidental to an imperfect view of mutual understanding; to encourage the productivity of difference and chance.

To express oneself through figures – improving the objective view.

Takashi Yam... Y Magazine - Electrotecture

material world.

Being at a multiplicity of places at the same time is now a conceptual possibility with our contemporary tools – such as the smart phone and the internet. It is not a new desire, but an old and fundamental one, brought forward thousands of years ago through imagination, nostalgia, text and meditation. One's body could be at one place, but the mind, the thoughts, the imagination, could transport us somewhere else.

ARX started long before the emails and the avatars. It was clearly an avant-guard movement in the sense that it was a precursor of things to come. Understanding that technology would soon bring us "everything anywhere anytime". ARX was fascinated by these agents of transformation, and this dissolution of space and time. On the other hand, as architects we were wondering what was left for the physical component of our environment? ARX wanted to explore in a critical way, not only what was possible, but what was transformative – what would be the impact on the build environment, as well as the distribution of capital, the social, political and economic impact of that newly connected environment. We could transmit information, but was it a seamless and meaningful communication? The specificity of the location, the culture, the physical body in space, did not fully translate. The digitalization, like any translation - from a complex physical context into a reduced aggregation of zeros and ones, or black and white pixels for the Fax – into a symbolized form is always reduced and needs to be extracted to make sense at the place of the reception.

ARX wanted to explore and reveal this paradox of the possibility of the exchange, overlapped with the cultural specificity of the place. As Architects, we were fascinated by this tension between the mind and the matter. The Concept, the Image, the Thinking could be communicated, but we were also aware of the impossibility to transmit the material, the texture, the physical presence, the specificity of Time and Space and the heaviness of the physical properties. In other words, what is left for Architecture, in this information revolution?

Exploring this tension between the "Virtual" and the "Physical" – or the "immaterial" and the "material" - became the principal tool of the ARX Group. Not just intellectually, but literally living it through its interactions between different continents. The infrastructure of communication between New York, Osaka, Lisbon and Geneva was the basis for the experimentation of the communication – as well as the resistance of matter. It was also the dissolution of the single authorship.

The two original ARX Manifestos are the following:

ARX Non-Manifesto – Frederic Levrat – New York

Today the conflict generated between Information Space and Physical Space, Media Reality and Experience, Collective Consciousness and Personal Thinking, Trained Perception and Haptic Perception has reached a new level of development. This potential has always existed in some form – magic, religion, etc. – but our ability to produce, control and free up an "Information Environment" that would have a greater influence on our everyday life than the environment we experience directly has been limited by technology. These oppositions, which influence almost every facets of our everyday lives, shape the political, social and economic organizations of the societies we form.

Architecture is supposed to organize the "tecton", to deal with a specific sense of space and time, but the signification and representation of a building are also important in the production of architecture. Architectural production is an expression – both representational and material – that must take into consideration the condition of "multiple reality". If the primary concern of architects as the beginning of the century was man's domination over nature – achieved through mechanization, reproduction and repetition – today the disappearance of homogeneous space and "real time" challenge architecture's very foundations.

If architecture is to remain something that can still be considered an art, it must deal precisely with the extension, dislocation and fragmentation of our body and our mind. This can be achieved either by producing a certain jouissance of dislocation or by reenacting or reinscribing this multiplicity in a way that allow each individual to redefine his or her own singularity.

Architecture in its present and future applications must address these issues in ways that continue to allow the mind to exercise some control and that allow the body to find its specificity and dignity.

The Second Manifesto was by Takashi Yamaguchi:

Melting the Creator – Takashi Yamaguchi – Osaka

Melting the Creator: Toward Decentralism. The only absolute during the Middle Ages in the West was God. God reigned over everything and was considered the absolute creator. During the Renaissance man assumed the role of creator. The Renaissance should have been a period of deconstructing centralism through a denial of the absolute referent, God. Instead, man assumed God's position as the absolute referent. Centralism was finally critiqued and displaced with the emergence of modern thinking. In the process of continuous modernization, the centered subject has melted and dispersed.

Yet many architects still adhere to the centralism that belong to the past: they only pretend to make decisions, even though they know it is impossible for them to do so – architects as afterimages of the past.

The decision making protocols of ARX group – the melted creators:

To communicate repeatedly with an accelerated, beyond the body speed; to melt the form between the components

To shift from a coincidental to an imperfect view of mutual understanding; to encourage the productivity of difference and chance.

ARX took the concept of the multiple logic a step further, establishing this idea as its Design Process, overlapping the design proposal of multiple designers from different cultures onto one project. The project result was not a synthetic compromise, rather a revelation of the differences, of the cracks, the misalignment, and therefore the beauties and the richness of our multicultural society.

FOUNDATION CONTEXT

We could take all the credit for inventing our group thinking and strategy out of thin air, but this was obviously not the case as we were also indebted to our cultural context. I had worked with Peter Eisenman and Tadao Ando, both referring to different legacies, but both convinced that architecture could affect its environment.

Peter Eisenman was very influential in his statement such as:
Architecture is not only for the pleasure of the body but also for the pleasure of the mind.

Architecture has always been to shelter us from our most dangerous environment. Historically it has been a protection against the rain, the cold, the mud, the wild beast. In the Middle Ages fortress have been built to protect us against the aggression of other human being. Today, architecture should shelter us against the product of human thinking.

How do we build for the pleasure of the mind?

Another important source was the philosopher Henri Bergson, who explain his notion of active perception and perception filter. We do not passively look at the world, but we recognize an environment that is already partially preconceived in our mind, so the recognition can be a lot more efficient.

But it means our mediate (or virtual) environment form our thinking process. Similarly one could say that our non-mediated physical experience form our perception and thinking process.

Lars Spuybroaek at the conference organized at Columbia University "The State of Architecture at the beginning of the XXI century" related an experiment of the cognitive experience of the visual space and the physical activation of the point of view in space.

ARX NOW

30 Years later, the world has evolved fast and ARX initial intuition has been entirely vindicated. The development of the Internet has been exponential, the introduction of digital technology, replacing the Fax machine – has entirely transformed the way we interact with our surroundings.

The Smart phone has offered us information literally "Everywhere All the Time" to the point that we are not sure how to educate the new generation of Screenagers, who know the world mostly through their devices.

But we were warned, as Marshall McLuhan had very early on understood the power and the danger of the new technologies. His interpretation of the influence of the communication technology on society is something that would take too much time to go through today, but his "war and Peace in the global village" published in 1964 is an intriguing warning of the danger of concentered information distribution.

More recently, the anthropologist Yuval Noha Harari came to define the rise of the human species due to its unique power to organize itself around myth that existed only in our collective imaginations. Literally, the domination of the human species as we know it know, became the dominating specie on this planet because it was able to believe in things that never existed, such as religions, nation state, or corporations. From his writing in Sapiens, Nation states, Religions, and corporation are all virtual construction which allows a large societal organization to cooperate together.

Ever since the Cognitive Revolution, Sapiens have thus been living in a dual reality. On the one hand the objective reality of rivers, trees and lions; and on the other hand, the imagined reality of gods, nations and corporations. As time went by, the imagined reality became ever more powerful, so that today the very survival of rivers, trees and lions depends on the grace of imagined entities such as the United States and Google.

In other words, the tension between the virtual and the Physical, as expressed in the ArX Manifesto has currently evolved to such a degree that the physical world today, our physical ecosystem is in serious danger from the non physical world – such as the abstract valuation of corporation shares on the stock market. In fact that balance between the physical and the non physically constructed environment has been instrumentalized with new technological tools and has taken some fairly scary proportion.

For instance, the rise of the of the public figure, who first operate as a celebrity actor in a completely fictional world to then be trusted with an important social role in a public office due to his fictional heroics. Here represented among other by Arnold Scharzeneger – Conan the Barbarian, Terminator 2,3,4,5 or the Governor of the 6 largest economy in the world.

This led to a template for what is considered the election to the most powerful position on the world, as commander in chief of the largest army in the world, and the largest economy in the world, among other responsibilities, mostly based on a media constructed environment.

Over these last 30 years we have witnessed some very powerful presence of the constructed information reality, which has generated devastating wars, based on fabricated stories which were not based on any physical evidence. Nevertheless, these information constructed environments, or virtual realities, justified and self-reinforced by the echo chambers of one media form to another, newspaper citing television, citing radio, citing website, as a proof of a logical reality, had very violent impact on the physical constructed environment. About half a million dead, a million injured, and close to 4 millions refugees only in Iraq, with similar numbers piling up in Syria and Yemen.

So how do we address this complexity of the Information manufactured environment in architecture?

We embrace it. Some of the largest budgets for new buildings are not to build new hospital or environmental friendly water purification plants, but to build fantastic backdrop to televised events, such as the Olympic games or the World Cup. Why would the capital of the most populous country in the world fight to get the 2008 Olympics, well just to be in the news, to exist in the digital world for just one month, not knowing what to do with the colossal – and beautiful - construction once the event is over.

Or we embrace the digitally animated large signage enhancing building "images" such as exemplified by Times Square in New York, where gigantic commercials invade the public space without much question about who own or control this urban public space.

In fact some entire cities urbanism have embraced the simple consumption of space as an image. Admittedly based in an arid climate – with no agriculture and very little oil – Dubai has reinvented itself as a dreamscape. As a place where people can invest their abstract capital into an image, a manufactured lifestyle.

Every construction has a name, a story, a marketing manager, an assigned lifestyle, a "virtuality". And this virtuality in everyway codifies and generates its physicality. The Palm Jumeirah for instance. A well marketed simple name, an image, flattened as a 2D plan, existing clearly in the potential investors head. All of the houses were presold in 48 hours, before the land was even "constructed". In everyway, the virtual, or image driven and constructed environment of marketing, propaganda and visualization managed to raise enough funds to allow the physical world to be enacted. The Palm Jumeirah is slightly larger than the City of San Francisco, emerging from the Persian Gulf and constructed in less than 5 years. The mental image as the generator of a physical materialization.

The question might be, what does it means to Live in an image?

I have spent time with my university student analysing cities like Dubai and neighbourhood like Times Squares, not cynically, but as actual example of our complex overlap of the information world and the physical world. We have to recognize today that what we call "reality' is a multi layered environment encompassing the virtual, the visual and the Physical realms.

ARX Kobe, ArX Osaka, ArX Portugal and ArX new York have been aware of this and has tried to address these issues over the last 30 years, each in their own interpretation. But ARX is not the only movement celebrating its 30 year anniversary. The summer 1988 was also the opening of the deconstructivist show at the Museum of Modern Art in New

York, curated by Mark Wigley and Phillip Jonhson. Based on the philosophical writing of Jacques Derrida, embracing the notion of complexity and the multiplicity of point of views, mostly due to the presence of multiple layers of information, Eisenman, Rem Koolhaas, Bernard Tschumi, Frank Gehry, Daniel Liebesking, Zaha Hadid and Coop Himelblau were well placed to address this notion of "disjunction". Surprisingly, their initial awareness of the multi layered environment got absorbed by the economic forces of the developers and the notion of the Media was not used as a condition of multiple logics but as a simplification tool for capitalist profit. From critical thinkers, questioning the social and philosophical role of the profession, they became transformed as Star-architects, bringing back the simplicity of the absolute Authorship and the name recognition as a saleable product. Therefore, they mostly became image providers for enhancing developer profit margins.

Another avenue in regard to the influence of new technologies onto the constitution of our architecture and urban environment can be found in the writing of William Mitchell. Seven years after the foundation of ARX, William Mitchell publishes the City Of Bits, Space, Place and the InfoBahn. His writing is interesting as he argues that new technology will make the physical city entirely obsolete. Digital Networks will allow us to be connected and have access to "everything, everywhere all the time". The theory sounds good, but the fact on the ground are quite the opposite. Never has humanity lived so densely in urban centres. Currently, over half of the world population is living in cities, an unprecedented condition in the history of human civilization. But why are we paying so much rent to live in the centre of Tokyo, Shanghai or New York? Why, if we can have access to "everything, everywhere all the time"?

Maybe it is because we do have unlimited access to information, because we are inundated with data and news, fake news and other layers of the information environment. We need a place to contextualize data, to understand and "experience" information. As we know, Information without context is meaningless.

What do we need a Physical City for in the XXI Century? Well it seems we need the Physical City as an interface to contextualize data. To make sense of information, the experience space and communication in an immediate condition. The Physical city has become the place to experience physically information. Here is a picture of the Champs Elysees in Paris, during the 1998 World Cup, where the citizen went to the street to celebrate and to try to understand what the information they had seen on their TV meant.

If this contextualization of information is the new role of the city, the education and experience of space, is used by all citizen. Nevertheless, it is the education sector that is the most interested by this condition, and we see the higher education institution investing in the physical cities. In New York, the very expansive centre of Manhattan has seen the rapid extension of the urban campus with Columbia University, or NYU, blurring the boundaries between the campus and the city.

In the digital age, I have come to the conclusion that the main function of the physical city is the Knowledge City, offering an interface between the abstract information and the physical environment.

If the City is a Physical interactive construct for the collective to "experience" information, how do we establish a similar function at an architectural scale?

Can Architecture be the Interface between the Mediated and the Personal Experience?

It gives an extremely important function to contemporary architecture, which happen to be critically located at the intersection of the information world and the physical world. Can we produce an architecture that reside somewhere between information space and physical space? That educate and protect us from the product of Human thinking? Architecture as an Education of our senses, as an Interface between the Mind and the Body?

I will briefly show three projects which attempts to address these issues at different scales: The Object scale, the spatial scale and the Building tower scale.

The first project, the Axonometric Chair, is questioning the notion of the Materialization of Representation, as a reversal process. Rather than drawing a physical object, I am building a representation of an object, extracting in three dimension the representation in 2D of a visual 3D construct. It is intentionally a very simple chair, which nevertheless question our convention of reading and the accepted cultural codes of representation.

I tried to send this chair to the Patent office in Bern, Switzerland to protect my design, but they returned my application asking why I was paying only for one chair and submitting three designs. I argued through a second letter

that it was three pictures of the same chair, which was the specificity of the design. Nevertheless, they returned the application arguing the images were not coherent. In other words, following the multiple logic of representation and of anthropomorphic physicality the images were too complex for its understanding.

The second project is a Showroom, located in the middle of Manhattan, in the Fashion District on 37 Street and 7 Avenue. New York is well known for its efficient grid. A symbol of efficient organization. The Orthogonal grid, not only in plan but in x,y,z, is the representation of the commodification of space as an orthogonal subdivision of capital. Therefore the logic of gravity and capital regulate all the space and is so easy to understand it almost offer no resistance. We understand space as we have been educated to experience orthogonal space. We can assume the physical distance of a room by projecting and interpreting our visual perception in an orthogonal room.

The project wanted to destabilize the perception, forcing the more personal education of the senses, forcing the experience of space. By creating the main wall as a folded surface, not only at an angle in plan but also in the vertical axis. The visual clues are suddenly much more complex and the imposition of a completely white finish, to the floor, the wall, the ceiling and the furniture, force an exploration of the space with the entire body.

Quite a number of visitors would actually use the tactile quality of touching the wall with their hand, while walking along the wall, negotiation and recording space as an experience between theirs mental, visual and physical understanding of the space.

The last project is for a large tower in Abu Dhabi, on a new island, recently developed. I had designed a few project for Dubai and Abu Dhabi, looking at the tower as an image production and the possible resistance of such consumption of the image. The relation between the surface and the volume, where the image-surface becomes the main condition of the vertical tower, exploring the notion of the hyper-surface, folding, etc. A few project attempted to question the idea of the surface, through compression or expansion.

The physical site on Reem Island was on a corner, between a boulevard and an open park. The volume had to be massed on the corner and the volumes ended up as a six sided diamond shape. The interesting part was that we always want to read a tower as an extruded rectangle.

The real desire of this project was again the resistance to the consumption of the simplified image. I wanted to question the hierarchy between the visual space and the physical space, or between verticality and an angled self-referential positioning. In other words, by questioning the hierarchy of visual space and physical space, I was attempting to question the ultimate parameter of the physical environment: gravity. Five similar volumes are repeated, each with a 5 degree rotation, where the top volume reside at 95 degree with the ground. But you would not know as you are looking at the sky.

30 years ago ARX was founded on the understanding that we could communicate across the newly connected globe. That we could test the relations between Information space and

Physical space, between mediated information and immediate experience.

Today I would say we have an Ethical duty as architects and urbanist to explore these relations between Information Space and Physical Space, more urgently than ever. Our profession is strategically located as an intersection between the Information Environment and the Physical Environment.

Trajectory of 30 years

TAKASHI YAMAGUCHI

JULY 1, 2018

This event is held to mark the 30th anniversary of ARX. The origin of the ARX formation can be said to signify a futuristic shift from human to non-human factors (say, computer program). It is similar to what Peter Eisenman had proposed about erasing the subjectivity in building creation.

The computer scientist and futurist Ray Kurzweil had predicted year 2045 as a critical point based on the the speed of technological evolution. Death and aging can be overcome by fusing three technologies of GNR (G = Genetics, N = Nanotechnology, R = Robotics Engineering), the fusion of humans and machines. In addition, he had predicted that the entire universe would show existence of intelligence.

In this event, we will hold exhibitions and symposiums on the theme of criticism for future technology, following this singularity hypothesis. What will new technology bring to us? I would like to investigate the problems relating to the evolution of technology.

In other words, in this age of convergence towards a singularity, how should we confront the emerging new technologies? I would like to discuss this problem by revisiting the thinkings of Peter Eisenman and ARX.

While exhibitions and discussions are being held at Osaka CASO and Yurakucho, the first session of such discussion had been held at the University of Tokyo. To begin, I would like to start from a specific problem rather than a generalization. First of all, I would like to talk specifically about the idea of architecture I have considered, comparing with those of Eisenman.

There is major difference in the ways Western European and Japanese worlds perceive and interpret realities. The Western European world would first believe in things that are truly existing, that are tangible and visible. In other words, they would first believe in their experience through perception. Then the subject would be interpreted by consciousness. In shifting between experience and conscious interpretation, the Western understanding of the world, as well as technological progression can move forward.

During the process, understandings and happenings in the past would always be scrutinized under critical reviews.

We Japanese do not have such a frame in capturing the world. Being a Japanese who had not equipped with such Western consciousness, I would like to show you the process of how I had evolved after being in contact with Eisenman's thinking. My architecture had departed from Eisenman.

Here I would like to show you a project of Eisenman. It is the Aronoff Center for Design and Art at University of Cincinnati. The project is like a series of rectangular parallelepiped frames leaving their traces. The project had begun in 1986 and was completed in 1996.

Diagrams like animations show that architecture changes over time. Attempts have been made to abstract the context of the site and into the interiority of the architecture. Here, the concept of Plato's chora, redefined by Eisenman, is continuously introduced between the undulation of the site and the existing building and the inserted building. As a result, the volume continuously responds to the surrounding environment and expresses a vibration expression.

Like an animation show, the progression of the frames give a sense of the passage of time to the architecture. It is an attempt to abstract the context of the site, internalizing the site's externality into the building. Eisenman had not first fixed imaget about what the building should basically be, and then tried to internalize the site's condition. This trajectory of thought got frozen to become the final form of architecture.

The concept of chora redefined by Eisenman is continuously introduced between the site and the existing building and the inserted building. As a result, the volume continuously responds to the surrounding environment, and the volume vibrates in time.

Such system of frames being projected consecutively onto the ground plane, had become a hint for us in the Berlin competition proposal submitted by ARX.

In our competition proposal, we had abstracted and altered the exteriority of place and time. like Eisenman, we had not first considered what the buildings should become. The architecture had emerged and materialised as a trajectory of the abstract time and history.

In other words, we sought to imprint new buildings by superposing the traces of the arcs and the grids and curves that settled in the history, exposing the traces. But there was something more important than that. That's because there was a plan to make the subject disappear when doing the project.

We have introduced time liquidity into the project. Introducing such time liquidity makes the past and the present juxtaposed in parallel. In order to eliminate the originality, including the subjectivity, everything will be made equivalent. Here, the superiority of the subject as an author is lost.

At that time, Eisenman had the thoughts of avant-garde architecture, on weakening the subjectivity in the creation of architecture.

The experience that I had at Tadao Ando's office was especially relevant.

I had doubts on the approach of the highly subjective architecture of Tadao Ando.

I suggested exploring the problem.

ARX had existed to address such issue. For us we had recognized the same issue.

Deconstruction, which is the theme of ARX, was to address such issue by blurring the subject as author. In which we had operated differently from Eisenman. Eisenman had operated blurring by just himself, a single architect. Through superposing his subjectivity from the past, in the present, and from the future; a singular subjectivity had to surpass itself in time in the creation of architecture. ("superpose" is coined by Eisenman)

Unlike Eisenman, we decided to blur the place, involving several entities in our design process. We had put our focus on the place rather than time. As a result, singular subjectivity had been abandoned. Several subjects were being shuffled, and any singular subjectivity had been dismantled. We had superposition of different subjects ("superposition" is coined by Eisenman). In addition, multiple entities in different places had been in continuous contact by telecommunications. And in a way Eisenman's concept had been employed —that is, retaining in the history of time lapse, even the same subject would be regarded as having different existences between past and present. Across space and time, multiple subjects would be made equivalent, blurred and superimposed. At that time, the Internet was just about to emerge. We had strong feeling about the meaning of the emergence of such telecommunication technologies. We had used the advanced technology critically, and the Berlin competition was completed in the process. It was 1992.

I had learned a lot through participating in this competition. And I got to know the limit of the operation –mainly, the unique fluidity of an idea got fixed and frozen into an object at the time when architecture was produced. I became very frustrated.

In our competition entry, we had succeeded to blur in the process, and yet the problem about finally getting an idea frozen into an object could not be surpassed. We had succeeded in trying new attempts in the process, and had wished for a brilliant result, and yet we had failed at the landing. Though we had got the prize, yet I was not completely satisfied at our own final proposal. After that, I was aware of and became critical at the basic problem of blurring, that is, on the shifting of the subjective position to blur.

And then, I had tried to introduce active record of temporality into the generation process, through dismantling the subject by blurring and by applying it on the program. It was 1997, and the result was published in SD magazine.

At that time, the emphasis of architecture in the United States was toward computing. But the concern was formal, using techniques like collage or overlay. The underlying principle was still traditional. Referencing to literary theory of architecture, I tried to decode architecture as text, focusing on overcoming the basic confrontation between the figure and the ground. The resulting shift was translated into the program during the generation process.

In 1997, I made an experiential project called cyberspace. The program was not generated by an overall masterplan directed from the top, but instead it was generated by adjacent relational logic, being determined mathematically. It was based on a dynamic computer program, rather than static collage and superimposition methods. As a result, critical dynamic program had been produced in contrast to traditional static and absolute architecture. The proposal was critical about the conventional design process focusing on proportional relationship between the part and the whole. The new result by introducing dynamic time element into architecture was that space was no longer a fixated entity, but a moving one.

And yet, the dilemma was that it took time to reach the final state of equilibrium, and what I had achieved was a possible transformation in architecture with the delay of time. I was not satisfied about the result, that the final form was still just an indicator of a wish to make something movable. That, I would like to re-visit the issue of this project in future.

By doing this project I came to aware of the new problems presented by the part-to-whole relationship program. That is, the danger of eroding the whole. Changing parts will risk breaking the integrity of the form. Besides the formal problem, integrated functions would fail, and the whole architecture would become dysfunctional. On top of that, aesthetic meaning will also be changed, there will no longer be an integrated aesthetic. Beauty based on proportional relationship will needed to be abandoned. The introduction of a new temporal dimension would lead to the emergence of new aesthetics. Beauty no longer exists as an integrated object, but it exists in the program, in the mathematics of production.

Introducing time into the generation process is no longer a criticism of subject superiority. I have embarked on a key issue of architecture, the integrality of whole and parts.
In conventional architecture, the part and the whole are controlled and fixated by proportion and geometry. However, by letting in relational changes in the generative process, the part and the whole got to change with time. The integration is no longer static, but ever changing with time. The discovery had changed the concept about integration as a final whole.

In 1998, I got my first chance to realize the concept.
It was a glass temple. In a sense, it was an inheritance of Eisenman's volume concept. According to Eisenman, volume contains motivation. And I tried to diagram the energy and the potential, by turning the energy potentials into tangible form. Again, we are blurring the inside and the outside. The building was completely buried into the ground, with a glass roof on top. By doing so, it became hard to distinguish between the inside and outside. The sensation became doubtful and unfamiliar. The transparent interior became part of the exterior, and yet the exterior would also become part of the interior. The spatial relationship was calculated by Boolean algebra using dots that defined density, and by that volume and void were generated through the binary confrontational figure and ground.

The next project is a multiplication project on the train line between Kyoto (2004) and Shinagawa (2006). The outline of the form would be no longer constrained by the so-called context of railway, but would be planned to reproduce like in a biological metaphor. Buildings would be assigned along the existing railway acting as "street context".

The boundary between where the internal and the external of the building meet, would be as if being transformed biologically according to the economic principles of real estate. The form would exceed the context of the location, and would be generated according to economic activity in the neighborhood.

In this project, we planned to incorporate economic activities in the neighborhood by equivalent exchanges. Through this exchange in capitalist energy, volumes surrounding the site may be exchanged with volumes on the railway. Hence volumes on the railway may get developed vertically, and green space may form in the surrounding area. It was an idea to redevelop the city without destroying the current urban context. At the nodes of the network, development tended to grow vertically.

The next project is a factory office completed in 2009. Although the whole volume is covered with the same material, each element in the louver unit can change to a different direction, and hence the whole surface can change. Fibonacci sequence is being used in determining the directionality and hence the randomness. By that we avoided concentrating the reflection of light towards one direction in the neighborhood.

The next project is a tower type foresting the dessert and ocean, proposed in 2009. These towers play a role of preserving and restoring the environment. Here, the building is a robot, a product of technology. It tracks the sun and the floor can be inclined. We also proposed that the floor may be convolved and stored.

Next, I will show you a louver system consisting of a number of units covering the skin of the building. It was proposed in 2011. This louver system is to be built with a robot. We also introduced dynamic responses by sensors programmed to cope with the environmental contextual changes, including wind energy, sunshine, outlook etc.

The next is a tea house, designed in 2015. Combining homogenous square members in the form of an X, fixated by tension by passing a wire through the cross section. The angles and directions of each element were determined by programming, and being generated as a whole. As long as we have the same square members and program, this system can be built in any part of the world.

Finally, I present a project that motivates space by the immaterial light.
Light was my theme from the Glass Temple. This is based on the previous planning of shops in Boston and New York, and the project of the grid at Ashiya restaurant that had been built. The program is placed on a grid, arranged in a wave pattern.

In the restaurant of Ashiya completed in 2012, we introduced dynamic movements, using this lattice group as a robot. This time, we employed the immaterial light as a motif. Light is projected among the grid groups arranged in a wave pattern. In the elongated space, the immaterial light changes based on the signal from brain wave. Brain signals direct changes in the light.

This lighting project is a challenge to non-materiality and the theme is about how the human physique may get extended into external space. This project is currently under construction in a hotel in Kyoto, and will be completed in October. You can see there. At the exhibition at CASO, I also exhibit the program as a light installation. As change of LEDs and laser beams are expressed by reading of the brain waves of people listening to music. Please see how the light would change under such program.

Time can only be interposed in processes. I finally came to understand this from the Berlin competition. By understanding that limit, I thought about the development of mobile architecture and robots. In the laboratory at the university, we have studied about how the human body may extend into and interact with space. How will the spatial potential be changed by the electroencephalogram data feedback? I would like to make it into architecture.

Let me summarize my summary.
First, let's talk about architecture in relation to technology Especially about subject and object.

Today's technology grasps the world only through human

rational reason and controls human being under that reason. The idea is to inherit the Western view of the world, which sees the world as the work of God, dominated by Logos. It also means inheriting the traditional metaphysics based on the Western belief that the existence of the world matches the present.

Architecture that value subject status and do not acknowledge its limitations tends to have technology dominating the object. As a result, there was a possibility that the existence that surpassed human beings would undermine human existence. That is, it suppresses humans. Technology is a double-edged blade. We are at a time when we need to consider these problems between subject and object. Without such a debate, blinding technology and disregarding the subject would lead to a crisis.

Program is a device that integrates all kinds of information for production. Conversely, diagram is a device that recognizes the world. Moreover, it will have the power to interpret and transform the world. Does the problem of diagram exist? For example, diagram cutting and projecting a changing world's section on a static screen. Is there any danger of sneaking in the creator's will behind impersonating the observer? But the converse is also true. It is also dangerous that diagram having the criticism of recognition of world is lost.

An algorithm is a mediator between human thinking and the computing power of computers. There are two aspects to the algorithm acting as such an interpreter. In one aspect, it is a mean for humans to tell a computer how to solve a problem. And on the other side, human thoughts could be transformed into algorithms.

There are dangers in exchange for convenience.

Program fundamentalists have begun to work with parametric devices that can be operated by anyone. The consciousness that persisted in the presence of the intelligent subject is being driven away. Program fundamentalists denied such subjects, transformed them into open subjects, and began treating them as something that could be touched by anyone. As a result, the possibility of subjectivity dwarfing and deterioration has been opened.

The existence of the subjectivity as an observer is important. Program fundamentalists tend to try to dominate objects all by programs. they want to eliminate all subjects.

However, the existence of a subject who is an observer and has a check function must be guaranteed.

Next, I would like to talk about physical problems, that is, physical expansion.

In architecture, universal geometric models always lead to a Vitruvian view of the world that has been tied to physical problems. Vitruvius argued that architecture should be a human body, symmetric, hierarchical, and of appropriate proportions. For this reason, he thought that the interiority of architecture had a clear boundary with the outside and was autonomous without being affected by exteriority.

In the near future, technology will accelerate further beyond the classic Vitruvian picture. That is, it is a body image that is continuously deformed. These body images have the intention to break away from universal geometric models.

In my laboratory, I am conducting research on the premise that the Vitruvian body is dismantled. With the development of technology for sensing information inside the body, such as brain waves and physical electrical signals, the possibility of the inside of the body continuing seamlessly to the outside is expanding.

The possibility of producing objects that contain parameters is opening up. By changing these parameters, objects with various variations are created. This ensures that the object maintains continuity and connectivity. This notion is consistent with Sanford Quinter's notion that the object is not fixed, but only one aspect of continuous liquidity, as well as Deleuze's origin, the concept of an object with time.
It would go back to Le Corbusier's vague definition of volume as not solid.

Deleuze's idea is interpreted as corresponding to the image of the world in which everything is fluidly continuous. In other words, it is the consciousness that various elements are not autonomous independently, but are connected equally and maintain their diversity and coexist in a continuous system.

But continuity may be an illusion. It is also very dangerous because it is simple.
In the place of "hierarchy eliminated and equivalently", there may be a danger of a rhetoric invading.

As a result of the continuity, each region's unique culture was destroyed. This combination of continuity and computer technology is already putting the world in crisis in the financial world. In the field of architecture, some people jumped into this consciousness. Thus, new aesthetics have emerged, but are creating confusion and contradiction.

With the emergence of quantum computers in the near future, the arrival of big data, advanced networking, and AI, An environment that exceeds singularity will come. In this future, further intervening agents will appear between subject and object. Such existence cannot be denied. Rather, it should be actively incorporated into the creative process. In the future, volumes will be subdivided into particles, quantumetric (intelligent particles agents) will appear. In the previous stage, segmentmetric (intelligent segments agents) will be performed . Such is performed by RoboTectonic. My lab's work has been in predicting these directions.

The necessity of changing over time should exist not only in the design process in the virtual space, but also in the real space. In that sense, I propose "flexible architecture in real space."

I think that invisible things such as energy density and potential are important, more so than forms. Based on such intangible conditions, I had proposed and built architecture.

Here it is my presentation about the relationship between technology and architecture in the near future, about the problems of the subject of production. I hope this presentation will further spark ideas and discussions in the future.

TYMDL | **Project / Event**

Parasite : Paresite - Exhibition Space -

言語化できない情報として、都市のポテンシャルを計測するプロジェクトである。ビッグデータは資本主義によって飼い慣らされた人々の欲望や総体的で均質的な情報であるが、そうしたものとは異なる次元の情報を獲得、解析し、建築空間へと再構築する試みである。

リアルな展示に重ね合わされた情報によって、リアルとヴァーチャルな世界を交流させる。

現在の VR や AR の方向を示す最初の提案であり、ミラーワールドやデジタルツインを形成する基本となるものであった。

IMAGE

EXHIBITION METHOD DIAGRAM

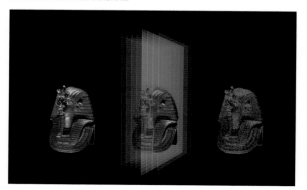

IMAGE

AERO-LOGICAL SKIN

このプロジェクトは、建築自らが外部環境の持つエネルギーを電気エネルギーへと変換し、スキン全体を通してニュートラルに供給できるシステムの提案であると同時に、従来のブラックボックス化された発電システムとパイプライン化された供給システムへの批判でもある。

アブダビに計画されたこのプロジェクトは、砂嵐に対応したエコロジカルなスキンである。砂嵐によってもたらされる風力によりユニット内のタービンが回され、ウィングを持ち上げることによって開口部が閉じ、外部からの砂の侵入を防ぐ。

CONFIGURATION DIAGRAM

Skin　　　▶　　　Double-skin　　　▶　　　Curve-skin　　　▶　　　Unitization

IMAGE

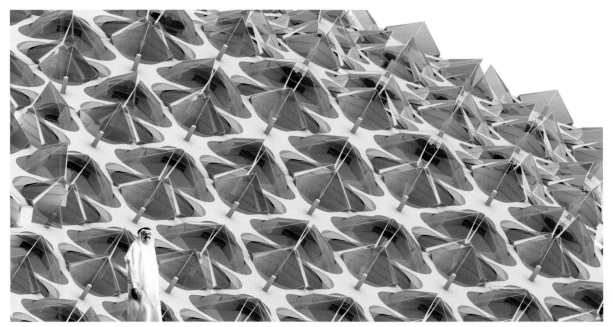

WIND SPEED DIAGRAM

+ : Passing speed

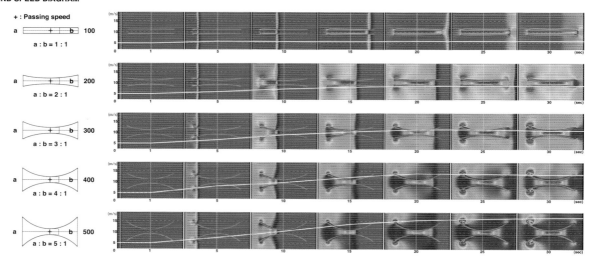

a : b = 1 : 1   100

a : b = 2 : 1   200

a : b = 3 : 1   300

a : b = 4 : 1   400

a : b = 5 : 1   500

IMAGE

MODEL

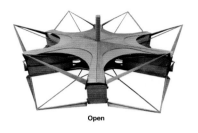

Open

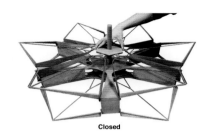

Closed

SAND REMOVAL SYSTEM

AIR-FLOW DIAGRAM

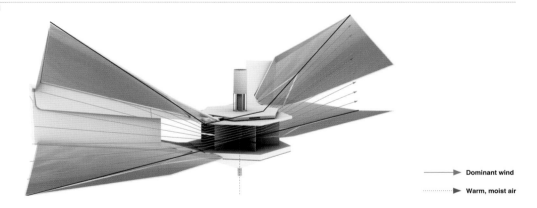

→ Dominant wind

┄┄► Warm, moist air

UP-DOWN SYSTEM

Self-Conversion Buildings

情報化社会となり様々なデジタルツールが普及する現代では、情報ネットワーク内でのコミュニケーションが増えており、ネットワーク内の個人間の関係性は常に変化していて流動的である。この流動的なネットワーク（ヴァーチャル）の中に、物理的な建築空間（フィジカル）をどのように構築していくかがこのプロジェクトの目的である。

回転運動を行い、部分から全体へと接続関係を変え、動線・視線・対話といったフィジカルな関係性を解体し、まるでシナプスのように生物的で流動的なネットワークを常に構築する新たな建築の可能性の提案である。

COMMUNICATION DIAGRAM

SPACE DEPENDENCE DIAGRAM

Fix

Flexible

- Network line
- Physical network line
- Dependence
- Parsonal space
- Communication line (Gaza , Circulation)
- Base line

UNIT IMAGE

EYE LEVEL DIAGRAM

FL+5570mm
FL+4455mm
FL+3340mm
FL+2230mm
FL+1115mm

IMAGE

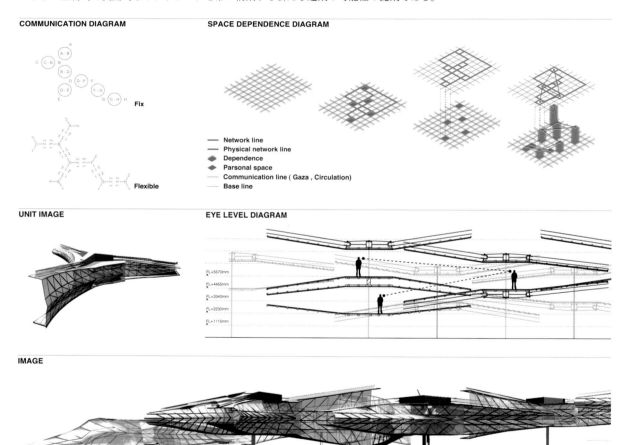

IMAGE

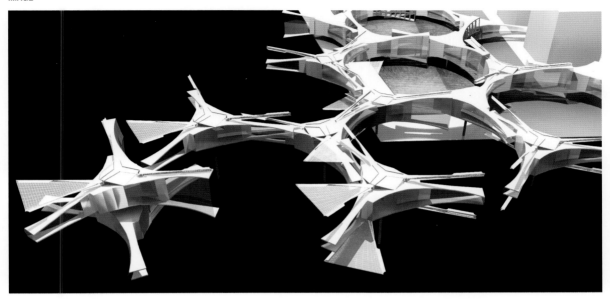

CIRCULATION PATTERN

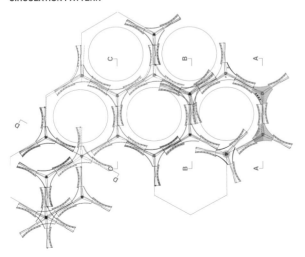

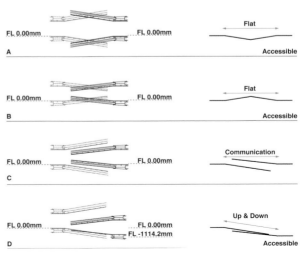

FL 0.00mm   FL 0.00mm   Flat

A   Accessible

FL 0.00mm   FL 0.00mm   Flat

B   Accessible

FL 0.00mm   FL 0.00mm   Communication

C

FL 0.00mm   FL 0.00mm   Up & Down
      FL -1114.2mm

D   Accessible

309

Scaling City

情報化社会への変容やモビリティの高速化によって、人の動きはより流動的で複雑化しており、現在の固定化された都市システムでは対応が賄えていないのが現状である。

このプロジェクトは、散逸されたノードとノード間のユニット化された交通機能で構成されている。より流動的で複雑化した人の動きに対応し、人が移動することによって形成される新たな都市空間の提案である。

このノードと交通機能との関係は、長く存在し続ける部分（フレーム）と取り換え可能な部分（ユニット）というメタボリズムの都市のフレームとユニットの関係性を批判し、都市の運動としてメタボリズムを再評価する。

MODEL CITY DIAGRAM

ATTACHMENT SYSTEM

UNIT SYSTEM

MOVEMENT DIAGRAM

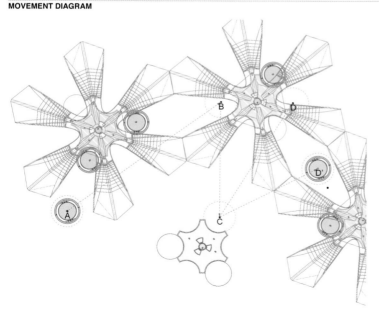

IMAGE

CIRCULATION

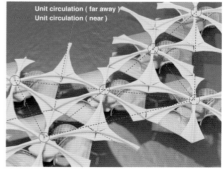

Unit circulation (far away)
Unit circulation (near)

IMAGE

MODEL

Unit

Structure

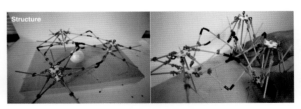

SECTION

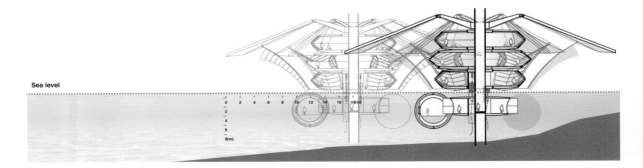

Sea level

0 2 4 6 8 10 12 14 16 18(m)

0
2
4
6
8(m)

Architecture of Automatic Fluctuate

生物は様々な環境や関係性の中で生存し、その環境の変化と共に進化を繰り返している。しかし建築は固定的なものとして存在し、常に変化する外部環境や多様化が進む内部機能に対して、変化せずに建築家が定めたデザインに従い続けている。生物の構造メカニズムを研究し建築に応用することで、自律的に変形する新たな建築の可能性を模索する。

このプロジェクトは、梯子状の神経系を持ち、各セグメントに感覚器官・神経系を備えた生物の構造メカニズムを建築に応用することで全体を知性のある集合体とし、内外の環境の要因によって形態が変化する新たな建築を提案する。

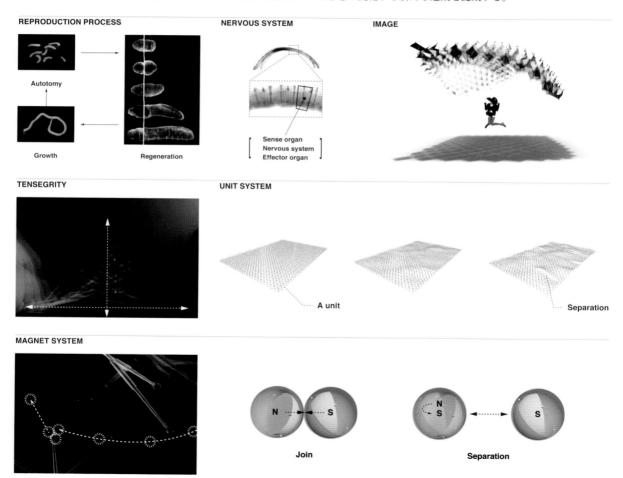

REPRODUCTION PROCESS

Autotomy

Growth

Regeneration

NERVOUS SYSTEM

Sense organ
Nervous system
Effector organ

IMAGE

TENSEGRITY

UNIT SYSTEM

A unit

Separation

MAGNET SYSTEM

N → ← S
Join

N S ← → S
Separation

Biological Reserch Project

これらのプロジェクトは、生物の構造メカニズムの研究から新たな構造・構法的な可能性を模索した上で、シミュレーションすることによって、新たな建築の形態やシステムを提案する。

SIMULATION

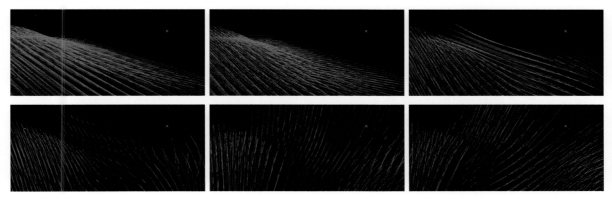

MODEL

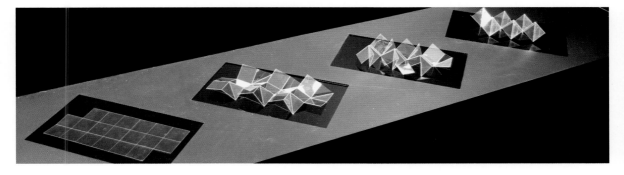

SIMULATION

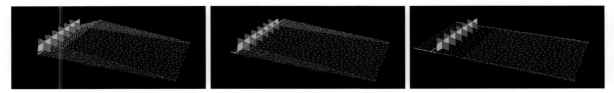

NEURO-POSITECH

様々な外部環境からの刺激は人間の脳内で処理され、電気信号に変換されることが知られており、コンピューター技術の発達によって、その電気信号を脳波（数値）として測定・取り出すことが可能となった。

フィールドワークを行い、様々な環境下においての脳波を測定した。

このプロジェクトは、脳波の数値を用いて空間が変化する新たな建築の提案である。空間が建築家に依存せず、人間の受ける外部環境の刺激に呼応し、形体が変化する。

DEFORMATION SIMULATION

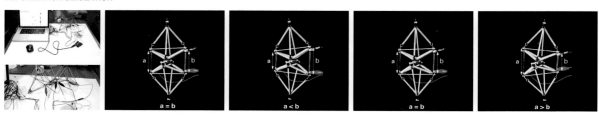

GRAPH

AFFECT SPACE FORM DIAGRAM

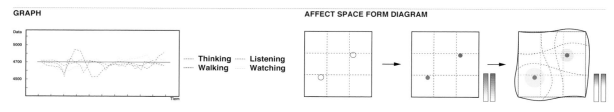

FORM VARIATION

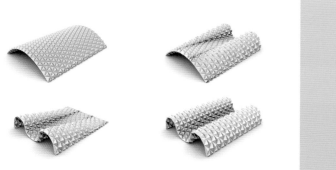

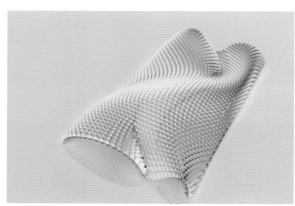

MODEL

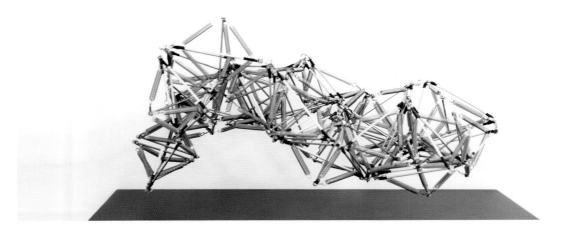

IMAGE

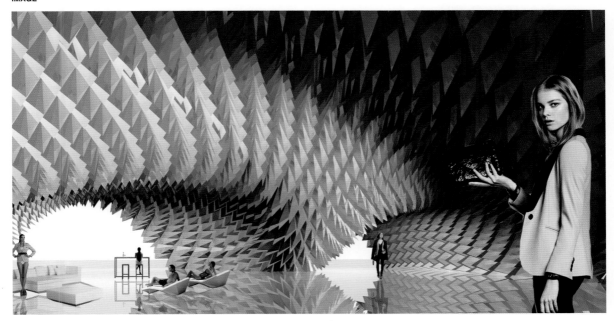

Brain waves Reserch Project

これらのプロジェクトは、フィールドワークで得た様々な環境下における脳波の値を測定し、プログラミングソフトを用いたビジュアライゼーションを行うことで、新たな建築空間を探求する試みである。

FIELDWORK

REPRESENTATION

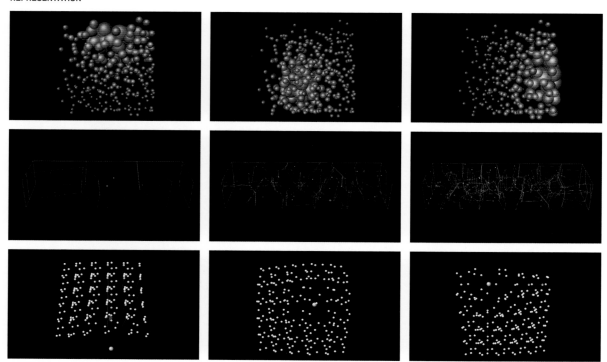

FIELDWORK

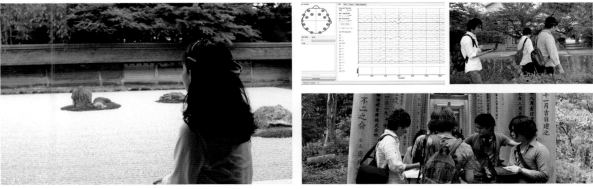

REPRESENTATION

Brain Waves Surface

従来の建築は、機能や行為によって壁や床等のサーフェイスで遮断されており、サーフェイスを介しての他者とのコミュニケーションは断絶されている。

このプロジェクトは、サーフェイスを分割（ユニット化）し、繊維状（ライン）に細分化することで、透過性与えて他者の存在を知覚させる。そして脳波の測定値がユニットの回転角度を変化させ、様々な開口部を生み出すことで、新たなコミュニケーションを構築する建築の提案である。

OPENING DISTANCE

   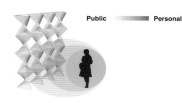

Public ▬▬▬ Personal

ROTATING SYSTEM

a1 wave

Wave	Angle
B wave	0°-120°
a3	120°-240°
mida	240°-360°
a1	360°
0 wave	360°

IMAGE

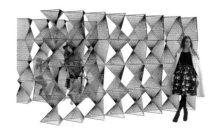

IMAGE

Green Cell - Parametric moving louver -

このプロジェクトは、「Green Cell」のサーフェイスをロボットユニットによって再構築することを目的としている。

サーファイスを構成するロボットは、モーターが内蔵されたロッドAとモーターのないロッドBがあり、モーターの働きが連動することによって、密度を変化させることが可能となる。

日光や風、風景への視線方向など様々な環境因子がパラメーターとして働き、ロッドの粗密によってそれらの環境因子を制御する試みである。

ROD SYSTEM

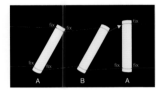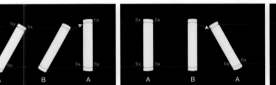

SIMULATION

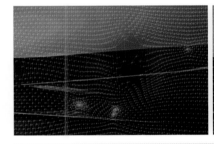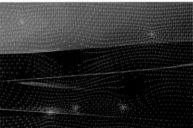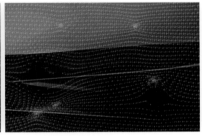

IMAGE

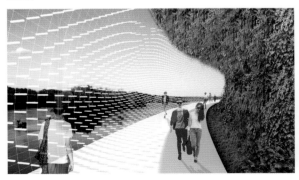

Ground Surface

このプロジェクトは、場所性としての環境と人との関係性を可視化し、互いの相互作用よって変化するグラウンドの提案である。ユニットは上面が硬質なサーフェイスと下面がグリーンのサーフェイスの2層で構成されており、人の通行量が多い箇所では硬質なサーフェイスが出現し、人の通行量が少ない箇所ではグリーンのサーフェイスが出現する。グリーンのサーフェイスはその植生によって場所性が可視化され、太陽光を効率的に吸収するために隆起し、人の通行量によって様々な地形へと変化する。

UNIT SYSTEM

GROUND PATTERN

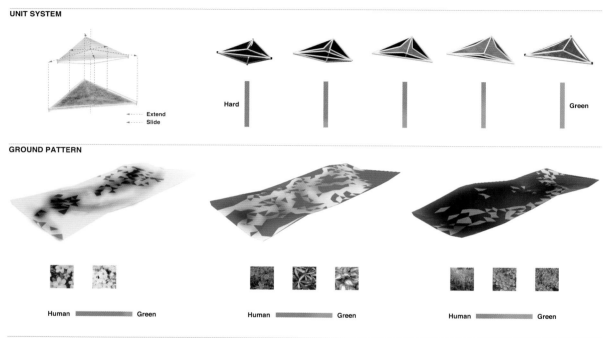

SURFACE SYSTEM

Reversible Architecture

このプロジェクトは、表裏が反転することが可能な機能を持つユニットの提案である。

触手のようなアームを回転させることで凹凸のある球体から凹凸のない球体へと形態を変化させるユニットは、変形の動きの中で異物を格納することができる。

このシステムは、スケールを変更することで、海面に漂う異物や体内に侵入した異物の回収など応用が可能である。

REVERSIBLE SYSTEM   **SHAPE DIAGRAM**

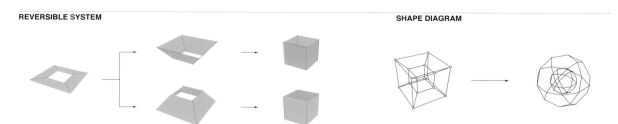

IMAGE

IMAGE   **DEFORMATION DIAGRAM**

   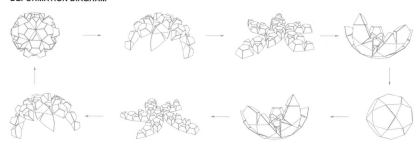

P-Robotic Architecture

このプロジェクトは、完全自律制御の分子型ロボット建築の提案である。

環境の持つエネルギーをデータ化することで、コンピューターで環境に基づく形態をシミュレーションし、移動距離を座標情報で分子型ロボットに送信することで分子型ロボットを制御する。

分子型ロボットは、2個が対になり、分子型ロボット内の1軸の回転運動だけで平面移動や立体移動が可能である。

TWO-DIMENSIONAL MOVEMENT

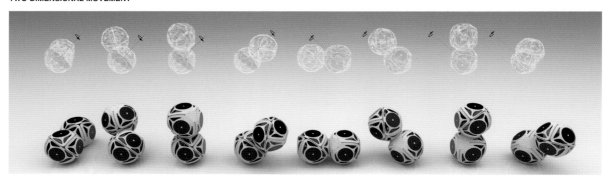

THREE-DIMENSIONAL MOVEMENT

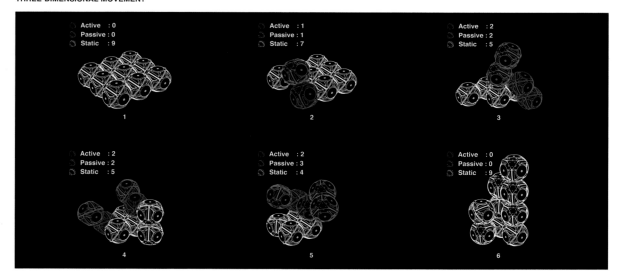

CINSTRUCTION SIMULATION

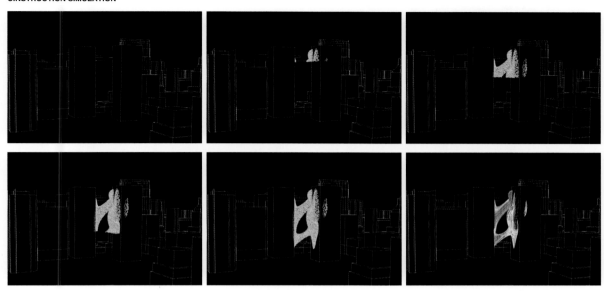

SOLAR POWER SYSTEM

UNIT DETAIL

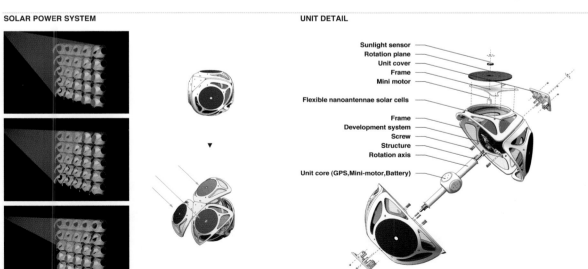

Sunlight sensor
Rotation plane
Unit cover
Frame
Mini motor

Flexible nanoantennae solar cells

Frame
Development system
Screw
Structure
Rotation axis

Unit core (GPS,Mini-motor,Battery)

Topological Folding House Project

住宅プロジェクトの構成を定義するため、プログラミングを用いてシミュレーションを行ったプロジェクトである。
住宅は一枚のプレートが折りたたまれた構成となっており、プレートは季節による太陽高度と開口部の形状との関係性の様々な
シミュレーションを経て決定されている。

DIAGRAM

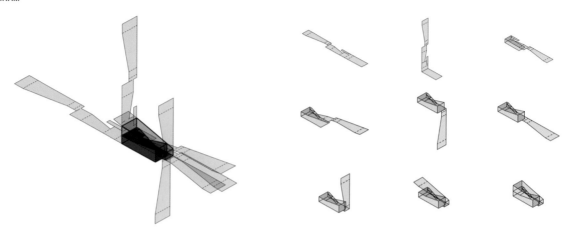

SIMULATION

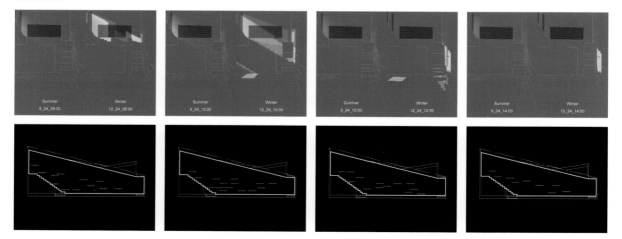

Parametric Tea House Project

仮設の茶室プロジェクトである。

世界のどこでも手に入る素材、専門的な技術が不要な工法、明解なシステムで構築されており、最小のエレメント数で成立するようプログラムされている。個々の角材の傾きと接地面に投影される軌跡上の位置は、正方形の畳の中心を基点に計算されている。

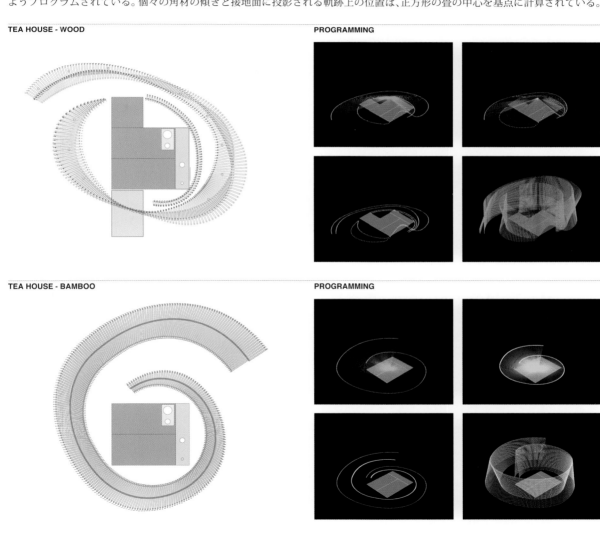

TEA HOUSE - WOOD

PROGRAMMING

TEA HOUSE - BAMBOO

PROGRAMMING

Living Architecture System

このプロジェクトは、従来のグリッドシステムに対する批判であり、新たなスペースとヴォイドの関係を構築する。
ベースとなる水平のプレートが水平・垂直方向に稼働することによって、様々な空間を構築することが可能である。プレート同士は連結と独立が可能であり、床面積を自由に操作することができる。さらには、プレート自体が垂直動線の役割を担っており、自由にレベルを操作することができる。

TWO-DIMENSIONAL MOVEMENT

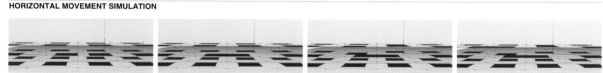

Base   Move   Pattern A   Pattern B

HORIZONTAL MOVEMENT SIMULATION

VERTICAL MOVEMENT PATTERN

MOVEMENT SYSTEM SIMULATION

MOVEMENT PATTERN

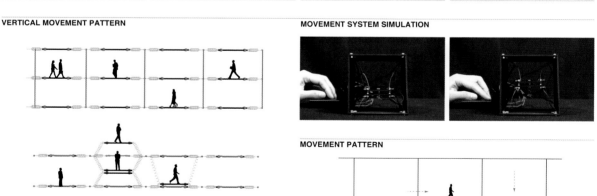

Space Configuration System

空間を隔てる面要素を線要素へと細分化し、それぞれを自律するアーム型のユニットロボットで構成することで、人の行動にインタラクティブに反応するアクティブな空間を構築するプロジェクトである。

人の動線に合わせて配置される従来の間仕切りシステムとは異なり、人の動線や誘導、指標のための変化も可能になり、コミュニケーションにも似た、人と建築とのインタラクティブな関係性の提案である。

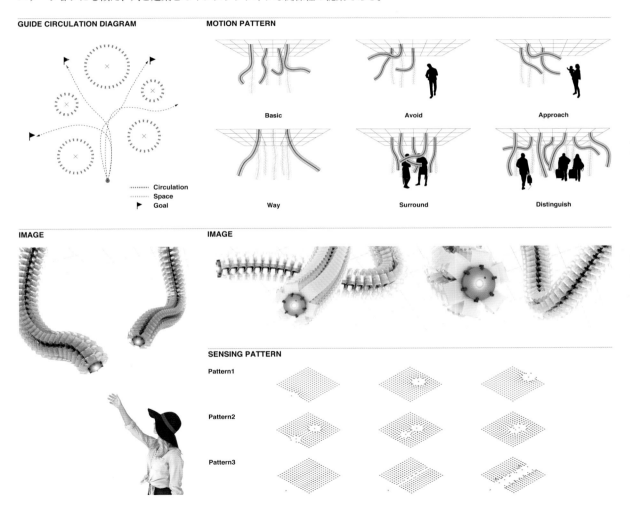

GUIDE CIRCULATION DIAGRAM

.... Circulation
.... Space
▶ Goal

MOTION PATTERN

Basic Avoid Approach

Way Surround Distinguish

IMAGE

IMAGE

SENSING PATTERN

Pattern1

Pattern2

Pattern3

Wearable Architecture

このプロジェクトは、ゴットフリード・ゼンパーの被膜の考えを現代のテクノロジーによって、人間の肌を覆うウェアラブルなものへと発展させ、身体内で処理されるデータに基づく形体を生成することで、より人間の身体情報に基づく新たな身体・建築空間の可能性の提案である。

感覚器官は人間の脳のセンサーとして働き、刻々と変化する周囲の情報をデータとして脳へと伝達している。脳内で処理されたデータは命令として筋肉へと伝達され、動きとして反応する。

生物構造を応用した被膜は小型３Ｄプリンターユニットによって構成されており、身体情報に基づく様々な空間を出力することが可能である。

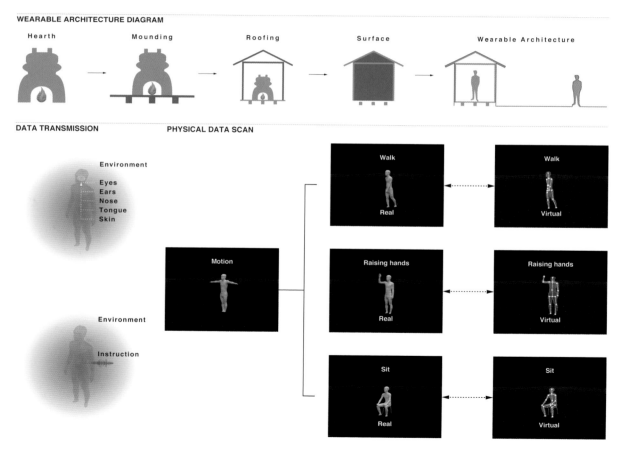

WEARABLE ARCHITECTURE DIAGRAM

Hearth → Mounding → Roofing → Surface → Wearable Architecture

DATA TRANSMISSION

PHYSICAL DATA SCAN

Environment
Eyes
Ears
Nose
Tongue
Skin

Environment

Instruction

Motion

Walk — Real / Walk — Virtual

Raising hands — Real / Raising hands — Virtual

Sit — Real / Sit — Virtual

IMAGE

MODEL

MODELING SIMULATION

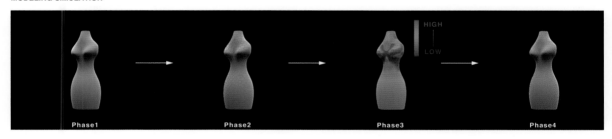

UNIT IMAGE

DETAIL

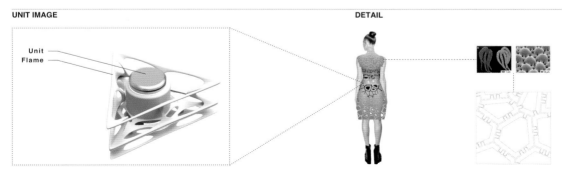

IMAGE

CONTROL PATTERN SIMULATION

Programming Louver Project

プログラミングによってパラメトリックな動きを持つルーバーを生成するプロジェクトであり、モダニズム空間を超えるための試みでもある。

ここでは、chora(コーラ)の考え方が二重化されている。身体の変化(脳波の変調)を元にコンピューター上でプログラムされた幾つかの波形が trace される。そして、長い直方体形状の矩形空間に imprint する。ヴァーチャル空間での trace がリアルな空間へと転写され、壁と天井へと格子波形として imprint されている。

Koshimo +

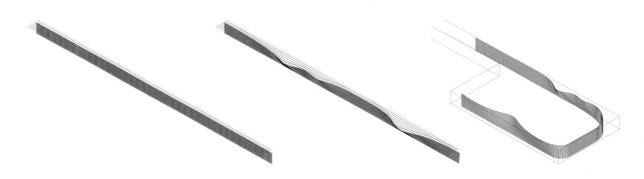

MOGANA

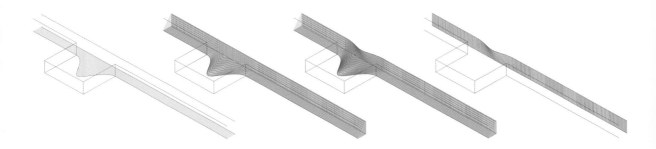

Programming Light Project

このプロジェクトは、リアルとヴァーチャル、trace と imprint、これらが交互に反転していく空間を構築することを目的としている。

ここで計画されている照明は、リアルな格子波形の天井形状を trace した上で脳波の測定値を用いることで、ヴァーチャル上で光の動きがプログラムされ、再度リアルな格子波形天井へと imprint される。

MOGANA

PROGRAMMING

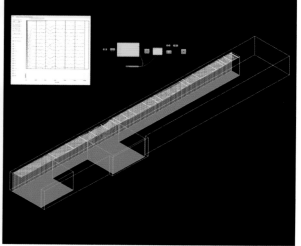

Immateriality Illumi-Brai-n-ation

建築と音楽との新しい関係を探る山口隆（建築家）と朝比奈隆子（音楽家）とのコラボレーションである。
Toward Singularity の展覧会において、人間の身体の内部性を外部性へと拡張することを表現したインスタレーションとして展示された。音楽を聴いた人間から発する感情の振幅を trace し、脳波パターンとして抽出し、サイバースペース上で幾つかのパターンへと変換する。そのパターンをリアルスペースへと imprint させ、光の動きとして空間内に充満させている。

IMAGE

PATTERN

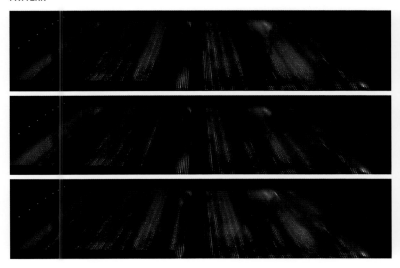

IMAGE

Medical Smart Emergent Project

このプロジェクトは、感染ウィルスを保有している人を個々に独立させて監視できるカプセル型の隔離システムの提案である。
さらに、医者や看護師への感染や２次・３次感染を未然に防ぐためのシステムの提案でもある。

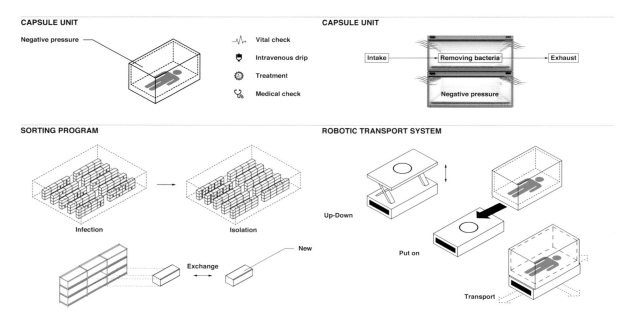

CAPSULE UNIT

Negative pressure

⎯⋀⋁⎯ Vital check

Intravenous drip

Treatment

Medical check

CAPSULE UNIT

Intake → Removing bacteria → Exhaust

Negative pressure

SORTING PROGRAM

Infection → Isolation

Exchange ↔ New

ROBOTIC TRANSPORT SYSTEM

Up-Down

Put on

Transport

IMAGE

IMAGE

FLOOR CONFIGULATION

EV

Expansion

Void

Capsule space

Treatment space

ISOLATION SYSTEM

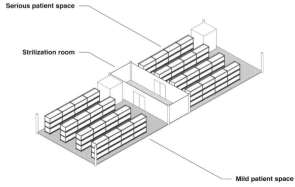

Serious patient space

Strilization room

Mild patient space

Technology × Future

DATE : 12, Mar. 16
LOCATION : Osaka Sangyo University,
Grand Front Osaka Knowledge Capital
SPEAKER : David Benjamin, Kunio Kudo,
Tadashi Shirasu, Takashi Yamaguchi

SEXY TECHNOLOGY

DATE : 11, Jul - 15, Jul. 16
OPENING : 10:00am (-18:00pm)
LOCATION : ASJ TOKYO CELL
SPEAKER : Hiroo Mori, Joji Kunihiro,
Takashi Yamaguchi

ROBOTIC ARCHITECTURE

DATE : 14, Feb - 17, Feb. 17
LOCATION : Grand Front Osaka ACTIVE Studio
SPEAKER : Giacomo Valentini, Takashi Sasaoka,
　　　　　　Hirofumi Tamai, Yoshihiko Sugimoto,
　　　　　　Tsukasa Takenaka, Takashi Yamaguchi

ART vs ARCHITECTURE

DATE : 12, Nov. 17
LOCATION : Grand Front Osaka Knowledge Capital
SPEAKER : Paul DeMarinis, Takashi Sasaoka,
Takashi Yamaguchi

Toward Singularity

DATE : 26, Jun - 8, Jul. 18 [Osaka]
24, Jun - 3, Jul. 18 [Tokyo]
LOCATION : SEASIDE STUDIO CASO[Osaka],
ASJ TOKYO CELL,
University of Tokyo [Tokyo]
SPEAKER : Kengo Kuma, Frederic Levrat,
Takashi Sasaoka, Nobuaki Ishimaru,
Takashi Yamaguchi

PARAMETRICISM

DATE : 16, Mar. 20
LOCATION : Main Hall, Osaka Central Public Hall
SPEAKER : Patrik Schumacher, Takashi Yamaguchi

東京オリンピック新国立競技場コンペで最初に選ばれたザハ・ハデッドの斬新な案は世界中に衝撃を与え称賛を得た。しかし、不幸にも白紙撤回になってしまった。

この問題で明かになった事は、ザハ案のような建築の多用性を認めない日本の産業構造であった。世界の流れは、多様性を認め、実現する方向にあるにもかかわらず、日本は効率性を求めるために多様性への対応を閉ざすのである。そのため、日本の技術は世界から遅れ始めており、危機的状況にあると思われる。

ザハの後継者であるパトリック・シューマッハは優れた理論家であり、文明の問題点に迫る。自動車メーカーのフォードが生み出した画一的大量生産の古い産業構造は、遅かれ早かれ、変化する多用性を帯びる未来の状況に対応できなくなる。新しい社会はパラメーターで対応可能な生産構造が基本になると言う彼の哲学を巡って議論したい。

TY&A+TYMDL | **Chronology**

ARX 設立

TY&A
TYDML

House I   House II   House III   House VI   **Wexner Center**

                                                                            Firehous La Villette

House X   **IBA Social Housing** Biocenter **Koizumi Sangyo**

                                                                            Guardiola House

EISENMAN ARCHITECTS   Cannaregio   Fin D'Ou T Hou S   Groningen Music-Video Pavilion

Publication_Gilles Deleuze
ニーチェと哲学

Publication_Jacques Derrida
幾何学の起源

Publication_Gilles Deleuze
カントの批判哲学

Publication_Peter Eisenman
THE FORMAL BASIS OF MODERN ARCHITECTURE

Publication_Jacques Derrida
エクリチュールと差異
声と現象
グラマトロジーについて

Publication_Gilles Deleuze
差異と反復
スピノザと表現の問題

Publication_Jacques Derrida
哲学の余白

Publication_Gilles Deleuze
アンチ・オイディプス

Publication_Gilles Deleuze
千のプラトー

Publication_Peter Eisenman
HOUSE X

Publication_Gilles Deleuze
フーコー
襞：ライプニッツとバロック

Exhibition
Deconstructive Architecture at MoMA

61 62 63 64 65 66 67 68 69 70 71 72 73 74 75 76 77 78 79 80 81 82 83 84 85 86 87 88 89 90

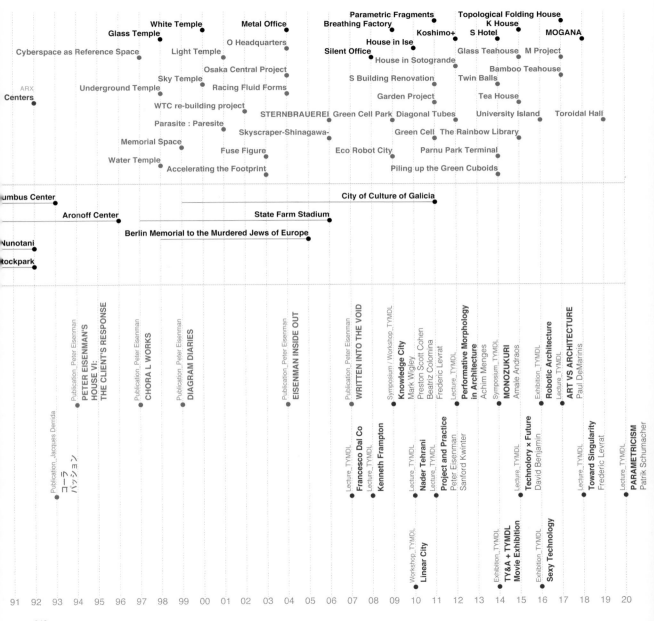

Cyberspace as Reference Space
Glass Temple
White Temple
Light Temple
Metal Office
O Headquarters
Breathing Factory
Parametric Fragments
Topological Folding House
K House
Koshimo+
S Hotel
MOGANA
House in Ise
Silent Office
Glass Teahouse
M Project
House in Sotogrande
Bamboo Teahouse
Osaka Central Project
Sky Temple
Underground Temple
Racing Fluid Forms
S Building Renovation
Twin Balls
ARX
Centers
WTC re-building project
Garden Project
Tea House
STERNBRAUEREI
Green Cell Park
Diagonal Tubes
University Island
Toroidal Hall
Parasite : Paresite
Skyscraper-Shinagawa-
Green Cell
The Rainbow Library
Memorial Space
Fuse Figure
Eco Robot City
Parnu Park Terminal
Water Temple
Accelerating the Footprint
Piling up the Green Cuboids

umbus Center
City of Culture of Galicia
Aronoff Center
State Farm Stadium
Berlin Memorial to the Murdered Jews of Europe
Nunotani
tockpark

Publication_Jacques Derrida
コーラ
パッション
Publication, Peter Eisenman
PETER EISENMAN'S
HOUSE VI:
THE CLIENT'S RESPONSE
Publication, Peter Eisenman
CHORA L WORKS
Publication, Peter Eisenman
DIAGRAM DIARIES
Publication, Peter Eisenman
EISENMAN INSIDE OUT
Publication, Peter Eisenman
WRITTEN INTO THE VOID
Symposium / Workshop_TYMDL
Knowledge City
Mark Wigley
Preston Scott Cohen
Beatriz Colomina
Frederic Levrat
Lecture_TYMDL
Performative Morphology
in Architecture
Achim Menges
Symposium_TYMDL
MONOZUKURI
Amale Andraos
Exhibition_TYMDL
Robotic Architecture
Lecture_TYMDL
ART VS ARCHITECTURE
Paul DeMarinis

Lecture_TYMDL
Francesco Dal Co
Lecture_TYMDL
Kenneth Frampton
Lecture_TYMDL
Nader Tehrani
Lecture_TYMDL
Project and Practice
Peter Eisenman
Sanford Kwinter
Lecture_TYMDL
Technolory x Future
David Benjamin
Lecture_TYMDL
Toward Singularity
Frederic Levrat
Lecture_TYMDL
PARAMETRICISM
Patrik Schumacher

Workshop_TYMDL
Linear City
Exhibition_TYMDL
TY&A + TYMDL
Movie Exhibition
Exhibition_TYMDL
Sexy Technology

91 92 93 94 95 96 97 98 99 00 01 02 03 04 05 06 07 08 09 10 11 12 13 14 15 16 17 18 19 20

TY&A+TYMDL | **People**

Takashi Yamaguchi   TY&A **ASSOCIATES**

山口 隆

建築家、山口隆建築研究所主宰。

1953 年京都市生まれ。 京都大学工学部建築学科卒業後、安藤忠雄建築研究所を経て独立。
1988 年ピーター・アイゼンマンのパートナーやコロンビア大学の理論家達とともに研究グループ ARX を結成し、「主体の解体」を目指して、ネットワーク上でテレコミュニケーションによる設計活動を始める。
フランス、イタリア、ドイツ、フィンランド、ルーマニア、ペルー、中国などから招待作家として展覧会を開催。
パリ・ラ・ヴィレット建築大学、ミラノ工科大学、清華大学、プリンストン大学、MIT などでレクチャーおよび設計デザイン教育をおこなう。東京大学客員研究員、ハーバード大学客員研究員、コロンビア大学客員教授を経て、現在に至る。

主な受賞として、日本建築設計学会賞（2018）、ベネディクタス大賞（2001）、パドヴァ国際建築ビエンナーレ・バルバラ・カポキン賞（2005）等。
主な作品として、清涼山霊源皇寺透静庵 (1998)、Metal Office（2004）、Breathing Factory(2009)、Parametric Fragments(2011) 等。
主な著書として、ネットワークプラクティス（翻訳 2014）、DIAGRAM-SIDE OUT（2016）等。

加藤 正浩
村田 純
疋田 訓之
畑 秀幸
中前 佑介
松原 優磨
Lu Zhe
岡江 良樹

木野島 佑亮	義基 匡矢	谷口 由祈子	松井 峻太
西村 賢	Sanna Ruotsalainen	谷口 遼太	渡辺 貴士
町田 康	Madhu Basnet	安井 慎吾	大野 直人
山本 大二朗	若山 貴司	Lu Zhe	奥田 葉月
宮崎 崇	出口 佳祐	岡江 良樹	梶原 尚人
Hai Kaigen	結城 賢作	阪口 真基	竹中 誠人
太田 琢也	上田 将勝	西川 菜都美	谷澤 雄飛
加埜 隆太	上村 昌史	西谷 直斗	松岡 優
松本 洋人	岡 貴士	菱田 祐真	吉川 海希也
猪飼 勇貴	林 秀幸	平川 賢治	朝野 のぞみ
植月 美幸	池村 礼乃	太田 拓	石川 真一郎
大月 仁志	芝野 優志	重村 茉代	神原 明日香
馬上 紘一	中前 佑介	南野 晋吾	高部 凌
濱中 順也	橋本 雄摩	西本 啓志	八尋 健太
畑 秀幸	古井 健司	平井 俊充	
Sauli Kosonen	松原 優磨	光井 郁哉	
Olli Raila	松本 研二	森川 夕輝	
松塚 庸平	Sanni Sipilä	上籠 勇海	
森下 悠也	今井 逸平	大堀 由貴	
井川 雄介	中谷 優太	奥 寛世	
梅田 将志	西村 弥剛	Vo Ngoc Thuan	
梅野 穣	百田 聖一	杉原 佑佳	
澤 和樹	Okko Saurama	富山 翔太朗	
三上 咲良	Johannes Koskela	堂地 愛梨沙	
山本 暁子	北出 隆哉	Sophoan Vuthika	

ROBOTECTONIC

2020 年 3 月 15 日　初版発行

著者：山口隆

発行人：岸隆司

発行元：株式会社 総合資格

東京都新宿区西新宿 1-26-2 新宿野村ビル 22 F

TEL 03-3340-6714 （出版局）

http://www.shikaku.co.jp/

企画・編集：Takashi Yamaguchi & Associates

編集協力：総合資格学院　なんば校（池田雄一）

株式会社 総合資格　出版局（新垣宜樹）

装丁・造本：Takashi Yamaguchi & Associates（中前佑介、岡江 良樹）

印刷・製本：シナノ書籍印刷 株式会社

Printed in Japan

ISBN 978-4-86417-345-2